GW01057418

Susan,

Hopefully you will
really enjoy this.
The Life & Times of
.... a star!

Piff ('06)

HEADLONG THROUGH LIFE

HEADLONG THROUGH LIFE

The Story of Isadora Duncan

Ean Wood

Book Guild Publishing
Sussex, England

First published in Great Britain in 2006 by
The Book Guild Ltd
25 High Street
Lewes, East Sussex
BN7 2LU

Typesetting in Garamond by
Keyboard Services, Luton, Bedfordshire

Printed in Great Britain by
CPI Bath

A catalogue record for this book is
available from the British Library

ISBN 1 84624 003 4

FOR MYRA
who was the first to suggest that
I write about the inspiring Isadora,
and who then had to live with her for
months while I did so,
lovingly and uncomplainingly

Contents

Acknowledgements

In preparing and writing this book I was helped by many people, who lent me books and videos (all of which I hope I have now returned), who answered my questions, and who guided me towards various vital sources of information. Among them I thank Nora Gohar, Alex Gohar, Bernard Marlowe, Veronica Hitchcock, Victoria Preece, Bill Campbell and John Holmstrom.

Among the many source-books I consulted I wish above all to acknowledge Fredrika Blair and Peter Kurth, whose well-researched earlier biographies pointed me in so many directions.

My grateful thanks also go to the staff at Book Guild Publishing, especially to Carol Biss, to managing editor Joanna Bentley, and to my copy editor, Gareth Vaughan, who drew my attention to many minor inaccuracies. Any that remain are my own fault.

Ean Wood

Chaper One

California Girl

Mention the name 'Isadora Duncan' to anyone of the many who have heard of her, and the chances are that they'll say (with slight inaccuracy), 'Ah yes – the dancer who was strangled when her scarf got caught in the wheel of a Bugatti.' (For a start, it wasn't a Bugatti – a member of the Bugatti firm, on hearing of the accident, commented sniffily that he was amazed the car concerned had enough power.)

Isadora's death was undoubtedly dramatic and bizarre, but there was much more to her than simply that. It was not even the major tragedy of her eventful life, although it did have the useful effect of keeping her name alive. Without it she might nowadays be as forgotten, except among historians of the performing arts, as, say, Harley Granville-Barker, the innovative London stage director of the Edwardian Era – an era that was also the time of Isadora's greatest influence.

Her life was colourful, passionate and disorganised. An imaginative, impulsive woman, she was instrumental in raising dance (in the public perception) from a cultured entertainment to a serious art-form. She helped to lay the foundations of Modern Dance. In the process she also influenced the way women dressed and behaved and regarded themselves. And above all, and all her life, she worshipped Art with a religious fervour. Not just dancing, although that was her own personal means of expression, but Art of all kinds. Art as a means of human communication – Art as enriching and reassuring – Art as the source of man's greatest joy and meaning.

She was born in San Francisco on 26th May 1877, and the city she spent her childhood in was both amazingly young and amazingly wild. A hundred years earlier, in 1776, before the area was even part of the USA, Spanish Franciscans, spreading north from Mexico (which had been a Spanish viceroyalty for centuries) had established a settlement there, seizing vast acres from the native Californians, then known as Indians, in the name of God. The Indians, naturally peaceable, accepted being converted and baptised without truly understanding what was going on, and before they knew what had happened were working from sunrise to sunset building dozens of Catholic missions on what had once been their land.

These missions became considerably wealthy. By 1834, for instance, the San Gabriel Mission was valued at eighty million dollars, embodied in seventeen substantial ranchos, each with vast herds of sheep, steers and horses, and with the hard work being done by three thousand Indians who lived in poor adobe huts and in effect were slaves. If they attempted to run away, they would be pursued and brought back 'dead or alive'.

This profitable state of affairs (for the Spaniards) was not destined to last. Mexico and its surrounding territories became independent from Spain in 1821, and fourteen years later America decided to annexe the territory that became Texas. This in time led to war between the United States and Mexico, and when the war ended, in 1848, the United States had won, and now owned not only Texas but also the future states of New Mexico and California. It was at around this time, only thirty years before Isadora was born, that they named the town San Francisco.

This was a good time to win California, because in January 1848 gold had been discovered there. This discovery led to the California Gold Rush of 1849–50, and San Francisco during the following years grew rapidly from a large settlement to a substantial city. In 1849 alone 50,000 new inhabitants arrived there (some sources estimate there were 75,000).

Those who came were not only prospectors, but whores and gamblers and speculating businessmen, all hoping to get their hands on any gold the prospectors found (which they generally did). Among the earliest whores was a shipment of three hundred 'undesirables' transported there by the government of France. Hundreds more arrived by boat from Chile.

San Francisco became a city of considerable lawlessness. Many of those who arrived in pursuit of gold, either by digging it out of the ground or by swindling or robbing those who had, were sailors off Australian ships, a great number of them former convicts, who simply jumped ship on learning of the riches that might be theirs. Violent and lawless, their gangs became known as the 'Sydney Coves' or the 'Sydney Ducks', although many also came from such places as Tasmania, then still known as 'Van Diemen's Land'. The ships they deserted, in a city desperate for buildings, became used as banks, offices, warehouses, hotels, jails and brothels. Another group, which terrorised the town in 1849, called themselves the 'Hounds'. These were mostly toughs from New York's notorious East Side, plus fugitives from the law in other states and deserters from the army.

In the lower (and more dangerous) areas of the hilly town, bordering San Francisco Bay, an area came to be nicknamed the Barbary Coast. Here, in the words of the city's historian Stephen Longstreet, 'the whores and their macks and the thieves lived in jerry-built huts and unpainted houses along the waterfront... To this district came all the human trash, the sea outlaws, the brutes, sadists and adventurers, black sheep, mountain men, exiles, escaped or uncaptured murderers.'

Even the law was lawless. Police and lawyers and the city government were mostly corrupt, voted into office by organised groups of villains. Groups of men banded together to set up private 'vigilance committees', which in effect led often to mob rule, riots and lynchings. These were, after all, the days of the Wild West, and the growing city was considerably isolated from the rest of America. The trans-continental railroad would not be completed until 1869, so the only ways to reach it from the east were by wagon train across the wilderness, or by boat. As there was then no Panama Canal, this meant sailing right round the southern tip of South America, or taking one ship to Panama, making the short overland crossing by mule and wagon, and then taking a second ship. None of which was easy.

As the more organised and successful hustlers became rich (in most cases by speculating in real estate and building property of all kinds), they colonised the hills above the town. And many became extremely rich. Darius Ogden Mills, for instance, owning the Bank of California, became the richest banker in the West, owning a controlling interest in the main source of all the gold, the famous Comstock Lode. There were, as one hostess wrote, 'Steel barons, coal lords, dukes of wheat and beef, of mines and railways.'

Another observer wrote of '...almost Sybaritic luxury and social splendor ... the constant round of brilliant banquets, afternoon teas and receptions ... Soon nothing remains for the wives of the Western millionaires but to purchase a brownstone mansion, and swing into the tide of fashion with receptions, balls and kettledrums, elegant equipages with coachmen in bright-buttoned livery, footmen in top-boots, maid-servants and man-servants, including a butler...'

These newly rich quickly set about civilising themselves, buying fine furniture and works of art, and importing prize-winning chefs from

3

Europe. Europe was then still regarded by Americans as the fountainhead of culture.

In September 1850 there arrived in San Francisco a cheerful, energetic and repeatedly unsuccessful hustler who in due course would become Isadora's father. His name was Joseph Charles Duncan, and he had been born in Philadelphia in 1819.

As well as being a hustler, a womaniser, and a lover of the good life, he had a lifelong devotion to the arts, in particular to poetry. This devotion he inherited from his own father, Joseph Moulder Duncan, who, when Joseph Charles was an infant, became a professor of belles lettres at a college in Maryland.

Unfortunately, the Duncan family were (and would continue to be) prone to bad luck. In 1827 the college was completely destroyed by fire, the Duncans losing almost everything they possessed. With his wife and his two young sons – Joseph Charles had a younger brother named William Lorenzo – Joseph Moulder moved to Manhattan, where they managed to escape an outbreak of cholera, but suffered financially again in 1837 when the New York economy collapsed.

Shortly after this, Joseph Charles, now nearly twenty, decided to strike out on his own (or almost on his own, because he took with him his younger brother William). Together they headed first for Indiana, then to Illinois, where they set up in business 'buying up produce and horses and hogs, shipping out stocks to St Louis and the then rapidly developing city of Chicago.' Joseph Charles also edited Illinois' first-ever literary magazine, containing fiction, poetry, anecdotes, reminiscences and biographical sketches. It was called *The Prairie Flower*, and failed within a year.

It was at about this time that Joseph Charles first got married, to a young woman from Virginia named Elmira Hill. Together they would have four children – Caroline, Harriet, William and Joseph. But by 1850, when Joseph Charles set off for the promising-sounding city of San Francisco, the marriage was effectively over. He went there alone.

Finding the freewheeling opportunities of the town to his liking, he at once helped organise a lottery. In this enterprise he quickly lost $225,000, but as many other speculators in the city were in the same boat, and as money was printed locally, he managed to survive and carry on.

Again involving himself in publishing, he would over the years edit three newspapers – the *Morning Globe*, the *Evening Globe* and the *Mirror*. For a while, after one of his printing presses was unfortunately destroyed by fire, he became what he called an 'art importer', running a wharfside establishment he called the 'Chinese Sales Room', which he advertised as selling 'Bandas and Pongees, Mantillas and Mantelets, Silks Embroidered by patient Hindoos, Work-boxes of Bombay, Scented Sandalwood, Grotesque Carriages from Japan, etc., etc.'

In the course of this enterprise he made a number of buying trips to Europe, and through contacts there somehow managed to arrange the sale of a number of rare miniatures of George and Martha Washington to the Tsar of Russia. One could not say he was short of enterprise.

Another person of lifelong enterprise who had arrived in San Francisco shortly after he did was the famous (or infamous) Lola Montez. Born in Limerick in 1818, her mother a disreputable milliner and her father a junior officer in the British East Indian Army, her real name was Marie Dolores Eliza Rosanna Gilbert (or so she claimed). Making herself available as a Spanish Dancer (but not very good at the actual dancing), she travelled widely across Europe, becoming the lover of Franz Liszt and, later, of Alexandre Dumas *père*.

In 1847 she briefly became the mistress of Prince Henry of Reuss, a small principality in Thuringia, and when he threw her out (for walking across his flower beds), quickly managed to attach herself to King Ludwig I of Bavaria. He was infatuated with her, arranging for her to dance at a command performance for his court, and within eight weeks had bestowed on her the title of Donna Maria de Dolorez Montez, Baroness von Rosenthal and Countess of Landsfeld. She also assembled a sort of harem of devoted male students.

It could not last. In 1848, at around the same time as gold fever began to grip California, riots over her growing power, incited by Ludwig's Jesuit advisers (the kingdom was Catholic), forced the king reluctantly to sign an order banishing her. Going to England, she married a cornet of the Life Guards, who happened to be extremely rich, but in Spain she stabbed him violently and he left her (she was prone to violence, often throwing things and almost always carrying a riding whip).

Hearing of the Californian Gold Rush, she sailed for America. There she married an American journalist named Hull, and on reaching California they settled in a cottage in the town of Grass Valley, some hundred miles north-west of San Francisco. Although they lived in high style, she needed to make some money, and took to touring the mining camps and dancing. Her speciality was her 'spider dance', wriggling and twisting and shaking a shower of rubber spiders out from under her short skirt. These she would then stamp on (while dancing) with her high-heeled slippers. The miners loved it, shouting out things like, 'Lola, gal, look

5

up-aways! 'Nother spider further up!' There is no evidence that her style of dancing in any way influenced Isadora.

But even with this small success, Lola's finances dwindled, and in 1856 she enlisted the help of Joseph Charles Duncan to arrange the auction of some of her jewellery. It has been claimed that he too briefly became one of her lovers. By this time she had had enough of Hull and thrown him out. After a number of quick liaisons she returned to King Ludwig in Bavaria, and in 1857 they were married. Doctors quipped that his main wedding gift to her was syphilis, of which she would die (back in America) in 1861.

By this time Joseph Charles Duncan had gone on to found the San Francisco Art Association, and was becoming known as 'the admitted authority on all matters appertaining to art on the Pacific Coast' (according to his son Raymond, the younger of Isadora's two brothers).

He wrote poems, which were published in magazines and anthologies, and he mixed with such lasting names as the novelist, satirist and versifier Bret Harte, then founder and editor of an ambitious but short-lived literary magazine, *The Californian*. Joseph Charles himself was the first to publish the poems of Ina Donna Coolbrith, who had arrived in California as a child with her parents, from Illinois in a covered wagon. By 1869, still in her twenties, she was helping Bret Harte edit another magazine, the *Overland Monthly*, whose contributors included a temporary San Francisco resident, Mark Twain. Years later, in 1915, the California State Legislature would name her the state's first official Poet Laureate, and in her old age, in 1928, she would remember Joseph Charles as the love of her life – 'so gentle, so great an idealist and so fine a poet'.

San Francisco was gradually becoming more respectable. During the first half of the 1850s a vigilante committee organised by a group of responsible citizens had succeeded, fairly violently, in imposing a measure of law and order – when it was disbanded, in August 1856, with a triumphal parade of 5,000, it was probably the only time on the American frontier when what was effectively lynch-law received civic approval.

The city was also continuing to prosper. As early as the 1850s it had begun to rival such established cities as New York and Boston as a shipping port. And because it was so isolated on the west coast it had remained little affected by the strife and hardship of the bloody American Civil War (1861–65). There was an element of luck in this, because California's isolation became much less in 1869 with the completion of the trans-continental railroad, its terminus across the bay from San Francisco in the small rural town of Oakland.

A San Franciscan who had fought in the Civil War was the man who would become Isadora's maternal grandfather, Thomas Gray. Originally from Ireland, he had come to the States in 1819, when still in his teens. Settling successively in Ohio, Illinois and Missouri, he had, while in St Louis, met and married a young woman who was also of Irish descent. Her name was Maggie Gorman. She was slightly-built, with strong features and what was described as a 'Spanish type of Irish beauty'. Together they had eight children – four boys and four girls.

Their last child, a girl named Mary Dora, was born in St Louis, Missouri in 1850, and a year later the family joined the hordes moving west to California. They were reasonably well off, travelling by boat to Panama, across the isthmus, and again by boat to San Francisco. There Thomas Gray continued to do well. Eventually he would build and operate the first ferry service from San Francisco across the bay to Oakland. By then known as Colonel Gray, from his wartime record, he would also be voted three times a delegate to the California State Legislature.

By the time Mary Dora (or Dora, as she was known) was twenty, in 1871, she had grown tall and handsome, had acquired an education suitable to a well-bred young lady, and had somehow met Joseph Charles Duncan. Even though he was then fifty, his easy charm and vitality won her heart, and on 21st January of that year they were married, his earlier marriage having presumably been dissolved.

This can't have entirely pleased the Gray family, who were all staunch Catholics. Divorce was bad enough, but the situation was made worse by the fact that Joseph Charles, if he was anything, was a Protestant – an Episcopalian. If there was any family pressure to prevent the marriage, Dora was quite strong-minded enough to resist it. As a writer for the *Oakland Tribune* remembered in 1977, 'she was a forerunner of the feminists, boldly printing her name on calling-cards and wearing low-cut dresses, much to her father's chagrin.

Together, Joseph and Dora would have four children, at roughly two-year intervals – Mary Elizabeth (1871), Augustine (1873), Raymond (1875) and Angela Isadora (1877). The name Isadora was the suggestion of one of Mary's devoutly Catholic sisters, suggested out of devotion to the learned St Isidore of Seville, who converted the Visigoths from the Arian heresy and died in AD 636.

By the time Isadora was born, her father, Joseph Charles Duncan, had succeeded to such an extent that in 1874 he had been able to found and become chief stockholder of a bank – the Pioneer Land and Loan

Bank. Also involved in it were various members of his family – his younger brother William, a son of his first marriage, the husband of one of the daughters of his first marriage, and his new father-in-law, Colonel Gray, who, on account of his prosperity and civic position, was made the bank's nominal president.

The bank aimed to cater mainly to the less well-off – to working men and servant girls – and it attracted them by paying a high rate of interest. Soon it had around three thousand depositors, and was housed in a handsome five-storey building on the corner of Montgomery Street and California Street.

Unfortunately, in 1877 a financial crisis hit the city, brought on by attempts to make its financial structure less based on wild speculation. Banks began to close, and Joseph began to panic. He invested recklessly in stocks and he raised inadequately-protected shares in an effort to stave off disaster. But on 8th October 1877 – when Isadora was only four months old – it crashed. Many poorly-off people were ruined.

So, at about the same time, was the Duncans' marriage. Joseph, who had gone in an instant from the hero of the poor to the most depraved criminal in the city, became wanted on several charges of forgery and 'false swearing'. He fled from the Duncan home and went into hiding. For four months he seemed to have totally disappeared, and when he was finally found, living in a rooming-house, it turned out he had spent much of his time roaming the streets of the city disguised as a woman, wearing a chestnut wig and a hat with a veil. The fact that the chief of police lived next door to the house he was found in did nothing to allay still-surviving fears of police corruption.

Over the next few years he would be brought to trial four times. At each of the first three the jury was unable to agree on a verdict, at the fourth he was acquitted on a technicality. But he never returned home, so by the time Isadora was properly aware of the world, her father was gone. Her mother was later to claim that the marriage 'might have succeeded' if he had not had so many women friends (during his disappearance she had found perfumed letters in his office), or if he had refrained from trying to keep solvent by melting down the table silver and pawning her jewellery. By the time of Joseph's final acquittal, he and Dora were divorced.

Five days after the bank failed, on 13th October 1877, the four-month-old Isadora was baptised (exactly one week after St Isidore's day). On the part of her mother, excusably somewhat distraught at the time (which might also account for the delayed baptism), this was a concession to family respectability rather than to devotion, because on the break-up of her marriage she had firmly rejected the Catholic church and become an outspoken atheist.

Although all four of Dora's children were intelligent and lively, it was obvious to all the family, from the time of her birth, that Isadora was more vital and alive than any of them. In the words of her elder brother Augustin (who had by adulthood dropped the 'e' off the end of his given name), she was 'a lovely child, sweet and kind. She was docile as a girl, too.' (By 'docile' he presumably meant 'sweet-natured' – there was never much hint in Isadora's character, at any age, of docility.)

She was known in childhood as 'Dora' or 'Dorita', and after her parents' divorce, when she was about three, her mother took her and her brothers and sister to live across the bay in Oakland, in a succession of cheap lodgings – in cheap hotels and rooming-houses and in cold-water apartments, and for one brief period in a remote rented farm in the Napa Valley (where they turned a barn into a makeshift theatre).

Why her mother's family did not do much to help her financially is not clear. Possibly her father, Colonel Gray, had himself lost money in the collapse of the Pioneer Bank, and possibly the family felt that, having gone her own headstrong way in marrying a non-Catholic, she had made her own bed and now should lie on it. Nonetheless, they did not disown her, and she remained in touch with them, especially her unmarried sister, Augusta. Isadora remembered her Aunt Augusta as 'remarkably talented', writing in her memoirs: 'She often visited us and would have performances of private theatricals. She was very beautiful, with black eyes and coal black hair, and I remember her dressed in black velvet "shorts" as Hamlet. She had a beautiful voice and might have had a great career as a singer had it not been that everything related to the theatre was looked upon by her father and mother as pertaining to the Devil.'

Dora attempted to provide for her family by using one of her few marketable talents – by advertising her services as a teacher of music (the education of a young lady was not designed to be in any way practical). In Isadora's words, 'Although she was an educated woman, she was barely able to earn a bit of bread for herself and her children by giving music lessons. Her earnings were small and not enough to feed us. Whenever I remember my childhood, I see before me an empty house. With my mother at her lessons, we children sat by ourselves, generally hungry, and in winters generally cold.'

Another way in which mother attempted to earn money was by

knitting. She would make hats and scarves and mittens, and sell them to local stores. In this she was not always successful, not being bred to be a saleswoman, and one day the young Isadora came across her mother sitting on her bed, weeping, her little garments unsold. Isadora had inherited more than her share of her mother's strong-mindedness, and this was one of the early occasions when it surfaced:

> I decided I would sell these things for Mother and at a good price. I put on one of the little red knitted capes and caps, and with the rest in a basket I set forth. From house to house I peddled my wares. Some people were kind, others rude. On the whole I had a success, but it was the first awakening in my childish breast of the monstrous injustice of the world. And that little red cap that my mother had made was the cap of a baby Bolshevik.

Their privations tended to weld the family closer together, and to increase their general confidence that to be a Duncan was really to be something special. This attitude was largely inherited from Joseph Charles, and none felt it more strongly than Isadora.

As part of this pride, Dora made every effort to keep around her family some remnants of their cultured life. They still had a piano, on which she would play music by great composers such as Beethoven, Mozart, Schubert and Mendelssohn. They retained a small library, and she would read to her children from fine authors and poets – from Dickens and Thackeray, from Shakespeare, Shelley and Keats, from Browning, Burns and Whitman. And hung over the bookcase, wherever they moved, was always a proudly-owned copy of Botticelli's 1478 painting, *Primavera*.

This depicts the Roman legend in which the earth-nymph Chloris is pursued by Zephyrus (the West Wind) and caused by his breath to generate her alter ego, Flora, goddess of flowers and the spring. The whole woodland scene is presided over by Venus, originally goddess of the fertility of plants. She is pregnant, and above her head hovers Cupid. At the left of the picture stands Mercury, also originally a god of fertility, and beside him are the three Graces – Aglaia, Thalia and Euphrosyne, the handmaids of Venus – wearing highly-imagined classical drapery as they dance in a circle to celebrate spring.

The picture stimulated the young Isadora greatly. As she remembered, 'It came to me what a wonderful movement there was in that picture, and how each figure through that movement told the story of its new life. And then as mother played Mendelssohn's *Spring Song*, as if by the impulse of a gentle wind, the daisies in the grass would sway and the figures in the picture would move.

It was obvious from early in her life that she was enormously responsive to movement. At the age of six, before she had properly learned to dance herself, she once 'collected half a dozen babies of the neighbourhood – all of them too young to walk' and having placed them on the floor in a row, taught them to 'wave their arms' in preconscious ecstasy. When her mother, amused, asked her what she was doing, she replied that it was her 'school of the dance'.

Overshadowing this early period of her life was the spectre of her missing father – the father whom she alone of the children was too young to have any memory of at all, the mysterious father of whom no-one would speak – except that her mother constantly warned all the children to beware of him, because if they met him he would kidnap them, and except that her aunts, her mother's Catholic sisters, insisted that he was a demon who had ruined their mother's life. Isadora, while in her early years imagining him as a picture-book demon, with horns and a tail, felt his absence keenly.

One day in 1883, also when she was six, the doorbell rang at the third-floor apartment where the family were then living. Isadora went into the hall to answer it, and as she recalled:

I saw a very good-looking gentleman in a top hat, who said:
'Can you direct me to Mrs Duncan's apartment?'
'I am Mrs Duncan's little girl,' I replied.
'Is this my Princess Pug?' said the strange gentleman. (That had been his name for me when I was a baby.)
And suddenly he took me in his arms and covered me with tears and kisses. I was very much astonished at this proceeding, and asked him who he was. To which he replied with tears, 'I am your father.'

Filled with delight, she rushed inside to tell the rest of the family:

'There is a man there who says he is my father.'
My mother rose, very white and agitated, and, going into the next room, locked the door behind her. One of my brothers hid under the bed and the other retired to a cupboard, while my sister had a violent fit of hysterics.
'Tell him to go away, tell him to go away,' they cried.

Amazed by this reaction, Isadora returned to the hall and, with all her six-year-old dignity, informed him, 'The family are indisposed and cannot receive today.' Whereupon her father took her by the hand and conducted her to an ice-cream parlor: where he 'stuffed me with ice-cream and cakes.'

She recalled that she was enchanted by him, although somewhat bewildered by the whole situation. Returning home she informed her unsettled family, 'He is a perfectly charming man, and he is coming tomorrow to give me more ice-cream.' But he didn't. 'The family refused to see him, and after a time he returned to his other family at Los Angeles.'

The last part is probably not quite accurate. What had happened to Joseph Charles Duncan was that after his acquittal he had stayed in the Bay Area of San Francisco, working as a broker, until in 1883 he decided to move south to the fast-growing town of Los Angeles, where there was reportedly just the sort of property boom that might give him an opportunity. He did not yet have a family there, and it seems likely that his visit to his ex-wife and his children was simply in order to bid them farewell.

Isadora later claimed she never saw her father again, although her brothers and sister were sceptical of this claim. He kept in touch with Dora and her family, and when he could help them financially, he did, once even buying them a small house in Oakland.

But whether Isadora met him seldom, or only that once, she inherited much of his character – his verve and imagination, his warm and outgoing personality, his combination of strength and gentleness, and his absolute refusal to ever be defeated.

Being as strong-willed and independent as she was, and coming from a household where there was so much that was important and life-affirming to be learned, Isadora found school a boring waste of time.

She had been attending the Cole Elementary School in Oakland from the somewhat early age of five (her later explanation was that her mother had lied about her age, needing school as somewhere to park her during the day). It was there, one Christmas when she was around eight or nine, that the teacher gave out candy, saying, 'See, children, what Santa Claus has brought you.'

Isadora, the young unbeliever, immediately objected that there was no such person as Santa Claus. Told that candies were only for little girls who did believe in Santa Claus, she retorted, 'Then I don't want your candy.'

Called to the front of the class and told to sit on the floor, she instead addressed the class in what she recalled as 'the first of my famous speeches', shouting, 'I don't believe lies. My mother told me she is too poor to be Santa Claus; it is only the rich mothers who can pretend to be Santa Claus and give presents.'

The teacher managed to send her to stand in a corner, where she continued chanting, 'There is no Santa Claus.' So she was sent home, and went, still chanting.

'Was I right?' she asked her mother.

'There is no Santa Claus,' her mother replied, 'and there is no God, only your own spirit to help you.'

Recalling the incident in later life, Isadora wrote, 'I never got over the feeling of injustice with which I had been treated, deprived of candy and punished for telling the truth.'

By this time her dancing life had begun in earnest. When she was very young, the first dancing she remembered was Irish. Her maternal grandmother, the former Maggie Gorman, she recalled, 'used often to sing the Irish songs and dance the Irish jigs.' Isadora learned to dance the jig from her grandmother, who, she later believed, had incorporated steps and gestures into it from what she had seen of the dances of American Indians, and perhaps 'a bit of "Yankee Doodle Dandy" when grandfather Colonel Thomas Gray came marching home from the Civil War.' (Grandmother Gorman was a strong character in her own right. Raymond once credited her with giving him 'the lesson of my life', by telling him, 'Raymond, you must never do what everybody does.' This lesson he certainly took to heart.)

From her very early days Isadora practised how to move, not just in dancing but in all the movements of her life – sitting down, standing up, walking, turning, kneeling, skipping, opening a door. At first she appeared stilted and self-conscious, but gradually her sense of how to move well became a part of her, and her style of dance gradually evolved out of it, the steps and gestures she used all being rooted firmly in the movements of everyday life. It all became such second nature to her that before long her brother Augustin would tell a family friend, 'Isadora knows exactly how she's going to look when she takes a pose. We think we know, but Isadora never makes a mistake.'

All four Duncan children – Elizabeth, Augustin, Raymond and Isadora – were keen on dancing, even though their characters differed. 'We are none of us alike in our family,' Isadora once said.

Elizabeth, where Isadora was tall, was tiny, 'with a bright bird-like face and a little-girl voice.' Almost as devoted to the dance as Isadora, her tragedy was that in her childhood one of her legs had become shorter than the other (either through illness or accident), and the resulting lameness would restrict her all her life to teaching and theorising about dance.

Augustin, known informally as Gus, was, as he admitted himself, somewhat conservative and 'not concerned in the innovations'. Handsome and somewhat stocky in build, he would have the most conventional life of the four, going on to become a successful actor and in 1915 a founder-member of the influential Theatre Guild – a semi-amateur group of aspiring playwrights, actors, directors and producers who got together to present plays they judged to be of artistic merit.

Where Augustin was stocky, Raymond was spare in build and somewhat sharp-featured. Like Isadora, he was a true original. Intelligent and sensitive, he would in time develop and preach a gospel of philosophic simplicity that had something in common with the hippy attitudes of the 1960s, rejecting the materialism of the modern world. His attitudes and Isadora's had much in common, and they would influence each other all their lives.

In 1885, when Isadora was eight, their mother managed to scrape up enough money to give the four children private dancing lessons. These were given in their home by a San Francisco dance instructor calling himself Professor Jay Massborn. Mother would play the piano while he taught them the popular social dances of the day – dances such as the waltz, the schottische, the polka, the mazurka and the galop.

Professor Massborn, an arrogant and short-tempered man, who according to Raymond affected 'an outdated sort of cassock', did not last long. He quit after a heated argument with mother on the subject of her tempos. Nothing daunted, the family continued practising on their own, with Elizabeth, now around fifteen, as their instructor.

But social dancing was not dance as Isadora was beginning to conceive it. She took to going off alone 'into the woods' or to a deserted beach. 'And there I danced. I felt even then that my shoes and my clothes only hindered me. My heavy shoes were like chains; my clothes were my prison. So took everything off. And without any eyes watching me, entirely alone, I danced, naked by the sea. And it seemed to me as if the sea and all the trees were dancing with me.'

School continued to be a bore. As she said, 'I remember that in the classroom I was either considered amazingly intelligent and at the head of my class, or quite hopelessly stupid and at the bottom of the class.

It all depended on a trick of memory, and whether I had taken the trouble to memorise the subject we were given to learn.' So while still quite young (at ten, she claimed), she informed her mother that it was useless for her to go to school any more, 'as it was only a waste of time when I could be making money, which I considered more important. I put my hair on the top of my head and said that I was sixteen. As I was very tall for my age every one believed me.'

San Francisco continued to grow and prosper, in spite of the fact that by the 1880s most of the gold in California had long been mined. It now contained many rich families. One such family, also living in Oakland, which they had moved to in 1880, were the Steins. Mr Stein was one of the directors of the city's cable-car company, built to transport people up the steep hillside from the San Francisco sea-front to the prosperous upper town. One of his children became the famous and experimental author Gertrude Stein, who later recalled that her family 'had ten acres where they had every kind of fruit growing, and they had cows and dogs and horses and hay making, and the sun in the summer dry and baking, and the wind in the autumn and in the winter the rain beating and then in the springtime the hedge of roses to fence all these joys in.' Years later, in Paris, Raymond would confess to Gertrude that Isadora and he had often sneaked into the estate and scrumped apples. (Gertrude's lifelong friend Alice B. Toklas was also a San Franciscan, born, like Isadora, in 1877.)

Isadora knew Gertrude Stein. Although she had removed herself from school, she continued to educate herself in her own way, and a large part of this process was through haunting the local library, as Gertrude also did. Both girls were helped and encouraged by the librarian, who as it happened was the poet Ina Donna Coolbrith, first published by Isadora's father.

As often happens with the very best of self-educated people, she would become at once ground-breakingly original and poor at separating bright ideas from barmy ones.

With so much prosperity (although San Francisco would continue to have its rough and dangerous waterfront community for years), most of the wealthy inhabitants continued in their pursuit of respectability, and to become respectable meant acquiring culture. Clothes, décor and furniture were imported from Europe. Theatres and concert-halls were built and flourished, the city having had a fondness for stage performances from its beginning, and at all levels of decency.

For a girl as restless and inquisitive as Isadora it was a place full of stimulation. She was reading, studying the great paintings of the past, attending plays, listening to classical music, and dancing, dancing, dancing. Gradually, and aided by her family, she was constructing in her heart a complete philosophy of dance – what it should be and what it should not be.

Chapter Two

Into the Real World

In around 1888, when Isadora was eleven, she joined her sister Elizabeth, then seventeen, in giving dancing lessons. At first they found the experience less than satisfying. The big dance craze in America in the 1880s was the waltz, which had been steadily growing in popularity since it first arrived there in 1816. Isadora disliked it, later calling it 'an expression of sickly sentimentality and romance which our youth has grown out of'. In fact she disliked ballroom dancing in general, on the rather unusual grounds that it was not sexy enough, that artistically it was a lie. In her words, she was 'amazed at the great restraint shown by the dancers, who, clasped in one another's arms, and moving to the most lascivious music, still continue to behave in the most orthodox manner.'

Furthermore, their pupils were mostly children and teenagers, attending the classes mainly to acquire a social accomplishment, and drilling self-conscious (or even reluctant) young people in the steps of conventional social dances was, not at all what either of them had in mind. As Elizabeth remembered, 'we soon recognised the necessity of coming up with a more vital approach... We went our own ways in order to pursue our impulses and our dreams.'

It was good that they were growing up in such a vibrant and freewheeling city, with a mother who herself was somewhat rebellious, because the freedom she encouraged in them allowed them to absorb many influences which nourished what they aspired to do, and helped them to work out what their aspirations were.

Underlying all these influences was the notion of Art as a cause, a calling, a belief. In the 1880s this idea was very much the fashion in America (although few adopted it so deeply and wholeheartedly as Isadora).

This attitude had been given great impetus by two connected events. One was the arrival in America in 1881 of the Gilbert and Sullivan

17

operetta *Patience*, satirising the affectations of the British aesthetic movement of the 1870s; the other was the arrival in 1882, to give a nationwide lecture tour, of the ambitious Irish poet, Oscar Wilde. Then aged twenty-eight, he had enthusiastically adopted aestheticism as a fashionable and congenial doctrine. The way in which the two events were connected was that Richard D'Oyly Carte, producer of Gilbert and Sullivan, had conceived the idea of following the opening in New York of *Patience* with a lecture tour by Wilde, then seen in Britain as the apostle of aestheticism.

Part of D'Oyly Carte's reason was that although America had several famous poets — Longfellow, Whitman and Emerson prominent among them — it had no obvious aesthete, as Wilde had made himself, and who was the butt of *Patience*. D'Oyly Carte wanted America to see what it was they were supposed to be laughing at. It says much for Wilde's shrewdness and sense of showmanship that he was quite prepared to go and propound his doctrines quite seriously in order to publicise, and be publicised by, a skit on them (not that *Patience* was all that damaging a skit — until after two-thirds of the libretto had been written it had had a clerical setting, being the story of the love-rivalry of two curates).

Cultured America had for some years been aware of Britain's aesthetic movement. This was in some ways an outcome of the teachings of John Ruskin and William Morris, that Art had the power to enlighten. Ruskin in particular had been preaching the idea that Art had a moral message — that great art reflected nature, and that in reflecting nature it gave rise to sensations that were either Beautiful, inducing thoughts of Love and Goodness, or Sublime, causing people to reflect on the awesome majesty of creation and thus on their own smallness in the scheme of things. This helped to cleanse the mind of pride and induce a healthy humility.

Many Americans had been aware of the teachings of Ruskin and Morris for some time, but by Wilde's era a change had taken place. People who had influenced him — such as his Oxford tutor Walter Pater, the London-American painter Whistler, and the French painter Degas — while they admired Art and the idea of Art as much as Ruskin, had revolted against perceiving it as having a moral message. Art to them meant to express oneself and the world around one in Beauty. 'Art for Art's sake' was their watchword, giving rise to such Wildeanisms as 'Those who find beautiful meanings in beautiful things are the cultured. For them there is hope.' and 'All art is quite useless.'

He arrived in America with such a message at just the right time. In the period after the Civil War, the country's heroes had become its military leaders, but by 1880 many people, especially women, were becoming a little tired of so much *machismo* (this change was probably first acknowledged at the Philadelphia Centennial Exhibition of 1876, whose avowed intention was to publicise 'the noble arts of peace'). The astute Wilde, sensing this growing change in attitude from the moment of his arrival in New York, announced, 'I think you have taken quite enough motives from war. You don't want any more bronze generals on horseback... Suppose you try the motives that peace will give you now.'

Although naturally he was mocked by some, to many he was seen as offering a new religion of beauty that would improve both public and private life. His visit did much to usher in an age of American aestheticism that would last for a dozen years, and while it lasted it was all-pervasive. Unlike the slightly earlier British movement, it permeated all levels of society, from the highest to the lowest, mainly among women.

Part of the reason why his teachings had an appeal for women was that not only was he preaching an abstract gospel of aestheticism, he was also extending it into the practical world of the home – two of his lectures were 'The Value and Character of Handicrafts' and 'House Decoration'. As he said in the course of one of them, 'Into the secure and sacred house of Beauty the true artist will admit nothing that is harsh or disturbing, nothing that gives pain, nothing that is debatable, nothing about which men argue.'

This was a considerable change from the prevailing attitude to the home, that it should above all be clean and practical, which was basically a male attitude. Women, enthusiastically adopting aesthetic principles, found that they were gaining a greater measure of control over their environment, and thus over their lives. Creating a living space that was a work of art was a step forward from merely being a housekeeper. It was a small escape from orthodoxy, and gave hope to the many women who felt under the domination of tyrannical Victorian husbands or fathers, or who found themselves shackled to ineffective or unreliable men. An attitude that, whether it came directly from Wilde or not, was by the 1880s strongly held by Dora Duncan. The ineffectiveness and unreliability of her husband Joseph had given her a contempt for the whole institution of marriage – a contempt she passed on to her children, especially Isadora, who not only came to regard marriage as oppressive and unnecessary, but in the field of dance regarded men as totally irrelevant, at least as far as she was concerned, as directors, tutors, choreographers, costume designers, or anything else.

Wilde's lecture tour began in New York in January 1882, and for the whole year he would tour and lecture endlessly, covering half of the USA and half of Canada.' Between 27th March and 5th April he lectured in San Francisco four times, and the city took to him.

Isadora, then almost five, was of course too young to have seen him, but his influence persisted. He had spoken, for instance, in praise of simplicity in women's dress, then corsetted, bustled, tight-sleeved, and over-decorated with bows and flounces. Beauty in clothing, he taught, should consist in perfect adaptability to the needs of the wearer. (Attacking Victorian conventions of style, he announced that women (and indeed men as well) 'should wear loose drapery'.

'Drapery' was a key word in aesthetic ideas of dress, and in praising it Wilde reached back to the beauties of Ancient Greece. He preached that dress should follow the lines of the figure like the earliest forms of Greek costume, as depicted in the surviving sculptures of that time.

Isadora and her family, especially her brother Raymond, were by their mid-teens well aware of Ancient Greece (partly through the classical subjects of Botticelli). Indeed, it would be a lasting devotion for both her and him.

A reverence for the Ancient Greeks had been growing in both Europe and America for years. Latin and Greek had been taught at universities and the best schools for centuries, so educated men had long been familiar with the moral philosophy and rich culture of the classical world. But two events during the nineteenth century gave a more concrete reality to this world.

The first was the bringing to England in 1806 of the collection of carvings from the ruined Parthenon by Thomas Bruce, the seventh Earl of Elgin. These swiftly influenced painters and architects, and inspired romantic poets such as Lord Byron to view Ancient Greece even more strongly as a lost golden age, a world of heroes, artists and sages, of wisdom and of a true simplicity rooted in nature.

The second, during the 1870s and 1880s, was the work of the pioneer archaeologist Heinrich Schliemann, whose excavations in Asia Minor in search of the legendary city of Troy unearthed a horde of thrilling artefacts, of jewellery, sculptures and decorated pottery. Depictions of these discoveries were much appreciated in America – the simplicity of the earlier time they came from was seen as cleaner and more wholesome than the decadent civilisation of Europe, from under whose domination the country had only relatively recently escaped.

Furthermore, Greece was seen as the cradle of democracy – a non-elitist society devoted to the serious and worthwhile pursuit of art and learning. To Isadora, and even more to Raymond, it seemed also to offer an antidote to the increasing mechanisation and money-grubbing of the nineteenth-century world they lived in.

California in particular became increasingly Greek-minded. After all, had not many residents and visitors commented on the similarity of the California coastline to the shores of Greece. More than a few Californians took to wearing sandals and cheesecloth garments in imitation of the Ancient Greeks, proclaiming the health-giving properties of fresh air and sunlight, and existing on a simple diet of fruit and nuts. Raymond would become a lifelong prophet of this lifestyle, and there was something of it in Isadora too, with her insistence on dancing in loose flowing costume, and in dancing barefoot on the shore (even giving her youthful dance classes, she was already dressing herself in a somewhat Greek-influenced costume, consisting of a short white robe tied with a sash).

Someone often said to have influenced her evolving attitude to dance was the famous professor of music and oratory at the Paris Conservatoire, François Delsarte, although Isadora, later in life was always at pains to deny any such influence.

Delsarte, who lived from 1811 to 1871, had minutely observed the postures, the gestures and the tones of voice of people in all manner of situations, both joyful and sorrowful, and especially when under stress, and from his observations had developed a set of 'rules of emotional expression' for the benefit of singers and actors (among his pupils were Jenny Lind, Georges Bizet and the great *tragédienne* Rachel.

In America, his teachings got an immense boost in 1885 when an American elocution teacher, Genevieve Stebbins, published a book, *The Delsarte System of Expression*. It took the country by storm and gave rise to a craze for 'classical statue posing' and 'emotive expression' through movement.

Isadora, denying Delsarte's influence on her, once in the Twenties allegedly told a friend that she 'didn't know what it was all about'. And in her youth, when the craze for his teachings was at its height, she once made fun of her sister Elizabeth when she came across her trying out Delsarte gestures. Probably she was right in her denial, although his attitude to expression through movement did to some extent resemble hers. He spoke, for instance, of gesture as the 'direct agent of the soul', and laid down such laws as 'To each spiritual function responds a function of the body' and 'There is nothing more horrible, or deplorable, than a gesture without meaning or purpose.'

One person who definitely did influence her attitude to life and art was the famous American humanist Colonel Robert Ingersoll. Ingersoll, a warm-hearted and witty man, was a lawyer who rose to become Attorney-General for the state of Illinois, and would almost certainly have become its Governor if he not been widely known as an infidel. During the latter part of the nineteenth century he published many essays and gave many lectures in praise of agnosticism, and by doing so became a great hero of Dora Duncan in her atheism.

Isadora too read him avidly, and it is interesting to read what he has to say on the subject of Art, partly as showing how pervasive the concept of Art had then become to many educated people. In his essay *Art and Morality*, for instance, he wrote:

> Art is the highest form of expression... At the foundation of the beautiful will be found the fact of happiness, the gratification of the senses, the delight of intellectual discovery, and the surprise and thrill of appreciation... Art civilises because it enlightens, develops, strengthens, ennobles. It deals with the beautiful, with the passionate, with the ideal. It is the child of the heart. To be great, it must deal with the human. It must be in accordance with the experience, with the hopes, with the fears, and with the possibilities of man... Genius is the spirit of abandon; it is joyous, irresponsible. It moves in the swell and curve of billows; it is careless of conduct and consequence. For a moment the chain of cause and effect seems broken; the soul is free.

This indicates how seductive the idea of Art then was to those who, like Isadora, had a natural urge towards spirituality coupled with the knowledge that there was no God. Belief in Art rushed in to fill the void.

The poetry that her mother had recited to the family from their infancy had made a deep and lasting impression on Isadora, especially that of Walt Whitman. She was proud of being an American, and his poems, filled with the raw energy and hope of a young people in a young country, and praising the individual at his best as an impersonal seer at one with Nature, chimed perfectly with her own feelings.

She once declared herself to be 'the spiritual daughter of Walt Whitman', and his poem 'Song of Myself' would become her private anthem:

I celebrate myself, and sing myself,
And what I assume you shall assume,

For every atom belonging to me as good belongs to you.
Do I contradict myself?
Very well then I contradict myself,
(I am large, I contain multitudes.)

Isadora herself, in her mid-teens, had not of course fully formed her philosophy of dance. Indeed, passionate as she was about dancing, it was not her sole performing interest. At the age of eleven, her brother Augustin remembered, she 'arranged a little tableau entertainment for children', in which pupils from her dancing classes posed with bows and arrows while she read Longfellow's short poem 'The Arrow and the Song': 'I shot an arrow into the air,/It fell to earth, I knew not where.'

This was, Augustin thought, her 'true beginning', although in fact there was nothing startlingly original about it. In late nineteenth-century America, children's pageants and *tableaux vivants* were commonplace – so much so that they were almost a cliché. Nonetheless, it was out of these that Isadora arose. She liked the idea of performances that mingled dance, music and poetry.

Naturally she watched every sort of dance that was to be seen, although little of it seemed relevant to the ideas that were growing in her mind about what dance should be. The dancing she saw in theatres and vaudeville houses she dismissed as 'inane coquetry'. The most popular performer in California in the 1870s and 1880s was the young vaudeville performer, Little Lotta Crabtree, who not only danced, but played the banjo and sang. But Lotta's dancing would have had little to recommend it to Isadora, believing, as she did, that 'dance was once the most noble of all the arts; and it shall be again. From the great depths to which it has fallen, it shall be raised.' After all, Lotta had originally been discovered and trained for the stage by Lola Montez, whose own dancing had little in it of nobility.

Above all, Isadora detested the ballet, her detestation made stronger by the fact that it was the one dance-form that carried an aura of artistic respectability. But ballet in nineteenth-century America (and indeed elsewhere) was not the developed and expressive form it later became.

It had begun in Italy, but got its greatest impetus in France during the long reign of Louis XIV, who adored it. It was in France that a whole system of conventional steps, gestures and positions was gradually developed, and it was there, from around 1830, that its great romantic era began. Among the dancers of that era was Marie Taglioni, originally from Italy, and it was she who first introduced *pointe* work as an expressive part of the ballet, rather than as an occasional exercise in sheer technique. Ballerinas began to wear ballet-shoes with blocked toes, as they do today, instead of the high heels they had previously worn. Succeeding years also saw skirts shorten into the modern tutu, made decent to the respectable by the earlier introduction of tights. With all this, male dancers at the same time somewhat faded in importance.

Until the early years of the nineteenth century ballet was mostly danced to existing music, but gradually composers began to write music specifically to be danced to, and by the end of the century it had become considerably spectacular, with lavish and expensive productions. The leading American ballerina by the 1890s was an Italian, Marie Bonfanti, whose most famous production was a five-hour spectacle called *The Black Crook* that included devils, demons and pyrotechnic effects, as well as certain styles of dancing that later would not have found their way into a conventional ballet. (She brought a revival of this to San Francisco in 1893, when it is at least possible that Isadora saw it.)

Ballet was then still a somewhat hybrid form, with overtones of operetta, and even of the opulent British pantomimes of the day. This was even more so outside the three countries that had become the great centres of ballet – Italy, France and Russia. Only those had properly established ballet companies, and even in those (with the exception of Russia) ballet was still regarded as a sort of handmaid of opera.

Some writers have excused Isadora's contempt for ballet by rather implying that if she'd come to it thirty years later, when it was a more developed art-form, she might have been kinder about it. But her dislike went deeper than its lack of cohesive development. Her whole urge was to found a dance based on natural movements, and to her ballet felt deeply unnatural.

The cantankerous painter-turned-essayist William Hazlitt, writing in 1826 of dancing he saw when visiting France, almost perfectly encapsulated her attitude, saying:

> The French, whether men or women, have no idea of dancing but that of moving with agility, and of distorting their limbs in every possible way, till they really alter the structure of the human form... The French Opera-dancers think it graceful to stand on one leg or the points of their toes, or with one leg stretched out behind them, as if they were going to be shod, or to raise one foot at right angles with their bodies, and twirl themselves round like a *te-totum*, to see how long they can spin, and then stop short all of

a sudden; or to skim along the ground, flat-footed, like a spider running along a cobweb, or to pop up and down like a pea on a tobacco-pipe, or to stick in their backs till another part projects out behind *comme des volails*, and to strut about like peacocks with infirm, vain-glorious steps, or to turn out their toes till their feet resemble apes, or to raise one foot above their heads and turn swiftly round upon the other, till the petticoats of the female dancers (for I have been thinking of them) rise above their garters, and display a pair of spindle-shanks, like the wooden ones of a wax-doll, just as shapeless and as tempting.

Isadora herself, when young and wanting to know all about all kinds of dance, did at one time try taking lessons from 'a famous ballet teacher in San Francisco'. It was not a success. 'When the teacher told me to stand on my toes I asked him why, and when he replied, "Because it is beautiful," I said that it was ugly and against nature, and after the third lesson I left his class, never to return.'

There was a further reason why she was against ballet, at least for Americans like herself. In her *I See America Dancing* (written towards the end of her life and with a title echoing her beloved Whitman's poem 'I See America Singing'), she wrote, 'The real American type can never be a ballet dancer. The legs are too long, the body too supple, and the spirit too free for this school of affected grace and toe-walking. It is noteworthy that all great ballet dancers have been very short women with small frames. A tall finely made woman could never dance the ballet. The type which expresses America at its finest could never dance the ballet. With the wildest turn of the imagination, you cannot picture the Goddess of Liberty dancing the ballet.'

It was quite obvious by the time Isadora was in her mid-teens that she, although the youngest, was the strongest character in her family, with intelligence, imagination and a burning desire to express her ideas to the world.

In a programme note of 1905, she gave a short sketch of her career to date (rather exaggerating her achievements, as writers of such notes naturally do), saying:

> Taught from the age of 11 years to 16 years – classes always growing – gave performances appearing both alone and with pupils – dancing singly and in chorus – and also the pupils danced and mimed small scenes – of mimodramas accompanied by Poems. The

dancing of these pupils was considered wholly remarkable and as something quite opposed to the dancing of the time – Press of that time wrote expressing admiration for this New Dance.

At age 14 made a tour of Principal Theatres of California – immense enthusiasm all along the route –

This, in spite of the exaggeration, does have some truth in it. She and her sister and brothers did make a tour of California theatres, although how 'Principal' they were is unclear. Probably not very, as this was their first recorded professional engagement. And the year was 1893, when Isadora would have been fifteen or sixteen, not fourteen.

The show that she and her siblings had assembled, with growing confidence, was not mainly dancing.' It also contained singing, poetry reading, scenes from Shakespeare, and sketches (melodrama, comedy and burlesque). Which implies that the four of them were providing most, if not all, of the evening's entertainment.

Later in 1893 the family fortunes took an upturn. Joseph Charles Duncan, having now been in Los Angeles for ten years, had got married 'for the third time (his new wife, Mary, being a sister of the wife of one of his sons from his first marriage), and, as he hoped, had prospered in real estate. As the *San Francisco Examiner* later wrote of this period in his life, 'When the boom in real estate came along he was in the forefront of the speculators. He bought and sold property day and night. At one stage of the boom he was reputed to be worth easily $250,000 in cash.'

Out of this wealth he again bought his ex-wife Dora and her children a house, this time a handsome and sizeable corner house in San Francisco. It was known as the 'Castle' mansion and it had large rooms suitable for dancing. In its grounds were a tennis court, a windmill, and a barn, which of course the family at once converted into a theatre, as they had done before at the farm they rented in the Napa Valley.

It was at around this time that Isadora first began to use that name. No longer was she 'Dora' or 'Dorita'. And by now she was clearly established as the genius of the family, dreaming, as she said 'of a different dance. I did not know just what it would be, but I was feeling out towards an invisible world into which I divined I might enter if I found the key.'

But it was hard for her to see how she might proceed to build a professional dancing career. At one point she went to audition for a road-company producer. Accompanied by her mother, she danced for him 'in a little white tunic'. Although she was adept at the social dances she taught and despised, she had nothing that a theatre professional would recognise as formal training, and whatever she danced for him, based on her own concept of natural movements in dance, the producer was unimpressed, telling Dora, 'This sort of thing is no good for a theatre. It's more for a church. I advise you to take your little girl home.' Whether or not he did say, as Isadora claimed, 'your little girl', she was by now not all that little. Approaching eighteen, she had reached her adult height of five foot six.

Whatever performances she and her family and pupils mounted in their home barn-theatre are not recorded. But during the two years that the Duncans lived in the Castle mansion they undoubtedly continued teaching dance and giving little performances of dancing, poetry and drama, while Isadora strove to refine her ideas.

One thing was becoming clear to her. She was increasingly dissatisfied with San Francisco. It was now more respectable than it had been forty years before (at least outwardly – the scheming partnership between politics and crime would linger on for years), but to Isadora its very respectability was small-minded, conventional and stultifying. Her family felt rather the same, her mother complaining, 'They don't understand Isadora. They just don't understand.' It was not the place to be trying to create a new approach to the sacred world of dance – to bring dance back from centuries of distortion to the nobility it had in Ancient Greece.

Her next move would be prompted by a new family disaster. In 1895 history repeated itself when her father, Joseph, again overreached himself financially. The real estate boom in Los Angeles ended, he lost his entire fortune, and the Castle mansion was repossessed. (Three years later, on 14th October 1898, when Joseph was seventy-nine, he and his third wife Mary, and their twelve-year old daughter Rosa, would all be drowned, along with 104 others, when the S.S. *Mohegan*, en route from London to New York, ran aground on the Manacle Rocks off Falmouth, in Cornwall. It was reported that there had been a dance aboard that night and that the crew were drunk.)

Shortly after the loss of their mansion, Isadora, now the family's leader, took charge. In her words, 'I called the family to a council, and in an hour's harangue made clear to them all the reasons why life in San Francisco was impossible.'

The result of this harangue was that in June 1895 Isadora and her mother uprooted themselves and headed for what they hoped would be the more sophisticated city of Chicago. Their plan was that Elizabeth, Augustin and Raymond would follow later.

27

To manage this, they did everything they could to get their hands on ready cash. They borrowed from friends, some of whom were as convinced of Isadora's genius as the family themselves. They sold, through another friend, some fine antiques they had acquired during their brief spell of prosperity. Isadora claimed she sold popcorn on the street to raise fare money, and then she and her mother left, with, she recalled, nothing but 'a small trunk, some old-fashioned jewellery ... and twenty-five dollars.' And of course her 'little white tunic'.

She had chosen Chicago because at that time it was regarded as the most go-ahead city in the USA. Two years before, in 1893, it had hosted the biggest world's fair then ever staged in America – the World's Columbian Exposition (so named because it was intended to honour the 400th anniversary of the famous voyage of Christopher Columbus).

This fair had been a mammoth success. Its theme had been electricity, and the entire show acquired the nickname 'The White City' from the way its classically-inspired white buildings were illuminated at night. It demonstrated Bell's telephone, Tesla's electric coil, Westinghouse's dynamo and transformer, and Edison's light-bulb. It was the fair that invented the midway, that broad central boulevard lined with attractions, used at fairs and fairgrounds ever since. On the midway were exhibitions from different nations – a German village, an Austrian city, an Irish pub, a Moorish palace, a Buddhist temple, a Chinese market, a Dahomeyan village. But the attraction that acquired more publicity than any other, more even than the giant Ferris wheel, was Little Egypt (the Darling of the Nile) with her scandalous coochee-coochee belly-dance.

By June 1895 the fair had been over for twenty months, but its magic in a way still lingered on, making Chicago for many Americans a city of hope and of promise for the future. This, in the actual city, was illusory. With the fair and its millions of visitors gone, the optimism quickly vanished, and the city's one-and-a-half million inhabitants reverted to concerning themselves mostly with the everyday ambitions of the business world.

Isadora had with her a letter of introduction from the San Francisco Press Club to its Chicago equivalent. Going there, she earnestly addressed the journalists she found, saying (or so she remembered), 'I have brought you a revelation from California. I have discovered the true movement of man. This movement, drawing its inspiration from nature and going up through the evolution of the psychology of modern thought, is the true revelation of the Dance.' This was the Chicago Press Club that not many years later would number among its members such cutups as Ben

Hecht and Charles MacArthur, who would immortalise hard-boiled Chicago pressmen in their play *The Front Page*, so it is hardly surprising that Isadora's impassioned and high-flown address (no matter what it was she actually said) was received with a cynical lack of interest.

She began spending the uncomfortably hot summer days touring the offices of theatrical managers, but failed even to get an audition. She and her mother's money ran out. She managed to get enough to pay room-rent for a while by selling a little collar of Irish lace off her dress. There was enough left over to buy a box of tomatoes, and for a week they lived on them and nothing else, her mother becoming so weak she could not stand. Eventually, deciding to take any work she could find, Isadora went to a domestic employment bureau, where she was turned down as totally unskilled.

Reluctantly, she managed to get herself an audition at a music hall. Reluctantly, because to her the dancing in music halls represented a debasement of all she was striving for. But at least the music hall she auditioned at was Chicago's leading one – the Masonic Temple Roof Garden. The audition was given by its manager, Charles Fair, who watched her dance in her little white tunic and said, 'Well, you're very pretty and graceful. And if you would change all that and do something with some pep in it, I'd engage you.'

When Isadora asked what exactly he meant by pep, he said, 'Well, not the sort of thing you do. Something with skirts and frills and kicks. Now you might do the Greek thing first, and then change to the frills and kicks, and it might be an interesting turn.'

Wondering where on earth she would get frills, and how she might get hold of them without any money, she wandered the hot streets till she came to the vast Marshall Field department store. As she told it:

> I went in and asked to see the manager, and I was shown into the office, where I found a young man sitting behind a desk. He had a kindly expression, and I explained to him that I must have a skirt with frills by the next morning, and that if he would give me credit I could easily pay him from the engagement. I do not know what inspired this young man to comply with my request, but he did so.

The young man she would meet from time to time for the rest of her life. He was Gordon Selfridge, later founder of the famous London store, and with his approval she collected 'white stuff and red stuff for petticoats, and lace frills'.

Back at the lodgings, her mother, still weak from hunger, sat up in bed and worked all night to make a costume. Next day, armed with it, Isadora returned to the Roof Garden and to Charles Fair, who had an orchestra standing by to play something with a bit of pep. But what was it to be? In her inexperience she had omitted to bring with her the music she was to dance to, or even to decide what it should be.

Hurriedly she suggested the then-popular Sousa march, *Washington Post*. The band played it, Isadora improvised what she described as her best attempt at a 'peppery' dance, and Charles Fair told her he would put her in his current show the next night, that he would pay her $20 a week, and would make a special announcement to introduce her.

He did introduce her, but not under her own name. She was introduced as 'The California Faun', and billed as that she began performing. Unfortunately, both the show and its audiences 'disgusted' her. After three weeks she could stand it no more and quit. But this first foray into the world of truly professional performance meant that at least she now had a little money.

By then she and her mother had found a community of part-successful artists, actors, poets and writers, of the sort known since about 1850, on both sides of the Atlantic, as 'bohemians'. They spent much of their time socialising at various clubs, and at one, aptly named the Bohemian Club, Isadora found friends. It had been set up by journalist Martha Everts Holden, well-known throughout the middle west as 'Amber'. Amber, liking the company of bohemians, and understanding that they were all broke, largely subsidised the club, providing free beer and sandwiches. Without these, Isadora recalled, she and her mother might well have starved.

Isadora found the bohemians more congenial than the other Chicagoans she had met. She even on occasion danced at the club, doing what she called 'my religious dance' (possibly on a billiard table). Unfortunately, the bohemians, while earnestly approving of anything that might be called art, were as baffled by her new style of dancing as anyone else. As Nesta Macdonald wrote in *Dance Magazine* in 1977, 'The general conclusion . . . was that the young woman had an idea, but that clairvoyance was required to understand it.'

It was at the Bohemian Club that she found the first love of her life. He was a Polish immigrant named Ivan Miroski, more than twenty years older than she was, 'with a great shock of red, curling hair, a red beard, and piercing blue eyes. He generally sat in a corner and smoked a pipe and looked on at the *divertissements* of the Bohemians with a slightly ironic smile.'

He began taking Isadora and her mother for picnics, during which he and Isadora would leave mother dozing under a tree while they went off for lengthy walks and '*tête-à-têtes*'. Isadora was by now a handsome, fresh-faced young lady, with long wavy brown hair, and before long the pair were, in her words, 'madly, insanely in love'. It was a very chaste and proper Victorian love, expressed mainly by hugging, kissing and holding hands, and according to the approved manner of the time, Ivan soon asked her to marry him.

Isadora hesitated. Madly in love with him she might be, but her greatest love was still the dance. She intended to make a success of her dancing career, and regretfully told Ivan that she thought they should wait until she had 'made a fortune'. She was also of course deeply mistrustful of the whole institution of marriage, although, as she wrote of the episode, 'I had not yet taken up the cudgels for free love for which I did battle later.'

By the time Ivan made his proposal she had already come to the conclusion that any success she might have was not to come from Chicago. It now seemed obvious to her that the place to be was New York, the biggest, richest, most active city in America. In fact it was not then properly a city – it was, and would be until 1898, a group of independent cities and boroughs including Manhattan, Brooklyn, Queens, the Bronx and Staten Island. It was a place that during the latter half of the nineteenth century had grown almost too fast for its own good, its population having increased from around 400,000 in 1847 to almost ten times that number, and by the 1890s it seemed almost overwhelmed by its own wealth. But its wealth made it a place where things happened, and it was Isadora's good fortune that in the late summer of 1895 Chicago was visited by the Broadway producer, Augustin Daly, and his company of players.

Augustin Daly's was then the most prestigious theatre company in America. It was also one of the last of the old-style stock companies, with a regular group of players, each belonging to a particular, almost traditional, stock type – leading man, leading lady, villain, ingénue, comic servant, etc. These would play their roles in a vast repertory of plays, sometimes dozens of them in a year. Daly was a determined opponent of the emerging star system, believing that to preserve theatrical illusion actors should not become celebrities (with the sole exception of his leading lady, Ada Rehan, who happened also to be his mistress). As he once said, 'I want my company kept at a level. I put them all in a line, and then I watch, and if one head begins to bob up above the others, I give it a crack and send it down again.'

31

Prestigious as he was, Daly was already beginning to be seen by ambitious young theatricals as something of a back number. Bernard Shaw, in 1897, when still a drama critic, would lump him in with Henry Irving as 'fit for nothing but to be stuffed and mounted under glass to adorn the staircase of the Garrick Club'.

All the same, to be hired by Daly remained a sure step to a theatrical reputation and, from the moment his company arrived in Chicago, Isadora (who had seen his company perform in San Francisco) began haunting the theatre door. Again and again she sent in a request to see him, and again and again she was told that he was too busy, but she might see his under-manager. She kept refusing this offer and demanding to see Daly, and eventually her persistence paid off.

There is no mention in her memoirs that she did a dance audition for him, but she does admit that she gave him a 'harangue'. 'I told him that I had the germ of a great idea, a revolutionary idea, which would awaken the world to an intimacy with the art of dancing.'

Her passionate enthusiasm did enough to awaken Daly to a cautious approval. He told her that he could offer her 'a little part in a pantomime' if she could get to New York by October. Also of course provided that when she got there she proved suitable.

Excitedly she wired friends in San Francisco. The wire read: TRIUMPHANT ENGAGEMENT. AUGUSTIN DALY. MUST REACH NEW YORK FIRST OCTOBER. WIRE A HUNDRED DOLLARS FOR FARE. The money duly arrived, as did sister Elizabeth and brother Augustin, 'who, inspired by the telegram, had decided that our fortunes were to be made.'

Ivan was 'desperate with grief' that Isadora was proposing to leave Chicago, but they swore eternal love, and she even softened the blow by encouraging him to believe that some day they would marry. Then it was on to New York.

Chapter Three

Building a Career

The Duncans – Isadora, Elizabeth, Augustin and their mother Dora – got to New York and found lodgings in what Isadora would describe as 'a terrible boarding-house' on Sixth Avenue. She danced for Augustin Daly and, being found suitable for his pantomime, was cast in it, although, to her disappointment, she was not to dance.

It was not a pantomime in the British sense of a lavish Christmas-time entertainment, based on a fairy tale, with songs and comedy and transformation scenes. It was pantomime in the true sense of a drama using gesture in place of words, and Daly had imported it from France, that stronghold of mime, importing with it its Parisian star, Jane May. Its title was *Miss Pygmalion*, and Jane May had also co-written it, in collaboration with Michel Carré *fils*, under the pseudonym Jean Herbert.

Isadora loathed it. She thought pantomime a foolish exercise, in which 'people substitute gestures for words, so that it is neither the art of the dancer nor the art of the actor, but falls between in hopeless sterility... When I was told that I must point ... to say YOU, press my heart to say LOVE, and then violently hit myself on the chest to say ME, it all seemed to be too ridiculous.' For her, movement was for 'lyrical and emotional expression' and what it expressed could no more be translated into words than music can. Nor could words be expressed properly by gesture.

Her feeling that the whole concept of pantomime was ridiculous made rehearsals under the disciplinarian Jane May doubly hard for her. One day she was reduced to tears when Jane May sent for Daly and told him that Isadora, 'had no talent whatever and could not possibly carry the part.' Seeing the tears, Daly patted Isadora kindly on the shoulder, saying to Jane May, 'You see, she is very expressive when she cries. She'll learn.'

Daly seems to have had a soft spot for Isadora, even though he had

33

little appreciation of how far she had already developed her ideas on dance. He even insisted, as part of her contract, that she should take dance lessons from time to time. Most of these were given her by the company's dance master, Carl Marwig, although she also on occasion was taught by Marie Bonfanti, she whose five-hour extravaganza, *The Black Crook*, had visited San Francisco in revival in 1893. Isadora must have loathed all these lessons, so different from the sort of dancing she aspired to. In her later life she never mentioned Daly's efforts on her behalf.

Rehearsals of *Miss Pygmalion* lasted for six weeks. The custom of the time was that actors did not start getting paid until the play opened, so the Duncans, in their 'terrible boarding house' were hard pressed to make ends meet. In fact they were soon evicted from it for inability to pay their rent, and found another lodging, on 189th Street in Washington Heights.

This was some little way from Broadway, and as the family had no money, every day Isadora had to walk. She didn't have any money for a mid-day snack either, so every day she 'used to hide in the stage box during the lunch hour and sleep from exhaustion, then start rehearsing again in the afternoon without any food.'

By the time the play opened, in November 1895, she was nearing collapse. But open in it she did, feeling most unaesthetic in 'a Directoire costume of blue silk, a blonde wig, and a big straw hat. Alas for the revolution of art which I had come to give the world!'

Some of the critics were as unenthusiastic about the piece as she was. The *New York Times* spoke of its 'excess of gesticulation', saying 'it carries with it no illusion of life, and it does not stir the emotions'.

It played in New York for three weeks, then, as was the custom in the Daly company, it began touring. Isadora found herself on the road, travelling 'weary miles' from town to town. Away from her family for the first time in her life, and with few friends among her fellow-actors who, she recalled, 'regarded me as queer', she found touring a hard and lonely life. The little spare time she had she spent mostly alone, either reading books (she remained a voracious reader) or writing letters to her great love, Ivan Miroski, still back in Chicago.

A particular hardship for her was that Daly expected his actors to provide their own food and accommodation. Isadora, obliged to limit her expenditure to fifty cents a day, could afford only the poorest lodgings, often finding herself in the sort of digs where men, 'mostly drunk', would try and get into her room. Of one such occasion she wrote, 'I was terrified and, dragging the heavy wardrobe across the room, barricaded the door with it. Even then I did not dare go to sleep, but sat up on guard all night.'

There was, however, an important bright spot. During her engagement with the Daly company, for the only time in her life, she was learning from professionals the discipline of performing. Quite soon she truly came to appreciate Jane May, who, while on tour, 'called a rehearsal every day, and nothing ever suited her.' Isadora, as she later wrote, 'could not help but admire the extraordinary and vibrant expression of this pantomime actress. If she had not been imprisoned in the false and vapid form of pantomime, she might have been a great dancer.'

But in spite of Jane May's efforts, *Miss Pygmalion* was not well received by either public or critics, and when the touring company returned to Broadway, early in 1896, Augustin Daly announced that to build up his coffers he was sending out another touring company immediately, to play several of his repertory standards, including the play that had always done well for him at the box office, since he first presented it in 1888, *A Midsummer Night's Dream.*

Daly was notorious, as many stage producers were throughout the 1800s, for taking considerable liberties with Shakespeare. He thought nothing, for instance, of amending any Shakespeare play in which Ada Rehan was to appear, cutting and rewriting it to make sure her star shone as brightly as possible.

His staging of *A Midsummer Night's Dream* was infamous among the discerning for its spectacular effects – smoke and shadows and falling mists, and fairies whose wands twinkled with tiny electric lights. Nor were they any happier with the lavishness of his music – he borrowed much of it from Weber's opera *Oberon*, and he built Mendelssohn's 'Wedding March', originally written to accompany the last act, and to celebrate the forthcoming nuptials of Theseus and Hippolyta, into a magnificent grand finale. The public loved it.

Isadora he cast as the First Fairy, and told her, 'If you like, you might dance in the fairy scene.' This was to come early in Act II, before the entrance of Titania and Oberon. Isadora, delighted, chose a piece of Mendelssohn to dance to (fortunately he was among her favourite composers), but all would not be plain sailing. Daly's fairies were to glitter, and he was insistent she wear a fussy costume, all gauze and tissue-paper and sparkles. Worst of all, she was to wear a pair of tinsel wings. Isadora, with her settled ideas on simple dress for dancing, objected to these in particular, saying she needed no tinsel wings. She by her dancing could 'express' wings, she told him. But he was insistent. The wings stayed.

Then came another problem. On the first night, delighted to feel she was making a beginning on her chosen road, she gave it her all. As she wrote later, 'Here, at last, I was alone on a great stage with a great public before me, and I could dance. And I did dance – so well that the public burst into spontaneous applause. I had made what they call a hit.'

Daly, backstage as she came off, was furious, shouting, 'This isn't a music hall!' What had happened, of course, was that she had broken his golden rule that no member of his company should make themselves stand out. He gave orders that, for the rest of the play's run in New York, and for the entire length of its tour, the stage lights would be dimmed during her dance. She performed as well as ever, but as she sadly remembered, 'Nobody could see anything on the stage but a white fluttering thing.'

As well as *A Midsummer Night's Dream* the company performed various other plays. In *The Geisha* she played a singer but, as she was hopeless at carrying a tune, was forced to mime. She danced as one of a quartet of women in *Much Ado About Nothing*, as a spirit in *The Tempest*, and was given a solo gypsy dance in *Meg Merrilees*, a dramatisation of Walter Scott's novel, *Guy Mannering*. She acted in *The School for Scandal*, and in *Twelfth Night* was again allowed a short dance. The tour took the company all over America, including Boston, Washington, Pittsburgh, Philadelphia, San Francisco (where naturally her performance was noted in the local papers), Atlanta, New Orleans and Chicago.

During the company's time in Chicago she was able to renew old acquaintances, which led to her giving several short performances of her dancing in private homes. And of course she was delighted to be back again with Ivan Miroski. To him she unburdened her dissatisfactions. It was now the summer of 1896, she had been employed by Daly for nine months, and she had realised that the commercial theatre could never in any way accommodate the sort of dancing she wished to present. As she perceived it, she was simply one of 'a Company of Marionettes, pulled by the hand of a master'.

It may be from her unhappiness at this time that, before setting off back to New York, she again gave Ivan her promise to marry him. In New York she told her family of this promise, and her brother Augustin, shrewder in the ways of the world than she would ever be, took it on himself to make a few enquiries about Ivan. These soon unearthed the fact that he had omitted to mention to Isadora that he already had a wife, who was alive and well and living where he had married her, in London.

Dora, for a moment exerting parental firmness, forbade Isadora ever to see Ivan again. The whole business was a 'terrible shock' to Isadora, and in her forlorn misery she agreed. She never wrote to, or heard from, Ivan again. (In 1898, on the outbreak of the Spanish-American War, he volunteered for service. Enlisted, he was posted to boot camp in Florida, and there died of typhus.)

In spite of her unhappiness at her life in the Daly company, she stayed with it for another twelve months, developing, as she later said, 'a perfect nausea for the theatre: the constant repetition of the same words and the same gestures, night after night, and the caprices, the way of looking at life.' She took to bringing with her to rehearsals a copy of the *Meditations* of Marcus Aurelius, in an effort to encourage in herself a spirit of Stoicism, but in this she was only partially successful. Feeling that her passion to develop the Dance, her whole *raison d'être*, was being thwarted, she became increasingly miserable.

There were compensations, although they were few. One was that in the summer of 1897 she had a small part in a production of *As You Like It* (as one of the 'Persons in the Train of Hymen') which took her for the first time away from America when the company went to England to perform at Stratford-on-Avon, as part of one of the annual summer seasons of Shakespeare introduced there in 1886 by the touring actor-manager Frank Benson.

Daly's attempts to give Isadora instruction in dancing continued. While the company were in England he arranged for her to have lessons with the dancer Katti Lanner. Lanner, who had studied with the Romantic ballerina Fanny Essler, was now dance director at London's famous music-hall, the Empire, Leicester Square. As Isadora detested both ballet and the dancing of the music-hall, this might have seemed like another bad idea. But as it turned out she did get something from Lanner, who was much respected for both her sense of music and her ability at mime.

Mime is subtly different from pantomime, being the art of expressing emotion through movement and gesture, rather than attempting to convey thoughts better expressed in words. And the dance that Isadora was feeling her way towards would have in it a strong element of mime, as well as being extremely responsive to music. She was sufficiently impressed by Lanner to refer to her later, when back in America, as her 'dancing teacher'.

Soon after the trip to Stratford, there came a day when, back in New York, Daly came upon Isadora quietly weeping in a backstage room. He asked her what was troubling her, and she began to pour out her sorrow and frustration, saying, 'What's the good of having me here, with my genius, when you make no use of me?'

During the course of her lament, he slipped a consoling hand down the back of her dress. She felt angry at this, but ignored it, continuing to complain till she felt she had made her point. When she stopped, he withdrew his hand, thoughtfully said, 'H'm,' and left the room. Within a few days Isadora had resigned from his company.

It was the late summer of 1897, and her plan now was to make her way as a solo performer. During her twenty-odd months with Daly she had managed to make some contacts in the New York theatre world, and using those she began to advertise herself as a 'choreographic philosopher'. She and her family decided that the thing to do was to hire what they called 'a studio', where Elizabeth could give dance lessons during the day, and Isadora could practise and perfect her performances during the evening (mother playing the piano for both). Being the Duncans, they rented a rehearsal room in Carnegie Hall.

To afford it, they economised by also moving out of their lodgings and sleeping there (on mattresses on the floor). To make ends meet they also from time to time sublet the room to others who wanted to use it. Augustin was seldom there, having by now become an actor and joined a touring company, and Raymond, who had by now also arrived from San Francisco, followed in his father's steps by venturing into journalism (while also sleeping in the rehearsal room).

Soon Isadora was at last beginning to attract attention. From time to time she gave performances in private salons, and in February 1898 these were remarked on by the *New York Herald*, which called them 'delightful entertainments', explaining (no doubt after a little help from Isadora herself) that she had 'revived the graceful art of the Poetic Greeks ... through the tripping of her feet, the swaying of her body, the expression of her sympathetic face.'

Isadora was by now developing her idea of improvising dance to the music that accompanied her – by letting it inspire her and using the sense of movement and gesture that was now so deeply a part of her that it was almost instinctive. She began to study the music of Gluck, who in the eighteenth century had done so much to reinvent opera. From him she learnt a lot about coordinating music and drama.

Other composers she responded to at the time included Mendelssohn and Johann Strauss, especially his waltzes (for all her drive and ambition she was a born romantic). She even enjoyed some sentimental popular melodies, such as those of Ethelbert Nevin, who composed the music for such well-loved songs of the time as 'The Rosary', 'Little Boy Blue' and 'Mighty Lak' a Rose'. Nevin also wrote more ambitious pieces, of the sort that could be described as 'tone poems'. Isadora considered him 'a great virtuoso composer', and took to dancing to his most famous composition, 'Narcissus'.

Nevin, then thirty-five and fatally ill (probably with tuberculosis) had recently returned to the USA from Europe. It so happened that he too was renting one of the rooms at Carnegie Hall and one day, early in 1898, he burst into Isadora's room shouting, 'I hear you are dancing to my music! I forbid it, I forbid it! It isn't dance music, my music. Nobody shall dance it.'

As Isadora recalled the scene, she took his hand and conducted him to a chair.

> 'Sit there,' I said, 'and I will dance to your music. If you don't like it, I swear I will never dance it again.'
>
> Then I danced his 'Narcissus' for him. I had found in the melody the imagining of that youth Narcissus who stood by the brook until he fell in love with his own image, and in the end pined away and turned into a flower. This I danced for Nevin. The last note had hardly died away when he jumped up from the chair, rushed towards me, and threw his arms around me. He looked at me and his eyes were filled with tears.
>
> 'You are an angel,' he said. 'You are a *divinatrice*. Those very movements I saw when I was composing the music.'

He set about arranging for her to give a performance, dancing to his music. Other musicians, as well as some singers and actors, were assembled, and on Thursday, 24th March 1898, they performed at Carnegie Hall. Isadora danced gracefully to three of Nevin's *Water Scenes* – 'Narcissus', 'Ophelia' and 'Water Nymphs'.

Writing of her personification of Narcissus, a reviewer described her as 'first startled, then charmed' on seeing herself reflected in the water. 'Becoming more and more enamoured, the dancer leans forward, seemingly viewing herself from side to side, sending kisses to the liquid image, stepping across the shallow brook and still finding the figure reflected from its surface... The first start, the gradually growing conceit, the turning and bending, the ecstasy of delight at finding himself so beautiful are all most convincingly enacted.'

She was now truly on her way. Shortly after the Carnegie Hall appearance she appeared in a series of what were called 'Lenten matinees' at the Lyceum Theatre on Fourth Avenue, and she made further appearances at Carnegie Hall. It was at around this time that she took to giving her audiences little lectures on her philosophy of dance, being one of the first to adopt what would become a common twentieth-century habit, that of artists (especially painters) issuing manifestos explaining what their art was aiming to express and be. At one Carnegie Hall performance she said (among other things) that after 'ten years' study' she had realised that dance wasn't 'dancing' but 'movement expressive of thought'. 'If dance is not to come to life again as an art,' she told her audience, 'then far better that its name should rest in the dust of antiquity.'

A socially well-connected American, then in her thirties and soon to embark on an illustrious writing career, was the future novelist Edith Wharton, and her attitude to prevailing styles of dance much resembled Isadora's. Invited, in the summer of 1898, to see Isadora dance, she declined, on the grounds that, 'Only two kinds of dancing were familiar to that generation, waltzing in the ballroom and pirouetting on the stage. I hated pirouetting and did not go. Those who did smiled, and said they supposed their hostess had asked the young woman to dance out of charity – as I daresay she did. Nobody had ever seen anything like it; you couldn't call it dancing, they said.' (Later, in Paris, Edith did catch up with Isadora, and admired her greatly, finding her dancing to be of a sort she 'had only dreamed of, a flowing of movement into movement, an endless interweaving of motion and music, satisfying every sense as a rose does, or a phrase of Mozart's.')

Edith had been invited to see Isadora because she was a member of the social elite to whom Isadora was fast becoming a fashionable new sensation, being invited to give salon performances both in the grand houses of New York and in such fashionable resorts for wealthy New Yorkers as Newport, Rhode Island. At these performances the piano music she danced to was usually provided by her mother, once rather ungallantly described on such an occasion as 'a large mama in a blue gown'. (Her mother's well-bred and matronly presence did, however, help in assuring her genteel salon audiences of Isadora's respectability.)

The undisputed leader of New York society was Mrs William Backhouse Astor Jr, and it was she who became Isadora's first patroness. It was at Mrs Astor's place in Newport that Isadora danced in the summer of 1898, and as she recalled, 'Mrs Astor represented to America what a Queen did to England. The people who came into her presence were more awed and frightened than if they had approached royalty. But to me she was very affable.'

This, however, was towards the end of the somewhat elderly Mrs Astor's dominant rule. Other wealthy Newport and New York hostesses were vying to replace her as the leader of fashion, in particular a trio who acquired the nickname 'The Great Triumvirate'. These were Mrs O.H.P. Belmont, Mrs Herman Oelrichs and Mrs Stuyvesant Fish, and all three raced to outdo the others by being the next to present Isadora.

Such rich ambitious women seemed to Isadora to represent at last her hope of establishing a dancing career. Soon she would be described in the New York papers as 'Society's Favorite Dancer', although she admitted herself that society, like so many others, seemed to have little idea of what she was attempting to do. She remembered a constant 'gurgle' from those Newport audiences of 'How perfectly sweet! How very pretty!' and as she well realised 'They had no art sense whatever.'

Fortunately for the nurturing of her art, she also continued to dance elsewhere. Towards the end of 1898 the periodical *The Director* was reporting that her dances 'had created a deep enthusiasm among the cultured people [of New York], and the manner in which they are heralded by the press as the arrival of a new creation in art has aroused a general and widespread interest.'

The upsurge in her fortunes allowed Isadora and her family to stop dossing down in their rented room at Carnegie Hall. They gave it up and booked themselves into two rooms at the Windsor Hotel, on Fifth Avenue between 46th and 47th Streets. Their rent totalled ninety dollars a week, which was (as so often) rather beyond what they could afford, but at the hotel they also had the use of a large salon on the second floor where Elizabeth was able to give 'Children's Classes for Cultivation of Movement and the Dance'. With Isadora's growing reputation, these classes never went short of pupils (sometimes she conducted the classes herself), but even so the family's finances remained precarious.

A woman, Marie-Louise de Meeus, who attended the classes as a child, recalled in *The Cornhill Magazine* in 1932 that complicated steps and 'tours de forces were rigorously excluded'. She remembered how Elizabeth 'made me realize how movement must invade my whole being, from the poise of the head through the poise of the body, running like a current down the limbs, even to the tips of the fingers.'

At around this time there was a mild crisis in the tight-knit Duncan family – or rather, there was an event in it that certain members elevated into a crisis. Augustin, continuing his acting career, had gone on tour in a production of *Romeo and Juliet*. He, now aged twenty-five and beginning to advance in the profession, was Romeo. His Juliet was a sixteen-year-old actress named Sarah Whiteford. They fell in love in real life and, while still on the road, were married. Not only that, by the time they returned to New York and Sarah was able to meet the family, she was pregnant.

As Isadora later wrote, 'This was taken as an act of treason. For some reason that I could never understand, my mother was furious. She acted in much the same way as she had done on the first visit of my father [note the word 'first']... She went into another room and slammed the door. Elizabeth took refuge in silence and Raymond became hysterical. I was the only one who felt any sympathy.' (Presumably mother, in addition to having outspoken views against marriage, was, like many mothers, jealous of another woman taking the affections of a beloved son, and was simply more honest than most in expressing her feelings.)

At around the same time as the family moved into the Windsor Hotel, Isadora gave another series of matinee performances at the Lyceum Theatre. At these she danced to recited passages from *The Rubáiyát of Omar Khayyám* (her performances would continue to mingle dance, music and poetry for some time, the poetry often read by her sister or a brother, and this romantic, sensuous and somewhat godless piece was a great favourite with all the Duncans).

At her performances in late 1898 she danced to the famous translation by Edward FitzGerald, but when she returned to the Lyceum with it in March 1899 it was in collaboration with actor-author Justin Huntly McCarthy, who had made a new translation. Their performance was billed as 'An Afternoon with Omar Khayyam, the Astronomer-Poet of Persia'.

In it McCarthy first gave a short talk on the life of Omar, after which Isadora danced to his reading of his translation, and for the first time a new thread entered the tapestry of her life, one that would remain for ever – she caused a scandal. As a critic observed, 'It was no fault of McCarthy's that certain society women of New York got up and left the theatre. Mr McCarthy was properly garbed and conducted himself in every sense as an elocutionist and a gentleman should.

It was, of course, Isadora who offended the women's respectability. Not only was her dancing uninhibitedly sensual, her costume was suddenly perceived to be indecent. Still wearing a version of her 'little white tunic', and still at this point in her career wearing soft flat ballet shoes (barefoot would come later), she had dispensed with the unnecessary and restricting tights that were deemed essential for stage dancing. It wasn't that she had suddenly abandoned them for this performance. Probably she had never encumbered herself with the things. More likely her passionate involvement in this particular performance had made it more shockingly obvious that her legs were bare.

The incident caused much discussion. Her morals were questioned, and one writer seriously advised her to abandon dancing to the *Rubáiyát*, suggesting she 'enlarge her present repertoire or arrange a new one' if she wanted to continue her career. The scandal did not, however, prevent another prominent socialite, Mrs Arend Van Vlissingen, from inviting her to Chicago to perform the *Rubáiyát* in a salon performance.

She did, of course have many other items in her repertoire. One, which she called *A Dance of Wandering*, was set to a melody by Paderewski, and early in 1898 her performance of it was described by the *New York Herald* as 'a spirit roaming through the forests, bewildered by the strangeness of her surroundings, trembling at every sound, the rustle of the leaves, the sighing of the winds.' The *New York Times*, of the same performance, observed that, while her movements were 'extremely graceful', they 'were more of the body and arms than the legs.'

The *New York Herald* gave a picture of another of her early performances, describing her dancing to the Johann Strauss waltz, *Voices of Spring*: 'The dancer bounds onto the stage with uplifted hands and face, the incarnation of the joyous spring breaking the icy fetters of winter. To the sensuous waltz music she springs hither and thither, scattering the seeds as she goes, plucking the budding flowers, breathing the life-giving air, exhaling a joyousness of nature which is wondrous in its grace and beauty.'

Isadora was proud of having been accepted by high society as a performer. For almost all her life she would cherish a photograph taken in 1898, showing her dancing on the lawn of a great house, with her mother at the piano and Elizabeth reciting, in front of an audience of millionaires and their wives. But there was another drawback to performing for such audiences, as well as their lack of 'art sense'. This was that they regarded performing for them as such an honour that their fees were correspondingly small. She complained, 'These ladies were so economical of their *cachets* that we hardly made enough to pay the trip and our board.'

For this reason and others, by the spring of 1899 Isadora was once again becoming disenchanted with a city, feeling that 'in all my experience in New York I had found no intelligent sympathy or help for my ideas.' This may not have been entirely true, but undoubtedly many New Yorkers did feel little sympathy for her earnest devotion to Dance. A typical attitude was expressed in *Broadway Magazine* later that year:

Miss Duncan holds forth at such ultra-fashionable places as the Waldorf-Astoria, Sherry's and Carnegie Lyceum. She spurns Broadway with a large, deep, thick spurn, that almost makes us ashamed of having anything to do with the thoroughfare. She is very, very classic, and is horribly, dreadfully afraid of becoming anything but absolutely and painfully refined. It can thus be seen that Miss Duncan occupies a rather unique position among American dancers. Long may she retain it.

More and more Isadora's thoughts began to turn to England. For one thing her father and his next family had been drowned off its coast only the previous October, so it was naturally on her mind. For another, she had enjoyed a certain feeling she found when she toured there with the Daly company in 1897 – a feeling that England was more responsive to Art than any place she had so far been in, and where she might find a more enthusiastic response to her ideas. After all, was it not the home of many writers and painters she admired and 'might meet there – George Meredith, Henry James, Watts, Swinburne, Burne-Jones, Whistler… These were magic names.' (Significantly, she does not mention Wilde, who in 1895 had been jailed for two years for an unspeakable crime. His downfall had hastened the end of America's flirtation with aestheticism, which was then declining anyway as the country entered a more belligerent era, symbolised in the Spanish-American War of 1898.)

Another reason for Isadora's dissatisfaction with New York was that the Duncan family were not finding themselves very happy at the Windsor Hotel. As she recalled, 'The Windsor was a gloomy hotel, and we found very little joy in living there and trying to meet these heavy expenses.' She remembered going, on the morning of Friday, 17th March 1899, to try and borrow some money from 'a very rich old lady who lived on the third floor'. The old lady refused, at the same time complaining about the Windsor on her own account, saying, 'I have stayed in this hotel for many years, but if they don't give me better coffee, I am going to leave.'

As Isadora drily remarked, years later, 'She did leave that afternoon, when the whole hotel went up in flames, and she was burned to a crisp!'

The fire was started when a guest tried to toss a lit match out of a second-floor window and accidentally set fire to the curtains. In an hour, while the St Patrick's Day parade marched past along Fifth Avenue, watched by a cheering crowd, the hotel burned to the ground.

Isadora and Elizabeth were giving one of their classes (also on the second floor) when the fire began. Their mother was at the piano as usual, and it was she who had the first hint that something was amiss, when she saw bodies flying past the window. At first she thought 'her eyesight was playing her a trick', but soon a maid entered the salon, accompanied by 'a puff of smoke', and calmly told Elizabeth that the place was on fire.

Mrs Duncan, Elizabeth and Isadora (and the maid) at once bundled the little girls they were teaching into their coats (for the lesson they were wearing flimsy tartan dresses and white satin slippers), told them to take hold of each other's hands and not let go, and shepherded them out through the smoke-filled hall and staircase to safety.

When it was all over, and the Duncan family was safely settled in the Hotel Buckingham, Isadora was interviewed by the *New York Herald*, who reported that, 'She said mournfully that she had saved only the dress she wore, a house gown of dark brown material with flaring Elizabethan collar. All of her costumes and those of her sister were lost as well as the bric-a-brac which they highly prized.'

This disaster, Isadora felt, in her usual dramatic fashion, 'was fate'. To England the family would go.

To accomplish this she immediately set about organising a series of benefit concerts, to be 'Given in Aid of Miss Isadora Duncan and Other Sufferers of the Windsor Hotel Fire'. The series continued for six weeks, the concerts being given at such prestigious venues as Delmonico's restaurant. When she was not herself performing, she circulated among the wealthy invitees, taking tea with them and begging for financial assistance. She worked herself into a state of exhaustion, later recalling that at one moment, 'In the heat of pressing my suit I became quite faint and fell over sideways. My tears fell into the chocolate and onto the toast.'

The result of all her efforts was that she succeeded in replacing her wardrobe (and that of her family), but was left with a surplus in cash of only around three hundred dollars, which was 'not even enough for second class tickets on an ordinary steamer'.

While the family were wondering how else they could raise money quickly, or what other arrangements they could make, it was Raymond who came up with the 'bright idea'. He suggested that, instead of taking an ordinary liner across the Atlantic, they could travel more slowly, but much more cheaply, on a cattle boat. And maybe even more cheaply if mother would agree to cook for the crew.

Mother bravely agreed, and everyone agreed, and soon Isadora, Elizabeth, Raymond and Mother had arranged a passage to England and set sail. Augustin stayed behind with his expectant wife and his acting.

45

Chapter Four

A Taste of True Success

Somehow the Duncans – Isadora, Elizabeth, Raymond and mother Dora – did manage to get themselves passage to England on a freighter transporting a couple of hundred cattle there. They sailed in May 1899, and for some reason decided to travel incognito, adopting from Dora's mother the surname O'Gorman together with various appropriate first names. The high-spirited Isadora became 'Maggie O'Gorman', and had an enjoyable voyage adopting a fictional personality and spending much time flirting with the Irish first mate while he was 'up in the lookout'.

At this time she was a graceful young woman of twenty-two. She still had something of a boyish figure, an oval face with handsome features, and a mass of long wavy chestnut hair. In fact she was so attractive that before the end of the voyage (which would have taken the best part of two weeks) the first mate proposed to her, saying, as she later recalled, 'Sure, Maggie O'Gorman, I'd make a good husband to you if you would allow it.' Naturally, she did not.

It was a happy trip for all of them. Quite apart from the excitement of embarking on a new adventure, they found the crew sociable and friendly. Mother, as planned, did the cooking, and seems to have received no complaints, while the captain kept the family generously supplied with 'hot toddies'. The only drawback was the cattle, whom Isadora described as 'struggling beasts in the hold, on their way to London from the plains of the Middle West, goring each other with their horns and moaning in the most piteous way, night and day.' This the family found upsetting, and Isadora later believed that this experience did much to influence Raymond into becoming a vegetarian.

Arriving in London threw them all, Isadora said, into 'a state of perfect ecstasy'. Never before had the Duncans (except for herself) been in a city with so much ancient wealth, with so much history and so much

Art, with so much to explore. They rented a room near Marble Arch, and all four enthusiastically set about behaving like tourists. They spent hours, she recalled, 'in Westminster Abbey, the British Museum, the South Kensington Museum [which that year would be renamed, by royal command, the Victoria & Albert Museum], visiting Kew Gardens, Richmond Park, and Hampton Court.' And they went on doing that, living in a haze of artistic idealism, until they ran out of money and were unable to pay their rent.

Their situation was forcibly brought home to them when they returned from 'a most interesting lecture on the Venus and Adonis of Correggio' to find that their landlady had locked them out. They had 'no money, no friends' and no place to spend the night. As Isadora recalled, 'We tried two or three hotels, but they were adamant upon the necessity of payment in advance, in default of luggage. We tried two or three lodging-houses, but all the landladies acted in the same heartless manner. Finally we were reduced to a bench in Green Park, but even then an enormous policeman appeared and told us to move on.'

For three nights, she recalled, they were homeless, snatching sleep where they could, wandering the streets, living on coffee and penny buns, and reading aloud to each other from *Journey to Athens*, by the celebrated Abbé Winckelmann.

Johann Joachim Winckelmann, born in Germany in 1717, had been a pioneer in arousing enthusiasm for the culture of Ancient Greece. The son of a cobbler, when young he became fascinated by the ruins of Pompeii, and decided to devote his life to the study of classical times. Although hampered in his chosen career by snobbish officials who resented his humble origins, he persevered to become Prefect of the Pontifical Antiquities of Rome, and Professor of Greek in the Vatican Library. He became an outstanding art historian, campaigned for the introduction of classical styles into architecture, and was a founding father of archaeology. He compiled a record of six centuries of life in Ancient Greece, intending to develop the facts he had assembled into a more mature and thoughtful work. But in 1768, before he could do so, he was stabbed and killed by a deranged young man he hardly knew, named Francis Arcangeli.

The Duncans were finding London a revelation in learning more about Ancient Greece. They were, as Isadora wrote, 'crazy with enthusiasm' about the Greek artefacts in the British Museum, 'where Raymond made sketches of all the Greek vases and bas-reliefs, and I tried to express them to whatever music seemed ... in harmony with the rhythms of the feet, and the tossing of the thyrsis' (this, in Greek called a 'thyrse', was a spear or wand tipped with a pine-cone and wound with ivy or vine-leaves, sacred to Dionysus and carried by his votaries, the Bacchantes, during their somewhat unrestrained rituals).

Isadora was developing her ideas of dance further. No longer seeking simply to copy the poses and imagined movements of Ancient Greece, she was attempting 'to steep [herself] in the spirit underlying them', to experience deeply 'the feelings that their gestures symbolised'. An essay she would write in 1903, 'The Dance of the Future', shows clearly how deeply she was observing and understanding:

> People have thought that so long as one danced in rhythm the form and design did not matter; but no, one must perfectly correspond to the other. The Greeks understood this very well. There is a statuette that shows a dancing cupid. It is a child's dance. The movements of the plump little feet and arms are perfectly suited to its form. The sole of the foot rests flat on the ground, a position which might be ugly in a more developed person, but is natural in a child trying to keep its balance. One of the legs is half raised; if it were outstretched it would irritate us, because the movement would be unnatural. There is also a statue of a satyr in a dance that is quite different from that of the cupid. His movements are those of a ripe and muscular man. They are in perfect harmony with the structure of his body.

After three days, the Duncans had had enough of sleeping rough. Intoxicated by the holy mission of Art and fortified by the belief that the world owed artists everything, Isadora led the family to the famous and expensive hotel, Claridges. It was still early morning, and as she recalled:

> I informed the night porter, who was half asleep, that we had just come on the night train, that our luggage would come from Liverpool, to give us rooms in the meantime, and to order breakfast to be sent up to us, consisting of coffee, buckwheat cakes, and other American delicacies.
>
> All that day we slept in luxurious beds. Now and then I telephoned down to the porter to complain bitterly that our luggage had not arrived.
>
> 'It is quite impossible for us to go out without a change of clothes,' I said, and that night we dined in our rooms.
>
> At dawn the next day, judging that the ruse had reached its limit,

we walked out exactly as we had walked in, but this time without waking the night porter!

Somehow the family again managed to get themselves into inexpensive lodgings, and fortunately for them it wasn't long before Isadora had a further inspiration. Exploring Chelsea, an area rich in artistic associations through such past and present residents as Turner, Rossetti, Whistler and Sargent, she sat down to rest on a bench in St Luke's churchyard, just off the King's Road. There her eye fell on an open newspaper, and in it she noticed the name of a wealthy society woman. She recognised the name, and observing that the woman had a house in Grosvenor Square, set off there, reflecting that if society women in New York would hire her to give private performances, so they would in London.

She was right. Within a few hours she was back at the lodgings with an engagement to dance the next weekend and a cheque for ten pounds as an advance fee (this would at the time have represented several weeks' wages for a clerk). She got there to find Raymond earnestly discoursing 'on the platonic idea of the soul', which he broke off on hearing her news to announce that the family must at once rent a 'studio' to live and work in, 'for we must never again subject ourselves to the insults of these low, common lodging-house women'.

They soon found an adequate place, a small house in Manresa Road, also just off the King's Road (and not far from St Luke's). They bought food, and Isadora headed for the West End to buy fabric at Liberty's to enhance her costumes. She bought 'a few yards of veiling' and became so enamoured of Liberty fabrics that for the rest of her life she used their silks for her costumes on all possible occasions.

She also decided at this point to make her costume more Grecian by abandoning the ballet flats she had previously worn. Instead she adopted golden sandals with golden lacing criss-crossing up to her calves.

Salon dancing in London turned out to be very similar to salon dancing in New York and Newport. Isadora's name soon spread among the ladies of fashion, and she had no problem getting bookings. Her mother of course played the music she danced to, and Raymond recited the poems. But her audiences remained obstinately unenlightened. As she wrote, remembering those days, 'The English are such an extremely polite people that no one even thought of remarking upon the originality of my costume and, alas! neither did they comment upon the originality of my dancing. Everyone said, "How pretty," "Awfully jolly," "Thank you so much," or something of the sort – but that was all.'

Nor was the living she could make any better than it had been in America. One day she would be 'dancing before Royalty, or in the garden at Lady Lowther's, and the next with nothing to eat. For sometimes I was paid, more often I was not.' On one occasion she was almost driven to despair when her hostess, after a charity benefit she had performed at, 'held up a huge bag filled with golden sovereigns and said: 'Look at the mint of money you have made for our Blind Girls' Home!'

The family were forced to live extremely frugally. 'There were long days,' Isadora remembered, 'when we had not even the courage to go out, but sat in their small house wrapped in blankets, playing chequers on an improvised chequer-board with pieces of cardboard. All the Duncans were prone to emotional ups and downs, easily depressed and easily elated. Things for them, Isadora included, tended to be either a disaster or a triumph, and of this period in her life she wrote, 'There were days, in fact, when we no longer had the courage to get up in the morning, but slept all day.'

Elizabeth was the first to crack. In September 1899 she decided to return to New York, where she had at least some reputation, and reopen her dancing school. But she would continue to support Isadora's great cause by sending whatever money she could spare back to London. The other three Duncans saw her off by train from Victoria Station, then returned to their house, so cast down by this partial break-up of the family that they 'spent some days of absolute depression'.

Rising out of it, Isadora continued to drum up what salon dancing she could, and she and Raymond continued to haunt the British Museum. One day, in a fit of high spirits, they were dancing together among the rhododendrons in a Kensington park when a strikingly beautiful Italianate woman in her thirties asked them cheerfully, 'Where on earth did you people come from?'

Isadora, elated from her dancing, replied airily, 'Not from the earth at all, but from the moon.'

'Well, whether from the earth or the moon, you are very sweet; won't you come and see me?' was the reply.

The woman was the actress Mrs Patrick Campbell, then at the height of her success and fame, and her invitation would prove to be of huge importance in Isadora's life.

She was a woman almost as dramatic and intelligent as Isadora herself, and possibly even more tempestuous. In 1893, aged twenty-eight and with very little acting experience, she had shot to stardom on the stage performing the title role in Pinero's drama *The Second Mrs Tanqueray* –

the first attempt by a British playwright to emulate the new realistic drama of Ibsen. Her success would endure – in 1912 Bernard Shaw would write *Pygmalion* with her specifically in mind to play Eliza Doolittle.

Not only did she hire Isadora to give private dancing lessons to her young daughter, Stella, she also introduced the Duncans to the world of London's artists – of painters, poets and authors (there were no professional dancers in London then, outside the music-halls). They had their own high society, considerably separate from the fashionable world for whom Isadora had been dancing, and she took to it at once, not only enjoying the elevated conversation (and the mingling with names that had long been famous to her), but also acquiring what would become a lifelong taste for champagne.

She and Raymond were introduced to the Park Lane salon of George Wyndham and his wife Sibell. George was a prominent Conservative Member of Parliament (the following year he would be appointed Chief Secretary for Ireland), and an author of the sort described as a 'miscellaneous writer'. Among the people Isadora met at the Wyndham's salon was the portrait painter Edward Charles Hallé. His father, who had died in 1895, was Karl (later Sir Charles) Hallé, founder of the famous Hallé Orchestra and first principal of the Royal College of Music, so Edward Charles was extremely well-connected in the world of the arts.

He was fifty-three when he met Isadora and, while not a particularly good painter, he was devoted to Art. Becoming a member of the Royal Academy quite young, he had in his late twenties joined in a revolt against it by several fellow-members who felt that painting and sculpture should be more faithful to life and its realities than the Academy preferred. It was this 'Secession' that had led to the founding, in 1877, of London's Grosvenor Gallery, so fashionable among the aesthetes of that day that it was burlesqued by name in *Patience*.

Through Hallé, Isadora met a number of eminent painters, including William Holman Hunt, John Singer Sargent (who, although born in Florence of American parents, had become British society's favourite portrait-painter), the recently-knighted Sir Lawrence Alma-Tadema, and George Frederic Watts. Knowing Sargent opened many doors in fashionable society to Isadora, but the two painters who helped her most in developing her ideas were Alma-Tadema and Watts.

Both shared her passion for the Graeco-Roman world. Alma-Tadema had been born in Holland in 1836, but had settled in England in 1870. His speciality was scenes of life in ancient times – Greek, Roman and Egyptian – rendered with an almost photographic clarity that tended to make his people (frequently near-naked nubile young ladies) seem somewhat artificial. Nonetheless, his knowledge òf those ancient times − of the clothing worn at different times and in different situations, of the architecture, furniture, domestic ornaments, jewellery and hairstyles, of the rituals of everyday life − was encyclopaedic. He frequently accompanied Isadora to the British Museum to look at the Elgin Marbles and the other classic artworks there (as, on other occasions, did Charles Hallé), and later in life she would describe him as her 'guide' to Greek art.

He was so knowledgeable, and his pictorial sense was so strong, that theatrical managers frequently came to him for advice for their spectacular productions. Frank Benson, producing the *Agamemnon* at Oxford, found invaluable his knowledge of the Greek garments, the chlamys and the chiton. In the same way, the actor-manager Herbert Beerbohm Tree, rehearsing for the title role in *Julius Caesar*, came to him for advice on how to correctly wear a toga (which he was finding a more intricate garment than it looked). He also thanked Alma-Tadema for helping bring Ancient Rome to the stage of Her Majesty's Theatre, saying he 'taught us the Roman handshake, the mutual grip of the wrist'.

Hallé was fifty-three and Alma-Tadema was sixty-three, and Isadora, still only twenty-two, found them much more fascinating to go round with than younger men, whom she found naïve and insipid. What she responded to at this point in her life was men with knowledge, experience, and a passionate involvement in their craft. As she would recall, she 'desired no other friends. Ordinary young men bored me exceedingly.' She developed a manner towards them that 'was so superior that they were completely frozen'.

George Watts did not bore her, even though he was now eighty-two. He came to dote on Isadora, and often she would visit his house-cum-studio, when they would walk in his garden while he talked of his life and his art.

It is interesting that the painters she responded to were all established, respected figures, whose style had been formed years before, and who were no longer in the forefront of new developments. But it is not surprising. She was not really interested in the craft of painting itself, and how it might be going forward, but in people who, like her, looked back to Graeco-Roman times as a golden age, who had striven to learn all they could about it, and had based their work on its attitudes. From them she could gather information for the road she had already decided to walk, following ideas of her own, developed in the isolation of her tightly-knit family.

53

Part of her growing understanding at this time was that there were two sides to her soul as a dancer – the Dionysiac and the Apollonian. One was creating art through abandoning oneself to instinct and passion; the other through calmness and almost contemplative harmony of movement. As she would explain, 'It is possible to dance in two ways. One can throw oneself into the spirit of the dance, and dance the thing itself: Dionysus. Or one can contemplate the spirit of the dance – and dance it as one who relates a story: Apollo.'

Watts was the most Apollonian of all the artists she met. He aimed to be a thinker in paint and stone, inviting the viewer to contemplate aspirations to resolution and nobility. Many of his works had moralising titles like *Hope, Mammon* or *Life, Death and Judgement*, and they were at heart more mid-Victorian than Ancient Greek, but he also painted many scenes from classical myth and legend – *Orpheus and Eurydice, Olympus on Ida* and *Ariadne in Naxos*.

Isadora, now that she was moving in the world of the arts, also began to attend the theatre, usually in the company of Charles Hallé. With him, and with his sister Maria, she saw the actor Sir Henry Irving in *The Bells*. Irving was so eminent in his profession that he was known within it as 'The Chief', and it was *The Bells* that had shot him to stardom back in 1871. The piece itself was a melodrama of not much literary merit, translated from a French original called *Le Juif Polonaise*, but Irving's performance in it of Mathias, the haunted Alsatian burgomaster who had committed a murder in his youth, was so strikingly powerful that for a while he was nicknamed 'The Unnerving Henry Irving'.

She saw Irving again, with his female equivalent for eminence and his frequent on-stage partner, Ellen Terry, in *Cymbeline*. Alma-Tadema had so much of a hand in helping design this that it was described (admiringly) as one of his paintings come to life. There was also for Isadora a connection with Watts, because in 1864 the sixteen-year-old Ellen Terry had married him, although the marriage had lasted only a year. Isadora admired her immensely for her carriage and movement on-stage, her womanly beauty and her air of spirituality.

A third great actor she saw was the Italian Eleanora Duse, then devotedly admired in London, even although she only ever performed in her native language (which led a few to wonder whether the admiration she excited was not to some extent self-generated by her admirers). Isadora saw her in the play that Mrs Patrick Campbell had made a success (and which had made *her* a success), *The Second Mrs Tanqueray* – translated, of course, into Italian. Duse was famous for the restraint of her acting, for the spare but telling use she made of gesture, and Isadora was vastly impressed. Remembering the performance years later, she wrote:

> At the end of the third act, where Mrs Tanqueray is driven to the wall by her enemies and, overcome with ennui, resolves to commit suicide, there was a moment when Duse stood quite still, alone on the stage. Suddenly, without any special outward movement, she seemed to grow and grow until her head appeared to touch the roof of the theatre... [It] was one of the greatest artistic achievements I have ever witnessed. I remember that I went home dazed with the wonder of it. I said to myself, when I can come on the stage and stand as still as Eleonora Duse did tonight, and, at the same time, create that tremendous force of dynamic movement, then I shall be the greatest dancer in the world.

Early in 1900, Isadora herself briefly returned to the acting stage. In February she joined the Frank Benson touring company (this probably came about either through her having played Shakespeare at Stratford with the Daly company, or through her friendship with Alma-Tadema).

Benson was then in his early forties. The son of a country squire, educated at Winchester and at New College, Oxford, he was rather a clean-cut athletic sort of chap (his great passion, alongside the theatre, was for cricket), and had entered the acting profession in 1882 with some sort of idea of making it respectable, of purging it of the rogues and vagabonds that he felt had infested it till then.

Mostly what he produced was Shakespeare and, like Augustin Daly, he was not above tampering with the sacred text, although, unlike Daly, his amendments were usually in the spirit of the piece, and introduced to remove passages that were either dull or confusing.

Like Daly, too, he seems to have taken to Isadora, introducing into his forthcoming Stratford production of *Henry V* a role in which she danced for the Dauphin in the French camp at Agincourt. It was, she recalled, 'a most picturesque and rather heretical representation of the French camp' and she herself was, in her own words, 'lightly clad'.

A little later she would appear again for Benson, this time in *A Midsummer Night's Dream*. In it she danced as an unnamed Fairy, and was given 'a good many lines to speak'. Whose lines, she did not say.

She did not much enjoy her times with the Benson company. Bursting with her ideas about the philosophy of Art and Dance, and stimulated by living in a world where these things could be discussed endlessly with passion and involvement, she came across to her fellow-actors as 'contentious'. Thus she was not very popular with them. And on her side, she felt that what she was doing, and wanted to do, was 'too spiritual for their gross, materialistic comprehension'.

Her appearances with Benson were no doubt undertaken purely in order to make money, for no matter how much progress she felt she was making in developing her dancing, money for the Duncans was still tight, and Isadora was the only one of the family who had any hope of earning much. It was probably for this reason that at around the time of her Benson performances she made a visit to the one dancing teacher she had admired, Katti Lanner, at the Empire music-hall, in an attempt to see if she could in any way perform there. Unfortunately, there wasn't.

Things got better when, early in May 1900, she found herself giving one of her own performances at the Royal Court Theatre, in Chelsea's Sloane Square. In her audience was the Prince of Wales, who in less than a year would be King Edward VII, and who had in fact seen her before making one of her salon appearances for the fashionable.

The magazine *The Lady*, reviewing her Royal Court performance, took the fashionable to task for the way in which, less than a year before, they had failed to perceive Isadora's quality, saying that they had failed to reward her with 'any great enthusiasm: Miss Duncan's dancing was either too unusual, or dancing in a garden too bold a departure. But the whirligig of Time has his revenges, and when Miss Duncan danced the other day in the "Teraph" [a teraph being a household idol or image revered in early Semitic religion] ... she achieved a triumph ... and is now talked of all over London.'

She had made a breakthrough, and it received further impetus a few days later when, on 17 March, she gave a performance arranged for her by Charles Hallé at the New Gallery in Regent Street, of which he was a director. The list of sponsors for her performance contained many eminent names – Holman Hunt, Alma-Tadema, the writers Henry James and Andrew Lang, and several female members of minor royalty, including Queen Victoria's third daughter, Helena, now Princess Christian of Schleswig-Holstein.

The gallery was somewhat floridly designed, with much variously-coloured marble and with tiles of a Spanish-Moorish pattern, and it was furnished with potted palms. Isadora danced round a fountain in its central court, accompanied by the reading of poems and by a small orchestra that, according to John Fuller-Maitland, music critic of the

London *Times*, 'on more than one occasion rendered the reading inaudible'. Tiles and marble do not provide an ideal acoustic setting.

The poems she danced to, both at the Royal Court Theatre and at the New Gallery, were not read by her brother Raymond, English audiences having had trouble understanding his Californian accent. Raymond was somewhat put out by losing his role in her performances, but as things turned out it would not be long before Isadora dropped poetry from her performances altogether.

John Fuller-Maitland, who was also one of her sponsors at the New Gallery, on the whole pronounced her performance there a qualified success, and in the wake of it gave her some valuable advice. As he recalled in his 1929 memoirs, *A Door-Keeper of Music*:

> It was luckily my place to notice her performance, and [in my notice] I ventured to [hint] that it would be an improvement if she would dance, not to poems (she used to announce that she would dance 'to an idyll of *Theocrates*'), but to good music, and specially mentioned the waltzes of Chopin. She introduced herself to me and asked me to recommend music that she could illustrate in her art. I told her how anxious I was to have a *rubato* of Chopin carried out in the dance; and she came and went through one or two of the Chopin pieces until she could get the right elasticity of rhythm.

It is possible that Fuller-Maitland unknowingly took a little too much credit to himself for introducing Isadora to Chopin – she had been dancing to Chopin for years – but it is also possible that he introduced her to several Chopin pieces that were unfamiliar to her. What is more certain is that he was high among those who suggested she should abandon dancing to poems. When she appeared next at the New Gallery, on 6th July 1900, making the first of two appearances there that month, he commented approvingly in the *Times* that 'almost all attempt to illustrate well-known stories or poems was dispensed with, and the reading, which has been felt as a wholly unnecessary and tiresome addition, was left out altogether.'

This suited Isadora. More and more she was moving away from dances that told a story or followed the emotional pattern of a poem, to expressive dances that abandoned traditional narrative. As a result of her discussions with Watts, Alma-Tadema and others, she began to evolve a different repertoire, and in particular a suite of dances based on famous paintings, usually of classical legends. She would depict such legends as Orpheus and Eurydice, Narcissus and Echo, Apollo and Daphne, and this suite she would continue to perform for years.

One of the paintings she chose was, naturally enough, the Botticelli *Primavera* – a painting that happened to be a great favourite with the Pre-Raphaelites, such as Holman Hunt. For her dance, Isadora would wear a costume based on that worn by Flora, the painting's central figure, and in portraying Botticelli's allegory of spring's awakening, she would also in turn embody all the other characters in the picture – Venus, Chloris, Zephyr, Cupid, Mercury and the Three Graces.

Her Flora costume was described in a London newspaper after one her earliest performances of *Primavera*:

> The robe appears to consist of several gauze slips worn one over another. The upper one has angel sleeves and is dim, pale green in colour, painted here and there with delicate flowers... Very Botticelli-like is the long, dark hair crowned with roses, and falling in curls to the waist. Ropes of roses wind about her body and the feet are shod in gold sandals.

This costume had in fact grown out of the conversations she had had with painters, and it had something of a Pre-Raphaelite appearance. Very quickly, however, she would abandon this approach and revert permanently to a more Ancient Greek style of dress for her performances.

The music she chose for *Primavera* was a Venetian lute song of the sixteenth century, and a description of her style of dancing at this time, as it emerged into maturity, was perceptively set down by the American dance historian, Elizabeth Kendall, writing in the late 1970s:

> London programs show that as early as 1900 she was finding those essential motions which formed her language, which she would fit together differently in each dance, and which she would also use as the basis for her teaching... In Renaissance art she experienced a new dimension and she began to show the movements of several figures within a space. She added to her language those gestures of surprise or suspended motion one sees in Renaissance canvases – the effects of figures on each other. One of the clearest signals she took is the stylization of 'I am being pursued' – a nymph pursued by a satyr, a Diana chased by Actaeon, Ariadne surprised by Bacchus... The gesture of this appears again and again in Duncan dances: the dancer in a sideways lunge, her hands fending off the pursuer as

she looks back over her shoulder. The pursuer is seen in the same dances (mimed also by the solo dancer): he lunges forward and reaches out towards the imaginary pursued. Gestures like these existed in Delsarte too; but Duncan's versions were broader – they were no longer gestures but motions because they led to other motions. Their purpose was not to transmit a mimed message but to show an action. It is extraordinary that a young dancer decided that by herself she could offer an audience not just the pantomimic intentions of one figure but the flow of question-response among several figures inside the formal space of a painting-frame or a stage.

Although her artistic development was now proceeding fast, filling her soul with excitement and a sense of achievement, her private life was still surprisingly calm and demure. A letter she wrote at this time to a recent friend, the poet Grant Duff Douglas Ainslie, is revealing:

> I have been leading a most orderly and charming existence in our little Kensington House, doing everything except going to the Parish Church that a demure Kensington Maiden should – If you come you will find me in white dress and a blue sash sitting in a pink parlor pouring tea... Town is quite horrid now – except the British Museum – when I can no longer stand the low ceilings in this cracker-box of a house I go there, where I can find everything I want – or everything I ought to want, which isn't the same thing.

Douglas Ainslie was an educated and well-connected Scot. Although he was then aged forty-four, she found him handsome, especially admiring his soft and 'dreamy eyes', and she began flirting with him, as in her letter. More and more she was enjoying flirting – she had flirted a little with Charles Hallé, with Alma-Tadema, and even with the aged George Watts – but the intensity of her flirtation with Douglas Ainslie seemed to her mother a little dangerous (after all, she herself had somewhat ill-advisedly married an older man). As Isadora recalled:

> Every evening at dusk [Douglas Ainslie] appeared at the studio with three or four volumes under his arm, and read to me the poems of Swinburne, Keats, Browning, Rossetti, and Oscar Wilde. He loved reading aloud and I adored listening to him. My poor mother, who deemed that it was absolutely necessary to act as chaperone on these occasions ... could not understand the Oxford

59

manner of reciting poetry, and after an hour or so, especially of William Morris, she used to fall asleep, at which moment the young poet would lean forward and kiss me lightly on the cheek.

Increasingly her romantic feelings about men were coming to the fore in her nature. She still, for instance, remembered with loving regret her Chicago bohemian, Ivan Miroski, and one afternoon, telling none of her family, she sought out his widow, whom she had discovered to be living in Hammersmith, at a boarding-school where she taught. Isadora, dressing as demurely as she could manage in a 'Kate Greenaway dress... A big straw hat on my head, and my hair in curls on my shoulders', made her way there. Mme Miroski was not expecting her, and Isadora recalled:

> Her welcome was not very cordial. I tried to explain who I was. 'I know,' she said, 'you are Isadora; Ivan spoke to me about you.' 'I am so sorry,' I faltered. 'He never spoke to me about you in any of his letters.'
> 'No,' she said, 'he would not, but I was to have gone out to him and now – he is dead.'
> She said this with such an expression of voice that I began to cry. Then she began to cry, too, and with that it was as though we had always been friends.

They spent most of the afternoon together, reminiscing about Ivan with gloomy pleasure, after which Isadora travelled back by bus to Chelsea. Sitting on the upper deck, she wept for her loss of Ivan and for the sadness of his 'poor little wife', but at the same time she confessed to glorying in a feeling of her own power, when contrasted to someone like poor Mrs Miroski – one of the sort of 'people who were failures, or who spent their whole lives waiting for things'.

One who had no intention of sitting round waiting for things was Raymond. Not only was he disgruntled at being dropped from Isadora's performances, he was also unhappy that it was no longer he who went to places like the British Museum with Isadora. He felt surplus to requirements in London, and announced his intention of moving on to Paris. Which he did.

Not long afterwards, Douglas Ainslie went to Paris too, although only for a week. Isadora sent a letter to greet him there on the morning he arrived, saying (in part): 'Not for a long week will you think of me but will see many wonderful Things and people and think beautiful Thoughts.

I remaining here will lose you Seven days and Nights ... only being happy in remembering the precious minutes you cared to spend with me – and wishing also that – what am I wishing?'

She sent him other letters too during the week, signing them all 'Terpsichore', and speaking in them of 'all the love and longing' he had aroused in her. Unfortunately, she slightly overdid it. The fast-growing strength of her passion alarmed the gentle poet, and on his return he regretfully informed her that its power was not reciprocated.

Isadora retreated for solace into her world of Art and Philosophy, feeling that, 'Ideas are eternally satisfactory, always there to welcome one, if one comes in the right spirit. People, on the contrary, are most unsatisfactory and cause pain.'

Meanwhile, Raymond, in Paris, had begun bombarding her with telegrams urging her to join him there. London was Anglo-Saxon, stodgy and inartistic, and there was nothing there to compare with the vibrant, forward-looking artistic life to be met and mingled with in the *vie de bohème*.

Depressed by the fact that her romance with Douglas Ainslie had proved to be nothing but a dalliance, and perhaps feeling that she had got all she was going to get out of London ('Town is quite horrid now'), she quite soon gave in to her brother's urging. In around September 1900 she and her mother left Chelsea and set off to join him in Paris.

Chapter Five

A Deeper Understanding

Paris in 1900 was, and had been for some years, a vibrant city, fizzing with energy and imagination, both in the arts and in simply enjoying life. The 1890s, the famous *Belle Époque*, had been the culmination of several previous decades of creative activity – a time of Art Nouveau and Impressionism, of the acting of Lucien Guitry and Sarah Bernhardt, of the cancan, of Montmartre as a centre of entertainment and bohemian life, of *boulevardiers* and pavement cafés and absinthe, of the Eiffel Tower (erected for the Paris Exposition of 1889), round which the rich Brazilian, Alberto Santos-Dumont, often piloted his miniature airships.

As it happened, Paris was holding another Exposition even as Isadora and her mother arrived there, and the city was thronged with visitors. Like any World's Fair, the 1900 Exposition, which ran from 14th April to 5th November, was something of a jumble, with displays of modern inventions alongside such things as a reconstruction of mediaeval Nuremberg and a Pavilion of Russian Alcohol. Its declared aim was to publicise the cultural and industrial creations of the whole world, to sum up what the human race had achieved so far in preparation for the confident leap into the Twentieth Century.

Isadora and her mother travelled to Paris by channel ferry to Cherbourg and then by train. There they found Raymond somewhat changed. As Isadora wrote, 'He had let his hair grow long over his ears, and wore a turned-down collar and a flowing tie... He took us to his lodging, where we met a little midinette running down the stairs, and he regaled us with a bottle of red wine.'

The little midinette swiftly disappeared from Raymond's life, because immediately he and Isadora were reunited they spent almost all their time in each other's company, more or less re-enacting the way they had behaved when first in London by setting about finding suitable lodgings, and haunting museums and art galleries. Now, however, Isadora was a little more disciplined, hunting out mostly those artworks, books or performances that seemed directly relevant to her developing theories of Dance.

Raymond had found work that she remembered only as 'printing-related enterprises', and it was probably because of this that the first lodging they found was a cheap apartment above a printing-press, which thundered through the night. Being a born romantic, and delighted at finding herself in the city of romance, Isadora declared that 'it sounded like the sea' and that the family should pretend they were at the seaside.

On her first morning, she and Raymond rose early and made their way, dancing, through the Luxembourg Gardens to the Louvre, she wearing a white dress and a hat she had bought in Liberty's. They loved the Louvre even more than they had loved the British Museum, wandering excitedly through the galleries like two children, shouting things to each other like, 'Look, here is Dionysus!' and 'Oh, look! Here's Medea killing her children!' The attendants were at first a little suspicious of their odd behaviour, but after Isadora explained to one of them (in a pantomime which would have been worth seeing) that she had come there only to dance, they were left alone as 'harmless lunatics'.

In subsequent days they visited the Musée de Cluny, the Carnavalet, and the Bibliothéque Nationale. Isadora worked hard at learning French, and soon was fairly fluent in it (although her tenses would always remain a little shaky – a defect that the French tended to find charming). Once she had become sufficiently fluent, she made her way to the library of the Paris Opéra. She explained who she was and that she wished to read books on dance, and, as she recalled, they 'took an affectionate interest' and dug out for her 'every work ever written on dancing' (which at that time wouldn't have been many). She read through them and made copious notes.

While working on her philosophy of Dance, she decided to extend her researches to philosophy in general. Returning to the Bibliothéque Nationale, she took out books on Descartes and Rousseau. She was interested briefly in Descartes' views on the soul and its relationship to the body (writing in the 1600s, he believed that the soul, while wholly distinct from the body, resided in the pineal gland at the base of the brain and could influence the direction in which the body, or parts of the body, moved), but soon she decided he was going to be of little help to her in her quest.

Rousseau, who wrote a hundred years later, believed that God spoke to man through the heart, which should be listened to, rather than to the intellect. This in practice tended to work out as 'if it feels good, do it' and was rather more to Isadora's taste, especially as, at about the time she arrived in Paris, she experienced a sort of belated puberty. She was then twenty-three and, as she recalled, 'My breasts, which until then had been hardly perceptible, began to swell softly and astonish me with charming and embarrassing sensations. My hips, which had been like a boy's, took on another undulation, and through my whole being I felt one great surging, longing, unmistakeable urge, so that I could no longer sleep at night, but tossed and turned in feverish, painful unrest.'

Suddenly she discovered she had another interest in life besides the Dance. She had become aware of her body (as she put it herself) 'as something other than an instrument to express the sacred harmony of music.'

It was the beginning of a development in her character that would give her problems for the rest of her life – a growing tension between her mind, through which she created her art (although it was expressed bodily), and her sensuality. As she once explained it herself: 'How I envy those natures which can give themselves entirely to the voluptuousness of the moment, without fear of the critic who sits aloft and separates and insists upon interjecting his view, when least wanted, to the coupled senses beneath.'

In the height of passion she would always find it difficult to subdue her active mind, perceiving herself, as if from a distance, with a certain cold detachment ('this unwanted commentary' she called it.) In her words, 'It ... has always been the experience of my temperament that, no matter how violent the sensation or passion, the brain worked at the same time with a lightning and luxurious rapidity. I have, therefore, never, in the slang sense, lost my head; on the contrary, the more acute the pleasure of the senses, the more vivid the thought.'

Her rising awareness of her sexuality was perfectly suited to the atmosphere of turn-of-the-century Paris, which had a strong undercurrent of eroticism. Many novels and stage comedies dealt with the 'four-to-five', the hour in which married women traditionally rendezvoused with their lovers – while of course maintaining an outward display of the utmost respectability. And it was only in the previous year that François-Félix Faure, the President of the Republic, had suffered a fatal heart attack while engaging in a sexual activity in his office at the Élysée Palace with his naked mistress, Mme Steinheil.

This world was, however, still a closed book to Isadora. In spite of the unconventionality of the household she had been raised in, and in spite of her bold exploration of Art and Life, she was sexually as innocent and uninformed as any respectable Victorian miss. This would shortly cause her several disappointments and frustrations, but meanwhile there was also the life of Paris to be explored.

She learned that the Paris Opéra was to give a performance of 'Greek Dancing', and hastened there with eager curiosity, only to be grievously disappointed, finding it to be simply 'modified ballet in white gowns'. After several similar experiences, she wrote to Douglas Ainslie, whom she retained as a friend in spite of the failure of their romance, 'I thought I might find some teacher, some help here, but it was all stupid, vanity and vexation – They do not dance for love – They do not dance for the Gods.'

Concentrating on her theories, as she was, the Universal Exposition held little interest for her – she had no desire to visit the Palace of Electricity or a Javanese temple or the *trottoir roulante* (a sort of early travelator, carrying people through the fairgrounds some twenty feet off the ground). But there was a performance of dance being presented there which would prove more rewarding to her than the Opéra's 'Greek Dancing'.

There had been for several years in Paris another American dancer, Loie Fuller, an ex-vaudevillian who had been so successful at the Folies Bergère music-hall that she now had a small theatre, built especially for her in the contemporary art nouveau style. She was not, at the time Isadora arrived in Paris, appearing herself at the Théâtre Loie Fuller. Instead it had been given over to the dance company, more than thirty strong, of two of her protégés – the Japanese actors Kawakami Otogiro and Sada Yacco, who were husband and wife.

Loie Fuller was no ordinary music-hall dancer. She had been born in a bar-room in Illinois in 1862, and her given names were actually Mary Louise. Starting her career working in rodeos and carnivals, by the time she was in her twenties she was a popular star of the American stage. Originally doing what was known as skirt-dancing, in which the swirling and flirting of the fabric of the costume was as important as the steps executed, she had developed this into a highly individual style where elaborate outfits consisting of many yards of unpatterned Chinese silk were manipulated by rods inside it, held in her hands. Using this technique she would start small and, whirling and spinning in the changing lights, would blossom into dozens of elaborate shapes, usually resembling flowers, such as orchids or lilies or elaborate seaweeds, but sometimes butterflies or even snakes.

And her dancing was not all. She was also a hugely influential pioneer of stage production, having quickly understood the possibilities of the new item of stage equipment, electric lighting. She used elaborate and dramatic lighting effects, making much use of coloured filters (and even Tiffany glass). She used ramps and mirrors, and even, after Marie and Pierre Curie (who were friends of hers) had isolated radium in 1898, equipped a laboratory of her own to experiment with the element's luminous properties, soon successfully presenting a 'Radium Dance'. (For her use of stage machinery and of electricity she would become much admired by those apostles of the Machine Age, the Italian Futurists.)

Isadora went to see Loie's Japanese protégés, who were presenting traditional Japanese Noh theatre, somewhat modified to make it accessible to western audiences. In fact the wife, Sada Yacco, who was the only woman in the cast, was a modification herself, because traditional Noh theatre employed no female performers. She was a brave and determined woman. Trained in youth as a geisha, she became virtually ostracised in her homeland, partly by appearing onstage at all, and partly because the tradition-bound Japanese objected to her modifying Noh theatre in any way (such as by reducing the running time of the piece she was most popular in, *The Geisha and the Knight*, from fourteen hours to two).

Noh, developed between the 14th and 16th centuries, has about 250 set pieces. Depicting mythical or historical stories, the plays have no dialogue, but use a combination of dance, mime, music and chanting – the slow, stylised dancing being the strongest element. Isadora was bowled over by Sada Yacco's graceful performance, recognising in it a perfect blending of emotion and control. She made exact note of many of the movements in the piece, calling them 'wondrous', and she would go back to see the company again and again.

Another exhibition arranged to coincide with the Exposition was the first major collecting together of the sculpture of Auguste Rodin. Rodin, then aged sixty, was regarded by many as the greatest sculptor of his day, although in his early days he had been heavily criticised for creating figures that were naturalistic rather than idealised, and for deliberately leaving many of them slightly unfinished, in order to link the medium from which they were made to the final image.

His knowledge of, and feeling for, human anatomy was enormous. As he said himself, 'I have always endeavoured to express the inner feelings by the mobility of the muscles. I obey nature in everything, and I never pretend to command her.' Isadora, as a dancer, responded to his work deeply. Entering the Rodin Pavilion, which was not far from the Théâtre

Loie Fuller, she felt she had stepped into 'a new world'. She was so bewitched that when she heard members of the crowd commenting on the lack of total realism, she took it on herself to harangue them, saying, 'Don't you know that this is not the thing itself, but a symbol – a conception of the ideal of life?'

Her London friend Charles Hallé came to visit Paris (and the Exposition). He had strong connections with the city, having been born there, although his family had moved to Manchester when he was only two. Among his connections was a nephew, Charles Noufflard. Hallé introduced Isadora to him, and after he returned to London in the autumn, Noufflard in turn introduced her to two of his friends, Jacques Beaugnies and André Beaunier. Through these three, Isadora was soon introduced to the world of the salon.

After a tradition lasting several centuries, the French salon was then approaching the end of its time, although there were still a number of wealthy hostesses who, on a set day of the week, would receive a *coterie* of regular guests, along with selected fashionable celebrities and a small seasoning of well-born pretty women. To become a guest at a salon meant one had entered an elite. Wealth and being of a good family were not enough – one had either to have achieved distinction in politics, literature or the arts, or have intelligence and charm and an ability to appreciate.

Running a salon successfully took time and money. A woman running one needed to keep up a prolific social correspondence, to be *au fait* with current affairs and with everything new in the arts, to be able to provide a superb cuisine and wines, and to have a suitably large drawing-room as a setting, with its own distinctive individuality and charm.

As in America and England, Isadora was soon performing at salons, and in Paris, where there was a respect for Art – or at least for the idea of Art – she was an immediate sensation (although even there she was not quite sure that her audiences really knew what she was driving at). *The New York World*, under the headline, HEROINE OF THE WINDSOR FIRE TAKES THE FRENCH BY STORM, was soon writing, 'The very best people in Paris have taken her up, and she has appeared in the most impenetrable drawing-rooms of the Faubourg St-Germain.'

One of these salons was that of Jacques Beaugnies' mother, Meg de Saint-Marceaux (whose day of the week was Friday), and there the Chopin she danced to was provided by the piano of Maurice Ravel, then aged twenty-five and only at the beginning of his composing career. Isadora always remembered the rapturous reception she first received there, with guests crying, '*Quel ravissement! Quelle jolie enfant! Bravo, bravo, comme elle est exquise!*' and she became a frequent performer there.

She performed at other salons as well, such as that of the Duchesse d'Uzès, a tiny woman who not only had a strong interest in literature and the arts, being for years the president of the Union of Women Painters and Sculptors, but who was also famous as the best sportswoman in Europe, said to be able to outlast any man in the saddle of either horse or bicycle. She would shortly become probably the first woman ever to be arrested for speeding in an automobile, being clocked doing twenty kilometres per hour in the Bois de Boulogne.

Her salon was high-spirited and not over-intellectual, and it may have been something in its atmosphere that impelled Isadora to deliver there one of her famous harangues, saying, 'When I am rich I shall rebuild the Temple of Paestum and open a college of priestesses, a school of the dance. I shall teach an army of young girls, who will renounce, as I have done, every other sensation, every other career. The dance is a religion and should have its worshippers.'

She became a success among '*le gratin*' (as the fashionable Parisian upper crust were known) with an ease that amazed her, and soon she was appearing at the most fashionable salon of the time, that hosted by the Comtesse Elisabeth de Greffulhe, who was one of the two models for Proust's Duchesse de Guermantes – the other being the rather more down-to-earth Comtesse de Chevigné, whose salon tended to lean towards politicians and witty writers than to the performing arts.

Elisabeth de Greffulhe was beautiful and clever, and the undisputed queen of the upper *monde*. She was a cousin of the vain and dandiacal Comte Robert de Montesquiou, patron of Proust since 1898 and part-model for his Baron Charlus, and she was a woman of many interests, in all of which she involved herself actively. Then only at the beginning of an illustrious career of encouraging and sponsoring, she would before long head a sub-committee to make possible the première of Debussy's opera *Pelléas et Mélisande*. She would bring first Chaliapin and then Diaghilev's Russian Ballet out of Russia to Paris, and would back the composers Mussorgsky and Stravinsky. She would discover Caruso, found France's Comité International du Patronage Artistique (which helped mount exhibitions for talented but impecunious painters), and popularise greyhound racing.

Isadora danced at her salon, but was not sure that the drawing-room, heavily rose-bedecked and somewhat overcrowded, was really an ideal setting for her. She recalled it as being, 'full of marvelously dressed and bejeweled women, [with] a front row of *jeunesse dorée*, whose noses just reached the end of the stage and were almost brushed by my dancing toes.'

Elisabeth de Greffulhe praised her dancing with enthusiasm, but Isadora wasn't sure if their impressions of Ancient Greece entirely coincided, writing later, 'The Countess hailed me as a renaissance of Greek Art, but she was rather under the influence of the *Aphrodite* of Pierre de Louÿs and his *Chanson de Bilitis*, whereas I had the expression of a Doric column and the Parthenon pediments as seen in the cold light of the British Museum.'

The strength and sternness of Isadora's devotion to her Art was indeed some way from the scented and sensuous interpretation of certain aspects of Ancient Greece in the Chanson de Bilitis (as witness her speech at the Duchesse d'Uzès' salon), although as it happened she too had read the currently fashionable poems of Pierre de Louÿs (whose structure he based on Greek forms he much admired). She had also read the poems of Sappho. But so innocent was she that their lesbian sensibility had escaped her totally. Writing late in her life she wisely interpreted her lack of understanding as an argument against censorship, saying that it proved 'there is no necessity to censor the literature of the young. What one has not experienced, one will never understand in print.'

Not that her speech at the Duchesse d'Uzès' salon was entirely true to the way she was now feeling. Renouncing every sensation but dancing was an emotional position she had moved on from. In her avowed determination to lose her virginity, she flirted with many men she met socially, but most of all with three young men she had met through Charles Hallé.

Charles Noufflard, Hallé's nephew, was tall, blond and pleasant. Jacques Beugnies she described as 'a pretty youth'. But the one of the three she went after most determinedly was the young writer André Beaunier, who was 'pale and round-faced and wore glasses'. 'But,' she recalled, 'what a mind! I was always a '*cérébrale*', and, although people will not believe it, my love-affairs of the head ... were as interesting to me as those of the heart.'

Be that as it may, she was eager to lose her virginity to him. He would come to the family lodgings bearing books and magazines, and did much to introduce Isadora to such French writers as Molière, Flaubert, Maupassant and Maeterlinck. They would ride buses round the city, exploring it. When they gazed at Notre Dame by moonlight, she recalled, 'He knew every figure of the facade and could tell me the history of every stone.' But still, exploit her unpractised wiles of seduction as she might, André remained unresponsive.

Once, when they were walking in the Forest of Meudon, to the south-west of the city, they sat down at a crossroads and amused themselves giving romantic names to the various paths. The right-hand one they called 'Fortune', the left-hand 'Peace', and the one straight ahead 'Immortality'. Isadora asked André the name of the crossroads where they sat. When he replied, 'Love', she declared, 'Then I prefer to remain here.'

At once he exclaimed, 'We can't remain here,' abruptly rose and, as she recalled, hurried off 'very fast down the road,' with Isadora following, crying out, 'But why, but why, why do you leave me?'

She tried organising a romantic champagne dinner. On another occasion she 'plotted to send Mother and Raymond to the Opera' and, inviting André to their lodging, dressed herself in her dancing tunic and wreathed roses in her hair. Nothing worked, and when he left she wept bitterly.

André too had moments of despair. When Oscar Wilde died, on the afternoon of 30th November 1900, he was desolated. 'He came to me white and trembling in a terrible state of depression,' Isadora wrote, saying that she 'had read and heard vaguely about Oscar Wilde but knew very little about him.' She asked André how it was that so famous a writer had come to die poverty-stricken in a miserable Paris hotel room, at which André 'blushed to the roots of his hair and refused to answer', saying only, 'You are my only confidante,' and leaving her with 'the strange impression that some uncanny calamity had befallen the world'.

Their relationship never did become more than 'cérébrale', and Isadora, summing it up towards the end of her life, wrote, 'When you recollect that at that time I was young and remarkably pretty, it's difficult to find an explanation ... and indeed I have never found one.' André would go on to become a friend of Proust's and a successful author.

Having failed with him, Isadora turned her attention to Charles Hallé's nephew, the tall blond pleasant Charles Noufflard. One night the two of them booked themselves into a rather disreputable hotel under assumed names and Noufflard, in Isadora's words, proved himself 'as enterprising as André was backwards in embraces and kisses.'

They undressed and got into bed, and as Isadora recalled, 'I found myself in his arms, submerged in a storm of caresses, my heart pounding, every nerve bathed in pleasure.' Which went on until something alerted Noufflard to the fact that she was a virgin. Immediately all his conventional morality asserted itself and he leapt out of the bed, lamenting, 'Oh –

why didn't you tell me? What a crime I was about to commit – No, no, you must remain pure. Dress, dress at once!' Ignoring Isadora's protests, he hurried her into her clothes and a cab.

At this time many of the rich and fashionable hostesses in Paris were American, and prominent among them was Winaretta Singer, who by marriage had become the Princesse de Polignac.

Only a few years older than Isadora, Winaretta had been born in Yonkers, the twentieth of the twenty-four children of the enormously successful inventor, Isaac 'Sewing Machine' Singer. An undiluted lesbian, she had first been married to the Prince de Scey-Montbéliard, except that it couldn't really be called a marriage because on their wedding night she had attacked him with an umbrella and threatened to kill him if he came anywhere near her.

Her second marriage, to Prince Edmond de Polignac, while no more sexual, was successful, he also being gay. They got on well, although in 1901, while the Duncans were still in Paris, he would die, by which time Isadora would know the couple well enough to attend his funeral.

By the end of 1900 the Duncans had got themselves an apartment in the rue de la Gaité where there was a room big enough for Isadora to practise and perform in, and one day Winaretta turned up there, abruptly and without warning. She swanned in, looking, Isadora recalled, 'like a Roman emperor'. Announcing who she was, she invited Isadora to dance for her there and then. Isadora did, and Winaretta swept out again, leaving at the door a payment of two thousand francs.

Generosity was the other thing Winaretta was famous for. As well as the payment she set about introducing Isadora to her social circle, and arranging a series of subscription concerts (at Isadora's apartment) to which came such famous names as the composer Gustave Fauré, the author and dramatist Octave Mirbeau, the politician Georges Clemenceau, and Rodin.

Rodin was fascinated by dancers, and Isadora was fascinated by both the sculptor and the man. She pursued him, as she admitted, 'like Psyche seeking the God Pan'. Rodin never needed much pursuing by attractive women, and one day when he had come alone to her studio to again see her dance, with just the two of them present:

He gazed at me with lowered lids, his eyes blazing, and then, with the same expression that he had before his works, he came towards me. He ran his hands over my neck, breast, stroked my arms and ran his hands over my hips, my bare legs and feet. He began to knead my whole body as if it were clay, while from him emanated heat that scorched and melted me. My whole desire was to yield to him my entire being and, indeed, I would have done so if it had not been that my absurd upbringing caused me to become frightened, and I withdrew, threw my dress over my tunic, and sent him away bewildered.

Probably it was the intensity of Rodin's approach that alarmed her, much as her own intensity had alarmed Douglas Ainslie in London, but in addition, no matter how desperate she was for sex, she was still a romantic, and for her Rodin's approach was too practical and direct.

Isadora's emotions at this time were in a state of considerable turmoil – not just with regard to sex, or to her work, but in general. She was a seething cauldron of feeling. One artist she admired passionately (and would for the rest of her life) was Rodin's closest friend, the painter Eugène Carrière, who lived in Montmartre with his wife and children. He was a warm-hearted and likeable man, as well as a fine artist, and Isadora built up a warm friendship with him.

Describing him years later, she wrote, with undiminished adoration, 'He had the strongest spiritual presence I have ever felt. When coming into his presence I felt as I imagine I would have felt had I met the Christ. I was filled with such awe. I wanted to fall on my knees, and would have done had not the timidity and reserve of my nature held me back.'

And timid she still was, apart from in her work, where passion drove her forward. The actress Lotte Yorska, who encountered her at Eugène Carrière's home, remarked, 'except for Lillian Gish, I have never seen an American girl look so shy.'

In 1901 the Duncans moved from the rue de la Gaité, where they had been living, into a larger apartment at 45 avenue de Villers, in the eighth *arrondissement*. It contained a vast barn-like room, with a long stage at one end, that was even better for Isadora's teaching and performing. The high-spirited Raymond painted Greek columns on the walls and, using tinfoil, made the gas jets on the walls resemble ancient torches.

There was of course a piano, and Mother spent hours playing preludes, waltzes and mazurkas, and on occasion the whole of Gluck's *Orfeo ed Eurydice*. Isadora was now digging deeply into herself to refine her ideas on the Dance, and on occasion had to ask her mother to stop the music for a while so that she could concentrate. Mother found the fierceness of her concentration somewhat disconcerting.

73

Isadora, in her memoirs, wrote:

> I spent long days and nights in the studio, seeking that dance which might be the divine expression of the human spirit through the medium of the body's movement. For hours I would stand quite still, my two hands folded between my breasts, covering the solar plexus. My mother often became alarmed to see me remain for such long intervals quite motionless as if in a trance – but I was seeking, and finally discovered, the central spring of all movement, the crater of motor power, the unity from which all diversities of movement are born... Motion is motivated by emotion, and must be expressed with the instrument of the entire human body.

She was making a great breakthrough in understanding, finding something that had long been missing in Dance, that perhaps had never been so fully understood before – that dancing should be rooted in spiritual truth, no matter what style of movement is used to express it. In her case, this strong realisation that her centre was located in her solar plexus led to an essential movement in her dancing being a raising of the chest in ecstasy. Her mature dancing style always seemed to emanate from the torso. Rather than simply interpreting music, as in her early days she had striven to do, her dancing now became an expression of the soul, whether in response to her surroundings or to her inmost feelings.

Music now served, as she once said, to 'start the motor in [her] soul'. But she would come to work towards a day when even music would be unnecessary, when the soul alone would suffice. As she once wrote:

> Imagine then a dancer, who, after long study, prayer and inspiration, has attained such a degree of understanding that his body is simply the luminous manifestation of his soul; whose body dances in accordance with a music heard inwardly, in an expression of something out of another, a profounder world. This is the truly creative dancer, natural but not imitative, speaking in movement out of himself and out of something greater than all selves.

These attitudes were the fundamental ones that would underlie the great Modern Dance of the Twentieth Century, no matter how much it changed in its details of movement from what Isadora would do. As the influential American dance writer John Martin would say of her in 1936,

'[Isadora's] uncovering of the substance of the dance as expressional movement is one of the monumental achievements in the history of the arts.'

She did admit that her basic theories were often difficult to explain to her pupils. As girls began to flock to her apartment, eager to learn from her, she would tell them, 'Listen to the music with *your soul.* Now, while listening, do you not feel an inner self awakening deep within you – that it is by its strength that your head is lifted, that your arms are raised, that you are walking slowly towards the light?'

One of her pupils at around this time was Princess der Ling, then in her teens and the daughter of the Chinese ambassador to France. Later she described the atmosphere of Isadora's lessons, saying:

> Her classes were growing by leaps and bounds... After a time so many pupils clamoured for lessons that she had to divide them up into three classes, tripling her labours, which were already beyond the capabilities of anyone else I could have named... The class would be lined up like soldiers. Isadora would tell them carefully, almost spelling out her lessons, exactly what to do, and just where each movement fitted in with the music... Fat girls, thin girls, tall girls, stubby girls; girls with knees, girls with calves, girls with neither knees nor calves! It seemed to me, watching, that none of them did correctly anything that Isadora told them, and that no two of them did the same thing. It must have seemed that way to Duncan, too, for at the very first movement she would say: 'Stop!... The arms must be exactly so, the curve of the limbs exactly so, the expression of the face, the curve of the neck, the position of the head ... exactly so.'

If Princess der Ling's memory was correct, there was obviously at this time still some gap between Isadora's developing philosophy of Dance and her practical method of teaching. Which is hardly surprising when she was doing so much to break new ground.

At around the time the Duncans moved to the avenue de Villers, early in 1901, another Irish-American woman, some six years older than Isadora, arrived in Paris. She would become Isadora's lifelong friend, and she called herself Mary D'Este.

Her real name was Mary Estelle Dempsey. Her father, Dominick Dempsey, was a Dublin-born merchant seaman who had settled in Quebec, where he met and married her mother, Mary Smythe. Mary

Dempsey, the last of their six children, was born in 1871. Her father Dominick died when she was young, and when she was five her widowed mother decided to move with her children to Chicago, where she had a sister who had married a saloonkeeper.

Mary was a vivacious, dark-haired child with hazel eyes. At ten, she left school and went to work wrapping toffee in a candy factory. An intelligent child, she developed a cheerfully aggressive manner that was not without charm.

Apart from her intelligence and charm, there were several reasons why Isadora would take to her when they met. One was her attitude to religion. Mary's mother, who was devoutly Catholic, and indeed had several nuns among her relations, had got herself a job in a Chicago convent, and one day, when Mary was in her early teens, she went there and happened on her mother scrubbing floors. As her son would later tell it, seeing her mother 'in a loathsome servile position, she developed an instantaneous allergy towards religion.'

Another was that, in spite of her limited schooling, she, like Isadora, was an avid self-educator who had become widely read and developed a love of music and the arts, having begun to learn piano at the age of nine from Italian neighbours. She had also developed a desire for a life of style and romance.

For this reason, while still in her teens, she had decided (being a born romancer) that, in her son's words, 'the name [Dempsey] was a misnomer, bestowed upon us in error by the vulgar Irish varlets of her ancestor, a distinguished Italian prince, unfortunately on the lam in Ireland because of a romantic duel. What these flunkeys were trying to say was "d'Este", the gentleman being a member of that celebrated Italian family – only they couldn't pronounce it.'

She began calling herself Mary d'Este Dempsey, and indeed used that name on her marriage certificate when, late in 1897, she married Edmund C. Biden, who was also from Chicago. (She may also have used it on a couple of earlier marriage certificates – one to a singer, that was annulled because she was only fifteen, and a second, in which she had a stillborn child and which was also annulled – but there is no clear evidence about either of these.)

Mary and Edmund had a son, Edmund Preston Biden, born in August 1898, but even before his birth it was obvious that the marriage was in trouble, because Mary, swept away on who knows what romantic tide, had married a shiftless alcoholic. Even when the boy was still an infant, she had started encouraging the attentions of one of Chicago's wealthiest men, a stockbroker, then in his mid-forties, named Solomon Sturges. In time he and Mary would wed, and her son would adopt his step-father's surname, going on in life to become the famous film-director Preston Sturges.

At the beginning of 1901, however, Mary's situation was that she had divorced Edmund Biden, and was being seriously courted by the wealthy Solomon Sturges, although they had not yet married. He was a gentle and kindly man, and when Mary expressed a desire to take young Preston and visit Europe, he offered her an allowance of $150 a month for as long as she was there, if she in return would promise to consider his offer of marriage.

Hungry for culture, and hopeful of maybe making a career in music or the theatre, she headed for Paris, arriving there in January 1901, booking into a poorly-heated, draughty room at the Hôtel Terminus. Some fellow-guests at the hotel, whom she had met on the ship from America, insisted she joined them at the Paris Opéra Ball, where, as she recalled, 'one Frenchman after another swept me off my feet, crying, "Oh, la belle Américaine, la belle Américaine".'

The next day, little Preston, then aged two, came down with a cold, and Mary approached an American named Donald Downey, who for an exorbitant fee would find lodgings for Americans in Paris. At his office she met a tall, majestic woman who exclaimed with delight, 'Is this your baby?'

It was Isadora's mother, who doted on children. Soon she decided that Mary was 'a darling', and that once she had got her lodgings arranged she must come and meet her daughter, who would adore her.

She and Mary went together to the lodgings that Downey had suggested – a dark, overpriced apartment on the rue de Douie, in Montmartre. Then Mrs Duncan bundled Mary and Preston into a cab and transported them to the apartment at 45 avenue de Villers.

There Mrs Duncan threw open the door with a great flourish, crying dramatically, 'Isadora, Isadora, look what I have brought you – Mary and her baby!'

As Mary remembered it, Isadora and Raymond 'both came forward, clasping me in their arms and dancing around in a circle as though I were some person they had been waiting for.' Mrs Duncan, taking baby Preston, raced to the piano, plonked him on the seat, and gaily played some tunes while the other three continued their whirling dance.

This meeting, Mary later wrote, 'Began the friendship which lasted all the rest of our lives.' Attempting to describe her feelings at the time, she explained:

Had I been ushered into Paradise and given over to my guardian angel, I could not have been more uplifted. Isadora was in her little dancing tunic, a colorless gauze of some sort, draped softly about her slender, ethereal form; her exquisite little head poised on her swan-like throat and tilted to one side like a bird, as though the weight of her auburn curls caused it to droop; a little retroussé nose that gave just the slightest human touch, otherwise I should have thrown myself on my knees before her, believing I was worshipping a celestial being.

Mary began spending long hours at the Duncans, and it was baby Preston who unwittingly drew the group even closer together. His cold worsened into pneumonia, which was rapidly cured when, as Mary recalled, 'Mrs Duncan came with a bottle of champagne of which she gave the baby a spoonful and every few hours thereafter she repeated this. The next morning the baby opened his eyes and looked up at us both with the sweetest smile in the world.'

After that, Mary and Preston left their 'dark, overpriced apartment' and moved in with the Duncans on the avenue de Villers. Mary would quickly become so obsessed with Isadora that she would begin to imitate her in everything, wearing the same kind of cloaks and hats and hairstyles, and even trying to walk like her.

Quite soon after Mary moved in with the Duncans, she found herself living at the apartment alone with Isadora, because Mrs Duncan and Raymond, taking little Preston with them, went off to stay at an inn in Giverny, a tiny village about fifty miles north-west of Paris. There they would be visited at weekends by such friends of the Duncans as Eugène Carrière and Winaretta Singer's husband, the Prince de Polignac. Isadora and Mary would also visit from time to time, but Isadora had her work to continue in Paris, and Mary remained with her as a faithful companion (also taking the occasional music lesson).

One other thing that Mary and Isadora had in common was a certain wild impracticality. As an earlier biographer of Isadora, Victor Seroff, wrote in 1971, Mary was 'a robust woman with a liberal amount of unspent energy, bringing with her wherever she went more noise and disorder than harmony and peace. In her approach to life, she thought everything 'terribly funny', except, perhaps, for one thing – she seriously believed that she was Isadora... While her intentions were sincere, their being carried out usually meant trouble and confusion.'

Mary was present during 1901 when another change occurred in

Isadora's presentation. She was to give a performance before an audience that included Georges Clemenceau (possibly one arranged at her studio by Winaretta), and accidentally spilled a glass of rye on the sandals she was to wear. As Mary remembered, 'We began to giggle and laugh, until try as we would, we could not get the sandals on... This was the first time that Isadora Duncan ever danced barefoot in her life and it created such a sensation, everyone raving over the beauty of her feet, that she adopted this for ever.'

Whether Mary was remembering accurately or not, this does give a picture of the headlong, creative, high-spirited, ecstatic world that Isadora had now created for herself. One day, Mary recalled, 'we climbed high in the hills and sat all day and listened to Isadora read Shakespeare and Shelley. Here was nothing but beauty and innocence... At this time Isadora knew nothing of love or lovers and I don't think the question of sex was ever mentioned between us.' (Isadora's conventional reticence no doubt accounted for this silence, because the subject was still constantly recurring in her mind.)

In the autumn of 1901 Mary decided that yes, she would marry Solomon Sturges and, taking Preston, she returned to Chicago. The wedding took place in October, in Memphis.

Early in 1902 Isadora's life changed again. Her brother Raymond, again becoming frustrated at her success alongside his comparative failure, took a job as advance agent for a concert tour of the United States. The performers at these concerts were to include the great Spanish cellist, Pablo Casals, and the American soprano, Emma Nevada, who happened also to be Raymond's lover.

Emma was billed as 'the Western nightingale' (an allusion to the late Jenny Lind – 'the Swedish nightingale') and as Isadora recalled, she 'sang like an enchantress and swept him off his feet.' Writing of her first awareness of their romance, she said, 'I noticed that little violet-scented notes were often poked under the door in the early morning hours, followed by the surreptitious disappearance of Raymond. As he was not in the habit of taking walks before breakfast, I put two and two together, and gathered my conclusions.'

Although her own love-life was proving disappointing, she was romantically eager to further her brother's, and conspired with the lovers in their surreptitiousness, helping them avoid the disapproving eye of mother. In return, Emma Nevada brought Loie Fuller to avenue de Villers so that the famous star could see Isadora dance.

Isadora danced for her and, as usual, gave a short lecture on her philosophy of Dance. 'As I did for everyone,' she later admitted, 'and would have done for the plumber had he come in.'

Loie was impressed, feeling (as she herself would say) that Isadora 'gave promise of great things.' She invited Isadora to join her troupe, which would also include Kawakami Otojiro and his wife Sada Yacco and their company, on a tour of major cities of Europe.

Isadora accepted with delight, as did her mother on her behalf, once she had been assured that Loie was 'a good woman' whose name had 'never been connected with any scandal' (which was not, as it happened, completely true, as in the early 1890s she had been involved, as the blameless plaintiff, in a notorious divorce case at which it emerged that her husband, a nephew of former President Rutherford B. Hayes, was not only married to two other women, but was also a pornographer, alleged to be addicted to 'unnatural practices').

Isadora quickly arranged to close down her classes and, leaving behind her mother, who at the time was suffering from a mild illness, set off by train, in a state of high excitement, to join Loie and her troupe in Berlin.

Chapter Six

Becoming a Legend

While Isadora had a burning ambition to create a School of Dance, Loie Fuller had already done so, in 1901, although it was in a looser and more informal way. In actual fact it consisted of a number of young women, described as her 'students', who toured with her, occasionally appearing in her productions, and to whom, as Isadora noticed, 'she was attached with extraordinary affection'.

Isadora later described meeting Loie and some of her students on her arrival in Berlin to join their troupe:

> I arrived ... at the Hotel Bristol, where, in a magnificent apartment, I found Loie Fuller surrounded by her entourage. A dozen or so beautiful girls were grouped around her, alternately stroking her hands and kissing her. In my rather simple upbringing, although my mother certainly loved us all, she rarely caressed us, and so I was completely taken aback ... I sat aloof, hearing strangely for the first time such phrases as 'my pretty; my dove; my darling; little one; sweetest; honey; dearest; darling,' which seemed the coin of their intercourse. Here was an atmosphere of such warmth as I had never met before.

Among the entourage were dancers of a wide variety of types, such as Sacchetto, a ballerina; Orchidée, a French chorine (described by Isadora as 'a child of nature'); and Gertrud von Axen, 'known for her waltzes'. There was also a dark young woman in a black suit, described by Isadora as circling round the others 'like some scarab of ancient Egypt'. This was almost certainly Gabrielle Bloch, who was for years Loie Fuller's closest companion.

Isadora's upbringing truly had been 'simple'. In spite of all the travelling and performing she had done, and the sophisticated city-dwellers she had socialised with, she had dwelt mainly within her own mental world of Art and cocooned by the protective and sympathetic clan that was her family. Even on tour with such as the Daly company, her fellow-actors had found her remote and withdrawn. So she found the exotic and emotionally-charged atmosphere of the Fuller troupe unfamiliar and somewhat disturbing, despite the fact that she enjoyed the 'luxurious life of champagne dinners and palatial hotel suites'.

The troupe, for their part, felt she was not as they were. Loie, while describing her later as a mystic and a visionary, saw her as arrogant. She found Isadora's perception of herself as an Artist pretentious, and was scathing about her personal appearance. Isadora, when not performing, was not clothes-conscious, probably from sheer lack of interest in something so mundane, and Loie described her as walking around in a grey Empire robe and 'a man's hat with flying veil', which everyone around her found 'absurd' (but it's only fair to say that all these things were written later, after they had parted with some bitterness).

Isadora's time in Berlin, in spite of her initial pleasure at being part of Loie's entourage, was not totally happy. For one thing, she did not respond to the architecture of the city, finding it too imperial and would-be imposing. Recalling her first impression, she wrote, 'These columns are not the Doric columns which should soar into the skies of Olympian blue. These are the Germanic, pedantic, archaeological professors' conception of Greece.' For another, she, like her mother in Paris, became mildly ill as soon as she arrived there. With what is not recorded but, whatever it was, for the moment it prevented her from performing.

Loie, oddly enough, was not in first-class physical shape herself. Isadora, while realising that Loie's dancing ambitions were on a much lower plane than her own, nonetheless admired her 'marvellous ephemeral art'. But it was an art that required much more athleticism and physical strength than anything Isadora was attempting to do, with all the whirling and spinning and manipulating yards of fabric on hand-held rods, and Loie's back in particular was giving her trouble. As Isadora remembered, 'She seemed to be suffering from terrible pains in the spine, for which her lovely entourage brought ice bags from time to time and placed them between her back and the back of the chair. "Just another ice bag, darling," she would say; "it seems to make the pain go."' Even though her programme of dances rarely lasted more than half an hour, she usually had to be carried from the wings after she left the stage.

Isadora was still too ill to dance when she went on with the company to Leipzig, and then to Munich, but by the time it arrived in Vienna she had recovered. Loie Fuller, a talented publicist, went to great pains to build up her reputation. She organised a private performance by Isadora, under the patronage of Princess Paulina Metternich, described by Loie herself as 'the most powerful woman at the Court of Austria'. In Vienna she was as pre-eminent an arbiter of taste as the Comtesse de Greffulhe was in Paris.

To the private performance Loie invited the American and British ambassadors, and representatives of 'the literary and artistic world' – journalists, artists and theatre-managers. It was to be held in the drawing-room of a hotel, and while the distinguished and influential audience (Loie among them) sat expectantly, Isadora failed to appear.

After what seemed to Loie an eternity, she excused herself and hurried to the room where Isadora was preparing herself to find out what was the matter. As she described it, 'I found her with her feet in warm water, in the act of dressing her hair. I begged her to hurry, explaining that she ran the risk through her negligence of offending a public which might definitely launch her.' (What Loie probably did not realise – few ever did – was that all her life Isadora suffered from crippling stagefright, sometimes having to be physically supported in the wings by a maid or dresser before making her entrance.)

Eventually Isadora did appear, 'calm, indifferent, and careless of whatever interest these people might have of her'. What was worse (to Loie) was that she 'seemed to have no clothing on to speak of... She appeared to me nude, or nearly so, so slight were the gauzes that covered her form.' Loie's account continues:

> She took her place near the orchestra, and while they played a prelude of Chopin she stood there motionless, her eyes cast down and her arms hanging listlessly at her side. Then she danced.
>
> Oh! how I loved it! To me it was the most beautiful thing in the world. I forgot the woman and all her faults, her silly fancies and absurd manners and dress. I only saw the dancer and loved her for the joy she gave me.
>
> She finished. No one spoke. My heart beat fast. I went to the Princess. She spoke to me softly. 'Why does she dance so insufficiently clothed?'

Loie hastily improvised an excuse, saying, 'I forgot to tell you how amiable our artiste is. Her baggage has not yet arrived, but rather than disappoint us here today she has consented to appear in her practising costume.'

She need not have worried. Few in Vienna were as disconcerted by the slightness of Isadora's costume as Princess Metternich was. On the contrary, word of this 'naked nymph' quickly spread through the city and Isadora became a *succès de scandale*. To those few who suggested that she should wear some sort of shift to hide the fact that her breasts were naked (under several layers of silk and gauze), she insisted that she would perform in the costume she felt was right for her dancing, or not at all.

With Loie Fuller's help, Isadora gave several more performances in Vienna. Presumably Loie's nervousness about the reception her costumes would receive diminished, but as things turned out she would not have to worry for long.

Isadora was beginning to feel she should move on from being part of the Fuller entourage, which she continued to find somewhat alien. This feeling crystallised after one particular young dancer, sharing her hotel room, appeared at her bedside and announced that she was going to strangle her (she had taken a strong fancy to Isadora, and possibly this was an expression of desperately unrequited love). Isadora asked permission to say her last prayers and, permission being granted, fled out into the corridor in her nightdress screaming. The young dancer, pursuing her, was seized by hotel staff. As Isadora wrote years later, 'in spite of my admiration for the art of Loie Fuller, I began to ask myself why I had left my mother alone in Paris, and what I was doing in this troupe of beautiful but demented ladies.'

Next day she sent two telegrams, one to Loie Fuller, announcing her intention of quitting, and one to her mother, begging her to come to Vienna. Her mother duly arrived from Paris, joining Isadora in the hotel (and causing Loie later to remark with some bitterness that she now 'had two guests instead of one.')

Fortunately, by this time Isadora had met a Viennese impresario, Sándor Grosz. She had explained to him her evolving ideas about what she was doing, saying, 'My dancing is for the élite, for the artists, sculptors, painters, musicians, but not for the general public.' In spite of this he felt she had commercial possibilities, and when she approached him he offered her a contract to make a tour of Hungary, then part of the vast, though somewhat ramshackle, Austro-Hungarian Empire. The tour was to be organised by Sandor himself, who would act as her manager.

Isadora accepted, and Loie Fuller felt betrayed. The tour she was making had landed her heavily in debt (largely because of the expense of transporting and catering for thirty-odd Japanese, who insisted on eating only Japanese food), and now one of her principal stars was deserting her without warning. Soon she would be back in America, appearing again in vaudeville, and the bad feeling that Isadora's defection created between the two of them would turn out to be life-long, Isadora some years later going so far as to deny that she and Loie had ever met.

Isadora began her Hungarian tour in Budapest, arriving there with her mother in the middle of March 1902. Budapest at that time was a civilised and sophisticated city, rivalling Paris and Vienna in its first-class hotels, garden restaurants and late-night cafés. It had an Old World charm – the women elegant and the men chivalrous. As the acclaimed Hungarian writer Gyula Krúdy, who moved to the city from the provinces in 1896 and adored it, wrote:

> Here the dancing in the theatres is the best, here everyone in a crowd may think he is a gentleman, even if he left jail the day before; the physicians' cures are wonderful, the lawyers are world-famous, even the renter of the smallest rooms has his bath, the shopkeepers are inventive, the policemen guard the public peace, the gentlefolk are agreeable, the streetlights burn till the morning...

Booked into a suite at the Royal Hotel, Isadora had a month to rehearse before her show would open, and Sándor Grosz made good use of this by inviting friends and colleagues to watch her rehearsing, and encouraging them to spread the word about 'the Little Dancer Poetess', emphasising her 'angelic face' and 'touching modesty' rather than her shocking barefootedness and lightness of clothing.

The pieces she rehearsed included her *Primavera* and another painting-based piece she had developed in London, *Angel with a Viol*. There were also some of her newer pieces based on classical legends, such as *Bacchus and Ariadne, Alcestis' Farewell* and *Orpheus*.

At one rehearsal, solely as a practice piece, she improvised a dance to Johann Strauss's *An der schönen blauen Donau*. Sándor Grosz, who was present at the time, having brought the actress Mari Jászai to see her, suggested she should add the piece to her programme. This immediately offended all Isadora's artistic sensibilities. As Mari Jászai recalled, 'By Heaven! You should have seen her wide eyes fill with indignation. In tears she told us: "Why should I tread the pioneer's thorny path in order to perform a commonplace, profane dance before a cultured audience? –

85

the kind of dance I've known since I was four? If that were my purpose, I'd go into vaudeville and make a lot of money." '

Isadora was booked to appear at the Urania Theatre, and was to give a run of twenty performances. Seats for all twenty were soon sold out, and after the first show, on Saturday, 19th April 1902, she received thunderous applause.

Next day, in the newspaper *Pesti Naplo*, one critic wrote, somewhat breathlessly:

> This new type of art ... is not merely a harmony of haphazard movements, it is already ... a codified art... She has discovered entirely new movements of the human body... This is, in fact, the magnificently free dance of nymphs on a Greek chalice where the feet carry the slender body with breathtaking ease.

And another, in the same edition of the paper, wrote, more analytically:

> At the beginning you perceive something unusual, almost strange. Generally, the speech of the feet is thought to be full of sensual enchantment. Her feet, however, though they are beautifully shaped, do not speak that language. They try to impart something which we feel we have seen once in a dream. And immediately her hands, her face, the lines of her magnificent body tell us wonderful things – in a word, they become eloquent of the soul itself... The audience gazed at her as if they would like to absorb through their eyes the sunlight and springlike flavour of her sweet soul.

Her second show, next day, was also rapturously received, and as the applause rang out, with hats and roses being showered onto the stage, she asked the orchestra to play *The Blue Danube Waltz*.

When they did, she erupted into a rocking, swaying dance of such ecstatic joy at being alive that, as she remembered, 'The whole audience sprang to their feet in such a delirium of enthusiasm that I had to repeat the waltz many times before they would behave less like mad people.'

Isadora was now an enormous success, so much so that her appearance on the streets would literally stop the traffic. Her popularity was enhanced by the fact that she liked Hungary, enthusing about the fine spring weather, the beauty of the scenery, and how much she was enjoying the food – the rich pastries, the cream cakes, the goulash.

One afternoon a small party was given in her honour, and among those invited was a young actor, Oszkár Beregi. In time he would become Hungary's most famous actor; even then, aged twenty-six and a year older than Isadora, he was a leading star of the Hungarian National Theatre. Ambitious, he had the idea that getting to know this 'exotic foreign dancer' might help him improve his English.

He arrived at the door of the apartment where the party was being held, and the maid who opened it to him went to fetch Isadora. Soon she appeared, wearing an Empire-style dress of light blue crêpe, and with her mother following close behind. As Oszkár recalled:

> At the end of the dim, shabby corridor a Renoir painting was suddenly coming to life and floated towards the door, dangling her hat on a band on her arm; she was accompanied by a refined, white-haired lady in a long, grey dress, a few steps behind her. I was standing stiffly in the doorway. I had never before seen a woman move in so free a manner. She was already standing in front of me, and without realising what I was saying, the words left my lips in English, as I proffered her the flowers: 'This is for you...'

Her hair, he remembered, 'was light brown, and her eyes ... her eyes were like those of a fawn: warm, radiant and innocent. She was smiling.'

He was deeply attracted to her from the moment they met, and Isadora was equally attracted to him. Her own memory of their first encounter, recorded years later, was suffused with romance:

> [I saw] over a glass of golden Tokay ... two large black eyes that burned and glowed into mine with such ardent admiration and Hungarian passion that in one look was all the meaning of the spring in Budapest. He was tall, of magnificent proportions, a head covered with luxuriant curls, black, with purple lights in them. Indeed, he might have posed for the David of [Michelangelo] ... From our first look every power of attraction rushed from us in mad embrace. From that first gaze we were already in each other's arms, and no power on earth could have prevented this.

At that first meeting, Beregi invited her to come that night and see him performing in *Julius Caesar*, which she did, and it would not be long before he would also be taking part in her performances, reciting lines from Ovid and Horace between her dances, his rich voice backed by the chorus of the Hungarian Royal Opera.

It was not long either, before, with mother safely asleep, Isadora took an open carriage through the night streets to rendezvous with this man she would refer to in her memoirs only as 'Romeo'. Years later, she recalled this life-changing assignation, which took place in the salon of his hotel suite:

At first Romeo was happy just reciting his roles, or speaking of his art and the theatre, and I was quite happy listening to him, but gradually I noticed that he seemed troubled, and at times quite upset and speechless. He clenched his hand and appeared to feel quite ill, and at such times I noticed that his beautiful face became quite congested, his eyes inflamed, his lips swollen, and he bit them till the blood came.

I myself felt ill and dizzy, while an irresistible longing to press him closer and closer surged in me, until, losing all control and falling into a fury, he carried me to the couch. Frightened, ravished with ecstasy, the realisation of sex was made clear to me. I confess my first impressions were a horrible fright, and terrible pain which seemed to resemble the pain of having many teeth pulled at once, but a great pity for what he seemed to be suffering prevented me from running away from what was at first sheer mutilation and torture.

That morning at dawn we left the hotel together, and taking a belated two-horse carriage, which we found in the street, we drove miles out, into the country. We stopped at a peasant's hut, where the wife gave us a room with an old-fashioned four-poster bed. Then, what was to me at that time, a ghastly, suffering experience continued, amidst my martyr's groans and cries. All that day we remained in the country, Romeo frequently hushing my cries and drying my tears.

I'm afraid I gave the public a very bad performance that evening, for I felt quite crippled. When, however, I met Romeo afterwards in the salon, he was in such a state of joy and elation that I felt repaid for all my suffering, and only desired to recommence, especially as he assured me tenderly that the pain would soon cease, that I would finally know what heaven was on earth. A prophecy which was soon fulfilled.

Both Isadora and Oszkár were ecstatically happy with each other, and with Isadora's success. Oszkár later recalled an evening when the two of them dined with her mother:

We were again at the Hotel Royal, in the drawing-room of their suite, the mother drunk with success, her daughter and myself, drunk no less. Dinner was served, white wine, red wine, champagne, up to three waiters bustled round us. Mr Grosz, the impresario, appeared. He brought money. He took it out of his briefcase and, sorting out the bank notes, he counted them out onto the large table. Isadora ran there, grabbed a handful of paper and metal coins, held them up high and let them drop back. She said laughingly, 'Money, money, money, you are nothing, money is nothing...'

Drunk with success or not, it was by now obvious to Isadora's mother that her daughter was heavily involved with Oszkár (not that Isadora was making any attempt to hide it). Mother didn't like it. Quickly she got in touch with her daughter Elizabeth in America, urging her to get herself to Hungary at once to try and talk some sense into her sister.

It wasn't long before Elizabeth was due to land at the Croatian port of Rijeka, one of the nearest ports to landlocked Hungary, on the Adriatic coast about 250 miles from Budapest. Isadora and Oszkár set off on a leisurely trip to meet her there and, after travelling less than half the distance, when their train stopped at the country village of Somogyszob, they impulsively alighted. Oszkár recalled the occasion:

'What a sweet little place it looks to be, and what a funny name it has,' said Isadora as we looked out of the [train] window... 'Don't you want to spend a night here...?' And, amidst ecstatic bursts of laughter, we were already standing down on the platform with our luggage, like two irresponsible teenagers, and waved our hands, flourishing our handkerchiefs, at the train as it left the station... Dusk was falling... The good woman [of the house where we found lodgings] sent us for a walk and, while we walked through the small village, she cooked a wonderful chicken paprikash in our honor. She also lit a fire in the fireplace because of the cool spring night.

I was lying on my bed with open eyes. Isadora put out the candle and began to dance. It was a marvellous dance. The shadow of her splendid young body was bending to and fro in the golden field of the wall illuminated by the light of the fire, music was furnished by the crackling of the logs, and the crackling sparks served as *pizzicati*. There, at Somogyszob, were our real nuptials. There, we did not have to be afraid of the door being opened on us, or of

89

the dawn. She was lying beside me, she went to sleep in my arms, smiling and exhausted.

They whiled away three romantic unforgettable days before resuming their journey and proceeding to Rijeka, where Isadora had her first view of the sea she had read of for so long in the classics – the Mediterranean. There they duly collected Elizabeth and she accompanied them back to Budapest.

Isadora was due to embark on a tour of Central Europe, arranged by Sándor Grosz, that would include in its itinerary the towns of Pécs and Debrecen (Hungary), Bratislava (Slovakia), Timisoara (Romania) and Oldenburg (Germany). She was desolate that Oszkár couldn't go with her, but her mother and her sister Elizabeth could, and did, reproaching her furiously all the time for her involvement with him.

The tour itself was a triumph. Seats sold out as soon as announced, even though the prices she was now able to command were high (which caused some resentment in some of the smaller and poorer towns), and Sándor Grosz continued to astutely publicise her, having her met from the train at every place she played by a victoria drawn by white horses and filled with white flowers – she herself being dressed in white, like (as she said) 'some visiting goddess'.

Back in Budapest, the tour over, she at once gave her mother and sister enough money to send them on an extended trip to the Tyrol, and rushed back into the arms of Oszkár, appearing openly around town as his mistress, attending performances and parties. In her words, 'I no longer recked the possible ruin of my Art, the despair of my mother, or the ruin and loss of the world in general.'

Reckless of convention, she began to crave children, pleading with Oszkár, 'Darling, I want a child. I want a child so much. A cow can have a calf, a cat can have kittens ... why couldn't I have babies ... why couldn't I?'

Once again, her all-or-nothing enthusiasm began to prove too much for a man. She began to sense a change in Oszkár, a feeling that his ardour was cooling. She continued to involve him in her performances, even hastily assembling a piece, set in Pygmalion's bedroom, in which he recited Pygmalion and she danced Galatea. But that rather backfired, as his notices were poor, the critics commenting that his words and her dancing did not properly meld, and that in any case his diction was sloppy. So as well as beginning to feel overwhelmed by Isadora's ardour, his professional pride was somewhat dented by her overwhelming success, both in performance and socially.

Nonetheless, he was still much in love with her, and their eventual break-up did not occur until Isadora began to chafe at simply starring in and around Hungary, when it now appeared that the whole world was ready to appreciate her Art. She wished to perform in other places, whereas he had a solid career with the Hungarian National Theatre.

'Oszkár,' she would implore him, 'the world belongs to us!... You want me to stay here?... Oszkár, this beautiful little country of yours, what can it give me ... when the world is waiting for me with banners, decked out in flags?' To which he naturally replied that if she wanted to be with him and have children, it would have to be as his respectably married wife there in Hungary.

Eventually, she recalled regretfully, 'during a long stroll in the country, sitting by the side of a haystack, he finally asked me if I did not think I should do better to continue my career and leave him to his. These were not his exact words, but that was his meaning. I still remember the haystack and the field before us, and the cold chill that struck my breast. That afternoon I signed a contract [with Sándor Grosz] for Vienna and Berlin and all the cities of Germany.'

After a last evening when she went to see him perform at the National Theatre and sat feeling as if she had 'eaten bushels of broken glass', she left Budapest (her mother and sister still being away touring) and headed back to Germany. It was September 1902, and it was five eventful months since she had arrived in Budapest.

Not only was she broken-hearted at losing Oszkár, she was also pregnant by him, and the journey to Vienna she later decribed as the saddest in her experience, saying, 'All joy seemed suddenly to have left the universe.'

To make things worse, one day she slipped and had a bad fall on the stairs of her hotel, which brought on a miscarriage. Sándor Grosz had her moved into a private hospital, where for several weeks she was laid up. Her performances were cancelled and for the moment she felt no particular wish to perform. It was some time before she even felt well enough, and plucked up enough courage, to send a telegram to Oszkár, telling him she was ill.

The day he got the telegram, immediately after he finished his evening's performance, he took a train to Vienna and next morning was with her. 'The nurse had spruced Isadora up,' he recalled, 'and she was sitting in her bed like somebody who was not even ill. But her smile, carefree at other times, looked now as if it were sorrowful. I was standing beside her bed. The nurse left us alone; I kissed her tenderly and laid her back on her pillows. She was just looking with those unforgettable, fawn-like

91

eyes, saying nothing, just looking. Finally, in a scarcely audible voice she said, "No baby...". I could not say a word. Neither did she say anything. We were just holding each other's hands.'

Oszkár's visit was probably as painful to Isadora as it was reassuring, knowing, as she now did, that they could never be together. He returned to Budapest, and she, suffering from all the emotional turbulence she had been through – her success there, her passionate involvement with him, the disappointments of losing first him and then their baby – had been robbed of all her vitality.

Sándor Grosz arranged for her to recuperate in the spa town of Františkovy Lázne, on the west edge of the Czech Republic, then too a part of the Austro-Hungarian empire. Not far from the German border, and known to Germans as Frantzenbad, the town was famous as a place for curing 'women's ailments', and gradually, among the Bohemian hills, Isadora's energy returned. By which time all the money she had earned had been spent on her hospital bills, and she had no option but to begin performing again.

The thoughtful Sándor Grosz, to make her return to performing less stressful, began not by booking her into major cities but into a series of spa towns – two in the Czech Republic, Františkovy Lázne and Mariánské Lázne (Marienbad), and one rather further away in Germany, Karlsbad.

While still recuperating in Františkovy Lázne, she was unnervingly reminded of how famous she had now become. She and Sándor Grosz and his wife were dining quietly together in a restaurant when word got round that she was there. Soon a crowd gathered outside to catch a glimpse of her, and went so far as to break the window so as to see her more clearly.

Recalling her decision to resume dancing, she wrote:

So one day I opened my trunks again, and took out my dancing tunics. I remember bursting into tears ... and swearing never to desert Art for love again... Probably skeptics will find this hard to believe, but it is true that from the experience of Budapest, for years after, my entire emotional reaction had such a revolution that I really believed I had finished with that phase, and in the future would only give myself to my Art... After that brutal awakening my senses slept; nor did I desire of them anything at all... I remember that I already thought about life like a man who has been to the wars with good intentions and who has been horribly wounded, and who, on reflection, says: 'Why should I not teach a gospel that will spare others such mutilation?'

Resuming dancing swiftly restored her spirits, and after her tour of the spas she returned to Vienna. There she was reunited with her mother and sister, with whom she was easily reconciled now that Beregi was out of her life. '[They] were delighted to see me again,' she recalled, 'although they found me changed and saddened.'

In her attempt to transform the pain her broken romance had caused her into a heartening message for others, she seized on the Greek legend of Iphigenia. Iphigenia is daughter of Clytaemnestra and her husband Agamemnon. When she is a young woman, and Agamemnon, leading the Greek fleet, is about to set sail from the harbour of Aulis to besiege Troy, he decides to sacrifice her to the goddess Artemis in order to ensure fair winds. But Artemis herself rescues Iphigenia and takes her to the land of the Taurians, where she installs her as her chief priestess.

As priestess, Iphigenia is compelled to conduct human sacrifices to an ancient wooden image of Artemis, and one day her brother, Orestes, unrecognised by her, is brought to be one. He has killed their mother, Clytaemnestra (and her lover, Aegisthus) and as a result has been tormented into madness by the furies. About to bring down her sacrificial knife upon him, Iphigenia suddenly recognises his voice, and sister and brother (now restored to sanity) flee, taking with them the sacred image, which they return to the Greeks, from whom the Taurians had stolen it.

Developing this theme of a woman battered by fate, but rising to priesthood and surviving, Isadora used for her music two operas by Gluck – *Iphigénie en Aulide* and *Iphigénie en Tauride*. The piece developed into one of her most powerful and successful.

Her confidence renewed, she went with her sister Elizabeth for a short holiday to the Croatian resort of Opatija, just to the west of Rijeka on the Adriatic coast, then headed for Munich, where she was to perform next.

When she arrived there, the reigning queen of dance was Cléo de Mérode, a Belgian dancer whose beauty was so spellbinding that she was adored in all the capitals of Europe, one reviewer of her ballet *Phryne* even heading his notice 'Gloria in excelsis Cléo'. Naturally it was rumoured that she had liaisons with nobility and royalty, although in fact it is likely that she had only two such affairs, both idyllic rather than mercenary, one with a French count and the other with a Spanish marquis.

Nor was she a mere 'exotic dancer', whose success depended on suggestiveness. What she danced was a sort of popularised form of ballet, or rather, of its earlier form, opera dancing. She was, in fact, entertainment, where Isadora was Art. For this reason, and to make the distinction quite clear to the public, Sándor Grosz insisted that seats for Isadora's performance cost considerably more than Cléo's did.

Late in 1902 she made her Munich opening at the Künstlerhaus, later describing it herself as 'the greatest artistic event and sensation that the town had experienced in many years'. She was hardly exaggerating. Audiences and critics were rapturous in their acclaim. She danced her *Iphigenia*, wearing a white Greek-style costume, short-sleeved and ankle-length and with crossed cords defining her breasts, and was such a success that Sándor Grosz was able to schedule six additional concerts.

Students took to her enthusiastically. When her carriage left the theatre each night they would escort it, singing songs and waving lighted torches. 'Often, for hours,' she remembered, 'they would group themselves outside the hotel window and sing, until I threw them my flowers and handkerchiefs.'

She had her portrait painted by von Kaulbach, and on 26th December 1902, back home in America, the *St Louis Sunday Gazette* reported (getting her name slightly wrong):

> The most talked of American girl now in Europe is Isadore Duncan, the Californian dancer – she of the bare and twinkling feet that have either scandalised or delighted so many thousands of spectators...
>
> Meantime, the demure little maiden is quietly raking in the shekels, getting higher prices for her unaided performances than are commanded by a Wagner opera... This pale, slender American girl ... who, while undeniably pretty, would herself be the first to ridicule any attempt to exploit her as a second Helen of Troy, sets whole communities by the ears...
>
> Her grace is indisputable. Never an abrupt movement, never a sharp angle.

Quick to pick up languages, Isadora had, by the time she left Munich, learnt enough German to be reading the philosopher Schopenhauer (1788–1860), who deeply admired both the Ancient Greeks and various eastern religions, notably Buddhism. He believed, developing the ideas of Kant, that the real world is an illusion, and that what a man perceives as his body is really a manifestation of his Will. Furthermore, that Will is indivisible, and that therefore we are all part of one Will, the Will of the universe.

Before leaving, she gave a closed lecture to members of the Künstlerhaus, speaking in a sort of English-German they found charming. She thanked them for judging her dancing (it was reported) 'not with their eyes, but with their fine imaginations'. At the end, they crowned her with laurel, and she left the hall earnestly discussing Schopenhauer and 'the relation of music to the will'. Then it was back to Berlin.

On her arrival, swept away by her new-found enthusiasm for German thinkers, she harangued the press, saying, 'I come to Berlin to learn. I come as an eager and thirsty pilgrim to drink from the Great fountain Head of German Knowledge and science. I come as a wistful weakling to be made strong by contact with men and women who have been cradled in the Birthplace of such giants as von Humboldt, Goethe and Kant.'

She had just started on Kant, reading his *Critique of Pure Reason* at bedtime over a glass of milk, and before she made her first dancing appearance in Berlin she addressed an audience of learned men ('white beards and gold spectacles' they were described as) in a closed session of the Prussian Academy of the Arts.

Her first performance, in January 1903, was given at Kroll's New Royal Opera House. She danced solo for more than two hours, delivering encore after encore, until the audience rushed the footlights.

Again many were students. As she remembered, 'Hundreds of young students actually climbed upon the stage, until I was in danger of being crushed to death by too much admiration.' As she left the theatre, they unhitched the horses from her carriage and drew it themselves down the Unter den Linden to her hotel.

As well as continuing her run at Kroll's New Royal Opera House (to similar receptions each night), she gave a number of select performances for those involved in the arts – for architects, sculptors, conductors, museum directors, for art and music critics. Not all were as responsive to her dancing as the general public, but any carping voices were lost amidst hosannas of applause. Back home, on 25th February, the *San Francisco Examiner* reported:

It is not in the rapidly whirling skirts of a fandango or the sand-scattering buck-and-wing dance ... that Miss Duncan has made her great hit. Berlin could not afford to risk her staid artistic reputation on anything so frivolous. Nothing less than Greek dances, Roman posturings and the most classic of gyrations satisfy the endeavors of Miss Duncan, and whether or not the archaeologists would admit the correctness of her dancing and her costumes, she has pleased the crowds immensely and her success is beyond question.

She was by then Berlin's leading attraction, and the city was entranced by her high-souled aspiration. Artists attempted to catch the spirit of her movement in paint or pencil. She began to be written about as if she were herself a priestess. Her dancing even began to be regarded by some as having a mystical healing power, and the sick and suffering were on occasion transported to the theatre to see her and receive her emanations.

To those of a less ethereal cast of mind she was celebrated as a leading symbol of female emancipation. It was the age of the New Woman, and serious attempts were being made to redefine the place of women in society, and to redress the repressions they lived under at that time – legal, sexual and political. They were then in many ways regarded as inferior beings, and even Isadora found herself wondering, 'Does the recognition of Beauty as the highest Idea belong wholly to the province of Man's intellect? Or do you think that a woman might also attain to a knowledge of the higher beauty?'

But the attitudes she had absorbed in her San Francisco girlhood stood her in good stead – her insistence on freedom in women's clothing, on sexual freedom and the irrelevance of marriage, on the right of a woman to do anything she wished in the world without the guiding hand of a man. Using her celebrity, she spoke up boldly for the advancement of women, linking it (somewhat loosely) to the most well-known and contentious scientific doctrine of the time, Darwin's theory of evolution.

As well as reading Darwin, she had continued her studies of German philosophy, having now found the philosopher who spoke to her more clearly and deeply than any other – Friedrich Nietzsche. She was introduced to him by the writer Karl Federn, who had reviewed and admired her work for some time, and who would for some years become almost a part of her entourage.

Nietzsche, who had died only three years before after a lifetime of ill-health, was an original thinker, although his teachings, like Schopenhauer's, have always tended to appeal more to artists and writers than to rigorous academic philosophers. A central part of his philosophy was that the human being of greatest value was the 'noble' man (not woman – while not exactly against women, he thought of them, as many men did at the time, as somehow lesser beings, saying, for instance, 'We take pleasure in women as in a perhaps daintier, more delicate, and more ethereal kind of creature. What a treat it is to meet creatures who have only dancing and nonsense and finery on their minds! They have always been the delight of every tense and profound male soul.')

His 'noble' man, a stern governing aristocrat, would learn to discipline and organise the chaos of his own passions, would protect lesser beings such as artists and poets, who know only how to do things, and would learn from his warriors about death in battle, and learn not to fear sacrificing them in the fight for whatever cause he found within himself to be right. He despised both Christianity and Buddhism for teaching that all men are equal, which he found a harmful and ignoble doctrine, tending to reduce everyone to the lowest level.

In spite of this, his writings are readable, and even poetic, and Isadora was drawn to him by his deep consideration of Art. Indeed, his very first book, published in 1872, when he was twenty-eight, was called *The Birth of Tragedy from the Spirit of Music*. In it he considered the Art of Ancient Greece as an intermingling of the Dionysian and Apollonian – the two major strands that Isadora had already felt and understood. 'Apollonian' to him indicated a pure and intellectual aesthetic approach; 'Dionysian' an intuitive approach through the passions.

He also had something similar to her deep understanding of dance. Indeed, he compared the wise man to a dancer, able to express the truth with 'lightness', and once he wrote, 'Count that day lost in which you have not danced.'

In Part Four of his most famous work, *Thus Spoke Zarathustra*, he wrote a section in which he imagines the prophet Zarathustra (who himself 'walks like a dancer') dancing with a female personification of Life itself. It begins:

Into your eyes I looked recently, O life: I saw gold blinking in your night-eye; my heart stopped in delight: a golden boat I saw blinking on nocturnal waters, a golden rocking-boat, sinking, drinking, and winking again. At my foot, frantic to dance, you cast a glance, a laughing, questioning, melting rocking-glance: twice only you stirred your rattle with your small hands, and my foot was already rocking with dancing frenzy.

My heels twitched, then my toes hearkened to understand you, and rose: for the dancer has his ears in his toes.

I leaped towards you, but you fled back from my leap, and the tongue of your fleeing, flying hair licked me in its sweep.

Away from you I leaped, and from your serpent's ire; and already you stood there, half turned, your eyes full of desire.

It is no wonder that Isadora fell for a writer who was not only a great thinker, filled with classical lore, but who could also write with such lush romantic passion about Life and Dance.

In March 1903 Isadora herself was invited to give an address to the Berlin Presse Verein (the Press Club) on 'The Dance of the Future'. This came about as the result of a letter she had written to the newspaper *Morgen Post*, vehemently rebutting a critical article entitled 'Can Miss Duncan Dance?'

Her brother Raymond had by then completed his job as advance agent for Emma Nevada's American concert tour, and rejoined Isadora, their mother and their sister. With his help, working from the stacks of notes she had made over the years, Isadora compiled her address. It began:

> I am asked to speak upon 'The Dance of the Future' – yet how is it possible? In fifty years I may have something to say. Besides, I have always found it indiscreet for me to speak of my dance. The people who are in sympathy with me understand what I am trying to do better than myself, the people who are not in sympathy, understand better than I why they are not.

The address was permeated with echoes from the philosophers she had been reading – from Nietzsche a sense of self-realisation and upward striving towards perfection; from Rousseau the concept of the 'Noble Savage', unconstrained by the shackles of so-called civilisation, and directly in touch with the purity and wisdom of nature. It went on:

> The movement of the free animals and birds remains always in correspondence to their nature, the necessities and wants of that nature, and its correspondence to earth nature. It is only when you put free animals under false restrictions that they lose the power of moving in harmony with nature, and adopt a movement expressive of the restrictions placed about them.
>
> So it has been with civilised man. The movements of the savage, who lived in freedom in constant touch with Nature, were unrestricted, natural and beautiful. Only the movements of the naked body can be perfectly natural. Man, arrived at the end of civilisation, will have to return to nakedness, not to the unconscious nakedness of the savage, but to the conscious and acknowledged nakedness of the mature Man, whose body will be the harmonious expression of his spiritual being.

This was stirring stuff, even in Germany where there would before long be a flourishing nudist movement, in which members of all strata of society would unite in throwing off their clothes in homes and health clubs, believing that air on the body was more natural and health-giving, and that this freer life would help release people from the neuroses arising from the pressures of modern society.

Isadora's address went on to vehemently attack the ballet ('an expression of degeneration, of living death') and to repeat her intention of founding a school – a school not just of Dance, but of Life, 'a theatre where a hundred little girls shall be trained in my art, which they, in their turn, will better. In this school I shall not teach the children to imitate my movements, but to make their own. I shall not force them to study certain definite movements; I shall help them to develop those movements which are natural to them.'

She concluded:

The dance of the future will be one whose body and soul have grown so harmoniously together that the natural language of that soul will have become the movement of the body. The dancer will not belong to a nation but to all humanity. She will not dance in the form of nymph, nor fairy, nor coquette, but in the form of woman in her greatest and purest expression. She will realise the mission of woman's body and the holiness of all its parts. She will dance the changing life of nature, showing how each part is transformed into the other. From all parts of her body shall shine radiant intelligence, bringing to the world the message of thoughts and aspirations of thousands of women. She shall dance the freedom of woman...

Oh, she is coming, the dancer of the future: the free spirit ... more glorious than any woman who has yet been; more glorious than the Egyptian, than the Greek, the early Italian, than all women of past centuries – the highest intelligence in the freest body!

Published later in 1903 as a pamphlet, this manifesto would gain Isadora much publicity, raising outrage (especially among devotees of the ballet), applause, and furious debate. As she wrote herself, in a letter to her old friend Douglas Ainslie, 'The journals write about it as seriously as if I were a Member of Parliament.'

She was now famous across Europe as a revolutionary dancer, a feminist (although her feminist ideas would always be expressed more in her general attitude than in a coherently developed philosophy), an apostle of simple dress, if not outright nudity, and as someone exciting, thought-provoking and outrageous.

While in Berlin she was flattered to receive a visit from Siegfried Wagner, son of the famous composer. He had a problem and felt she was the one to help him with it. He was helping his mother, Cosima, to run the Bayreuth Festivals held every summer to perform his father's operas, and his problem lay with his father's most popular opera, *Tannhäuser*. When this had last been presented at Bayreuth, in 1891, the dancing in the Bacchanal scene, at the beginning of Act One, had flopped badly (which was why it hadn't been presented there since).

Siegfried felt that Isadora was the very person to re-choreograph the Bacchanal, and swiftly she agreed that she would, although not this year (1903). As her work would involve working with a classically-trained corps de ballet, and as she detested ballet, this at first seems a strange decision for her to make. But as she later told a friend, it was very simple. She was young, passionately involved in her studies, and eager to meet great musicians, artists and scholars.

It is also possible that she was favourably disposed to the idea because her great idol, Nietzsche, had for years been a friend and admirer of Wagner (although they fell out permanently in 1882 when Wagner wrote *Parsifal*. This Nietzsche objected to because it was Christian in feeling, and worse, because it was insincerely so, the atheist Wagner using Christianity only for dramatic effect). Having agreed to come to Bayreuth at some unspecified date, Isadora duly received a written invitation to do so from Cosima Wagner herself.

Visiting Vienna for a brief series of performances, she appeared at the Karl Theater, alternating appearances there with the famous actress Eleanora Duse, whose on-stage restraint of gesture she had so much admired in London.

In the spring of 1903 Isadora decided to return to Paris, and celebrate her success by performing for the city that she loved. This she did over the 'entreaties and lamentations' of Sándor Grosz, who himself wished her to build on her reputation by embarking on a lengthy tour of Germany. Their partnership came to a temporary end, partly because of this disagreement, but also possibly because she now had her sights firmly set on 'destiny', rather than on sordidly making money. As she later recalled of her attitude at this time:

I felt that I was only at the gateway of the study of my Art. I

100

wanted to study, continue my researches, create a dance and movements which did not then exist, and the dream of my school, which had haunted all my childhood, became stronger and stronger.

As with many people just emerging from a time of widespread religious belief, the emotional pattern of Isadora's mind would always remain Christian, even though she had no belief in God. To follow the dictates of Art was to her the spiritual equivalent of following the Word of the Lord, and deep inside she believed that doing so could not help but lead to Glory – in the true sense, not necessarily in a worldly one. This was an attitude that would in later years cause her considerable trouble.

Raymond resumed his role of her manager, and when they returned to Paris, with mother and sister Elizabeth, the whole Duncan clan were again reunited, because there as well were Augustin, his wife Sarah, and their daughter, now three years old and named Temple. Also in the party was the German writer Karl Federn, who had introduced Isadora to Nietszche and become an admiring part of her world.

Isadora was now reasonably wealthy. In her words, 'There was a sum in the bank which seemed to me inexhaustible.' Which was perhaps not the healthiest way of looking at things.

For her performances, of which there would be ten, she hired the Théâtre Sarah Bernhardt, in the place du Châtelet – one of the largest theatres in the city. This was mistake enough, but what she had also failed to take into account was the curious self-absorption of Paris. No matter how celebrated a performer (or writer, or musician) might be elsewhere, in Paris you were nobody until the citizens decided you were somebody.

True, she had a small and influential band of admirers from the fashionable world of the salons where she had danced, but to the great mass of the general public she was an unknown quantity.

Nor was that her only problem. Raymond, in his capacity as manager, became high-handed with the conductor of her orchestra, with the result that words were exchanged and the conductor stormed out, taking the musicians with him. What made things worse was that he had also been composing original music for a new version of the legend of Pan and Echo, and the score for that too went with him.

In desperation, Isadora sought out the French-born but London-based composer Arnold Dolmetsch, who happened to be in Paris at the time. She had collaborated with him briefly when she herself was in London, and she now begged him to compose her a new piece. He agreed, and worked far into the night to provide one.

Realising that tickets were selling poorly, on the eve of her first night Isadora went with Raymond to the École des Beaux-Arts where they handed out free tickets to the students to paper the house.

At the last minute Isadora decided that the Dolmetsch piece was unsuited to her dance, and so bravely elected to dance *Pan and Echo* with no music at all. Mabel Dolmetsch, Arnold's wife, recalled the performance years later:

> The airy flights of the nymph in her diaphanous draperies and floral garlands were effective and charming, despite the absence of music. But when (still thus attired) she suddenly assumed a sinister frown, and twiddling her fingers to suggest the manipulation of a wood instrument, broke into uncouth gambols, a ripple of incredulous laughter ran through the audience.

Nonetheless, at least some of her audience must have appreciated her unaccompanied performance, because there came a night at the Théâtre Sarah Bernhardt when Isadora's orchestra walked out on her, and the audience demanded she perform her whole programme unaccompanied. Which she did.

But all in all her run was a considerable financial failure. It ended on 13th June 1903, and in a graceful speech to her audience after her last performance, she told them, 'I thank you all for having understood me... And I danced the last dance better than the first ones because I felt in sympathy with you. And so I thank you, I thank you.'

In that speech she also referred to dancing and sculpture as being sister arts, an understanding that was reinforced two weeks later when she was invited to the town of Vélizy to celebrate the award to Rodin of the Légion d'Honneur. The celebration, attended by his friends and students, was held in a local restaurant, in whose garden, for the occasion, was his sculpture of *St John the Baptist Preaching*.

On the train to Vélizy, Isadora had met a young English sculptor, Kathleen Bruce, who later recalled that, after the meal and the speeches of congratulation, someone suggested that Isadora should dance. This she did, on the grass of the garden, accompanied by fiddle music and ending her dance by falling at Rodin's feet. He took her hand and pressed it to Kathleen's, saying, 'My children, you two artists should understand each other.' (Kathleen Bruce, in only a few years' time, would become the wife of Scott of the Antarctic.)

In spite of the awkward failure of his and Isadora's attempt to make love, Rodin retained a lasting affection and respect for her, regretting, later in his life, that he had never made drawings of her while she was actually in front of him and dancing (he did make sketches of her from memory, but only in repose). Describing her, he once wrote, 'It may be said of Isadora Duncan that she attains sculpture and emotion effortlessly ... Suppleness, emotion, these high qualities, the soul of the dance, are her complete and sovereign art.'

She, for her part, always revered Rodin and felt almost abashed in his powerful presence, saying once, 'He is too great for me. As soon as he appears I feel like a nymph before a centaur ... before the very force of nature.'

Her profligate season at the Théâtre Sarah Bernhardt, and her constitutional inability to manage her finances, meant that by this time the 'inexhaustible' sum she had had in the bank was now completely gone, and she and her family were flat broke. So broke, in fact, that one night she was embarrassed, while giving a dinner party in her hotel suite, by the arrival of bailiffs sent to collect a debt.

Shortly after this embarrassment, she headed back to Germany and made a tour there for Sándor Grosz lasting several weeks. This duly returned her to solvency, but on her return to Paris she became imbued with a new idea. Still intent on developing her theories and discovering her destiny, she decided to take a break from performing and make a spiritual pilgrimage with her family to the place she now realised she should have headed for long ago – Greece, the cradle of all she revered.

Chapter Seven

Building a Temple and Dancing an Opera

It was decided that the whole Duncan family (except for Augustin's wife and his three-year-old daughter, Temple) would make an expedition to Greece together – Isadora, Raymond, Elizabeth, Augustin and their mother. With them too would go the young sculptor Kathleen Bruce, whom Isadora had met on the train when they both went to visit Rodin.

Raymond was as much a Graecophile as Isadora was, if not even more so, and shortly before the family set off for Greece he had undergone a conversion. On a short holiday in Normandy, in the company of a hired valet, he had invited the valet to come swimming in the sea with him. To which the valet had replied, 'I can't. I'm in livery.'

Whether or not this was simply a diplomatic excuse, it struck Raymond with the force of a revelation. 'That,' he recalled, 'was an eye-opener. I learned what clothes do to and for a man. I had a smart Bond Street wardrobe and I turned them all over to ... the valet. I bought some thick white linen and cut a hole for my head to slip through. They wouldn't let me on the beach. I said to myself, if people are so blind that they can't see the man, only his clothes, I intend to live long enough to show them the man.'

From then on he adopted what would be a lifelong habit of dispensing with conventional modern dress in favour of a loose, flowing Graeco-Roman tunic, his feet covered in self-designed leather sandals and his hair long.

For their actual time in Greece he insisted that all the family join him in adopting Ancient Greek costume, and before leaving Paris all five Duncans created for themselves garments resembling, as nearly as they could manage, the peplum (an oblong of cloth about twelve feet by six, wrapped round the body and pulled up over the shoulders), the chlamys (a long mantle worn for travelling) and the waist-length tunic.

Isadora took to the ancient style enthusiastically. Of the family's adopting it, she later wrote, 'We had decided that even the Directoire [Empire-style] dresses which I wore, and Raymond's knickerbockers, open collars, and flowing ties, were degenerate garments. To me it seemed sacrilege to touch the stones of Grecian temples with the high-heeled shoes of a decadent civilisation; to sweep with the silk petticoat of the twentieth century the sacred marbles of the Acropolis.'

She promised Sándor Grosz that she would return some time to make further appearances in Germany, and she and the rest of the party set off for Greece in the late summer of 1903, travelling first by train to the Adriatic port of Brindisi, on the heel of Italy. From there they sailed south through the Strait of Otranto, into the Ionian Sea, and landed on the Greek island of Lefkada, famous in legend as Leucas, where the poet Sappho was said to have thrown herself to her death from a sacrificial rock, after her advances had been rejected by the beautiful youth Phaon.

The Duncans were now in the very home of the civilisation they had adored for so long. They were all intoxicated to be there, and excitedly began wearing their historical clothing. One of the neighbouring islands to Lefkada is Ithaca, reputedly the birthplace and home of Ulysses, and when the group decided to hire a fishing smack to take them to the Greek mainland, they felt they were sailing the same seas as Homer's great hero had. Raymond undertook to guide the boatman, using a mixture of pantomime and Ancient Greek, and as Isadora recalled, 'The fisherman didn't seem to understand much about Ulysses, but the sight of many drachmas encouraged him to set sail, although he was loath to go far, and pointed many times to the sky, saying, "Boom, Boom," ... to inform us that the sea was treacherous.'

Their voyage took them about 30 miles into an almost-landlocked lake of sea called the Amvrakikós Kolpos (the Ambracian Gulf). At the inland end of it, in its south-eastern corner, they landed at the town then known as Karvasara. The name comes from the Turkish word 'kervansaray', or 'caravanserai', meaning an inn for travellers. The Turks were civic-minded, and built many of these inns along their main highways, including those in Greece during the centuries they occupied it, so Karvasara was on a main highway and was a good place for the Duncan party to land. (Since 1903 the Greeks have removed most of the Turkish names from their towns, so this one is nowadays known as Amfilokhia.)

Although the Duncans were well aware that the Greece of 1903 was no longer the Ancient Greece of Artists and Philosophers, they still held it in reverence, and when they landed at Karvasara, all of them knelt and reverently kissed the soil of the mainland. The local countryfolk were somewhat amazed at this oddly-dressed band of visitors, and as Isadora remembered, 'the first landing of Christopher Columbus in America could not have caused more astonishment.'

Their behaviour must have caused as much astonishment as their appearance because, having hired a two-horse cart to carry their luggage (and the fifty-year-old Mrs Duncan), they started making their way from village to village as a sort of celebratory pilgrimage, rejoicing that they were on their way to bring back to Greece the glory of its greatness. They swept the dusty roads before the cart with laurel branches, they hugged villagers they met, they danced in village squares, and, half from exuberance and half in earnest, they fell to their knees offering up extemporised prayers to the old gods who to them were the gods of Art – 'Salute, O Olympian Zeus! And Apollo! And Aphrodite! Prepare, O ye Muses, to dance again!'

The simple inns they found to sleep in were infested with bugs, but nothing could damp their enthusiasm. 'We sped along on the light wings of youthful feet,' recalled Isadora, 'often leaping and bounding before the carriage, accompanying our steps with shouts and songs of joy... Often our emotions were so violent that we could only find expression in tearful embraces.'

From Karvasara they made their way to Agrinio, about 25 miles to the south, and then a similar distance to the coastal town of Mesolongi, known to romantics as Missolonghi. This was the place where the poet Byron had died of a fever in 1824, having just arrived there to support the Greeks in their fight to be free from Turkish rule. The romantic Duncans paused solemnly on the shore to honour his memory ('with full hearts and tearful eyes,' remembered Isadora).

The next stage in their journey was to cross the Gulf of Corinth to Patra, where they became impatient at the slowness of their progress and, relinquishing their two-horse cart, boarded a train for Athens, arriving there late at night.

They booked themselves into a suite at the Hotel Angleterre, but slept little, soon rising to greet the dawn. Climbing the steps of the steep small hill called the Acropolis, they beheld on its crest the Parthenon, bathed in morning sunlight. They were awestruck. In Isadora's words:

The sun was rising from behind Mount Pentelicus, revealing her marvellous clearness and the splendour of her marble sides sparkling in the sunlight. We mounted the last step of the Propylœa and gazed on the Temple shining in the morning light. With one accord we remained silent. We separated slightly from one another; for here was Beauty too sacred for words. It struck strange terror into our hearts. No cries or embraces now. We each found our vantage-point of worship and remained for hours in an ecstasy of meditation which left us all weak and shaken.

She felt, she said, 'born for the first time in that long breath and first gaze of pure beauty'.

Not every experience they had in Athens was so sublimely spiritual. Many Athenians found their ancient clothing hilarious and, while most of them persevered with it, the conservative Augustin soon reverted permanently to conventional dress.

As they had done in other cities, the family spent their early days in Athens visiting museums and art galleries. They made excursions to nearby historic places such as Colonus, a mile or so north of the city, celebrated for once having had a temple dedicated to the sea-god Poseidon, for having had a grove sacred to the Furies, and for having the tomb of Oedipus. They went further, to Eleusis, which was thirteen miles from Athens, and danced the whole way. Once the centre of the cult of the corn goddess Demeter, a magnificent temple had been dedicated to her there. (The religious rites devoted to her are remembered as the Eleusinian Mysteries because nobody is quite sure what they were.)

They frequently revisited the Acropolis, and sometimes, in the ruined theatre of Dionysus at its foot, Isadora would dance before the empty stone benches, feeling, she told a reporter for the *New York World*, that forty thousand Greeks were there watching her, 'the spirits of those who lived in those glorious times.'

As well as the Acropolis they climbed several of the other hills around Athens. So greatly did they admire the views of the city from these hills that they took to spending whole nights camping out on them (while still renting their suite at the Angleterre), and gradually a plan evolved that the whole family would settle permanently near Athens. They would buy land and build a temple there, living as a sort of commune.

Isadora, in the hotel suite, gave an interview to the press. Reclining on a sofa, with her feet shod in sandals, she was described by one somewhat smitten reporter as having 'a wondrous figure, slim but rounded. There was a finely shaped head with a coil of glorious hair setting against the back of the neck, two arms exquisitely moulded – the very classic simplicity of the costume only made the wearer the more beautiful, the more graceful.'

In the interview she declared, 'Ah, you cannot imagine how ineffably happy I am in beautiful Athens. I came here to realise my life's dream; to be in a place sacred to the imperishable traditions of Greek art and Greek culture; to steep myself to the lips in the mysteries.' She assured the reporters that she loved Athens so much that she would stay there till the end of the year, and then, after returning to Berlin for a season of performing, would return and remain permanently.

Asked if she wasn't cold in her Ancient Greek costume, she replied with high-minded contempt. 'Cold! Who could be conscious of such things amid these surroundings? ... *Cold?*'

The Duncans began to develop a detailed philosophy for their communal life. One thing they vowed was there would be no marriages among them, although, in a concession to Augustin they allowed that those already married should remain married.

Augustin was proving less wholehearted about things than the rest of the family. No only was he refusing to wear ancient garb, he was admitting to missing his wife and daughter. As Isadora recalled years later (with some wryness about her youthful zeal), 'We considered this a great weakness on his part, but consented – as he was already married and had a child – that there was nothing for us to do but send for them.'

Raymond, of course, was determinedly earnest about the life they were planning to lead, and was the ring-leader in developing a rigid code of rules for it. In Isadora's words:

> We accepted Augustin's wife with ill-concealed reservation. But for our own part, we drew up a plan in a copy-book, which was to exclude all but the Clan Duncan, and therein we set down the rules for our lives... We did this somewhat on the same plan as Plato in his *Republic*. It was decreed to rise at sunrise. We were to greet the rising sun with joyous songs and dances. Afterwards we were to refresh ourselves with a modest bowl of goat's milk. The mornings were to be devoted to teaching the inhabitants to dance and sing. They must be made to celebrate the Greek gods and give up their terrible modern costumes. Then, after our light lunch of green vegetables – for we had decided to give up meat and become vegetarians – the afternoons were to be spent in meditation, and the evenings given over to pagan ceremonies with appropriate music.

They began walking the countryside around Athens, searching for suitable land to buy, and quite soon, some five miles to the east of it, as they were climbing a 'barren hillock' on the wooded slopes of Mount Hymettos, Raymond looked back at the city, dropped the staff he had been walking with, raised his arms and cried dramatically, 'Look, we are on the same level as the Acropolis!'

From the hillock, known for centuries as Kopanos, they were looking directly at the eastern portal of the Parthenon, some two-and-a-half miles away. It was obviously the place where they should settle, and at once they set about attempting to buy it. 'But,' as Isadora recalled, 'there were difficulties... First, no one knew to whom the land belonged. It was so far from Athens, and frequented only by shepherds tending their flocks and goats.'

They persevered, and eventually managed to establish that various parcels of land making up the hillock were owned by five different sheep-herding families. These families, concealing their surprise that anybody would consider their land worth buying, put their heads together and 'asked a sum entirely out of proportion.' But the Duncans were determined to have the site. They agreed to pay what was asked and, to make the signing of the contract into a suitably dramatic ceremony, they celebrated it by inviting all five families to a banquet where, Isadora remembered, 'we had lamb on the spit, and other kinds of tempting food. We also served much *raki* – the cognac of the country.'

On Kopanos, they decided, they would build a temple, which would also serve as a dwelling-place and as a theatre. They would pay the inhabitants to help them, and the stone, Raymond declared, must come from the quarries on Mount Pentelicus, some nine miles to the north. That was where the white marble to build the Parthenon had come from, in the fifth century BC. He swiftly designed the building, basing it on Agamemnon's palace at Mycenae. Like that, it would have walls two feet thick, and soon, wrote Isadora, 'each day could be seen a long procession of carts, carrying these red stones, winding their tortuous way from Pentelicus to Kopanos.' The stones were red because in the interests of economy Raymond had elected to use the poorer red stone from the base of Mount Pentelicus, rather than the fine white marble from higher up. Which was as well for Isadora, because it was her earnings from performing which were still subsidising everything.

As work proceeded on the temple, the whole atmosphere for the Duncans was one of holiday. Kathleen Bruce, writing in 1949 (by which time she had become Lady Kennet), recalled 'days of apparent indolence, seeding time, and nights too, of character! Sleeping out of doors undoubtedly adds to the interest of life... There were days when we rode bareback on ponies on the lovely beach beyond Phaleron, riding into the sea and falling off by intent into the water.'

When the cornerstone of the temple was laid, an Orthodox priest conducted a ceremony to bless the project, slitting the throat of a black cockerel to wet the stone with its blood. The Duncans, even though atheists, cheerfully went along with the ceremony, happy to keep on good terms with their neighbours and employees. After the priest had conducted his symbolic rite with the cockerel, wrote Isadora:

> Then followed prayer and incantation. He blessed all the stones of the house and, asking us our names, he uttered a prayer in which we frequently heard the names *Isadora Duncan* (my mother), *Augustin, Raymond, Elizabeth,* and *Little Isadora* (myself)... Great barrels of wine and *raki* were opened. A roaring bonfire was set ablaze on the hill, and we, together with our neighbours, the peasantry, danced and drank and made merry all through the night.

The building of the temple naturally aroused interest in Athens itself. Fashionable people would come to see how the work was progressing. On one occasion the king himself, George I, rode to Kopanos with his entourage. The Duncans, Isadora remembered, were unimpressed, 'For we were living under the reign of other kings, Agamemnon, Menelaus and Priam.'

She did deign to go into Athens and dance for the Royal Family, but even so admitted she preferred to mingle with the students of the city, who would congregate in front of the Hotel Angleterre (the Duncans did not spend every night camping out on the hillside), and would throng round the carriage if the family went for a drive 'and acclaim our Hellenic tunics.'

One problem that had emerged with the site for the temple was that the hill of Kopanos was waterless. They tried digging wells but, in spite of several attempts, found none. Water would have to be brought. But through the digging they did of wells and foundations, relics were unearthed that delighted Raymond by indicating that in ancient times there had been a village there.

He was having the time of his life, endlessly planning for the future and investigating the past. He became friendly with Angelos Sikelanios, the Greek poet, and with his sister Penelope, who was deeply immersed

111

in history and in art. She was red-haired and beautiful, and before long would become Raymond's wife (his antipathy to marriage having proved ephemeral).

Isadora, as 1903 began drawing to a close, became less happy. As had happened in Hungary, she was beginning to feel confined – as if, in spite of all the beauty and history around her, she was no longer in the big world that needed her message. She was also uneasily aware that, after five months in Greece, her money was running out.

One day, she later recalled, as she was ascending the 'sacred hill' of the Acropolis, the sad feeling struck her that 'we were not, nor ever could be, other than moderns... I was, after all, but a Scotch-Irish-American.' Nonetheless, she felt she had learned something important from her time in Ancient Greece. In an essay she wrote at the time, called 'The Parthenon', she remembered one of her visits to it, saying:

> These columns which seem so straight and still are not really straight, each one is curving gently from the base to the height, each one is in flowing movements, never resting, and the movement of each is in harmony with the others. And as I thought this my arms rose slowly toward the Temple and I leaned forward – and then I knew I had found my dance, and it was a Prayer.

It was decided that she and the family would return to Vienna, except for Raymond, who would remain to oversee the completion of their own temple on Kopanos. Contacting Sándor Grosz, she asked him to arrange a new series of appearances for her.

While in Athens, on one of their visits to the theatre of Dionysus at the foot of the Acropolis (on a moonlit night), the Duncans had heard a group of ragged urchins amusing themselves by singing. The family were enchanted by what Isadora described as the 'unearthly quality' of the boys' voices, and before leaving for Vienna she decided that she would dance there a performance of Aeschylus' tragedy *The Suppliants*, and would take with her ten such boys to sing as her chorus (she had long been looking for some way to make use of the classical Greek chorus in her dance performances).

So before leaving Athens she held a series of nightly competitions to choose the best ten boys she could find and, having found them, made the necessary arrangements to take them with her and her family (except Raymond) to Vienna.

The Suppliants tells the legend of Danaus, whose twin brother Aegyptus was king of Egypt (which he named after himself). Aegyptus had fifty sons and Danaus had fifty daughters (in each case by a variety of mothers). Danaus was sent to rule Libya, and dissension arose between the brothers over their inheritance from their father, Belus. Aegyptus proposed that, in order to reconcile them, his fifty sons should marry Danaus' fifty daughters, but Danaus, rightly suspecting a plot, fled from Libya, eventually reaching the Peleponnese, where he declared himself king and became a powerful ruler.

Aegyptus now sent his fifty sons there, telling them not to return till they had punished Danaus and his entire family. Arriving at the town of Argos, the sons begged Danaus to relent and let them marry his daughters. When Danaus refused, they beseiged the town, and eventually, from shortage of water, Danaus was compelled to do as they asked. A mass-marriage was arranged, and during the wedding feast he secretly doled out sharp pins to his daughters, for them to conceal in their hair. At midnight every daughter except one killed her husband by stabbing him through the heart. The exception was Hypermnestra who, on the advice of the goddess Artemis, spared her husband Lynceus because he had refrained from taking her maidenhead (he later killed Danaus and reigned in his stead).

The show opened in Vienna, with Isadora alone dancing, supported by her chorus of ten boys. 'As there were fifty "daughters of Danaus",' she later admitted, 'I found it very difficult to express, in my slight figure, the emotions of fifty maidens all at once, but I had the feeling of multiple oneness, and did my best.' The audience remained lukewarm, demanding that she dance *The Blue Danube*. Isadora attempted to inspire them by a harangue from the stage, exclaiming, 'We must revive the beauty of the chorus.' But still they shouted, 'Nein. Mach nicht. Tanze. Tanze die Schöne Blaue Donau. Tanze noch einmal.' When she did, they applauded her over and over again.

At least her Viennese appearances were a financial success, and, in her own words, she and her boys departed to perform in Munich and then Berlin, 'laden with new gold'. In both those places exactly the same thing happened. But during the Berlin run the boys became increasingly difficult. As she ruefully recalled:

The little Greek boys themselves were feeling the effects of their unaccustomed environment. I had received several complaints from our worthy hotel proprietor of their bad manners and the violence of their tempers. It seems that they asked continually for black

113

bread, black ripe olives, and raw onions, and, when these condiments were not in their daily menu, they became enraged with the waiters – going so far as to throw beefsteaks at their heads and attack them with knives.

In desperation, she moved them from the hotel into the family's Berlin apartment, installing cots in the parlour for them to sleep on. But it wasn't long before she received complaints from the police that 'our Greek boys were surreptitiously escaping from the window at night, frequenting cheap cafés and making the acquaintance of the lowest specimens of their compatriots which the city held.'

This was a long way from her own high ideals of the cultured life, and even from the enchanting quality of the boys' voices in the Athenian moonlight, because, to make things worse, some of their voices were now breaking, and the overall sound of her chorus was deteriorating sadly. As she remembered, 'One could no longer excuse it on the grounds that it was Byzantine. It was simply a fearful bad noise.' So one day she and Elizabeth assembled the whole bunch, bought them new clothes and one-way tickets to Athens, and sent them back there by train.

Abandoning Aeschylus, Isadora resumed her earlier repertoire. She was still wildly popular, especially in Austria and Germany – so much so that imitators were springing up all over Europe. Sándor Grosz kept begging her to let him arrange tours for her, to let people see that she was the original, to stop ruminating about the Ancient Greeks and think about her career. Isadora found this attitude Philistine, recalling:

He continually bombarded me with entreaties to travel, and continually came in, wailing with anguish, showing me newspapers which told how, in London and elsewhere, copies of my curtains, my costumes, and my dances were being ... turned into certain success and hailed as original. But even this had no effect on me.

She was still adding to her repertoire, and one item she added at this time became one of her most controversial, at least in Germany. She began to dance to some of the music of Beethoven's Seventh Symphony. It is possible that her attention was drawn to this piece because its Finale was described as 'the Apotheosis of the Dance' by Nietzsche's former friend and idol, Richard Wagner. Whatever her impulse, to interpret major concert works in dance was a significant innovation at the time, and her doing so caused considerable controversy.

She performed to sections of Beethoven's Seventh first in Munich and then in Berlin, and the German public, even the students who were her stoutest champions, were shocked that she would dare to do such a thing. Beethoven was to them such a towering figure that her attempt to add dancing to what was already a complete work of art seemed to indicate that she was blindly unaware of its perfection. In a typical reaction, the illustrated paper *Jugend* caricatured her dancing heavily and enthusiastically on Beethoven's head, with the caption '*Lerne leiden, ohne zu klagen*' ('Learn to suffer without complaining').

Shortly afterwards, however, when she went to Paris and performed to three of the symphony's four movements at the Trocadéro, she was an amazing success. At last the Parisian public took her to their hearts (it helped, of course, that they were less Teutonically sensitive to the glory of a German composer). The orchestra that accompanied her, the Colonne Orchestra, was then regarded as the finest in Paris, and in the same programme she also danced to sections of Beethoven's *Moonlight* and *Pathétique* sonatas, as well as making several enthusiastic harangues from the stage. In one she explained how hard she had been working over the past year, saying, 'But it is still not enough. The Art of the Dance is a very great thing and what I am doing is only the beginning. It is like a little girl making her first steps. I hope to do better next year; and I hope above all to teach young pupils who will outstep me and realise all that I foresee.'

She was scheduled to give two performances, but demand to see her was so great that a third was added. At the end of the second, the rapturous applause she received so overwhelmed her that tears filled her eyes and for once she found herself unable to speak.

Even with this success, having returned to Berlin, she continued to refuse Sándor Grosz's pleas to make an extended tour of Europe. Her mind was still on continuing to study, and on extending her understanding of dance. With the result that the next thing she did was to take up Siegfried and Cosima Wagner's offer of going to Bayreuth and working on the Bacchanal section of *Tannhäuser* for the summer 1904 Festival.

The opera, whose full title is *Tannhäuser und der Sängerkrieg auf dem Wartburg* (*Tannhäuser and the Contest of Song at the Wartburg*), is set in the thirteenth century, in the Bavarian Valley around the castle of Wartburg, whose Landgraves were lovers of art and music. Tannhäuser, a famous poet and minnesinger, has been enticed by Holda, the Goddess of Spring (who in time became identified with Venus, Goddess of Love), into her palace in the heart of the Venusberg mountain.

When the story opens, he has been there for some time and is beginning to tire of her pagan charms and long for the purity of the real world again. After the overture, when the curtain rises, we find him reclining in the arms of Venus, while nymphs, sirens, satyrs and bacchantes dance around them.

This was the scene that Isadora was to appear in and help restage (it ends when Tannhäuser tears himself away from Venus, with the cry that his hope lies in the Virgin Mary, and her court disappears, leaving him prostrate and alone before a cross in a peaceful valley beneath the Wartburg).

Studying the scene, Isadora perceptively saw that it 'expresses all the frenzy of voluptuous longing of a *cérébrale*. The closed grotto of the satyrs and nymphs ... was the closed grotto of Wagner's mind, exasperated by the continual longing for a sensual outlet which he could find only within his own imagination.' This gave her the key to how she would present the scene – her underlying concept. Rather than indicating the scene literally, she would 'depict' it as happening in Tannhäuser's mind.

She set off for Bayreuth in May 1904, but not alone. That same month, her friend Mary D'Este, with her five-year-old son Preston, had returned to Europe to rejoin the Duncan Clan. She and her husband of two-and-a-half years, the rich and amiable Solomon Sturges, had come to an agreement whereby she would henceforth spend half the year with him in America and the other half touring Europe.

On her arrival in Berlin, Preston was left at Isadora's apartment in the care of Mrs Duncan (as was Augustin's daughter, Temple), and Isadora and Mary set off at once for Bayreuth. At Isadora's suggestion, they were dressed identically, in 'loose flowing garments, blue shawls and white capes, with bare feet and gold sandals' – a conceit that somewhat rebounded on Isadora, because the two looked so alike that many people, including Cosima Wagner, commented that they looked like sisters. Which Isadora found irritating.

They entered the picturesque Bavarian town in style, riding from the railway station in an open carriage with Isadora waving happily to the gathering crowds. The carriage took them to the Villa Wahnfried, Wagner's last home and the place where he had been buried in 1883. Since then it had been devotedly preserved by his widow, Cosima, everything kept as far as possible in the exact state he left it. When Isadora and Mary arrived, Cosima gave them a guided tour, in which the most important sight was of course the great composer's grave.

They were to stay at Phillipsruhe (Phillip's Rest), the former hunting lodge of King Ludwig of Bavaria, in the Hermitage Gardens, and during her stay there Isadora would earn something of a reputation for debauchery among the staid Bavarians, mainly from her habit of receiving guests while reclining on a sofa. As she herself later explained, Phillipsruhe 'contained many couches and cushions, rose-coloured lamps and no chairs. It was looked upon by some as a Temple of Iniquity... The village people considered it a veritable witches' house, and described our innocent revels as 'terrible orgies'.

When not rehearsing, Isadora and Mary mingled enthusiastically with Cosima's social circle. In the words of Preston Sturges' biographer, Donald Spoto:

> They met a number of colorful celebrities that included the composer Engelbert Humperdinck (best known for his opera *Hänsel und Gretel*); the conductors Hans Richter and Karl Muck; the king and queen of Württemberg and the Ab-Princess of Meiningen, sister of the Kaiser; and the actors and musicians in rehearsal. Preparing dinner for Ferdinand of Bulgaria, brewing coffee for Siegfried Wagner, listening to music and poetry in the summer evenings – that time was remarkable for what Mary, with perhaps unconscious irony, called 'the joy and sheer beauty of its unreality.'

Cosima Wagner was a highly intelligent woman of remarkable determination. Born in 1837, the illegitimate daughter of the composer Franz Liszt and of the French Countess Marie d'Agoult, she married the conductor Hans von Bülow, and then caused a major scandal by divorcing him in 1869 to marry Wagner. (She had met him nine years before, and at the time of her divorce they already had two illegitimate children of their own).

When Isadora met her, she was sixty-seven, but still a force to be reckoned with (especially in Bayreuth). As Isadora remembered, 'I never met a woman who impressed me with such high intellectual fervour as Cosima Wagner, with her tall, stately carriage, her beautiful eyes, a nose perhaps too prominent for femininity, and a forehead which radiated intelligence.'

Cosima's impression of Isadora is also on record: 'While she thinks about the music, she is not musical, and she does not dance rhythmically... She belittles the importance of the right costume and surely her figure needs a flattering costume. Nevertheless, contradictions, stubbornness, limitations notwithstanding, we have a personality before us of true artistic importance.'

117

This assessment deserves comment, demonstrating, as it does, two strong personalities at slight odds. Cosima was mistaken in believing that Isadora belittled the importance of the right costume – Isadora had thought long and hard about the sort of costume that was best adapted to her dancing movements. The difficulty was that her filmy Greek-influenced costumes were not what Cosima believed her late husband had in mind for his *Tannhäuser*.

They were also somewhat revealing, which caused something of a scandal in respectable Bayreuth. On the opening night Cosima had asked her to wear a chemise under her costume, but Isadora had refused. Asked sarcastically by Cosima if all American women dressed as she did, she replied, 'Oh, no, some wear feathers.'

What is also interesting is Cosima's comment about Isadora's figure needing a flattering costume. This is one of the earliest hints that by 1904 Isadora was losing the boyish figure of her early twenties and beginning to put on the weight that would be something of a problem to her for the rest of her life. (Only a couple of years later, caricatures of her in German periodicals would depict her as positively portly.)

As to Isadora's not being musical, and not dancing rhythmically, this comment again stems from conflict between two strong personalities. While Isadora's dancing did not strongly emphasise rhythm, she was from childhood deeply sensitive to music. Even if her interpretation of Wagner's music was not in accord with Cosima's jealous devotion to it, she responded to Wagner deeply. In the weeks of preparation for the Festival, she attended the rehearsals not only for *Tannhäuser*, but for all the other operas to be presented. As she recalled, she found herself 'in a constant state of intoxication... My mind was saturated with these legends, and my being was vibrating with the waves of Wagner's melody. I reached that stage where all the outward world seemed cold, shadowy, and unreal, and the only reality for me was what took place in the theatre.'

From time to time in rehearsal Mary D'Este would dance Isadora's role as one of the three Graces (partnered by two German ballet dancers), so that Isadora, watching with Cosima, could assess it. On one such occasion Cosima turned to Isadora and remarked on how alike she and Mary looked, saying '*Wie schön*, but how she resembles you!'

Again Isadora was annoyed. Mary recalled that she 'flew onto the stage, shaking me by the two shoulders: "Don't ever do it again,' she cried. 'Never, never."' Later, driving back to Phillipsruhe, she returned to the subject, saying, 'It's awful, even the very expression of my eyes. No, I will never teach anyone again. They only succeed in making an imitation of me.'

There seem to be two reasons for her becoming so upset. One being the natural resentment of a performer at having someone else seen as a duplicate of herself – as if part of her individuality was being stolen from her. The other stemming from her passionate belief in dance as a true vehicle of expression – that dancers should not imitate the steps or postures of other dancers in any way, but search deeply into their own experience of the world so as to find their own.

Isadora's plan for restaging the Bacchanal never really worked out. Not only was Cosima resistant to changing anything from the way it had been done in Wagner's time, she was also deeply suspicious of 'concepts' (such as Isadora had had) in presenting a piece – especially a piece by Wagner. In Cosima's view, once given to a singer who wished to discuss his role: 'Phrase according to sense, pronounce each word distinctly, observe the indicated rhythm exactly! Then you've done your part; everything else is contained in the work itself.' The 1904 Bayreuth production of *Tannhäuser*, apart from Isadora's own dancing, remained almost exactly the same as the one presented there in 1891.

This meant that the dancing of the Bacchanal remained an unresolved mixture of two contrasting styles. One critic, named Busching, writing in *Die Musik*, remarked that the contrast between her 'athletic, liberal movement' and the 'shackled dislocation' of the conventional ballet dancers was more repellent than enlightening, although he praised her new approach to the piece as lighting the way to the future, saying that what she had danced as 'a single Grace ... should and will be danced by all who take part in the Bacchanal in the future, at least in Bayreuth.' (Naturally she was unpopular with the corps de ballet, who, she later claimed, scattered tacks on the carpet on which she danced, hoping she would cut her feet.)

At the end of June 1904, Mrs Duncan arrived in Bayreuth with the two children, Mary's son Preston and Isadora's niece Temple, later described by Preston as 'my first and desperate sweetheart'. But Isadora had sweethearts of her own. For a start, her Hungarian lover, Oszkár Beregi, had come to Bayreuth to be with her, and they had enthusiastically resumed their affair, although it no longer had for either of them quite the passionate involvement it had had in Budapest.

The children and Mrs Duncan did not stay with Isadora and Mary at Phillipsruhe, but were lodged nearby, in a private hotel that was also in the Hermitage Gardens. On one occasion, during a break in her performing schedule, Isadora, with Oszkár and Mary, took them on a short holiday to the small island of Heligoland, far out in the North Sea, off the northern coast of Germany. Leaving Oszkár on the main island, the women and children were rowed to a nearby small island for a day's swimming. After which the children were left on the small island, to spend the night at an inn there, while Isadora and Mary returned to Heligoland to spend a sociable evening with Oszkár. Unfortunately, a fierce storm blew up, and Isadora and Mary, alarmed, had themselves hastily rowed back to where the children were. They were only just in time. Just as they got the rescued children into the rowing boat, great waves swept right over the smaller island. The children were got back to Heligoland and put to bed with hot tea and whisky (as Preston observed of his childhood 'I never seemed to stop drinking').

Shortly after the party returned to Bayreuth, Oszkár returned to Hungary, and went out of Isadora's life for ever. He had so far been her only lover, and after he left she entered a period when her sensual longings became, as she had perceived Wagner's to be, mental rather than physical, existing vividly in her own imagination. She relapsed, she said, 'in a curious manner, to the state in which I was as a virgin.' This state of mind was intensified by her ongoing attempts to 'indicate' carnality during her performances in *Tannhäuser*.

She did, however, have two intense platonic relationships. One was with Cosima's son-in-law, Heinrich Thode, who was an art historian, and Isadora would describe their friendship as *cérébrale*. His wife, Cosima's daughter Daniela, was a cold remote woman, and their marriage has been described as 'grim'. He himself was anything but. The English stage designer Gordon Craig, who met him with Isadora in Berlin later in the year, described him in a letter to his mother, Ellen Terry, as 'a delightful man, brimming full of fun – a writer and keen enjoyer of music & drawing & dancing & jolly books.'

While Isadora was in Bayreuth he was writing a book about Saint Francis of Assisi, and he would read each chapter to her as he completed it. He also read to her from his biography of Michelangelo, written earlier, and read her the whole of Dante's *Divine Comedy*. 'He was like a man in a dream,' she remembered fondly, 'and regarded me with eyes filled with prayer and light.'

When she wrote of him years later, it was with such intensity of romantic feeling that it is hard to believe that they never became lovers.

As I returned his gaze, suddenly I was uplifted and, with him, traversed heavenly spheres or paths of shining light... The feeling of delight through all my nerves became so poignant that the slightest

120

touch of his arm sent such thrills of ecstasy through me that I turned sick and faint, with the sweet, gnawing, painful pleasure. It revolved in my head like a thousand whirls of myriad lights. It throbbed in my thoat with such joy that I wanted to cry out. Often I felt his slight hand pressed over my lips to silence the sighs and little groans that I could not control. It was as if every nerve in my body arrived at that climax of love that is generally limited to the instant; and hummed with such insistence that I hardly knew whether it was utter joy or horrible suffering. My soul partook of both, and I longed to cry out with Amfortas, to shriek with Kundry. [Amfortas and Kundry are both characters in Wagner's *Parsifal*. Amfortas is the ruler of the kingdom of the Holy Grail, and Kundry is the enchantress who, with the magician Klingsor, seeks to destroy Parsifal.]

Her other intense friendship, was with the biologist and evolutionist Ernst Haeckel, who was then aged seventy, and greatly respected by many Germans. Although it was less charged with sensuality, it was this friendship that caused shocked comment among the Catholic population of Bayreuth, which included Cosima Wagner, because Haeckel, as well as being an enthusiastic populariser of science (and inventor of the word 'ecology'), was also an outspoken anti-Christian, for instance describing the idea of an afterlife as 'ludicrous'. Not exactly an agnostic, still less an atheist, he described himself as a 'monist', believing that there was no personal God, but that matter and spirit were one and indivisible.

Isadora had come across his popular writings in London, and had long had among her bedside books his *Riddle of the Universe* and his *Natural History of Creation*. He had celebrated his seventieth birthday shortly after she arrived in Bayreuth, and she, along with many others, had sent him a letter expressing her good wishes. In it, she said that his work had brought her 'religion and understanding, which counts for more than life.'

Haeckel replied, and a lively exchange of letters began between the two, she addressing him with genuine humility as 'Dear Master' and signing them 'All my love, Isadora Duncan'. This correspondence led to her inviting him to be her guest in Bayreuth, and at the end of August he arrived there. She went to meet him at the railway station, and recalled:

He possessed a magnificent, althletic figure, with a white beard and white hair. He wore strange, baggy clothes, and carried a carpet bag. We had never met, but we recognised each other at once. I was immediately folded in his great arms, and found my face buried in his beard. His whole being gave forth a fine perfume of health and strength and intelligence, if one can speak of the perfume of intelligence... That afternoon, before the astonished audience, I promenaded during the entr'acte, in my Greek tunic, bare legs and bare feet, hand-in-hand with Ernst Haeckel, his white head towering above the multitude.

His very presence there scandalised Cosima, and things were made no better when Isadora later that day approached Haeckel, saying, 'Oh, Herr Professor, you looked today like a god!'

'Why, look who is here!' he replied. 'My goddess!' Such flippant reference to gods and goddesses was felt by Cosima as a further affront. With her stiff and uncreative mind she could not see, as Isadora could, that a truly religious feeling towards gods and goddesses can exist regardless of whether or not one believes they actually exist.

Isadora's relationship with Cosima deteriorated even further when, one day at luncheon, speaking of Wagner, she announced that 'the Master's mistakes were as great as his genius'. Exuberantly sharing her thoughts, she went on to refer in particular to Wagner's fundamental vision of opera as *Musik-Drama*, a powerful unifying of music and action, declaring it to be 'nonsense' and going on to say, 'It is impossible to mix in any way, one with the other. *Musik-Drama kann nie sein* [Music-Drama can never be]'.

Recalling the occasion, she admitted, 'I had uttered such blasphemy that nothing further was possible. I gazed innocently around me, to meet expressive visages of absolute consternation.' It is no wonder that she was never again invited to appear at the Festival.

Mary too had found herself a lover in Bayreuth, a Maltese tenor called Alfred Erwin von Bary, who was there to sing both Parsifal and Tristan. But by the end of the Festival she was becoming bored and looking for new adventure. So when it finished, in September, she rather abruptly dumped him in order to set off with Isadora (and her son, Preston) on a tour of Italy.

They went first to Florence, where, as Mary remembered, they 'danced gaily through the deserted streets ... singing at the top of our voices.' Then they went on to Venice where, as it was November and Mary's six months in Europe were up, her husband Solomon came to collect her and Preston and take them home to Chicago.

In October, Isadora returned to Berlin, taking a lease on a large apartment at 11 Hardenbergstrasse for herself and all the Clan Duncan (except Raymond, who was still temple-building in Greece), and began another tour arranged by Sándor Grosz. She also, shortly after her return, bought a spacious three-storey villa, with the idea of at last establishing a school of dance. It was at 16 Trabenerstrasse, in the suburb of Grunewald, lying to the south of Berlin and in those days still heavily forested.

The tour that Sándor Grosz had arranged for Isadora was mainly of German cities, although she did also play a short season in Budapest and another (for the first time) in Warsaw. But something about her time in Bayreuth, and in particular her time with Heinrich Thode, had changed her. In spite of the lack of physical activity in the relationship, theirs had been a deep involvement, and she missed bitterly 'the keenest pleasure and intensity of love' that she had had with him. As she later wrote:

> I left Bayreuth, but I carried a potent poison in my blood. I had heard the call of the sirens. The yearning pain, the haunted remorse, the sorrowful sacrifice, the theme of Love calling Death – all were hereafter to obliterate for ever the clear vision of Doric columns and the reasoning wisdom of Socrates... The spiritual ecstasy with which [Thode] had inspired me in Bayreuth gradually gave place to an exasperated state of uncontrollable desire.

It was in this frame of mind, with its echoes of *Tannhäuser* and the Bacchanal, that she met Gordon Craig.

Chapter Eight

A Genius of Stage Design

Isadora had chosen Grunewald as the setting for her school because it had been, since the 1880s, when the first large houses were built there, something of an artistic colony, attractive to lovers of nature because of the seclusion offered by what remained of its ancient forest. In fact it was the composer Engelbert Humperdinck who had drawn her attention to the villa she bought. It was in the process of being built alongside his own, and Isadora made a swift offer for it when, as she said, 'it was just passing from the workmen's hands.'

She bought it during November 1904, putting down a deposit and arranging to pay for it in a lengthy series of instalments. Although it would make use of her fame by being called 'The Isadora Duncan School', it was actually viewed by her and the rest of the Clan Duncan as a family enterprise. In particular, her sister Elizabeth would be the Director, supervising its day to day running. The family were assisted in planning the enterprise by Isadora's admiring friend, the German writer Karl Federn, who acted as adviser for the academic curriculum.

A prospectus that the family inserted in a number of German newspapers, inviting would-be pupils to apply, described the school and Isadora's hopes for it:

> The building is a three-storey structure with a large basement and top floor. All the rooms are spacious and airy and the many windows allow free access of sunlight and fresh air...
>
> The children are boarded and educated free of charge; this includes clothes and other necessities. Besides their dance training personally conducted by Isadora Duncan, the pupils will also receive academic instruction from a competent public school teacher and in addition, in order to stimulate their artistic sensibilities, there will be regular

visits to museums with lectures on art. Two governesses are in charge, and the management of the school is in the hands of Miss Isadora's sister, Elizabeth Duncan.

This free, non-profit dance school, founded by Isadora Duncan and entirely supported by her financially, is not a philanthropic institution in the ordinary sense but an enterprise dedicated to the promotion of health and beauty in mankind. Both physically and spiritually the children will here receive an education providing them with the highest intelligence in the healthiest body.

Being new, the villa was of course unfurnished, and the Duncans swiftly set about furnishing it. It was to be a boarding school, for girls aged eight to ten, so they bought, as she said, 'forty little beds, each covered with white muslin curtains, drawn back with blue ribbons.' Blue and white were chosen to be the school colours, and were seen everywhere – in the girls' uniforms and in their dancing costumes, and in the profusion of images of happy dancing children with which the Duncans decorated the halls and the dormitories – images to reassure and encourage their prospective pupils. These were copied from anywhere they could find them, and there were, Isadora recalled, 'paintings of children dancing on Greek vases, tiny figures from Tanagra and Bœotia, the group of Donatello's dancing children . . . and the dancing children of Gainsborough.' On a pedestal in the centre of the front hall was a tall statue of an Amazon.

Isadora's hope was that these beautiful images would influence her pupils, as the *Primavera* had influenced her in her childhood. As she explained:

> All these figures have a certain fraternity in the naïve grace of their form and their movements, as if the children of all ages met each other and joined their hands across centuries, and the real children of my school, moving and dancing in the midst of these forms, would surely grow to resemble them, to reflect unconsciously, in their movements and their faces, a little of the joy and the same childlike grace. It would be the first step towards their becoming beautiful, the first step towards the new art of the dance.
>
> I also placed in my school the figures of young girls dancing, running, jumping . . . exquisite images in terra cotta, with flying veils and flowing garments . . . They represented the future ideal to attain, and the pupils of my school, learning to feel an intimate

love for these forms, would grow each day to resemble them, and would become each day a little more imbued with the secret of this harmony.

Her ideas about education were not confined to dance, or to training dancers. Her ambitions were more general. Dance to her was simply 'the foundation of all other studies', and her ultimate aim was to give a child 'a knowledge of itself'. 'What I want,' she wrote in the Twenties, 'is a *school of life*, for man's greatest riches are his soul, his imagination.'

Her attitudes in 1904 were in the forefront of educational theory. Till late in the nineteenth century, the attitude to children, in Europe and to a lesser extent in America, was that they were light-minded and usually sinful, prone to (in the words of Max Beerbohm in 1899) 'lies and sloth, untidiness and irreverence, and a tendency to steal black currant jam.' They were regarded as imperfect adults, who should be brought to adult perfection as swiftly and sternly as possible.

This attitude, first challenged by philosophers and theorists a hundred years before, gradually began to change in the practical world of education in around the 1890s. Many of the thinkers that Isadora had read had considered the situation – Kant, Rousseau, Whitman, Nietzsche and Robert Ingersoll among them – and she had pondered their thoughts deeply in the light of her own view of humanity. She had also read and been influenced by the influential Friedrich Froebel, founder in Germany of the kindergarten movement.

When it came to the detail of lessons in the classroom, she was, however, a little hazy. As she wrote herself, 'When asked for the pedagogic program of my school, I reply, "Let us first teach little children to breathe, to vibrate, to feel, and to become one with the general harmony of nature. Let us first produce a beautiful human being, a dancing child."'

Officially the school was declared open on 1st December 1904, but that was before Isadora had had time to interview any of the candidates, so at first it had only one registered pupil, her niece Temple, then aged five.

The interviewing would not take place for several weeks, and before that happened there was a dramatic change in Isadora's life. Early in December her beloved Heinrich Thode was visiting Berlin, and to welcome him she held a reception at the Duncan apartment. To it came the brilliant English stage designer, Gordon Craig. He had been brought by a young woman invited by Isadora – Elise de Brouckère. Elise was the daughter of a Belgian senator, and she knew Craig because her sister

Jeanne had appeared in operas he had directed in London. She introduced him to Isadora.

Craig had been brought to Germany by the influential Count Harry Kessler, by profession a diplomat, but by inclination an art-lover and entrepreneur. Kessler knew everyone who was anyone in anything. He had seen Craig's work in London, had been impressed by it, and had arranged for Dr Otto Brahm, director of Berlin's Lessing Theatre, to hire him as designer for a production of *Venice Preserv'd*, Thomas Otway's blank verse tragedy of 1682.

The arrangement didn't work. When Craig submitted his first two set designs to Brahm, Brahm objected that one of the sets had no door. Craig, whose sets were expressionistic and devoted to the gospel of simplicity, pointed out that there was an opening, offering a perfectly good way in and way out.

'Yes,' said Brahm, 'but I see no door handle or lock. You cannot have a door without a handle.' This complete misunderstanding of his aims and theories in stage design caused Craig to stalk off the production in high-minded indignation, muttering darkly about lawsuits. He went to lodge for a while with Count Harry Kessler in the city of Weimar – the great centre of classic German culture, some 125 miles to the south-west of Berlin – then, with Kessler's help, returned to Berlin to mount an exhibition (his first) of his designs for sets and costumes, and his woodcuts of English landscapes. This was running at the time he met Isadora.

Then aged thirty-two, Craig was a tall, slender, strikingly handsome man, with a sensitive and poetic cast to his features. He was charming, quick-tempered and talented, and the instant Isadora met him her deep platonic involvement with Heinrich Thode was replaced by a new and wilder involvement, one that was even deeper and by no means platonic. 'Here,' as Isadora recalled, 'I found an answering temperament, worthy of my metal. In him I met the flesh of my flesh, the blood of my blood... This was not a young man making love to a girl. This was the meeting of twin souls.' (She had, as it happened, seen him onstage in London, playing a small part in *Cymbeline*, but at that time he had made no impression on her, overshadowed as he had been by his mother Ellen Terry and by Henry Irving.)

In a notebook he began a couple of weeks later, devoted to his impressions of her, Craig wrote of their meeting:

> I entered the room with my eyeglasses off – so I could not see very well – I was introduced first to her sister Elizabeth – then to

her – & her mother & so on – then to Sarah her sister-in-law. And Sarah's daughter, Temple, & Sarah's husband-lover Augustin Duncan...

Owing to my short sight (when without glasses) at first I took Elizabeth for the famous dancer I had heard about & was struck by her strangely harsh accent – I felt puzzled but told myself at once that often it is the small and insignificant women who are remarkable. 'What sort of dance can she put up' thought I – & then I came to Isadora. Augustin Duncan I took to at once as most people did owing to his personal charm – Isadora talks a lot of nonsense that 1st day – shows me gods – & pictures and all... A book with dancing figures – She was in fine spun robes – simple & lovely. (All this time I have not seen her dance, & find she is a nice Greekish lady & a fine American girl by nature, and I am sure I shall be bored by her dancing.) She then talks on & on about the way she likes her theatre to be shaped – curving her arms to describe something. (This curving of the arms was a movement of embracing an immense ball.) She at once suggests the amateur-hypnotic lady & I should distrust her if she were not beautiful & Beauty is the only thing we can entirely trust. This reference to her beauty is rather strange, for in features she was not beautiful, but in *movement* she made up for [its] lack.

Writing years later, he was more detached and mocking, claiming to have been only dimly aware of her dancing before they met. As he recalled:

I had heard [in Weimar] that there was some sort of governess who had taken to dancing in an artistic manner – at whom some people laughed, while others crowded in thousands to see her dance... She and I met in December 1904 – in Berlin. She took quite a liking to me and I thought she wasn't such a bad sort of governess after all... She didn't impress me as anything learned: a governess generally says 'Hic, haec, hoc' before half an hour has gone by, but Isadora said none of these things. So I took it that Weimar was just a bit stupid, and I asked Isadora how she did.

She said, 'I'm all right – how are you?' 'I'm fine,' I said. She then asserted that I was her '*lieber Mann*' – her dear husband. She began singing this to all and sundry – the room was full of the sundry. She then called for her coach, like poor Ophelia, and said to me, 'Hi! You come along .. you *mein lieber Mann.*' And down we went, down the spacious staircase leading to the vast hall which conducted to the street.

A coach awaited us. We got in and after saying 'To Potsdam,' leant back in the spacious coach and began to sing. We were not drunk; we had not touched wine or any stuff out of bottles – we were, I grieve to say, only happy.

Isadora's memory of their meeting differed as to which of them made the initial running. In her account:

I, like one hypnotised, allowed him to put my cape over my little white tunic. He took my hand; we flew down the stairs to the street. Then he hailed a taxi and said, in his best German, 'Meine Frau und mich, wir wollen nach Potsdam gehen.' ['My wife and I wish to go to Potsdam.']

Several taxis refused to take us, but finally we found one, and off we went to Potsdam.

A third, and probably the most accurate, account of this romantic meeting was given by the writer Karl Federn, in *Der Berliner Tageblatt* in 1928. As he told it, Isadora and Craig had been looking for an excuse to slip away from the reception for some time, and their opportunity came when Karl and his sister were leaving in a car that had room for two other people. Isadora and Craig joined them and, in high spirits, the whole party decided to drive to Potsdam.

Whatever the case, Isadora and Craig had each fallen for the other. They spoke the same language – the language of Art – and shared a host of thoughts and references. As with most couples who share this sort of spiritual kinship, from the moment they met they barely stopped talking to each other, often at the same time.

All the way to Potsdam they talked, on their way to look at Sans Souci, the palace that Frederick the Great had built there. As Craig recalled years later, 'we neared the palace where Voltaire and Frederick talked. But Frederick and Voltaire never talked as much as we did – we talked a sort of three-ply, if you can guess what I mean. We said a lot of words and looked a thousand more.'

In Federn's recollection, they arrived back in Berlin at 8 a.m., and decided to visit Elise de Brouckère at her flat at Spinchernstrasse 7. There they all had a cheerful champagne breakfast.

After the breakfast, as Isadora was unsure of the welcome she would get from her family after staying out all night, Elise went to call on them and returned to report that they were angry and upset about her staying out all night. She suggested that Isadora spend the day and the next night where she was, in the hope that things would by then have calmed down.

Isadora accepted her offer. Craig spent most of the day there with her, and Elise took four photographs of the pair of them together.

Soon they would use pet names for each other, she calling him 'Teddy' (as many had in his boyhood, his original name being Edward) and he calling her 'Topsy', possibly after the little slave girl in *Uncle Tom's Cabin* who has no memory of being born but supposes she 'just growed'. If this was his reason, it may have been in light-hearted allusion to her frequent insistence that she hadn't invented her style of dancing, simply discovered what had 'existed before'. (The notebook he kept, recording his impressions of her, he labelled *Book Topsy*.)

Some of the earliest of these impressions ran:

ISADORA. A woman of brains & beauty – not a little woman, nor a huge one – but the right size –

The expression on her face changes & seems to me to be at times the faces of very many women I have known... Each day I suddenly recognise a familiar face in hers – or a familiar voice – it's queer.

I think she is really Aphrodite, which accounts for it. She is the calmest thing I have ever seen in a woman.

Craig was the son of the great actress Ellen Terry. In 1865 her teenage marriage to the painter G.F.Watts had disintegrated (after only a year). The couple separated, without divorcing, and three years later, not yet greatly successful in her acting career, she temporarily retired from the stage to elope with the flamboyant English architect and stage designer Edward Godwin. By him she had two illegitimate children – first a daughter, Edith (usually known as 'Edy'), and then, in 1872, Edward.

In 1874, after their affair had lasted six years, Godwin abruptly abandoned Ellen Terry, who all her life would remain deeply in love with him. Needing to support her young family, she returned to the stage and, four years later, got her biggest break when she became Henry Irving's long-time leading lady at London's Lyceum Theatre, which he also managed. In 1886 Godwin died and, with her life's love gone for ever, Ellen Terry set about trying to regularise her marital status. The next year she was finally divorced from Watts and married the actor Charles Wardell (known to the public as Charles Kelly). Unfortunately, this marriage too would not last long, her new husband being so fond of the bottle that she '...gave him three-quarters of what I earned and prayed him to go.'

All this time nobody seemed quite certain what Edy and Edward's surname was. Was it 'Godwin' or 'Terry' (or maybe even 'Watts'). This uncertainty was resolved in their teens when together they decided to adopt the surname 'Craig', taking it from Ailsa Craig, the famous rock off the west coast of Scotland, which had fascinated them as children. So in 1888, aged sixteen, when his newly-married mother got around to having him christened, Teddy formally became 'Edward Henry Gordon Craig'. The other two Christian names came from his godparents, Lady Gordon and Henry Irving (not then knighted).

With such a strongly theatrical background, naturally Edward was drawn to the life of the theatre. As early as the age of thirteen, in 1885, he had gone across the Atlantic to Chicago, to appear with his mother in a melodrama being presented by the Irving company and based on Thomas Hood's poem *The Dream of Eugene Aram*. He revered Irving, regarding him as the nearest thing he had to a father – an attitude made easier by the fact that Irving and his mother were deeply attached to each other – perhaps even at times lovers.

At seventeen, he joined the Irving company himself and, sent on summer tours of the British provinces in junior versions of the main company, found himself playing such major Shakespearean roles as Romeo, Petruchio, Hamlet and Macbeth. But soon he realised that he had nowhere near the acting talent that his mother or Henry Irving had, and his driving ambition led him to abandon performing in favour of developing his ability to draw. Allowed £500 a year by his doting mother to get all his 'whims and fancies' out of his system, he quickly taught himself to make woodblocks, bookplates, posters and illustrations. Soon he followed his father's example (the father he had never seen since he walked out in 1874) and involved himself in stage design.

Edward Godwin had been something of an innovator in the field. Reacting against the prevalent Victorian taste for elaborate stage settings, such as those used by actor-managers like Irving and Herbert Beerbohm Tree, with ornate furniture and real plants, trees (and even animals) set against vast painted backdrops, he had argued for more simplicity. He had also argued for the abolition of that key symbol of the Victorian stage, the footlights.

132

Gordon Craig (to use Edward's professional name) carried all this further. As well as arguing, like his father, for greater simplicity and the abolition of footlights, he moved towards the idea of stage settings that would be 'a near abstraction of spaces and planes, with elevations disposed in curves and angles that evoked ... the essence of the work being played.' Seeing a stage performance as essentially an animated work of art, he would eventually argue for elimination of acting as generally understood, the actor to be replaced by what he termed the *Übermarionette* – a puppet-like performer who would be a 'supremely beautiful creature – something like a Greek statue', under the sole control of a godlike director – such as himself.

In 1897 he founded the magazine *The Page* to expound his ideas, and from 1899 he was designing and directing stage productions. Some were operas, presented by the Purcell Operatic Society, which he co-founded with Martin Shaw, later a distinguished composer and musicologist, and compiler of the influential *Oxford Book of Carols*. Among these operas were Purcell's *Dido and Aeneas*, presented in 1900, and Handel's *Acis and Galatea*, presented in 1902.

After that he mounted plays, such as Laurence Housman's nativity play *Bethlehem*, Ibsen's verse play *The Vikings at Helgeland* (all Ibsen's early plays were in verse) and Shakespeare's *Much Ado About Nothing*. All these productions were largely subsidised by his mother, who once cheerfully remarked, 'He is a donkey, but he's a *white* one.' None was a great financial success, and many of them lost money, so Craig now found himself in the odd position of being both hugely respected and a bad investment.

He and Isadora had much in common. They shared a passionate belief in Art, and in the creation of Beauty as its deepest expression (a legacy from the Aesthetic Movement which had shaped their ideas). Both were largely self-educated, with a good grounding in the classics, and both thought of themselves as socialists, eager to overthrow the established order (she in dance, he in theatre). Each revered the memory of a little-known father, and each had been hailed by sections of the public as a 'genius' – although on that first ride to Potsdam both agreed that they would not be taken in by such a silly illusion.

Although afraid he would be bored by her dancing, it was only a couple of evenings after they met that he attended, at her invitation, one of her performances. It was advertised as a *Chopin Abend*, and Craig was delighted to find himself as bowled over by her dancing as he had been by Isadora herself.

She danced to the 'Mazurka op 17, no. 4', and against it on his programme he jotted down the word 'Faultless'. When she danced to the 'Mazurka op 33, no. 4' he noted 'amazing – it is so beautiful'.

His enthusiasm for this performance remained with him for life (although it disconcerted him that a woman could be a truly original artist – a thing that all his life he emphatically declared was impossible). Years later he recalled:

> She was speaking in her own language ... and so she came to move as no one had ever seen anyone move before... No one would ever be able to report truly, yet no one present had a moment's doubt. Only this can we say – that she was telling to the air the very things we longed to hear, and till she came we never dreamed we should hear; and now we heard them, and this sent us all into an unusual state of joy, and I ... I sat still and speechless.

He was also impressed with the simplicity of her staging, which she had been gradually refining since she was young. As he noted in *Book Topsy*, her set consisted of 'Grand piano, wooden Greek columns about $5^1/_2$ feet high ... nice dark grey curtains, same height hung between each pilaster all very modest and useful.' [In fact the curtains were not exactly grey, but a sort of slate-blue.]

Isadora's ideas so closely resembled his own that Craig was even a little perturbed. Entering her loge after her performance he burst out (as Isadora remembered), 'You are marvellous! You are wonderful! But why have you stolen my ideas? Where did you get my scenery?'

'What are you talking about?' she replied. 'These are my own blue curtains. I invented them when I was five years old, and I have danced before them ever since!'

'No!' he said. 'They are my *décors* and my ideas! But you are the being I imagined in them. You are the living realisation of all my dreams.'

Isadora's mother, who was present, was sufficiently charmed by all this to suppress for the moment her concern about her wayward daughter, and politely invited him back to 11 Hardenbergstrasse to have supper. Naturally, he went. As did the writer Karl Federn. In *Book Topsy* Craig recorded his impressions:

> The next thing she does is to —— no, I will not write it — but I remember it, and how she discovers (bless her) that I am just an ordinary gentleman — for her anyhow!!!

134

All the people at the table are good souls & poor bodied persons (except for Augustin) – she has a good soul and a good body – is young in both, fresh in both, & while everyone talks a lot of lies we 2 go on talking either frank rubbish or all sorts of truth. She had the blessed sense of humour.

Anyhow we know that we know each other. She does not deceive me – much: & she can read me with ease. I flatter her – I say 'It is flattering the Greeks of 2000 years ago to say she is like a Greek dancer.' She says 'now that is nice' – yet knows it's only a nice speech & yet feels & knows that I mean it.

And what is more I *do & did* mean it. Because she is genius, & better than her it would be impossible to be. Then after supper they all dance waltzes – she sits and won't dance except alone – the waist business not appearing to fit her.

So she sits with me and her old literary friend [Federn] & we talk.

Near the time when I go she gives me a picture of herself & writes on it 'with Love Isadora'.

Oddly – or perhaps not, given the era – Craig found this dedication rather forward, and went on:

A regular hussy of a girl, one would say if one thought about it – but that only proves that to think is often a mistake – and leads to error. She can write it so because she knows I read it well. No – put it differently – say she always signs her photographs so – by the manner in which the 'with love' is taken, she judges the man; perhaps so: but all the same he/she knew what she was writing.

An interesting point in Craig's observations is his mentioning Isadora's sense of humour. She had always been lively and vivacious, even in the full flood of her youthful earnestness, but her commitment to her cause tended to make her somewhat solemn, even priggish. The earnest commitment she never lost – it was her very centre – but as she grew into maturity a light-hearted wry playfulness became more and more clearly a part of her character.

The day after Craig attended her *Chopin Abend* she returned the compliment by going with him to the gallery where his work was being shown. Craig recorded the occasion in *Book Topsy*:

60 drawings were shown on the walls, 13 of them sketches of

English Landscapes. Some 31 were scenes & costume designs. All in white she walks round with me & looks at each drawing – curiously interested or bored, I don't know which – nor do I care but I guess she is feeling things – that is something – the rest feel nothing and talk a lot. She goes away – I took her to the door & I can still see her look as the large door closed slowly she with her eyes on me to the last, I my eyes on her – this moment has often returned to me ... this farewell meeting in our particular land – and I go to write her a letter in the café ... I tell her I must write a line – Just to speak – not because I have anything to say – I tell her I am just amazed! I ask her to come *once* more & see my *studio* drawings. She is *white* before my drawings which are so black. It was I remember a letter of love if ever a letter held love in it. I cannot post it, it is too late: I go round to her house – rush upstairs, leave it & tear off again.

Next morning (as agreed) 4 of us (Augustin, Sarah, Isadora & I) (we are 2) are to meet to drive out.

The 3 others call for me in carriage & 2 jolly horses. I join them – everyone is in such good spirits & they laugh so much they almost drown my spirits. I am stupidly thinking often of my letter which seems so foolish now these others are near us ... & now that she & I are so near...

We visit her new school. The lilies (painted) on the walls revolt me – The others approve of it *all*. I find it all ugly except her. We lunch & laugh. Then we dance along by the trees & generally behave like 6 & 7-year-old children. We salute passing strangers who seem quite happy to see us happy – Then we return – we have tea – & she tells me the fairy story of Psyche – it breaks off like all fairy tales & as all the others go I have to go too.

Craig invited her to come to his studio and see some more of his drawings, and on 17th December 1904, Isadora accepted his invitation. She hired a carriage to take her there. It was at 11 Siegmundshof – an immense room on an upper floor, described by Craig in *Book Topsy* as 'empty – except for books & sketches – no carpets – no armchairs. A very tall studio with 2 windows facing south I think – for I recall the great sun of morning.' On one wall of this high room was a railed balcony, reached by way of a flight of stairs.

Isadora arrived at four in the afternoon, and immediately she arrived the two of them set off in the carriage for an hour's drive through the

Berlin streets, decorated for Christmas and blazing with lights. As Craig recalled years later, speaking of the lights, 'I can see them now! – & I can hear her now, talking, talking, – not saying much – but the heart talking millions to the minute – & I can hear the wheels of our carriage ... & forget as I forgot then all but just that hugging arm – that great friendly heart.'

They went to a café for tea, then were driven back to the studio. Isadora dismissed the carriage, they looked at Craig's drawings for a while, then had supper. It was quite clear to both of them that they were going to sleep together, but for a long time they talked, deliciously delaying the moment. They were to sleep on the wooden floor of the balcony. Craig recorded:

> Our bed was 2 carpets on which [we put] a fur cloak (hers) with my overcoat as pillow & 2 blankets and a sheet as covering.
> We do not sleep much all night, it is too lovely to have her there –
>
> *18th Dec.* In the morning – we sit in the sun ... sit there ... talk a little ... but look ... Sit still – kiss & rest contentish. [In Craig's diarising, 'kiss' was generally a euphemism.]

After a luxuriously idle day (it was a Sunday), they dressed and set off for the Duncan apartment, where there was to be another reception, in time to arrive there at about five o'clock.

> We walk along happy & as she says 'It's wonderful how independent & free virtue can be & feel' & we laugh for that's *just it.*
> Since we were born to lie holding each other, the scriptures of nature are only being fulfilled.
> At her house is a reception. About 50 to 80 people. We enter: she slips in and bathes.
> The Reception happens. She like a queen – cold – cool – lovely – everyone else excited & struggling to have 2 minutes conversation with her –
> By 6:30 everyone is gone & we dance into each other's arms.
> Everyone very chilly towards us in the house. Mothers, sisters, cousins & aunts. Only Sarah [Augustin's wife] is alive. The rest dead.
> Then she goes out in the evening to another Reception... I was going – but can't stand the fussy people all around us.

137

She goes alone – writes to me in the evening after she gets back.

In the letter she wrote, she sympathised with him for not attending the second reception, saying, 'Dear you were quite right – it was a sort of Blasphemy to go among a lot of people only dear Frau Begas gave the party in my honor … it was Horrid.'

What had been even more horrid for her was the reaction of her family to her deepening involvement with Craig. 'Chilly' was a mild word for it. They were outraged – her mother and her sister Elizabeth in particular, but also Augustin and her mother's sister Elizabeth, whose married name was Lightner, and who was known as 'Aunt Lizzie'. Aunt Lizzie had recently arrived in Berlin, and would remain there, eventually taking part in the running of the school.

The whole family rounded on Isadora for her behaviour. It was as if she was their own personal property, and anyone else claiming any part of her, especially a lover, was to be repelled at all costs. The next day (19th December), when Isadora went off again with Craig, mother called the police.

There was little the police could do, of course. Isadora was now twenty-seven, and what she was doing, while regrettable, was in no way against the law. Mother had to content herself with trying to keep her daughter out of the public eye, which she did by inserting an item in the newspapers saying that Miss Isadora Duncan's performances would be cancelled until further notice, as she had been taken seriously ill with *Mandelentzündung* [tonsillitis].

Isadora, as it happened, was quite happy about this, as she was beginning to find even her abundant supplies of energy seriously under strain. Quite apart from setting up the school, and giving occasional performances, and attending receptions, and making enthusiastic love to Craig, she was also booked to travel to St Petersburg (then the capital of the Russian Empire) and give two performances there, one on 26th December and one on 29th December (which in Russia in those days, using the Old Style calendar, were 13th and 16th December).

The cancellation of her Berlin performances (and of course receptions) gave her a little respite, and she and Craig were able to be together on, as he wrote, 'December 19, 20, 21, 22, 1904. – our perfect time… In those nights she gives herself to me & reserves nothing.' It had restrained the lovers not at all that, the next time Craig called at the apartment for Isadora, after the newspaper announcement, Mother had greeted him with the melodramatic words, 'Vile seducer, leave the house!' (One wonders how, in the high-minded Duncan household, she had contrived to see or read a melodrama).

Shortly before leaving for Russia, in a further letter to Craig, Isadora wrote, 'Thank you Thank you Thank you for making me Happy. Whole complete I love you love you love you & I Hope we'll have a dear sweet lovely Baby – & I'm happy forever.'

A later, shorter note simply said, 'Isadora loves *you* loves you.' On receiving it, Craig wrote on the back of it, 'Home here at 5 o'clock – good God – & find myself saying "if only she were here." She is not here – she is rushing through space, away from me – Oh, you *dear* one.'

He then received a third, and even more rapturous, letter, posted just before she boarded her train – accompanied by a secretary, her maid (Anna), and her pianist (Hermann Lafont):

Dearest Sweetest Spirit
    You will never know how beautiful you are. Only I know that. You will never know what an immense Joy *Giver* you are. All that joy is with me. You have given joy & love unspeakable. What shall I give you in return – All that I have in my power to give & that is not enough – but perhaps you will find a cold empty corner for it...
    We were born in the same star and we came in its rays to earth, & now for a little I was in your heart & then I wandered far away & now I am back. That is our History.
    No one could ever understand it – but us.
    Good night.
    I am your love if you will have me – if not –
    but I am
    Your Isadora

She wrote again to him from the train:

    I'm being borne away away away.
    The clouds are flying past – Am I transformed to a grey bird flying always North – I think so – or am I just your Isadora who loves you Yes you.

The journey, which took about a day and a half, seemed to her endless. 'All night long,' she wrote, 'the train has been not flying but going pim de pim over Great fields of snow – vast plains of snow – Great bare

Countries covered with snow ... and over all this the Moon shining – & across the window always a Golden shower of sparks – from the locomotive – it was quite worth seeing and I lay there looking out on it all & thinking of you – of you you dearest sweetest best darling.'

In St Petersburg she was booked into the Hotel Europe, off Nevsky Prospect. When she arrived, on the morning of 25th December (12th December in the Russian calendar), the staff first showed her into the bridal suite, but she 'stoutly refused to stay in it' alone (she would have had little difficulty with language, because at this time in St Petersburg it was fashionable to speak French). After a bath, and after having repelled a number of Russian well-wishers and celebrity-hunters, she went to bed for a while. Later in the day she again wrote to Craig:

> Dreadful lots of people came but I was quite savage & frightened my little maid out of her Wits – telling her to make 'em go away at once – Then I closed my eyes – & such a Wonderful thing happened – I could *feel you breathing*. You sweet you dear – it's almost too nice to write about but I could. After that they woke me up and I had to come & see awful people who talked at me. They've all gone thank the Gods...
>
> O *you* you darling – I've just got your telegram – You Sweetheart – I love you I adore you – I am nothing without you... I think the best thing to do with St Petersburg is to forget it – and pretend I'm not here. I'll not see it – I swear I won't – Darling – Sweetest Love – I shut my eyes think of it and heard your Breathing – but when I awoke I was alone – alone alone –

Both she and Craig were besotted, but her misfortune would be that she was also deeply in love. Blindly in love. During their long conversation that first evening in his studio, Craig had admitted to her that he was going to marry someone else in about four months' time. To which she had simply replied (Craig noted) that she did not believe in marriage.

Possibly his talking of a forthcoming marriage was meant as a kindly warning to Isadora that he knew himself, and knew that he was not capable of being her soul-mate for life. But if there had been an ounce of wariness in her soul – which there was not – that would have been a moment to be wary. For a start, his announcement was less than the whole truth.

He was already married. His wife's name was May Gibson, and he had married her in 1893. Five years later, while she was pregnant with their fourth child, he had left her for a beautiful young actress, Jess Dorynne. Her he also abandoned, also when she was pregnant by him, running away in 1902 with a British violinist from an Italian background, Elena Meo. With her he would remain all her life – at least in the sense of always returning to her between affairs. When he met Isadora, Elena was carrying their third child, and it was she he had promised to marry when he got divorced from his wife (a promise he never kept).

The fact was that Gordon Craig, as well as being a relentless womaniser, was spoilt and bone-selfish. As a result of his mother's misfortunate love-life, he had largely been raised in an all-female household. This, as Isadora would find out to her cost, gave him a deeply ambivalent attitude to women. On the one hand he found them a source of pleasure and inspiration – something to be pursued and possessed. On the other he found them something to be feared and avoided, a menacing power that could consume the spirit.

In particular, something deep within him resented his mother's huge fame and popularity. It has been suggested (perhaps straining a little too hard after subtle insight) that his passionate rejection of ornate Victorian stage-settings was an attempt to destroy the milieu in which she had triumphed, and that his concept of reducing actors to mere puppets, subservient to the will of the artist-director, was in some sense also aimed at her.

Desperately missing Craig, Isadora nonetheless enjoyed some things about St Petersburg, finding the city, as she wrote to him, 'very fine, covered with snow and the air like Champagne.' She was to dance at the Hall of Nobles, which faced her hotel, and her appearances there were a triumph. They were more than a triumph. They helped alter the course of Russian ballet, and thus, eventually, the dance of the world.

Ballet had come to Russia via France, and had been adopted enthusiastically. The great ballet-master and choreographer at the time of Isadora's visit was Marius Petipa, who was himself French, and had created such classics as *The Sleeping Beauty* (1890) and *Nutcracker* (1892), both with music by Tchaikovsky, and *Raymonda* (1898), with music by Glazunov.

But under Petipa (and others like him) Russian ballet had petrified – 'buried in its own greatness', as the dance historian Walter Sorell put it. Describing Petipa's work, he explained, 'He perfected the pas de deux, believing in dancing for the sake of dancing and in virtuosity heightened to a spectacle.'

It was art as craft, not Art as Isadora perceived it, reaching for something

141

higher and deeper from within. Another dance historian, Prince Peter Lieven, in his history of Diaghilev's company, the Ballets Russes, describing the Russian Romantic ballet that preceded Diaghilev's great days, wrote, 'It must be admitted that the cultural level of the Russian ballet was not high; ballerinas and male dancers were not educated people, their interests were all limited, and they were not concerned with art outside the narrow sphere of their concerns.'

Nonetheless, dance was popular in Russia, and although it was reported in the press that Isadora did not approve of the ballet, many flocked to the Hall of Nobles to see her, many with some idea that she was some sort of barefoot health reformer, others who had heard that she danced almost naked. The hall was sold out for both her performances, with a mixture of nobility, socialites, art patrons and of those who were creative in the arts – poets, painters, writers, musicians, and dancers.

Among the audience for her first night were the impresario Diaghilev and some of his colleagues, including the artists and stage designers Alexandre Benois and Léon Bakst, and the twenty-four-year-old dancer, soon to become a major choreographer, Michel Fokine.

Against her blue backdrop, on a thick rug, and with a stage decorated simply with a few cigar-like poplars and some fragments of classical columns, she danced her Chopin programme, accompanied by a solo piano. The theatre critic Nicolai Georgievitch Shebuyev, writing pseudonymously in the *Petersburg Gazette*, gave one of the most perceptive and detailed descriptions of her dancing that survives:

A rosy light shone out at the rear of the stage on the left, and pale violet tones began to gleam on the blue backdrop. The sound of Chopin's Mazurka (B-major, op.7, no.1) made one's nerves tingle, and onto the stage there entered a sylph. A bit of pink-blue gauze mistily enveloped her slender waist, and veiled yet revealed her bare feet. She is not at all beautiful, but her face is ... exotic ... and on it, with equal expressiveness, joy, sorrow, a tear, a smile, are fleetingly born and quickly die.

She emerged and swam like an Undine, swaying in time with the beat, waving her hands with the beat, smiling, diving with the beat – and suddenly she flew up like a bird and soared carefree, joyful, chirping soundlessly – no: tunefully, rather – for her dancing merged into a single chord with Chopin's Mazurka. And then she floated down again from the sky – touched the cold surface of the river – shuddered – and swam again, green and graceful, proud of her cold, nymphlike beauty. And dived again – and once again froze, her arms stretched forward at the finale.

That was all.

But on analysing what at first seems little, one finds much.

First, the marvellous plastic sensibility. Her body is as though bewitched by the music. It is as though you yourself were bathing in the music. Then, the expressive hands. Have you ever heard of mimicry by hands?... And yet Duncan's hands are as expressive as her face. And the legs? For after all, it was the legs, the bare feet, that were supposed to be the sensation of the evening... Actually, the legs play the least important role in these dances. Here *everything* dances: waist, arms, neck, head – *and* legs. Duncan's bare legs and bare feet are like those of a rustic vagabond: they are innocent: this is not a *nudité* that arouses sinful thoughts, but rather a kind of corporeal nudity.

For the Mazurka in A-flat (op.17, no.4) [the one that Gordon Craig had found 'Faultless'] there came onstage a figure severe and sorrowful, looking intently upward, all her being yearning for heaven while her hands seemed to beg, trying to seize something. Then suddenly her eyes flashed with Bacchic ecstasy – the flame died – there was another flash – then once again a look of serenity and prayer...

With the Mazurka in A-flat (op.33, no.4) [the one Craig found 'amazing' and 'beautiful'] she danced an entire tragedy. As she entered, consternation was on her face – the face of a bewitched Trilby; in her dancing, fear, tears, horror alternated with a morbid, decadent, compulsive *Presto*. And when, with this tragic look in her eyes, she approached the footlights and rose on her toes, she seemed to grow taller – majestic, fateful. This number moved the audience more than any of those preceding it.

The last of the Mazurkas was that in A-sharp major (op.24, no.3), lacelike, woven of soft, catlike, stealthy leaps; and there was a sort of caressing languour in her swaying movements that was at once feminine and maidenly.

Even more interesting are the four Preludes (op.28, nos.4,7,20,6). To the first of them she listens, standing at the piano... To the second ... she stretched with the utmost grace, and thawed. The third was a funeral dance: the wailing woman, shattered by grief, now seeks forgetfulness in dancing, now is tormented by memories, and, at the end, falls to the ground, exhausted. There is no dance for the fourth Prelude – only a mood, the mood of autumnal leaves and autumnal tears, autumnal beauty and sadness.

The best number of all, however, was the Polonaise in A-sharp major, op.53. This was the dance of Diana. In a short red gauze tunic, her legs bare, she leaps, gambols in a round, shoots from a bow; there are occasional flashes of something animal...

Duncan has no ballet technique; she does not aim at *fouettés* and *cabrioles*. But there is so much sculpture in her, so much colour and simplicity, that she fully deserves the capacity audience which she is already assured for next Thursday.

Isadora herself was dissatisfied with her performance. Writing to Craig immediately after it she said, 'The yellow dog and the gas man liked it, and so apparently did all the Kings & Queens in the audience – (It was full of Imperial Loges and Kings and things like that).' Her muscles, she bewailed, were 'quite Capoot'. She couldn't 'dance worth a Cent!!!!!!' Drawing a weeping face at the foot of the letter, she wrote, 'This is how I feel about a "great success". These is tears.'

Nonetheless, she had been a success – although at the time there was no way she could have known how great a one. Most important for the world of ballet was her influence on the young Fokine. As Diaghilev later remarked, 'Fokine was mad about her, and Duncan's influence on him was the initial basis of his entire creation.'

Not that that was entirely true. Fokine and other leading young Russian dancers were already looking for a way to go forward before she arrived in St Petersburg. And of course they already had an armoury of technique far beyond, and irrelevant to, anything that Isadora aspired to do. But as Fokine said years later in his memoirs, she showed him and others 'that all the primitive, plain, natural movements – a simple step, run, turn on both feet, small jump on one foot – are far better than all the richness of ballet technique, if to this technique must be sacrificed grace, expressiveness, and beauty.'

From her Fokine also learned to use neglected parts of the body. As Lynn Grafola observed in her 1989 book, *Diaghilev's Ballets Russes*, arms, torso, neck, head and hands all came to life under Fokine's direction – famously in *The Dying Swan*, which he choreographed for Anna Pavlova in 1905 – giving fluidity, emotion and a revived romanticism to the clockwork motions of the past.

But Isadora also embodied a deeper principle – that dance was as important in its own right as music or storytelling, and no mere accompaniment (as it had been viewed). After her, in the critic A.B.Walkley's words, 'it was no longer subject to music, but took its place.' Isadora began to be seen as part of the artistic trend of the early Twentieth Century. It would be observed that '[her] art has many points of contact with impressionism in painting, just as Nijinsky's has with the forms and masses of Cézanne.'

She herself, while in St Petersburg, softened a little in her unrelenting disapproval of ballet, impressed by some of the great dancers she saw. Invited to the salon of Mathilde Kschessinska, *prima ballerina assoluta* of the Maryinsky Theatre, and accepting an invitation to see her perform, she confessed herself 'astounded', saying that Kschessinska seemed 'more like a lovely bird or butterfly than a human being.'

She similarly admired Anna Pavlova, whom she saw in *Giselle*, and whose invitation she accepted to come next day and watch her practise at the barre. At which point her reservations began to reassert themselves. Describing Pavlova's practising, she wrote, 'She seemed to be made of steel and elastic. Her beautiful face took on the stern lines of a martyr. She never stopped for one moment. The whole tendency of this training seems to be to separate the gymnastic movements of the body completely from the mind.' (Years later, Pavlova would write, '[Isadora] came to Russia and brought freedom to us all.')

No doubt with her own school in mind, she accepted an invitation to come and watch the young pupils at the Maryinsky school. Here she was even less impressed, recalling years later 'all the little pupils standing in rows... They stood on the tips of their toes for hours, like so many victims of a cruel and unnecessary Inquisition. The great, bare dancing-rooms ... were like a torture chamber.'

Her second concert was as great a success as her first. She performed her *Dance Idylls*, and as the *Petersburg Gazette* reported: 'Gentle elegy and bacchic dancing equally charmed the spectators: there was not a single crude gesture, not a single exaggeration... The barefoot dancer was presented with several gorgeous baskets of flowers and many bouquets. The farewell curtains lasted for a long time, and the applauding public would not go away.'

She took twenty curtain-calls, then asked in the wings for a lighted candle. One was produced, and she asked what was the Russian for 'Good-night'. On being told, she returned to the darkened stage, holding the lighted candle, and wished the audience '*Dobroi Nochie*'.

All through her time in St Petersburg, her mind dwelt on Gordon Craig. Her train back to Berlin and him was to set off on the day after her second performance – on Friday, 30th December. Waiting eagerly to leave, she wrote him a letter, saying somewhat ruefully, 'I think that as an inspiration for a Dancer *you* are not a Success. You give me only one inspiration and that is to rush away from all Publics and the like and rush to you – & then die or what ever.'

She also sent him a telegram saying 'SOON SATURDAY NIGHT', followed by another saying 'TOMORROW LOVE'. And as the crawling train crossed the German border she wrote:

> Darling – This darned old train is 3 hours 3 centuries 3 eternities late late late – We will arrive about ten and the secretary & the maid will *yank* me up to Hardenberg Strasse – but I will slip away as soon as I can & come to No. 11... Darling I've come back Back Back from the Land of Snow & Ice – I think I've discovered the North Pole... The only thing that has kept me ... half alive is your sweet picture – and now I will see you you You – Imagine since yesterday Early morning in this train – Years & centuries *coming to you.*

As Isadora had affected the course of Russian ballet, so Craig had affected her. Their affair had aroused her sexuality far beyond anything she had felt before, even for Oszkár Beregi. Both were highly-sexed. Years later Craig would remark to one of his sons (Robert), 'Isadora was the only woman I knew, Bobby, who was not a tame cat, and whose ardours matched my own.'

And both, in early life, found their sexual ardour difficult to reconcile with their drive towards artistic creation. Craig would come to terms with the difficulty more quickly than Isadora would. In his 1957 book, *Index to the Story of My Days*, he would write, 'These sudden attacks bewildered me, and much later on I saw some relation between sex and creative ability in any work... It is a huge power which, properly guided, lends its strength to the creative artist – this is very certain. What else it assists I cannot say – but wrongly dealt with it damages those who attempt to crush it. It is not a thing to quarrel with – you must make friends with it.'

Isadora, certainly at this time in her life, felt her sexual appetites to be at war with her drive to develop dance. 'There is too much feminine in my composition,' she wrote in one of her letters to Craig, 'that's it – a silly mixture.' (In her case there was also a strong maternal drive – a deep love of children and a burning desire to have babies of her own.)

146

Arriving back in Berlin, late in the evening of Saturday, 30th December, she did as she had promised, slipping away from her family as soon as possible, back to her lover and the balcony in his studio.

Chapter Nine

A Dance School in Grunewald

Right from the beginning of 1905, Isadora embarked on a hectic touring schedule, earning all the money she could to pay for the school, its staff, her family, her personal staff, and Gordon Craig.

It was a recurrent pattern in Craig's life to sponge off whichever woman was most deeply involved in his life at the time – a pattern that had begun with his mother. In a letter to a friend at around this time he wrote, 'I'm not making a penny, but living like a Duke.' In another, written in early February, he wrote, with arrogant self-satisfaction, 'As you may guess, I am not paying my own hotel bills & haven't a sou in the world – but I'm damned if I'll starve or sit on a stool & wait for things.'

On 5th January he and Isadora were together in Cologne, where she was to perform. Staying at the Dom Hotel, they had fun with a new game they had invented, writing alternate lines of dialogue on the hotel stationery. In a typical exchange, Isadora wrote, 'I've drunk enough here God knows.' To which Craig responded, 'But God will never tell.'

From Cologne she and Craig returned to Berlin, setting off again on 15th January by train to Dresden. Everywhere she appeared at this time, she ended her performance by making a speech from the stage inviting people to bring any little girls they wished to enrol in her school to an audition – usually in whatever hotel she was staying at. At Dresden she gave three performances, and from the auditions she held at the Hotel Bellevue selected two seven-year-old girls as pupils. A third girl, aged ten, she hunted down herself.

This girl's name was Theresa Kruger. Like the majority of the pupils whose mothers would bring them to audition for Isadora, she was fatherless, her father, a Prussian cavalry officer, having died when she was a baby (she being the youngest in his family). Theresa was stagestruck, and at the time Isadora was in Dresden was taking part in a Christmas pantomime called *The Sea King's Daughter*. During the performance, Isadora, wearing her Greek costume, took her seat in a box next to the proscenium.

As Theresa recalled in an interview years later:

> I was dancing the part of the Pearl, trying to outshine the Coral, the Shell, and the Phosphorescent Fish… I wore a headband with a large pearl in the centre, that shook as I turned my head from side to side – which I was supposed to do slowly. As I did this, for some reason I became amused in a child-like way, and began to move my head faster – in a sharp, one-two count – which seemed to me to be more appropriate for the music. Carried away with the motion, I found myself almost under the proscenium loge, near the 'white angel', who was smiling so sweetly at me. I forgot my dance completely! All I could do was stand there and shake one foot and then the other…
>
> I did this repeatedly, because I was so enthralled by the apparition in the box. My sister came over and whispered, 'If you do that again, the dance master will not have us in his group – never mind who is in the box!' 'But,' I said, 'if she is not an angel, then she is Penelope' – whose statue my sister and I had often seen in the royal gardens of the museum.

Next morning, unannounced, Isadora turned up at the Kruger home, still, as Theresa recalled, wearing her Greek robes. 'Possibly not since Christ had anyone been seen walking around in such clothes, and here it was the dead of winter, with five feet of snow on the ground.'

Isadora, without beating about the bush, told Theresa's mother that she wanted her daughter to become one of her pupils, and she invited the Kruger family to attend her next performance. They went and, as Theresa remembered, 'The huge audience in the theatre was spellbound, and my mother, realising the beauty of it, said to me, "My dear child, do you want to learn to dance like that?" When I said, softly, "Yes," she replied, "It means you will have to leave us."

Two days later, Theresa, as instructed, arrived at Isadora's suite in the Hotel Bellevue, as did the other two Dresden girls. She remembered the door being opened by Gordon Craig, and him calling out, 'Isadora, your children are here!'

During the last week in January, Isadora was performing (and promoting her school) at the Thalia Theatre in Hamburg. There she collected five future pupils, among them the one who would go on to be the most well-known, Irma Erich-Grimme.

Irma was eight, and not especially stage-struck, although her widowed mother was. Her father, who had owned a foodstore, had died two years before, leaving her mother to provide for Irma herself and for five older children by a first wife, who had died. The family were not finding it easy to make ends meet.

One evening, after Irma had already been put to bed, her mother happened on one of the adverts for Isadora's school in a local newspaper. Immediately she roused her daughter. Only the day before, she had tried to get her enrolled in the Hamburg Municipal Theatre School, only to have her rejected for being far too young. Reading the advert aloud, she stressed that the school was accepting pupils aged from six to ten (the ages Isadora had decided on had a tendency to become younger – soon she would accept girls as young as four).

Irma, who had never heard of Isadora Duncan and had very little interest in dancing, was reluctant and sleepy, but her mother cajoled her into expressing interest. It was necessary to make a quick decision because Isadora's audition was to be held the following day. It was a distressful night for both mother and daughter, for Irma, if accepted, would be expected to stay at the school, without holidays, until she was eighteen.

The connections on their long journey to the audition were bad, and by the time their tram arrived at Isadora's hotel, the Hamburger Hof, they were late. Isadora's maid opened the door of her suite and informed them that the tryout was over. But mother pleaded, the maid went to confer with Isadora, and returned to say they were admitted.

They found themselves in a room full of parents and children, and as Irma recounted in her 1965 memoir, *Duncan Dancer*:

> On entering the famous dancer's room, I felt a pleasant sensation of warmth and the fragrance of numerous baskets of fresh flowers. The instant she stepped forward to greet me, in bare feet and ankle-length white tunic, I had eyes only for her. With childish pleasure I noticed the white ribbon she wore in her light brown hair. I had never seen anyone so lovely and angelic-looking or anyone dressed in that way...
>
> In a soft voice, speaking in halting German, she told mother that the tryout was over. Mother once again gave her excuses, and Isadora must have relented, for she told me to remove my clothes quickly

151

so she could have a look at me. Mother knelt down and promptly started to undress me, right there in front of all those people. It happened so quickly I didn't have time to be scared. In her haste to comply with Isadora's request, mother had difficulty with the many hooks and buttons that encumbered even children's clothing in those days.

After she had removed the black stockings, the high-buttoned shoes, and the last petticoat, I stood exposed in a cotton camisole and a pair of lace-edged underpants, from which dangled long black garters. I felt terribly ashamed when, thus accoutered, I was made to stand alone in the centre of the room. But not for long. The lovely vision in the Greek tunic returned and asked my name.

'Come and stand here in front of me, Irma, and do exactly as I do.'

The soft strains of Schumann's *Träumerei* came floating to my ears as Isadora Duncan slowly began to raise her bare arms to the music. She watched me closely as I imitated her gesture and then, after a while, she seemed no longer to pay attention to me. A faraway look had come into her eyes as, lost in the music, she raised her beautiful arms and with a swaying motion of her body moved them from side to side like the branches of a tree put in motion by the wind...

A nod to the musician at the upright piano, and the tempo changed to a lighter rhythm, an allegretto. She swiftly changed the mood and darted away, skipping gracefully around the room. All eyes, I was fascinated watching her circle round me like a bird... Uncertain what to do next, I remained where I was. Still dancing, she beckoned to me and called out gaily, 'Follow me! Follow me!'

Her radiant personality was contagious. I lost my self-consciousness and bravely skipped after her, trying my best to do exactly as she did. I undulated my little arms in emulation of her for all I was worth. But, in that absurd déshabille with the long black garters flapping against my legs at every step, I must have looked comical. I heard her laugh when she stopped abruptly and said, 'That is enough, my dear. Go and put on your things.'

While mother dressed me, I kept looking back over my shoulder at the lovely vision in white who had cast such a spell over me. She slowly went from one child to another of the many assembled there and deliberately made her choice as if picking flowers...

I glanced with envy at the girls she had chosen. Would she want me too? I wondered, secretly yearning to go with her wherever she went, for this was something I now wanted to do more than anything else. However, she passed me by. She turned instead with sudden animation and interest to a young man, sketchbook and pencil in hand, who had been quietly sitting in the background observing. He whispered a few words, which caused Isadora to turn around and look at me. She came over to where I stood beside mother, anxiously waiting for her to notice me. She smiled, took my hand in hers and leading me to the group of girls she had selected, gently said, 'And Irma, I will take you, too.'

The young man was of course Gordon Craig and, as Irma found out from Isadora years later, what he had said was, 'Take her, she has the eyes.' Next morning, Irma and the other four successful applicants returned to the Hamburger Hof and were fitted out with the school uniform – tunic and sandals and a little hooded woollen cape. Dressed alike, and enjoying the simplicity of this new dress, the five looked, Irma recalled, like sisters.

Isadora had already returned to Berlin, and the girls were shepherded to the train by her maid, Anna. When they too arrived in Berlin, Isadora was waiting for them at the station, sitting in a closed carriage. The girls climbed in and were driven to the school, where they were briefly left alone in the entrance hall with its statue of the Greek Amazon. As Irma recounted:

> We remained there waiting for what seemed an unconscionable time.
>
> Then something happened. Over to one side some sliding doors opened a crack, and out peered a small monkeylike face, brown and wrinkled. This face stared at us for a minute; then the doors opened wider, and a small woman stepped out. Outlandishly attired in a long red Chinese coat embroidered all over with flowers and parrots, this strange apparition mysteriously approached, limping slightly. She slowly circled around the little group, huddled together for protection...
>
> Without a kind word of greeting ... this odd creature poked her funny face into each one of our faces for a silent scrutiny and then disappeared as mysteriously as she had come, closing the sliding doors behind her.

153

It was sister Elizabeth, the school's director, who would always be as cold and forbidding to the pupils as Isadora was warm and welcoming. The children in the early days of the school, being told that this was Miss Duncan, assumed that 'Miss' was her first name, and so took to referring to her as 'Tante Miss'. 'Tante Miss' she remained, making no objection to the name.

After Elizabeth's unnerving appearance, Irma and her fellow-Hamburgers were relieved when two cheerful nursemaids appeared, and soon the children were shown round, introduced to the other pupils already there, fed, and put early to bed. Irma was sad that Isadora had never reappeared, but as she was lying in her bed she 'noticed a shadowy vision tiptoeing silently from bed to bed, bending over each child.' It was Isadora. As Irma wrote, 'At last she reached me... She placed a cookie between my lips and kissed me. "Good night, darling, sleep well," she murmured, and was gone.'

The children would not see Isadora again for several weeks. Within a couple of days she would be back in Russia, this time accompanied by Craig.

On this trip she was to give performances not only in St Petersburg, but also in Moscow and Kiev. But several things were now different. For a start, the mood of St Petersburg had changed. During the brief month she had been away, on 22nd January 1905 (9th January in Russia), the city had been the scene of the massacre known as Bloody Sunday.

Trouble was close to the surface in Russia at this time. The country was disastrously involved in a war with Japan (basically over disputed territories), and at home there were already the first stirrings of what would grow into the Revolution of 1917. Activists, Lenin among them, were already organising dissent, and those in power, especially the aristocracy, were quite understandably jumpy.

Among the peasant population there was much poverty, and on that Sunday a large but peaceful deputation of workers, led by Father Gapon, had marched to St Petersburg to present a petition to Tsar Nicholas II at the Winter Palace. Someone, whether the Tsar or one of his officers, commanded troops to fire on the demonstrators. Over a thousand were killed outright or died later of their wounds, and twice that number were injured.

Isadora, in her 1927 memoirs, claimed to have witnessed the aftermath of this tragic affair, saying:

Here I was, in the black dawn of Russia, quite alone, on the way to the hotel, when suddenly I beheld a sight equal in ghastliness to any in the imagination of Edgar Allan Poe.

It was a long procession that I saw from a distance. Black and mournful it came. There were men bent and laden under their loads – coffins – one after another. The coachman slowed his horse to a walk, and bent and crossed himself. I looked on in the indistinct dawn, filled with horror. I asked him what this was. Although I knew no Russian, he managed to convey to me that these were the workmen shot down before the Winter Palace ... because, unarmed, they had come to ask the Tsar for help in their distress – for bread for their wives and children. I told the coachman to stop. The tears ran down my face and were frozen to my cheeks as this sad, endless procession passed me... If I had never seen it, all my life would have been different. There, before this seemingly endless procession, this tragedy, I vowed myself and my forces to the service of the people and the down-trodden. Ah, how small and useless now seemed all my personal love desires and sufferings! How useless even my Art, unless it could help this.

There are slight problems with this account. Quite apart from omitting Gordon Craig, Isadora appears to be somewhat exaggerating the number of coffins she saw. 2nd February, the date when she and Craig arrived in St Petersburg, was more than three weeks after the massacre took place, and, even allowing for a number of victims dying some time after they were shot, it is unlikely that the procession of coffins could have been 'seemingly endless'.

Nonetheless, she undoubtedly did see some coffins being borne in procession, and what she saw that day did affect her for life. It brought out all the socialist attitudes that she had had since, when she was about five, she thought of herself as a 'baby Bolshevik' (although the term was not then in use). Later they would become more prominent in her life, as would her relationship with Russia.

The other change she found in Russia on this second visit was that attitudes to her dancing had somewhat altered. Those who appreciated it, and learned from it, such as Fokine and Diaghilev, were still her wholehearted supporters, but there was now a strong backlash coming from those who adored the conventional ballet, from those who felt her light costumes were scandalous, and, perhaps most of all, from those who felt that dancing to established pieces of classical music was disrespectful and wrong.

Her first performance in St Petersburg was disastrous. In the first part, her pianist, Hermann Lafont, was far from his usual self and gave her a below-par accompaniment. Worse, in the second half, when she danced, as she did so often, to passages from Beethoven's Seventh Symphony, she was accompanied by the Petersburg Philharmonic, and its conductor, the violinist Leopold Auer, made no attempt to hide his contempt and hostility towards what she was doing. He refused to so much as look at what she was doing onstage, and conducted in such a perfunctory manner that the orchestra's performance was listless and uninspiring. Uninspired, Isadora danced poorly. As the critic Shebuyev, who had reviewed her so understandingly and well only a few weeks before, noted, 'her dancing lost its brilliance, faded, wilted.' In consequence, she decided to omit Beethoven from her programme of performances in Moscow.

Her reception there was mixed. At one performance the audience booed her for her scanty costume. She stopped dancing and upbraided them, saying, 'This is impolite and unkind. This offends me as a woman. Those who do not like it may leave.'

Another performance, however, was a success, although at first it did not seem as if it was destined to be. Present in the audience was the great Konstantin Stanislavsky, then aged forty-two, and the co-founder and director of the Moscow Art Theatre. In his 1924 autobiography, *My Life in Art*, he recalled:

> I appeared at Isadora Duncan's concert by accident, having heard nothing about her until that time, and having read none of the advertisements that heralded her coming to Moscow. Therefore I was very much surprised that in the rather small audience that came to see her there was a tremendous percentage of artists and sculptors with Mamontov at their head [Savva Mamontov was a railway magnate and patron of the arts], many artists of the ballet, and many first-nighters and lovers of the unusual in the theatre... Unaccustomed to see an almost nude body on the stage, I could hardly notice or understand the art of the dancer. The first number was met with tepid applause and timid attempts at whistling. But after a few of the succeeding numbers, one of which was especially persuasive, I could no longer remain indifferent to the protests of the general public and began to applaud demonstratively.

When the intermission came, I, a newly baptised disciple of the great artist, ran to the footlights to applaud. To my joy I found myself side by side with Mamontov, who was doing exactly what I was doing, and near Mamontov were a famous artist, a sculptor, and a writer. When the general run of the audience saw that among those who applauded were well known Moscow artists and actors, there was a great deal of confusion. The hissing stopped, and when the public saw that it could applaud, the applause became general, and was followed by curtain calls, and at the end of the performance by an ovation.

From then on Stanislavsky never missed a single one of the Duncan concerts. On this occasion, however, her run was curtailed. On 17th February, Craig happened to be walking through Red Square when the unpopular governor of Moscow (and uncle of Tsar Nicholas), Grand Duke Sergei Alexandrovitch, was killed there by a terrorist's bomb. As Craig wrote to his mother a month later, 'I only escaped being bombed [myself] because no one had enough courage to throw at such a guy.'

A period of public mourning was declared. Theatres were closed, and the rest of Isadora's scheduled appearances in Moscow were cancelled. She did perform in Kiev, but on the whole was relieved to quit Russia and return with Craig to Berlin.

Once back there, she immediately set off on another short tour of Germany, this time unhappy at being without Craig. From Frankfurt she wrote to him, 'Pillow soaked with tears – no sleep. Why aren't you here? Great Big Beds – 2 of them – Hélas! – Poor little me – *alone* ... Anna is rather awed by my general gloomy mien & trembles with fear at my frown. She says *es war viel netter wenn Herr Craig war mit* [It was much nicer when Mr Craig was with us] – *Netter* – My Gods I should think it *war netter.*'

By 25th February she was missing him so much that she sent him both a telegram and a letter begging him to come and be with her. In the letter she said, 'It just struck me as a Blooming Farce your not being here & I sent a telegram asking you to come. I wonder if you Will?'

Craig's answer was tetchy and evasive. He wrote, 'Of course it's a blooming farce... How do I know whether or not I will come? I've sworn to go and work but swears are no use where you are... Come back quick and work with me. How else shall we – can we – be together – and even *then* how is it possible.'

Once again Isadora's overpowering need to give and receive love and warmth was beginning to discourage a man – not that the self-indulgent and promiscuous Craig needed any discouragement. Already he was beginning to distance himself somewhat from her. A passage in *Book*

Topsy shows how well he knew himself himself and reveals his attempts to prepare an exit:

> In the first days I used to laugh gaily whenever she grew deadly serious about 'mein lieber mann' & 'Hochzeit' [wedding] & all the rest of it for I used to say to her, 'we are *not serious*' 'we cannot be *serious*' – & she would take up the refrain 'no, not serious' & then her arms round my neck & mine round her we would kiss lightly or youthfully – never once can I recall her teeth meeting mine – or the tip of her tongue – not once – she kissed as much with the eyes as with the lips.
>
> 'no, no' – week after week, 'not serious, Topsy,' 'It can't last Topsy – love never lasts does it Topsy –' & then she would be apt to turn the talk or take a rather offended tone – She could not admit then that love never lasts & could she have really seen into my heart & head she would have seen there the same refusal to believe that our love could die. Only I had begun to provide for the future catastrophe so that when it came up I should be able to stand up to it. This she did not know – how could she.

At the same time he was itching to further his work. His mind was bubbling with ideas. As his son and biographer, Edward Craig, wrote, 'in 1905 he had too much to think about to give all his mind to any one project... It was a period of a hundred schemes.'

He was considering editing and publishing another theatre magazine, 'so that through that publication I might in time come to change the whole theatre – not plays alone, but playing, sceneries, construction of theatres – the whole thing.' He was planning productions – *The Tempest*, *Macbeth*, a collaboration with the great Berlin producer Max Reinhardt to produce Shaw's relatively recent play, *Caesar and Cleopatra*, a production of Sophocles' *Elektra*, to star Eleanora Duse. This last he did make some progress with, drawing designs for sets and sending the drawings to Duse, then in her native Italy, for her approval. Unfortunately she soon withdrew from the project, having decided that Elektra was not a sufficiently commercial piece to take on tour.

Still on tour herself, Isadora was feeling disoriented by the strength of her feelings for her absent lover. As she wrote to Craig from Hanover, 'I feel such extraordinary convolutions going on – one moment I feel I could live on bread & water on the highest mountain top & *think*, and the next as if I'd like to bask all my days in a valley with flowers & *kiss*

– & the changes come so quick & unexpected that I feel a bit rattled. Battled – rather say.'

Even books she had long loved now seemed meaningless to her. She had taken with her a copy of Walt Whitman, but as she bewailed to Craig, he now made her 'feel like a tissue paper fool.' She tried her beloved Nietzsche, but as she wrote from Göttingen, 'Nietzsche is [not] the thing for Mother's child to read.' In the same letter she said:

> Oh you you you – I am slipping away from myself and becoming nothing but a longing and reflection, and I tried to tell you the other day my *work* was the principle thing. *Work* – I haven't a thought or feeling left for it – that's the truth – it's this Infernal feminine Coming out at all places.

That letter ended with a relatively casual 'Come if you can', but more often she pleaded for his presence, sometimes in baby-talk – 'Topsy me comes if you telegraphs' or 'I feel dreful'. One letter begged, 'Teddy Come along – I'm trying to Hexry you [German *Hexerei*, meaning 'witchcraft'] – do you feel it? I Want You to Take The Train & Come – come come come come come...'

Eventually her few weeks' touring was over and she was able to speed back to Berlin. By which time Craig had embarked on another scheme. He would open a theatrical booking agency which would generate a steady income for him. It was to be called Direktion Vereinigter Künste (United Arts Management), and as its manager he had hired a twenty-nine-year-old American, now living in Berlin. His name was Maurice Magnus, and he was a live wire – short, energetic, sociable and dubious (one of his claims about himself was that he was a morganatic descendant of the Hohenzollerns – the German Imperial Family to which Kaiser Bill belonged).

Together, he and Craig opened an office (in the building where Craig had his studio), hired a secretary, printed stationery and registered a telegraphic address, ironically choosing the hated word FOOTLIGHTS. The money for all this activity would of course come from Isadora, as would Maurice Magnus' wages, agreed at three pounds per week, rising to five when bookings started to come in.

To add to Isadora's burdens, all was not well with the Clan. First there was her mother, who was growing more and more unhappy. Her unhappiness, which she expressed by criticising and complaining, stemmed largely from Isadora's increasing success and independence – an independence that was making her mother feel useless and unwanted. Isadora, in her memoirs, attempted to account for her mother's growing bitterness:

> For the first time since our voyage abroad, she began to express a longing for America, and said how much better everything was there – the food and so forth... I think that this turning of her character was probably due to the habitual state of virtue in which my mother had lived, for so many years devoting herself only to her children ... Sentimental and virtuous, she could only suffer and weep.

Among her siblings, Elizabeth was bitterly opposed to her relationship with Gordon Craig. Augustin, although he was functioning as Isadora's business manager, was having difficulties with his marriage to Sarah, which was showing signs of falling apart, and although Raymond, still building the family temple outside Athens, seemed happy enough with his wife Penelope, Isadora was not sure she really approved of her. According to their fellow San Franciscan, Gertrude Stein, who had emigrated to France in 1902, and now lived in Paris, 'she found the girl too modern a Greek.'

It didn't help that Raymond was dependent on Isadora to subsidise himself and his wife, as well as the continuing work on the temple. Rather bitterly Isadora wrote, 'and all the time my Brother my wise little Brother boy is singing to his goats on the hill side while his little Greek girl plays on the flute.' (Not only that – unknown to Isadora at this time, the little Greek girl had just become pregnant.)

In the middle of March, another weight was added to her emotional burden. Happening on a letter Craig had received, she learned that his lady in London, Elena Meo, had given birth in January to another of Craig's children (his eighth). Not only that, she learned that he was sending Elena money (money earned by Isadora), and had promised to return to her as soon as his agency business got on its feet. (As it turned out, he would visit her exactly once during the next year, and that for only a few days.)

Desperate to have a baby herself, the news of Elena's new child filled Isadora with perfectly understandable fury, and she stormed at Craig. But her anger didn't last. Soon it was replaced by contriteness and, once again touring Germany, she wrote him a letter saying, 'Dear – I feel awfully ashamed – ashamed is not the word. I feel dust & ashes – it was an awful kind of rage that took possession of me... I'm afraid you will never be able to think of me in the same way again.'

160

Only a few days later, on 16th March, she was writing to him again, this time from Magdeberg, assuring him that she accepted his union with Elena and giving it her blessing. She wrote, 'Save me from the *Green Demon Jealousy!* And the *Red Devil Desire for Complete Possessorship* and the ten & twenty thousand friends who accompany them.'

She began to worry that Craig no longer wanted her. After a brief stop back in Berlin, she wrote him a touching letter from Brussels, begging him to 'persue' her so as to reassure her of his desire, and saying:

> I think I is an Amazon.
> If you like the persuing idea you'll have to put up with me persuing at the same time & Clash Bang Crash *Collision* in the Middle –
> So long –
> Come along . . .
> I mean
> You must Come along and *persue me*
> Please Persue Me –
> I'll pretend to fly fine
> If you'll only persue me –
> I'll be more fun than a fox hunt.

What is pitiful in all this is that while Isadora was desperately trying to reconstruct her mind and emotions in order to accept Craig's chronic unfaithfulness as an inescapable part of the man she loved, he, with his deep and abiding self-centredness, was recording his gradual withdrawal from her in a secret notebook he labelled *Confessions*:

> I am in love with one woman only [by which he meant Elena], and although others attract me how could it ever obliterate what exists in her of my heart and soul . . . But I am keenly attracted to another woman [Isadora], who may be a witch or a pretty child (and it really doesn't matter which) and I find it hard to be away from her. She not only attracts me, she revolts me also. One moment I instinctively smile with her and love to be with her, and the next I want to be away from her and I shrink from her. It is not that she is at all ugly or repulsive – but merely that I am delighted with her or bored.
> When she talks about herself incessantly for a quarter of an hour – when she drinks more wine than she needs or wants – when she

cuddles up to other people, men or women, relations or not relations – it is not that she does so repulsively but I see that they are equally attracted as myself – and I object to be equally anything in such matters.

And my confession is that I have a contempt for her and do not like to feel I have a contempt – because I find her so dear and so delightful.

Still I cannot trust her, and even friendship, much more love demands absolute trust.

Not that I love her – it is not possible to 'Love' twice.

And that is perhaps where a clever idiot would get mixed, for though I do not love her, I tell myself and her that I do – Still I also tell her that I am unable to tell what love is....

Love is something a bit less restless and wayward than this. Love regards no other thing or person except through the eyes of the loved one....

Love which torments is not love. Love is all which is dear and beautiful, without flutter or excitement, without excess of laughter or tears, something at ease and gravely sweet – And where love is there is no love for any other thing.

The man was thirty-two.

He did still join Isadora on her tours when his schedule permitted. He did in fact 'persue' her to Brussels, where he stayed for three happy days, and after he returned to Berlin she wrote to him, for the moment still in her happiness, 'The people here are very gay, and the students pass singing & crying out – also the noise of the bells and the cars. All this Life – Wonderful and delightful life – Life is splendid – above all things to be *alive.*'

And again, a day or so later, 'Did I say you have no heart? But I couldn't have said that – have I not often heard your heart beating – happy me.'

And again, telling him she had begun work on a 'Marvellous Book!', she wrote, 'Had a wonderful torrent of ideas falling over each other – Don't know if they are of any worth... It's all a matter of magnetic forces ... Wonderful. Aren't we wonderful – Love Love Love Love Love. Waves – love waves – I've been writing about dance waves – sound waves – light waves – all the same.'

In April 1905 she performed in Holland for the first time, in Amsterdam. Holland was then a country little interested in dance, and her appearances there were carefully planned. Many items about her appeared in the Dutch press before her arrival – anecdotes from her life, excerpts from interviews, and reviews of her performances elsewhere.

At her opening night, which took place on 12th April, the house was sold out, and she performed one of her most accessible programmes – her *Dance Idylls*, followed by a suite of dances from Gluck's *Orfeo ed Euridice*, and ending with the dance that audiences always seemed to enjoy most, *Der schönen blauen Donau*. She had somewhat softened in her attitude to what she would often refer to as 'that infernal Blue Danube', and told a Dutch interviewer, 'The public that didn't understand the earlier dances, and who have been sitting there all evening, should be given something.'

The Dutch audiences received her enthusiastically, and she adored Holland, writing cheerfully to Craig, 'Dutch country so pretty, tulips and hyacinths – fields – and all like somebody's back garden ... Amsterdam is really too wonderful with all the houses leaning side ways on one another or just falling forward.'

Her only problem had been that, as in some other countries, the best Dutch orchestras refused to play for her, for the usual reason, that they felt classical music was sacrosanct, and should not be danced to.

Back in Berlin, Craig was restless about his career, discontented that he was not achieving more, and wondering which of his many projects to pursue. By the time Isadora returned from her short visit to Amsterdam, he had decided to write a book setting down his philosophy of Theatre. He was going to write it using a dialogue form, reminiscent of the dialogue-writing games that he and Isadora played, and as he wrote it he frequently discussed it with her (all his life he would be gracious in admitting how much Isadora's views on staging and performing had influenced his own, for instance in her belief that all Art should be simple and beautiful and rooted in Nature).

Being full of his subject, which he been thinking about obsessively for years, he completed the book in only twelve days. He called it *The Art of the Theatre*, and it would become a major success, establishing him as a leading theorist in the world of the drama, and giving him a reputation as an author that would prove a useful source of additional income for the rest of his life.

By the end of April, Isadora had gathered eighteen suitable pupils at her school. 'I don't know exactly how we chose those children,' she wrote later. 'I was so anxious to fill the Grunewald and the forty little beds, that I took the children without discrimination, or merely on account of a sweet smile or pretty eyes; and I did not ask myself whether or not they were capable of becoming future dancers.' (She never would fill all forty beds – the most pupils the school would ever have would be twenty.)

A helper at the school at this time was Isadora's friend Mary D'Este, who had returned from Chicago to spend her annual six months in Europe (although this time it would stretch to almost a year). Depositing her young son Preston with a family named Rousseau, who had a school in Joinville, east of Paris, she hastened to Grunewald and again involved herself in every aspect of Isadora's life.

As to the staff at the school, in addition to Elizabeth as Director there were two 'governesses', Fräulein Lippach and Fräulein Konegen, who supervised every detail of the girls' lives (apart from their schooling and their dancing lessons) from morning to night. Presumably these were the two that the young Irma Erich-Grimme thought of as 'nursemaids'.

The girls, whose ages ranged from four to twelve, rose at 6.30 a.m., and before breakfast, wearing blue one-piece bathing suits, did an hour's limbering-up exercises at a ballet barre. After breakfast, every weekday morning, came four hours of schoolwork, taught by state-certified teachers. The girls learned something of history, literature, mathematics, natural science, languages, music, and singing.

In out-of-school hours they learned to sew and knit, and to draw, carrying sketchbooks with them whenever they went outdoors. The drawing seemed something of a joke, as few of the girls had any natural ability, but in fact it had its purpose. It took pupil Theresa Kruger years to realise that 'sketching was just a ruse to get us to concentrate on natural movement. Trees and grasses bending in the wind carry a message for every dancer. If she is observant, and even if she isn't, the rhythm and pulse of nature are bound to affect her.'

Two afternoons a week the girls were taught by a Swedish gymnastics teacher, improving their balance, co-ordination and stamina by doing such exercises as handstands, somersaults and push-ups. Dance itself formed a surprisingly small proportion of the curriculum. It too took place twice a week, from four to six on Wednesday and Saturday afternoons. For their lessons the girls wore short cheesecloth tunics. (Curiously, and rather against the spirit of the school, the most usual punishment given for such delinquencies as idleness or talking during the long periods of the day when talking was forbidden, was being barred from a dance class. Perhaps Isadora, or maybe Elizabeth, thought that this would emphasise the importance of dancing in life.)

The dance lessons, during Isadora's frequent absences, were given by

Elizabeth. Irma, in her memoirs, recalled that 'For a long time I puzzled, trying to figure out how Isadora expected us to learn to dance from her lame sister.' Wearing her long Chinese coat, which did something to disguise her lameness, Elizabeth would on infrequent occasions lift the hem of it to briefly demonstrate a few steps of one of the social dances she had been teaching for so long – a waltz, maybe, or a polka or a gavotte. Mostly she sat in front of the class 'on a Greek bench', tapping out her instructions with a stick, and sometimes demonstrating a difficult pattern with her fingers.

In spite of this type of teaching, which seems so different from anything that Isadora preached, another pupil, Anna Denzler, recalled in an interview that Elizabeth 'did have a very deep understanding and appreciation of her sister's art. And though she rarely showed us a step, she did draw out of us little children the artistic quality needed to perform Isadora's abstract art of the dance.'

She was a strict and sarcastic teacher. As one of her closest friends, the American socialite Mabel Dodge, once recalled, 'No one *dared* to be clumsy anywhere near Elizabeth. It was a crime.' 'Touch the hills!' she would cry. 'Reach out your fingers till you can touch the hills... Up! Up! Don't stay down on the *ground* when you can go so *high! UP!*'

The meals were vegetarian (or so the theory went – in fact meat was served once a week). A typical evening meal might consist of carrots or Brussels sprouts, beans and cold cooked cabbage, or perhaps macaroni. For dessert there would be prunes or sago pudding.

Naturally a few of the girls found the regime of the school too much to take, and some who came left after only a few weeks. But there was always a slow steady trickle of newcomers, found by Isadora through her constant publicising of the establishment during her tours.

Where Elizabeth had become cold and forbidding, to the extent that the girls tended to run away if they heard her coming, Isadora was all warmth. The children worshipped her, and longed for the occasions when she would be there to be among them and teach them.

Anna Denzler recalled her as 'love personified', and Theresa Kruger recalled her as 'my angel in white', saying, 'I always had the impression that she had been sent to me from on high. When she greeted us with her quiet musical voice, she instantly gave us the effect of having been dipped in warm radiant sunshine.'

With her deep love of children, she often seemed more like an unruly pupil than like the school's founder. On one occasion, when things were going particularly well with Gordon Craig, she burst dramatically into a classroom, interrupting the lesson, and asked, 'Tell me, children, what is the greatest thing in life?'

Naturally they chorused, 'To dance!'

'No,' she beamed. 'Dancing is not the greatest thing in life. The greatest thing in life is – LOVE! Is it not true?' With which she swept dramatically out, leaving the lady schoolteacher crimson with embarrassment. Hastily she took a bible from her desk drawer and read out the passage from First Corinthians that ends 'And now abideth faith, hope, love, these three; but the greatest of these is love.' She explained that that was the sort of love Miss Duncan meant. Somehow the girls were not convinced.

Craig, still working, with the help of Maurice Magnus, to establish United Arts Management, suggested to Isadora at around this time that Maurice should act as her agent in arranging her tours. As the suggestion came from Craig, she agreed, the deal being that ten per cent of her receipts should go to the agency. Unfortunately, Magnus's idea of being an agent consisted almost entirely of socialising with the rich and famous. This he felt would itself ensure success. He would turn out to be almost useless as a businessman, and over the succeeding months Craig would fire him, rehire him, and fire him again on several occasions.

In June 1905, with the school beginning to establish itself, and encouraged by how well its pupils were progressing, Isadora began soliciting subscriptions from anyone she felt might have money or influence. Her aim was to buy a vacant lot near the school and on it build an annexe, giving her room for twenty-five more pupils. She also hoped that the school might have enough capital to be self-supporting, thus lifting from her the burden of financing it.

Soon she managed to attract quite a number of subscriptions. Money came mainly from people in the arts, like sculptors and musicians, and from wealthy and well-connected Berlin women, among them several ladies-in-waiting to the Kaiserin Augusta, wife of Wilhelm II.

But although such backing was welcome, it was not as much as the school had hoped for, so Isadora arranged that on 20th July 1905 her girls would perform at a fund-raising concert at Kroll's Opera House. It would be the first time they would perform in public, and naturally they found the whole idea exciting. As Irma recalled, 'Isadora gave us new silk tunics in pastel shades of blue, pink, and yellow to wear for the occasion, making us discard the cheesecloth ones entirely. Also we had small wreaths of rosebuds for our hair.'

At the concert, Isadora danced first, then the girls performed to two lively tunes from Humperdinck's children's opera, *Hänsel und Gretel* – 'Rosenringel' and 'Tanzreigen'. They were a resounding success. As Irma recalled:

> When we finished the audience responded with deafening applause.
>
> The shock of this unexpected noise descended upon us with the suddenness of a thunderclap. We turned for reassurance toward the wings, where, near the proscenium arch, we had espied the lithe figure of our idol, who had been watching our dancing and for whom alone we had danced. Sensing our childish alarm, she quickly advanced towards us smiling, her light draperies floating behind her. Arms filled with long-stemmed roses, she stopped in our midst and took a bow while the gaze of her little pupils turned towards her as flowers towards the sun.
>
> The audience clamored for encores. When the music began again, Isadora quickly whispered to us to dance towards her, one by one, from the opposite corner of the stage. We did so, and as each child skipped up she handed her a pink rose. With the flowers in our hands, we then circled round her as she posed in the center of the stage, arms outstretched as if to embrace us all in a loving, maternal gesture.

Craig was in the audience, and years later, in a talk on BBC Radio, he added his memory of this first public appearance, saying, '[She] called her little pupils to come to her and please the public with their little leapings and runnings! As they did, and with her leading them the whole troupe became irresistibly lovely... To see her shepherding her little flock, and keeping them together and especially looking after one very small one of four years old, was a sight no one there had ever seen before and, I suppose, will never see again.'

After the success of this performance, Isadora's pupils would perform publicly more and more frequently, both with her and without her, eventually appearing not only in Germany, but in Holland, France, Switzerland, Russia, Finland and England.

Things between Craig and Isadora were running fairly smoothly for the moment. In August, it being a particularly hot summer, they went for a holiday together in the relative coolness of Tutzing, a little way south-west of Munich, and on the edge of the Bavarian Alps. As Craig noted at the time, 'There was a well-managed hotel there – and there I sat and cut wood [made woodcuts] and Isadora read books.'

On 10th October, exasperated by the inadequacies of Maurice Magnus, Craig fired him again and agreed with Isadora that in future he himself would arrange bookings for her and manage her tours. The deal agreed between them was that he would receive half her earnings, out of which he would pay her expenses – 'theatres, lighting, orchestra and orchestra direction, advertising, railway and carriage expenses.' She, for her part, agreed to dance 'not less than twelve times a month' and to prepare, by the end of the year, a new programme.

Four days later Craig received a shock. On the night of 13th October, after performing in Tennyson's *Becket* at a theatre in Bradford, Sir Henry Irving unexpectedly collapsed and died in his hotel. (The next evening, Ellen Terry, appearing in a play at the Gaiety Theatre, Manchester, had to deliver the line, 'I had a beautiful husband once, black as the raven was his hair.' At which she broke down, the curtain was lowered, and the audience filed out without a sound.)

Craig, who had revered his mother's old acting partner, was devastated, writing to a friend, 'The old Angel dead, and howling forbidden to us of the masculine gender – and I cannot tell you the state I am in, unrelieved – may my immortal Henry float away and away wherever fancy allows.'

Isadora did her best to lift him out of his unhappiness, but only a few days later had to leave Berlin to make a second visit to Holland. This time she danced in both Amsterdam and The Hague, and in both places was again enthusiastically received. But the success of her previous appearance had drawn attention to her, and brought detractors out of the woodwork. Their loud objections were not only to her dancing to the classical repertoire, but to her bare legs – and even to her dancing at all. One critic wrote, 'Holland by nature is not a dance-oriented country... We are a reserved population with, generally speaking, introspective, mainly quiet, dignified citizens.'

As a result, the only orchestra she was able to hire to accompany her, the Haarlem Municipal Orchestra, was of poor quality. Even though she considered it third-rate, and often threatened to dismiss it, it played for all her performances on that tour.

At the same time as she was touring Holland (the end of October), her pupils were appearing without her at the Theater des Westens in Berlin. Reviewer Max Osborn, writing in the *Nationale Zeitung*, described their performance:

When the curtain went up, a winning little child with her dark hair combed over her ears, a narrow fillet of gold on her head, a dainty frock of gauze over her white undergarments, and bare legs and feet, which tripped lightly and daintily over the carpet, flitted into the room to the strains of a melody by Schumann. This was Temple Duncan, a niece of Miss Isadora Duncan. She was quickly followed by a second and a third elf-like figure, as daintily and airily clad as the first, until, gradually, the whole stage was filled with a score of similar figures. They flitted past and played a game of touch like iridescent butterflies with variegated wings; they curtsied and bowed – then leaped and danced like sprites ... ran hither and thither, flinging about their slender little legs under their short-skirted frocks... They mirrored the notes of the music by unstudied movements full of the most delightful rhythm, making one feel as if every trill and harmony had turned into flesh and blood...

For the most part all the [dances] were carried out with marvellous accuracy, as though learned by rote, but often the severity of the figures relaxed and the little ones skipped about at their own sweet will. This had a special charm and even a special interest of its own, for it showed clearly how well they had learned to move. Indeed, it must be admitted that there was a general absence of anything like stiltedness or affectation. The whole thing was like some voluntary game played by gay and frolicsome children, but directed by someone who could enter lovingly into a child's idiosyncrasies and capacity for expression.

By this time, Isadora's brother Raymond, whose wife's pregnancy was by now well-advanced, had decided that a Greek hilltop was not perhaps the ideal place for an *accouchement*, and had moved with Penelope to Paris (still wearing the toga-like classical costume that he would retain all his life). They took an apartment not far from the one where Gertrude Stein was living, and Raymond sent Isadora a plaintive note, begging for more money and telling her that Penelope 'would have to go to "Pauper Hospital"' if she didn't help out. Which of course she did. The child, a son, was born in November, and Raymond and Penelope named him Menalkas, a name used in the writings of both Virgil and Theocritus, and which came to symbolise a shepherd or rustic.

To add to Isadora's burdens (such as Raymond), at the beginning of 1906 the school began to attract unfavourable publicity. Prudish objections were being aired in the press, not about her own dancing costumes but about the costumes of her pupils, both on-stage and off.

Their simple, rational everyday dress had been drawing attention for months, as far back as the spring of 1905. Irma recalled:

> I can still see the shocked expressions among the local population, especially women, when we Duncan pupils first appeared in broad daylight with the coming of spring, appareled in tunics and with our bare feet in sandals, on the open streets of Berlin. Pitying exclamations like, 'Oh, you poor, poor little children! Why, you must be freezing to death with so little on!' engulfed us. Approaching our innocent governess with threatening gestures and looks, they shouted after her, 'It's cruelty, that's what it is! We ought to get the police after you. Cruel! Cruel! Cruel!'
>
> Unfortunately, that wasn't by any means the end of it. No one had reckoned with the other children of the neighbourhood, mostly boys, who subjected us poor victims to what amounted to a minor persecution. Like the Christian martyrs of old, we were actually stoned. Frequently (and this was most humiliating) the children pelted us – in this era of horse-drawn carriages – with something else entirely! ... We often panicked, despite heroic efforts on the part of our chaperone to fend off these wild hordes of insult-screaming juveniles.

This was bad enough, but early in 1906 public objections to their on-stage costumes also began to gather momentum. On 9th January the *Kölnischer Zeitung* complained that when the children danced, their 'sense of modesty was not protected.' And the Kaiserin herself, a notoriously pious woman, went on record as being outrageously shocked at children performing bare-legged. This remark attracted wide publicity, and the police stepped in to investigate the situation. They invoked a recently-passed Berlin by-law forbidding children of school age to perform on-stage without special permission, and further performances were banned.

Fortunately this ban applied only to Berlin, and it was soon lifted after Isadora marshalled such allies as Cosima Wagner, Heinrich Thode and Engelbert Humperdinck to support her cause. The special permission was granted.

Nonetheless, there was a growing sense among the less-informed public that there was something scandalous about her and her activities, and things got no better for her when, still in January, she discovered to her delight that Craig had made her pregnant. She feared that this news might not fill him with unmixed delight, but did her best to reassure him by reminding him that a baby of her own was what she had long wanted more than anything in the world.

Realising that her pregnancy would unavoidably mean she would have to cut down on her performing during the year, and thus reduce her and Craig's income, she told him in an apologetic letter, 'Dr says I can probably dance again next Dec 1 – Listen that isn't so bad.'

Unfortunately, the news of her condition soon leaked out, and she found herself under fire from those very Berlin ladies who were the financial supporters of the school. As she recalled, 'When they learned of Craig they sent me a long letter, couched in majestic terms of reproach, and said that they, members of the good bourgeois society, could no longer be patronesses of a school where the leader had such loose ideas of morals.'

The letter was hand-delivered to her by one of the school's patrons, Giulietta Mendelssohn, wife of the wealthy banker Robert Mendelssohn. As Isadora recalled, she 'looked at me a bit unsteadily and, suddenly bursting into tears, threw the letter on the floor, and, taking me in her arms, cried, "Don't think I ever signed that wretched letter. As for the other ladies, there is nothing to be done with them. They will no longer be patrons of this school. Only they still believe in your sister, Elizabeth."'

As Isadora wryly reflected years later, 'If they knew the truth, they wouldn't.' For the truth was that Elizabeth had embarked on an affair of her own. It was with an Austrian musicologist, Max Merz, who, after seeing one of Isadora's performances, had offered her his services at the school. Isadora, accepting, had brought him there, where he was immediately latched onto by Elizabeth. She became his lover, and effectively they began running the school together, making decisions that frequently Isadora, when away touring, knew nothing about.

Nevertheless, having Elizabeth approved of by the sponsoring women was an asset. With Isadora's consent, Elizabeth founded a 'Society for the Support and Maintenance of the Dance School of Isadora Duncan'. It was headed by the school's next-door-neighbour, Engelbert Humperdinck, and although it was nominally a fund-raising organisation, it also stood by to act as an administering body, able to take over the ownership of the school from Isadora, if the scandal over her pregnancy worsened.

Isadora was, and remained, furious about the attitude of the pious and respectable, regarding it as pure hypocrisy. In her memoirs she recalled, 'These women so aroused my indignation that I took the Philharmonic Saal and gave a special lecture on the dance as an art of liberation.' There is a strong possibility that this lecture was based on an essay she

171

had written, 'The Dancer and Nature' (which had started life as the 'Marvellous Book' her mind had been filled with in Brussels the previous year).

Craig too was having problems. In January his plans for producing *Caesar and Cleopatra* in collaboration with Max Reinhardt had fallen through (almost entirely through his own insistence on having total artistic control). This in turn had caused Count Harry Kessler to become tired of his obstructive arrogance, and to send him a letter strongly implying that their association was at an end. In part it said, 'Reinhardt has written to me, saying he is sorry and amazed at your changing your mind. I much regret it too, as I cannot help thinking this decision of yours a great mistake. However, you must know best, and so I can only wish that you may soon find some other way of realising your plans.'

In a letter to his old London friend and colleague, Martin Shaw, Craig wrote, 'Reinhardt, Kessler, Duse, all of them monkeys. I demand my theatre & my rights from the whole pack.' And in another, 'I am as it were cut off from the Theatre – I who possibly happen to *be* THE THEATRE – Queer.'

Craig had long been badgering Martin Shaw to come to Berlin as a friend and ally, and aid him in his enterprises, and in February 1906 Shaw finally did so. A Londoner, he was amiable and intelligent. In a 1929 book of reminiscences, called *Up to Now*, he recalled his first meeting with Isadora, after one of her Berlin performances:

> The theatre was crowded and the audience in a state of ecstatic delight throughout. Isadora provided the whole programme. This in itself is remarkable. I doubt whether any other dancer has ever been able to carry through a whole evening's entertainment unaided...
>
> After the performance I was taken round to see the wonderful creature in her dressing-room. She looked at me with the untroubled gaze of a child and spoke a few words of welcome in an American accent which the extraordinary sweetness of her voice robbed of the least suspicion of harshness. All her movements were deliberate, reposeful, never for an instant hurried or nervous. One simply could not imagine her catching a train.

It was arranged that, for so long as Isadora was able to continue dancing, Shaw would become her conductor. He did, and went with her that spring as she performed in Germany, Belgium and Holland, as well as in the Scandinavian cities of Copenhagen and Stockholm.

It was as well she did have Shaw with her for moral support, because, after their initial performance together, in Nuremberg, the orchestras they encountered were dismal. In *Up to Now*, Shaw recorded that in Augsberg the local philharmonic was made up entirely of army officers. 'They were most anxious to oblige,' he wrote, 'and I liked them, although their playing was, as might be expected, slightly heavy and mechanical.'

In Holland she was again constrained to use the Haarlem Municipal Orchestra, and while they were no better than before, at least she had Shaw to sympathise with her and to try and lick them into some sort of shape. Which wasn't easy. As he recalled, 'The players were seated in a room that just held them comfortably – and no more. It was impossible to tell whether [they] were sounding the right notes or not. Added to this, every single one of them had a lighted cigar in his mouth, even the wind players.'

They were so poor that at one performance Isadora stopped dead in the middle of a dance and began to harangue them. As Shaw told it, 'This was naturally jolly for me! The orchestra sat and listened to her with Dutch phlegm. At the end of her speech she relented and said she would try [the] dance again. But this I refused to do, and we went on to the next item and somehow finished the programme.'

Isadora, in her condition, found the tour exhausting, spending most her time asleep when not performing. On her return to Berlin the question arose of what peaceful town could she find to have her baby in.

At first, while attempting to decide on a good place, she stayed with some friends of Robert and Giulietta Mendelssohn, a Dr and Mrs Zehme, in their home near Leipzig, in central Germany. Although the house was comfortable, and she was well looked after, she did feel under pressure from the Zehmes, owing to their conviction that she ought to give up the baby for the sake of her career – either by having an abortion or by letting the Zehmes adopt it. Neither of which she had the slightest intention of doing.

Craig, busy about his own affairs, was little help. Nor, on 12th June, did he bother to go to London when his mother was fêted at a matinée at the Drury Lane Theatre to celebrate her fifty years on the stage (she had made her first appearance when she was eight). He was inclined to blame her for devoting herself more to her own career than to his – as he felt she had also done in the case of his late father and in the case of Sir Henry Irving, whose loss he was still mourning. Women in general, he felt, were deficient in devotion.

173

Isadora, still with the Zehmes, although delighted to be carrying a child, viewed the effects of pregnancy on her body with some alarm. As she recalled in her memoirs:

> The child asserted itself now, more and more. It was strange to see my beautiful marble body softened and broken and stretched and deformed... My hard little breasts grew large and soft, and fell. My nimble feet grew slower, my ankles swelled, my hips were painful. Where was my lovely, youthful naiad form? Where my ambition? My fame? Often, in spite of myself, I felt very miserable and defeated. This game with the giant Life was too much.

For a while she had considered the Italian area round Lake Como as a suitably quiet place to have her baby in, but eventually she settled on the town of Noordwijk, on the north-west coast of Holland. She had become fond of Holland, and besides, Noordwijk was remote and isolated, away from publicity. She rented a cottage on the dunes of the seashore, called Villa Maria, and went there accompanied only by a cook.

Craig visited her just after she moved in, but soon went. He did, however, leave behind his dog, Black, to keep her company. For company she also for a while had her niece, Temple. She had wanted to invite several other pupils from the school as well, but Elizabeth, edgy about possible adverse publicity, would not permit this.

At the time, one of Craig's pressing concerns was to oversee the translation of his book, *The Art of the Theatre*, into Dutch, and with this end in view was spending a lot of time in Amsterdam berating his publishers. Although Amsterdam is only about 25 miles from Noordwijk, he visited Isadora only infrequently and briefly. The beginning of July found her writing him imploring letters – 'When you comin to see yo poo ole Rabbit?'

Her sense of isolation from him was not helped when, later that month, he went off for ten days to England, to visit both his mother and his devoted Elena. Towards the end of that time, he at last wrote to Isadora, who sent him a heartbreakingly desperate reply:

> Dearest – Just rec your letter – you can have no idea how anxious I have been – *10* days without a line – I thought you were run over by a London cab – I thought you *ill* – I thought the boat had gone down in the storm Saturday night – I pictured all sorts of fearful things that had happened to you – till I got a bad fever and

the nurse had to take my temperature every minute. Now I see I was quite *silly*, but you know just at this time ones nerves are not under control... For you dear heart I am so glad you are well, and also glad you see your dear Mother or see any that you love, and I can only repeat – if there is anyone you care for very much who feels unhappy and wants to come with you she can have half my little house with *all my heart*. It will give me *joy* – and Love is enough for all.

To fill her endless lonely hours of waiting, Isadora wrote. She compiled a series of five hundred exercises for the benefit of the pupils at the school, and after watching Temple playing on the shore (where she had scandalised some of the local residents by dancing naked), she composed an essay, 'A Child Dancing'. One of the things she observed in it was, 'She dances because she is full of the joy of life. She dances because the waves are dancing before her eyes, because the winds are dancing, because she can feel the rhythm of the dance through the whole of nature.'

Towards the end of August, with the birth of her child expected at any moment, she wrote desperately to her sculptor friend, Kathleen Bruce, asking her to come and be with her. As Kathleen recalled in her memoirs:

> It was a queer cry, childish and pathetic. Would not, could not I come to her? Her need was very great ... I went at once. I found her pitiful, helpless, and for the first time, endearing. 'Poor darling, what is the matter?' 'Can't you see?' Cried the dancer spreading high her lovely arms. Slowly, and with many a lie the story came out at last... Her baby was due in a month or two. She had dared tell nobody, not her mother or her sister... She was lonely and miserable.

While at Noordwijk, Kathleen observed Craig on his brief visits with some distaste, and noted that while he was there Isadora put on a brave face, but as soon as he left she 'sank back exhausted into the monotony of the long wait.'

Isadora's letters to Craig do not show the full depth of her despair. By now she was sinking into severe depression. One episode was especially bad. The press had discovered where she was, and the day before a reporter had attempted to get her to give him an interview. That night, wrote Kathleen:

175

I woke in the small hours aware that all was not well. I lay still for some time, telling myself that there was nothing unusual afoot. I heard nothing. Nevertheless, after a little anxious listening I got up and peeped very quietly into Isadora's room. The bed was empty. There was no light in the house. The front door was open. I dashed down our usual sandy path to the sea ... and there, straight ahead in deep water and some way out, I could surely see dimly a head and two hands and wrists extended. The sea was calm. I rushed in. The figure ahead did not move. As I neared it, calling, she turned around with a gentle, rather dazed look, and stretched out her arms to me with a faint, childish smile, saying, 'The tide was so low, I couldn't do it, and I'm so cold.' ... With infinite and patient care ... I undressed and rubbed [her down], filled hot-water bottles, and made hot drinks, murmuring soothing and lullaby-like consolation. 'There, there, go to sleep ... There, there ... We'll forget all about it.'

The baby did not arrive, as expected, at the end of August, but over three weeks later, on 24th September 1906. Isadora's labour, overseen by the local doctor, was long and agonising, but at the end of it she had a beautiful daughter – 'a perfect miniature,' she said, 'of Ellen Terry.'

When she asked Craig what name they should give the child, he replied, 'Call her anything you damn please – Sophocles, if you like.'

Chapter Ten

A Libido Unleashed

After the birth of her daughter, Isadora stayed in Noordwijk for five or six weeks, recuperating from her difficult labour, which had left her, she wrote to Craig, 'weak on my pins'.

At the time she left the seaside villa, towards the end of October 1906, he was in Rotterdam, organising an exhibition of his drawings at the Kunst-kring. Which naturally left him no time to help Isadora pack and move.

She arrived back at Grunewald at the beginning of November, with a blue-eyed baby girl whose presence naturally caused curiosity. If questioned, Isadora would answer evasively, saying such things as, 'Soon she will be the youngest pupil in the school.' Or, if pressed further, would explain that the baby was the grand-daughter of Ellen Terry. As to the baby's name, that had still not been decided upon, so for the moment she was known by the nickname of 'Snowdrop'.

Not having danced for some months, Isadora was now seriously hard up, and left Holland with many bills unpaid. Furthermore, she and Craig had borrowed money from the school, and although this money was in a sense hers, Elizabeth and Max Merz desperately needed it back.

Craig, unaware that Isadora was still too frail physically to resume dancing, continued to urge her to perform, and to prepare a new programme, as they had discussed. In the meantime, his own projects were beginning to bear fruit, after several years when he had done nothing but plan and prepare. As well as having written a successful book and mounted his exhibition in Rotterdam, there was a distinct possibility of his designing sets for the famous Eleanora Duse.

Duse was a surprisingly retiring woman for such a successful actress. She often abandoned the stage for considerable periods, claiming not to miss acting at all and once insisting that her ideal place to live would be on a boat in the middle of the ocean, with no human beings in sight. It was in November, during one of her periods of inactivity, that she had come to Berlin and met Craig at the house of Robert and Giulietta Mendelssohn. As Duse spoke only Italian and French, and Craig was not fluent in either, Isadora, who had worshipped Duse since seeing her perform in London, went with him to act as interpreter.

They had several meetings, discussing the theatre with, Isadora recalled, 'mutual enthusiasm', before Duse asked Craig if he would design the sets for a production she was planning of the late Henrik Ibsen's *Rosmersholm*. Initially it would be performed for just one night, at the Teatro alla Pergola in Florence, although there would later be other single performances in other cities.

Once they got down to serious discussion, Isadora, as interpreter, found she had a job on her hands. Both Duse and Craig had firm and differing ideas about how the set should be designed.

Ibsen, in the second half of his writing career, had become one of the influential creators of naturalistic drama, and one would have thought that much of the strength of a play like *Rosmersholm* derived from its having a realistic setting. But Craig was a visionary. Resting his concept on the subtlety and intensity of Ibsen's characters, he decided that, as he wrote at the time, 'It shall be made into a dream, a dream – DREAM.'

The play takes place entirely in the living-room of the house of the title, described in Ibsen's text as 'spacious, old-fashioned and comfortable.' The set Craig designed was described by his son and biographer, Edward, as 'a dark greeny-blue interior with an opening at the back looking out onto a misty "beyond"; the mistiness even pervaded the interior and the walls, which seemed more like great curtains merged into the floor like the roots of huge trees.' Isadora remembered it as 'a great Egyptian temple with [an] enormously high ceiling, extending upward to the skies, with walls receding into the distance. Only, unlike an Egyptian temple, at the far end there was a great, square window.'

When Craig showed his sketch of this to Duse, she objected, saying, 'I see this as a small window. It cannot possibly be a large one.' Isadora dutifully translated this to Craig, who said angrily, 'Tell her I won't have any damned woman interfering with my work!'

Diplomatically, Isadora translated this to Duse as, 'He says he admires your opinions and will do everything to please you.' Duse began to enlarge on her objections, and these Isadora (who seems to have secretly enjoyed the situation) translated to Craig as, 'Eleanora Duse says, as you are a great genius, she will not make any suggestions on your sketches, but will pass them as they are.'

With such subterfuge, she managed to make the [...] success, and keep the project, at least for the time being[...] and Craig, and baby Snowdrop, were on their way to Flo[...] the set's construction. On arrival, Craig instructed Isador[...] job would be to keep Duse away from the theatre whil[...] in progress.

Hiring two workmen he found on the street, he set to work. And Isadora did manage to waylay Duse each time she seemed to be getting dangerously close, saying things to her like, 'In a little while – You will soon see. Have patience.'

Soon the set was complete, and the nerve-racking day of the unveiling arrived, neither Craig nor Isadora being sure of what Duse's reaction would be.

When the massive set was revealed, there was a gasp from those present. Duse gazed at it speechlessly, and then Isadora saw that she was moved to tears. After a while, she strode to the stage and called, 'Gordon Craig! Come here!'

Craig joined her. She shook him by the hand and announced dramatically to everyone, 'It is my destiny to have found this great genius, Gordon Craig. I now intend to spend the rest of my career devoting myself only to showing his great work.' She then went on 'to denounce the whole modern trend of the theatre, all modern scenery, the modern conception of an actor's life and vocation,' declaring that, 'only through Gordon Craig will we poor actors find release from this montrosity, this charnel-house, which is the theatre of to-day!'

For a woman whose whole keynote in performance was quiet resignation, this was a surprisingly dramatic speech, but her enthusiasm was genuine. Craig was able to write to Martin Shaw, 'She has asked me to work with her in joy and freedom [and] to do three more Ibsen plays at once.'

The rest of the cast seemed a little unsure and on opening night, which took place on 6th December, so were the audience. When the curtain rose, revealing Craig's set, there was a moment of stunned silence, followed by puzzled murmuring. But, rather as had happened at Isadora's performance the night Stanislavsky first saw her, a strong voice rose above all the others, exclaiming, '*Bella, bella*'. It was Tomasso Salvini, then Italy's leading actor (and a frequent stage partner of Duse). Hearing him, the audience became hushed and respectful, and the performance was a considerable success.

Later, Craig wrote to Martin Shaw, saying, 'It was a success, and is. Duse was magnificent – threw her details to the winds and went in –

she has the courage of 25! ... The pleasure I got from seeing Miss Duncan watching my work with Duse was *infinite*.. I care not now whether anyone approves or disapproves of one point in my plan or a hundred – because I have that which *glows* to *accept* it without approval or disapproval.'

The episode highlights how very much Craig and Isadora were on the same wavelength artistically, and how much each admired the other's work, no matter how their personal relationship was foundering. A few weeks later, Isadora, writing to Craig, said, 'I can't tell you what I felt when I witnessed your wonderful work in Florence. Probably you have no idea how truly great & Beautiful it was. It was like something supernatural that a man with a thousand million *geni* at his disposal might create & I felt conscience stricken too that I had perhaps been the cause of you wasting some of your time on me – It would be a *Sin*.'

She was writing to him from Poland, because again she had begun touring, in spite of the fact that she was still weak and exhausted. Returning from Florence to Berlin, she had given her baby into the care of her mother, sending them, with the baby's nurse, Fräulein Kist, to stay in San Remo, on the Italian Riviera. Then she had gathered her music and scenery and costumes and set off by train for Warsaw, where she was due to make her first appearance on 17th December.

Poland in those days was part of the Russian Empire, with Warsaw having the status of a provincial capital, and on this trip she had difficulty obtaining a Russian passport. As she wrote to Craig, 'I spent one day going half way to Warsaw & back and the next in rushing around all the Consuls American & Russian trying to get a passport, completely *Capoot*.'

Part of her difficulty may have arisen from the fact that newspapers had cottoned on to the news that she had a baby and no husband. Poland being a staunchly Catholic country, this news did not go down well there. Indeed, the director of the Warsaw Philharmonic, which had been hired to accompany her, wrote to Craig (still functioning as her agent) demanding to know the name of her husband. Craig replied that this information was 'Not the affair of the public.'

Isadora had not been able to fully admit to Craig what a weakened state she was in. As she wrote years later in her memoirs:

I was not in the least prepared for the ordeal of a tour... The first separation from my baby, and also the separation from Craig and Duse, were very painful. Also my health was in a precarious

180

condition, and, as the baby was only half weaned, it was necessary to have the milk drawn from my breasts with a little machine. This was a ghastly experience for me, and caused me many tears.

Not only that, during her train journey she had developed toothache. Nonetheless, her first performance, two days later, went well. She wrote to Craig, 'I slipped into my old dresses & my old dances last night like a Charm. After rehearsing orchestra all day – & great agony of spirit – suddenly I found myself dancing like a miracle. Art or whatever you may choose to call it – every little finger movement came in its old place. I was hardly conscious of my body at all ... last night was a real Joy!'

But things soon got worse. Of her next night's performance she wrote, 'Dear heart – as much as I joy in your presence I am *glad* you are not here. This is all *too much suffering*... I got through the performance some old way tonight but it was awful.'

Her toothache meant that during her few weeks in Poland she would visit the dentist ten times. Also her digestion was upset. Unable to keep food down, she tried eating such things as oysters and raw eggs as a simple invalid diet. Which made her worse. To Craig she wrote, 'Been dreful ill. Dr says *poisoned* oysters caviar or something – Am up & better now – [castor] oil every hour all day yesterday – spare you details.'

Nor were things running smoothly at the theatre where she was appearing. She had disagreements with the orchestra (possibly because at this time she was attempting a musical sacrilege by having some of Chopin's piano pieces arranged for orchestra, and Chopin was, after all, a Pole). She also had difficulties with the theatre director, the house manager and the backstage staff. And with the Polish agency that had arranged her bookings. Some of these disagreements were financial. After various deductions, the money she eventually received for her appearances totalled only one-third of her agreed fee, which meant that on her whole visit she barely broke even. On top of this, she was unable to make her scheduled appearance in the city of Lodz because, as part of the continuing rumbles of unrest in the Russian Empire, there were riots there. All theatrical performances were cancelled.

She left Warsaw on 10th January 1907, delighted to be returning to Berlin and Craig. She wrote to him, 'no woman in Siberia could be more pleased... Yes I want those kisses I do – I'm coming right along... Get that Brass Band out I'm coming.'

At the same time she was considerably concerned that he had booked her to set off on a tour of Holland almost immediately. Her health really wasn't up to it, and at one appearance in Amsterdam, where her tour began, she had to abandon her performance while dancing to a Chopin waltz. Visibly upset, she explained to the audience that she was ill, that her illness had prevented her rehearsing properly with the orchestra, and apologised for a ruined evening.

The audience applauded her generously, but she had to be taken back to her hotel in a state of collapse. Two days later, on 29th January, Craig was with her. The rest of her Dutch tour was cancelled, and she would remain resting in Amsterdam for several weeks.

In her memoirs she wrote, 'I think it had something to do with [my] milk. What they call milk fever.' (This fever, sometimes occurring in women who have recently given birth, was at one time thought to be caused simply by milk swelling the breasts, but is now believed to be due to an infection.) But she had also been suffering from severe menstrual cramps, made worse by the fact that during the prolonged birth to her daughter some of her internal tissues had been torn. In the light of modern knowledge it seems clear that her whole hormonal balance was seriously upset.

Unfortunately, Craig was unable to stay with her for more than a few days, because he had to return to Berlin and then go on to Nice, where Duse was preparing another performance of *Rosmersholm* (since Florence, she had also given one-night performances in Milan and Genoa).

Craig arrived at the theatre in Nice to discover that his set – the set that Isadora had found so 'great & Beautiful' – had ruthlessly been cut down by Duse to fit the smaller stage. As his son and biographer, Edward Craig, wrote, 'His fury knew no bounds, and after telling everyone in the theatre what he thought of them in English, with the introduction of various French and German words such as "cretins", "imbeciles" and "dummkopfs", he rushed off to find Duse.'

'What have you done?' he stormed at her. 'You have ruined my work. You have destroyed my Art! You, from whom I expected so much.' After much more of the same Duse had had enough. Angrily she dismissed him from her presence, and that was the end of their association. Her next performance of *Rosmersholm*, in Vienna, would be on a set by somebody else.

Isadora, still an invalid, had herself brought to Nice, hoping if possible to sort out the situation, or at least to reassure and comfort Craig. But she herself was too downhearted to be much comfort. 'She is so troubled,' Craig wrote to a friend. 'She's down, *down*.' Finding her company depressing, he fled to Florence, the city which had seemed so hopeful to him only a couple of months before. He moved into a villa lent to him by Charles Loeser, an American art collector, and would essentially base himself in Florence for the next seven years (in a succession of borrowed dwellings). Writing to him from Nice, Isadora said, 'So you have a villa. Bedad! It sounds very imposing.'

Although he was detaching himself emotionally (and geographically) from Isadora, he retained his admiration for her Art, and continued to function as her agent. From Florence he suggested that she resume her tour of Holland by 10th March, and a letter from her in Nice, dated 23rd February, gives her reply:

It kills me to say it but I'm afraid March 10th is impossible – O Lord! – I am still lying very flat & *pains* all over –
I came 'unwell' yesterday 22 ... I will be in bed a week more, the Dr says, & then it will be at least 2 weeks before I am strong enough to walk – practice – dance – ...
All this is despairing – the constant pain & constant powders. I feel a bit discouraged. Last night I was a bit cracky!

A few days later she was writing:

The Dr now says it's a form of nervous prostration. What next? He has just been here – he says no performance possible till the first of April! Otherwise he says I would only fall ill again & hints it would then be a profitable commission for the Undertaker!

And later again:

Getting well is really hard work. My spirits feel equal to anything & then I find my feet dragging & body like lead – Enough to make one Swear Horribly. I am so impatient to be strong – I want to feel the earth spring under me again – I do not wish to die yet or even by halves – but repeat to me those magic words – say you love me & my old husk will fall off. I will bloom up anew for you.

But Craig had decided he was at one of those moments in his life when it was time to make a clean sweep of the past and move on. All the signs were there. Not only did he seem to be entering into a period of productivity in his work, but in March 1907 his mother had married

183

again. She had married an American named Usselmann, who acted successfully for years under the name of James Carew. He was three years younger than Craig himself.

In Florence, starting a new chapter in his life, Craig began having affairs with other women. News of these filtered back to sister Elizabeth in Grunewald and, never having liked or trusted Craig, she passed on any such gossip to Isadora.

Isadora, realising that her sister was 'stage-managing', did her best to rise above her hurt by being philosophical. As she wrote to Craig, 'There are lots of clever and prettier people in the world than I – Heaps – if I turn out to be jealous of them all I will soon be dead – from the strain.' But years later, in her memoirs, she admitted, 'Visions of Craig in all his beauty in the arms of other women haunted me at night, until I could no longer sleep. Visions of Craig explaining his Art to women who gazed at him with adoring eyes – visions of Craig being pleased with other women – looking at them with that winning smile of his... Taking an interest in them, caressing them... All this drove me to fits of alternate fury and despair.'

To Craig, however, at the time, she forced herself to sound calm and accepting:

> Dear, you need not worry about me. It is true I am still somewhat ill & [in] a great deal of pain but your power of giving me joy is so great that the dear lines you write me make up for all else. It is perhaps just from having to lie so still & being so much in pain that I have more joy – it sounds a bit Irish but it is really so – life dulls things a good deal & this being in a way half out of life Love shines more clear – So don't worry about me – *I'm not unhappy*.

At least her health shortly took a turn for the better. 'The neuralgia pains have suddenly left me. Queer – Gone as suddenly as they came.' It wasn't long before she was able to return to Berlin, be joined there by her mother and her baby, and begin a period of convalescence. She had given up her apartment and taken up living in her school. Soon she was writing to Craig, 'had a good rest – & I feel so well again. I take long walks in the woods with Temple & we both dance for joy of all the opening buds.'

At around this time Isadora's friend and disciple Mary D'Este, and her son Preston, now aged eight, returned to Europe. They had not managed their annual trip in 1906 because, just as they were about to sail from

New York, Mary's husband, Solomon Sturges, had been involved in a bad road accident, breaking several bones including his skull. Mary returned to Chicago to nurse him through a long slow recovery. But the accident had left Solomon prey to erratic behaviour. He had come this year to Paris with his wife and stepson, and while there had climbed out onto a window-ledge and theatened suicide. Mary had arranged for him to be shipped back to Chicago, while she and Preston travelled on to visit Isadora. They spent some weeks around the school, where young Preston, somewhat reluctanctly, for a while adopted Greek costume.

In another letter to Craig, Isadora wrote:

> I practice a little each day. The beginning is like breaking stones. One loves to work when once begun, but it is so difficult to reach the right state to begin – sometimes I wish I might dissolve into a mist rather than begin again...
>
> To wrench oneself from Time & place and self & enter where time & place & self do not exist – that is a great pain – but then also a great reward. Is anything comparable to the feeling of having come in contact with that eternal idea of Beauty – a wrench, an awful suffering, a feeling of battering for ages against an impassable barrier, & then suddenly & sharply a glow, a light, a connection with the idea like entering into a God – a happiness indescribable, triumphant.

And in the midst of all this painful yet triumphant journey towards health and vitality, there is also her unbearable yearning that it might yet be all right between them:

> As for you – you must follow what your Demon says, I would not dare to say ... (the Baby is now howling like a veritable Bogie. There – I turned her on her Tummie & she stopped – now she's trying to chew the end of this paper – Well, that's a kiss for Papa –) I can't live without you: that's true. I think my Body & Soul contains parts of you & I long for you, but I'd rather you be a million miles away from me & know you *happy* or at *least* happy you know what I mean.

Craig, still navvying away to make good his escape, reminded her in a letter of the existence of Elena Meo in London, by writing that Nelly (Elena) had been ill and needed his help. Isadora replied:

185

I thank you for what you wrote me about N. I have often wanted to speak to you about her. I know it is a good heart & filled with love for you – and I have often thought of her and I thank you because it shows ... you have forgiven my stupid jealousy of which I have been many times ashamed – but I swear to you there is no vestige of it left. Perhaps it was the pain of the Baby which cleared it all out – only love is left... I mean I can't write what I mean but you know. It's just Love Love Love.

She was well enough to dance again in Amsterdam on 3rd April. Craig sent her a good-luck telegram, and next morning she wrote telling him, 'Everything went well last night. My legs were a bit *weak & wobbly* but I took great joy in dancing & thought of you & danced to a harmony of Love.'

She went on to give concerts in The Hague on 4th April, in Utrecht on the 6th, in The Hague again on the 8th, in Leyden on the 10th, and in Haarlem on the 12th. These six performances should have given her a useful bankroll, but her booking agent for Holland, whose name was Stumpff, insisted that their contract stated he was simply to *provide* an orchestra, not *pay* for it. That was her responsibility. He took it out of her fee, and she could do nothing but accept the situation. She wrote to Craig, 'Let Stumpff revel in his old guldens. I will go up to Berlin as this hotel simple robbery. I will send you by bank tomorrow what is left of the fray – And I will send you a list of my expenses etc. – ...'

She went to Berlin, where she was happy to be reunited with her baby daughter. Then she was off to Stockholm to give a series of performances between 4th and 15th May. She stayed at the Grand Hotel, and Craig joined her there, although it must have been a stiff and unsatisfactory reunion. They travelled back together to Germany, parting in Heidelberg – he to Florence, she to Grunewald. And that was the end of their love-affair, although Isadora had not yet fully realised it, and although they would continue to support each other's work. Craig was working on designing a marionette theatre – a development of his idea that the ideal actor would be a sort of super-puppet – and Isadora promised to send him money towards the project.

Summing up their relationship towards the end of her life, Isadora wrote:

His love was young, fresh, and strong, but he had neither the nerves nor nature of a voluptuary, but preferred to turn from

186

lovemaking before satiety set in, and to translate the fiery energy of his youth to the magic of his Art...

One never spent a dull moment with him. No, he was always in the throes of highest delight or the other extreme – in those moods which suddenly followed after, when the whole sky seemed to turn black, and a sudden apprehension filled all the air. One's breath was slowly pumped from the body, and nothing was left anywhere but the blackness of anguish...

It was my fate to inspire the great love of this genius, and it was my fate to endeavour to reconcile the continuing of my own career with his love. Impossible combination! After the first few weeks of wild, impassioned lovemaking, jealousy, that green-eyed serpent, possessed him; and I may say that I was a martyr to his difficult moods and caprices. He was jealous of my family, jealous of my School, jealous even of my ideas... And yet Gordon Craig appreciates my Art as no one else has ever appreciated it. But his *amour propre*, his jealousy as an artist, would not allow him to admit that any woman would really be an artist.

Craig, in his own memoirs, written thirty years after hers, was still striving to justify his behaviour towards her, saying, 'Why should I suppose she might help? Because I supposed she could understand – and she did not understand any deeper than did the others. I was wrong to expect it of anyone... How very idealistic – how absurd.' At least he felt the need to justify.

During the summer of 1907 Isadora, with her brother Augustin taking over the role of her manager, danced mostly in Germany, but with little financial success. Attendances were poor and Augustin was not a good organiser. Still in touch with Craig (and sending him money), she wrote, 'Gus is good & dear but not very *quick*. Dates fix themselves and vanish in the most irritating fashion.'

And in another letter, 'I have seldom in my life spent a more disagreeable time since – since you left. I telegraphed you yesterday to know if when things are fixed up here I should meet you somewhere or go on to Berlin until performance there... Must do one or other as money is given out. Those small affairs in Heidelberg & Baden only paid hotel bill.'

On 28th June she did perform in Berlin, with her pupils, but that had its problems because in order to obtain their 'special permit', they had to show a rehearsal to a police official. As Isadora reported to Craig, 'We put all the little girls in long dresses & he looked in vain for a single leg.'

12th July 1907 found her dancing again with her pupils, this time outdoors in Mannheim, at a vast festival celebrating the city's 300th anniversary. They made only two thousand marks (half of which Isadora sent to Craig, apologising for the amount being so small). 'Making money in summer,' she told him, 'is like trying to hold water in a sieve. Things are beginning to go forward but we need that *Business* man.'

Apparently Craig had been hoping there would be a meeting between them, perhaps so that she could apologise for hampering him in his work by sending so little, for he wrote, rather rudely, 'I expected to see you the day after Mannheim – but I expect you have lost the map – or your head – or some other trifle.'

To this she replied, 'You will have to tell your people there that they must wait till winter – there is no other way... I wish I could write something to comfort you... Dearest Dreamer, this is a pretty silly world & I'm afraid you needed someone a bit stronger than your poor Topsy to help you.' Which letter Craig believed showed the influence of Elizabeth, more in the lack of forthcoming money than in Isadora's confession of weakness.

Some people tend to feel aggrieved towards those they have injured, and by the time Craig came to write his memoirs, over fifty years later, he had worked his self-justification into:

> Damme if Madame Duncan didn't let me down & ... What's worse sent no word of excuse.
>
> From that day I have never forgiven this: I don't mind what anyone does or says to me – but if they in any way show disrespect for my work once I am at work (when warm at it) then click goes the apparatus & it's all over between me & whoever has played me the trick.

But Isadora was not yet fully aware how great was the distance Craig had placed between her and himself. In September, after her summer of performing, she went to Venice for a short holiday and, as Venice is not so very far from Florence – some 120 miles – she hoped to see him, writing, 'I bathe in the sea & am feeling much better and stronger. If at the end of the month you don't come I will & see you – *if* you want me. Do you?' (She underlined the word '*if*' fourteen times.)

Presumably Craig's reply touched again on how badly let down he felt by her, for a few days later she was writing, 'Don't expect such wonders of people, our ancestors were only lately throwing coconuts at each other's

188

heads & swinging by their curly tails.' To which he replied angrily, 'And so I expect too much of people... Rather do I think we have gone back a stage or two since we hung by the tail and caught fleas as an art.'

Even an artist as perceptive as Isadora can be blinded by hope, and even after such a letter she eagerly made her way to Florence and to Craig. She found their meeting short and painful, and after twenty-four hours left the city. Craig, recording their meeting at the time, wrote, 'I had found it impossible to kiss her as in the grand days. Maybe she had heard that the tears of a woman soften the heart of a man who loves her and whom she loves – but I gave no sign that I had seen any tears: from head to foot I suffered, but my cloak hid that.'

Isadora wrote to him from Cologne:

> Dear Ted you have a funny effect on your Topsy! You fill me with a Longing & Pain that are terrible. I felt I would rather *die* than leave Florence, & each jog of the train was like torture. It is probably better that I am not there. I have no strength when I am near you – I only want to fly into you & die... All my heart's love to you – & what I can't express.

The realisation that Craig was not for her, and probably never had been, threw her into what she later described as a 'frenzied state'. Now thoroughly awakened to the joys and satisfactions of making love, she missed sex. But she also missed the enjoyment, the sense of togetherness and rootedness, of having a loving sharing partner.

Believing that she would never find another man who was perfect for her in every way, as she felt Craig would have been, she gradually came to the conclusion that she would never find a partner in life, and that the next best thing would be to have a succession of lovers who were able to be partial partners – as if they, added together, might make up some fraction of the complete man she had hoped for. This approach to life would eventually merge in her mind with ideas about freedom for women – for the New Woman, as the ideal was known at the time. In 1922 she would tell a New York reporter, 'One cannot make rules for life, or rules for marriage. Life comes, and one lives, each day. I am opposed to marriages. I believe in the emancipation of women.'

The first in her line of temporary lovers was not long in appearing on the scene. Only a week or so after her disastrous parting from Craig in Florence, she was performing in Amsterdam when, as she recalled in her memoirs:

189

He entered one afternoon: fair, debonair, young, blond, perfectly dressed. He said, 'My friends call me Pim.'

I said, 'Pim! What a charming name. Are you an artist?'

'Oh, no!' he disclaimed, as if I had accused him of some crime.

'Then what have you? A Great Idea!'

'Oh, dear no. I have no ideas at all,' he said.

Here was my remedy. I had signed a contract to tour Russia – a long, arduous tournée, not only through North Russia, but South Russia and the Caucasus as well, and I dreaded the long journeys alone.

'Will you come with me to Russia, Pim?'

Pim would. A Dutchman from The Hague, his real name was Willem Noothoven van Goor, and, in Isadora's words, 'His golden hair [was] like a bed of golden tulips; his lips like rose tulips; and when he embraced me I felt as though I were floating away on a bed of thousands of tulips in the spring of Holland.' Although predominantly homosexual, he was for Isadora an accomplished and affectionate lover, offering her, she wrote, no romance or idealism, just 'pure delightful pleasure'.

Before they set off for Russia, in October 1907, she had to accept other future absences from her life. Her brother Augustin and her mother had both decided to return to America, and by the time she returned from her Russian tour they would both be gone. The Clan Duncan was at last disintegrating.

Augustin had been finding his life rather at a standstill – being a not-very-effective business manager for his sister did not promise much in the way of a career – and he had decided to go back home and resume his life in the theatre. Although his marriage to Sarah was increasingly rocky, she went with him. Their daughter, Temple, remained at the school.

Isadora's mother, increasingly irritable and depressed, had become more and more homesick for San Francisco, a feeling that had been intensified the previous year when news reached Europe of the disastrous earthquake and fire there on 18th April 1906.

Isadora continued to correspond with Craig, partly out of her enduring love for him and partly to keep in touch with the father of her daughter. Writing of her mother at this time she reported, 'Wild horses would not hold her. She has cost me a small fortune & now I think dear brother Gus may take care of her for a time.'

This was a difficult period for Isadora. For the first time in her life

190

she was alone. Since infancy, apart from short tours with Augustin Daly and Loie Fuller, she had been part of a close-knit family. Now she had neither family nor lover, for Pim was not truly a lover, simply a barrier against loneliness.

Stopping in Warsaw with Pim, en route to Russia, she wrote to Craig again, saying, 'I have been en fête perpetual here – champagne & dancing – it was the only alternative to suicide. The only way possible to stand Varsovie was to be continually *drunk!*' (Craig noted in the margin of this despair-racked letter that he thought she was a great fool.)

Accompanying Isadora to Russia in a professional capacity was Craig's on-and-off colleague in United Arts Management, Maurice Magnus, acting as her manager. In St Petersburg they were also joined by sister Elizabeth and the pupils from the school. It had been Isadora's sudden inspiration to have them dance at the end of her performances as a means of publicising the school and helping drum up funds for it. She was tired of shouldering most of its financial burden herself, and was looking earnestly for either a rich man or a public body to provide its backing. At the end of each of her Russian engagements she would step forward and implore the audience, '*Aidez-moi! Aidez-moi!*'

When she and her company reached Moscow, in January 1908, she visited the Moscow Arts Theatre, where she was received by its director and co-founder, Stanislavsky, as a guest of honour. She raised the question of her school perhaps becoming part of his organisation, but he could offer no hope of that happening. He did, however, suggest that the Russian state might be prepared to offer support, and advised her to approach the Director of the Imperial Theatres, Vladimir Telyakovsky (and warning her 'not to abuse the old Ballet too much.') She did try Telyakovsky, but without success.

In other ways, however, her association with Stanislavsky was a fruitful one. He was, in 1907, at the beginning of working out his theories about the craft of acting that would eventually be published in two influential books – *An Actor Prepares* (1936) and *Building a Character* (1948) – and create the approach to acting known in America as the Method. He and Isadora had many long conversations about performing and, as he recalled in the 1920s:

The necessity to see her often was dictated from within me by an artistic feeling that was closely related to her art. Later, when I became acquainted with her methods as well as with the ideas of her great friend Craig, I came to know that in different corners of

191

the world, due to conditions unknown to us, various people in various spheres sought in Art the same naturally born creative principles...

It became clear to me that [she and I] were looking for one and the same thing in different branches of art...

[At one] time, speaking of a performance of hers that was just over, during which visitors had come to her dressing-room and interfered with her preparations, she explained:

'I cannot dance that way. Before I go out on the stage, I must place a motor in my soul. When that begins to work my legs and arms and my whole body will move independently of my will. But if I do not get time to put that motor in my soul, I cannot dance.'

Isadora's hard-won understanding of how to dance with true expression and involvement helped crystallise Stanislavsky's growing ideas about acting, and he later credited her with being one of his major inspirations.

She also explained to him in some detail the Ideas of Gordon Craig, and did all she could to encourage Stanislavsky to invite Craig to come to Moscow and work with the Arts Theatre.

While in Moscow, she rather lost the attentions of her friend Pim, who embarked enthusiastically on what Maurice Magnus would describe as a 'violent friendship' with a discarded lover of Anna Pavlova's named Joseph Ravicz. For a while Ravicz also became one of Isadora's lovers.

She made a play for Stanislavsky too. As she recalled, 'One night I looked at him, with his handsome figure, broad shoulders, black hair, just turning to grey on the temples, and something within me revolted at always playing this rôle of Egeria.' (Ægeria, a prophetic nymph, or minor goddess, was said to have advised Numa Pompilius, second king of Rome, in establishing forms of worship, and her name thus became poetic shorthand for a wise female counsellor.)

Isadora openly pursued Stanislavsky, drinking with him late into the night and doing all she could to be vibrant and amusing. Eventually, one night she invited him to a restaurant. There, she insisted on a private room and, once in it, ordered champagne. It wasn't long before she threw her arms round his neck and kissed him full on the mouth. He returned her kiss, but tenderly, not passionately, and from then on politely kept his distance. He was, Isadora decided, 'too much married.'

Towards the end of January, still in Moscow, she wrote in one of her letters to Craig, 'Everything here is freezing – something unthinkable, the cold ... long, long stretches of snow & finally the Sea – all frozen.

I asked myself when I saw it – Why am I a dancing dervish & why am I up here at the North Pole?'

Her tour of Russia was in two parts. Late in February she and her company returned to Grunewald, but by April she was back, again accompanied by Maurice Magnus, but this time without Elizabeth and the children (or Pim). She toured Kiev, Tbilisi, Kharkov, Rostov and the Crimea, explaining in a letter to Craig, 'I am trying to make enough money to rest from June to October without dancing & stay quiet some place with the Baby.'

The baby had now finally been given a name. She was to be called 'Deirdre'. This was a name that until recently had mostly occurred only in Irish legend, but this was the time of that upflux of somewhat mystical Irish consciousness, expressed in all the arts, that was known as the Celtic Revival. Among its leaders, both George William Russell (who wrote as 'AE') and W.B.Yeats had written plays called *Deirdre*, and soon the name became a fashionable one.

The school at Grunewald was continuing to cause Isadora anxiety. Quite apart from her difficulty in earning or attracting enough money to support it, and she was feeling continuing pressure from the puritanical views of respectable Germans, from the Kaiserin down.

So towards the end of April, setting off with her children for another performing and fund-raising tour around Holland, Belgium and France, she made the decision to dismiss the teaching staff from the school and close it down. In order not to disturb her pupils, they were not informed until they reached Paris, when to their surprise they were taken by omnibus to a small house alongside a church – its former rectory. This, they were told by Elizabeth, would be their home for the time being.

Isadora's hope of a quiet rest-period after June did not materialise. It was suggested to her by the American-born Duchess of Manchester that she might be able to attract financial support for the school if she danced in England, and a tour there was soon arranged. She (and her pupils) would be under the management of Charles Frohman, one of Broadway's most powerful producers of musicals and revues. Martin Shaw would come along as her musical director, and she would also take with her her baby daughter Deirdre.

Isadora was a little nervous about appearing in England, being aware that during her time in London she had failed to build much of a reputation. As she wrote to Craig, 'Wish me luck! We open Duke of York Theatre July 6, under Charles Frohman – it has all been arranged inside of one week & I feel dizzy... If only we have a success ... I am frightened to death – Pray for us.'

There was, however, one reason why she was pleased to be performing in England with the Frohman publicity machine behind her.

By this time (1908), in the wake of her success, there were maybe a dozen women calling themselves 'art dancers' and appearing on the stages of Europe and America. But they were debasing what she was striving to create.

There was Maud Allan, for example. A Toronto-born dancer, some four years older than Isadora, she had approached her in Berlin in 1904. She had then been dancing in Europe for about a year, with little success, and her attitude to dance was similar to Idaora's – she regarded it as an art form in its own right.

Presenting herself as an admirer and fellow-dancer, unable to afford theatre seats, she asked if there was any way she could watch Isadora dancing. Generously, Isadora gave her free tickets to several of her performances. And was none too pleased when, some weeks later, Maud Allan joined the growing band of Isadora copyists, dancing barefoot in Greek costume to such composers as Mendelssohn, Strauss and Chopin, and worse, publicising herself as having been Isadora's pupil.

Even using such devious means, Maud's career had failed to prosper, so in 1907 she abandoned any hope of making a living by purely artistic dancing, and prepared a decidedly *risqué* number, to music specially written by the Belgian composer Maurice Rémy, based on the story of Salome and her dance of the Seven Veils.

The popularity (and notoriety) of this biblical story had begun in 1891 when Oscar Wilde retold it as a play in verse. Banned from performance in England by the Lord Chamberlain's office (whose approval was needed in those days), on the grounds that it was illegal to depict a biblical character on-stage, it was published by Wilde in book form in 1893, illustrated by Aubrey Beardsley with somewhat irrelevant drawings whose sexuality caused even more scandal than the play itself.

In 1907 Richard Strauss composed his opera, *Salome*, based on Wilde's play, and that too was banned in England. It was also quickly withdrawn from the repertory of the Metropolitan Opera in New York. So the story was a wonderfully scandalous one to base a suggestive dance on, and although Maud Allan might not have been the first dancer to do so, she was soon the most famous among the numerous Salomes that dominated the music-hall during the years from 1907 to 1910. A London newspaper somewhat overheatedly described her performance:

Her feet, slender and arched, beat a sensual measure. The desire that flames from her lips and bursts in hot flames from her scarlet mouth infects the air with the madness of passion. Swaying like a white witch with yearning arms and hands that plead, Miss Allan is such a delicious embodiment of lust that she might win forgiveness with the sins of her wonderful flesh... Before her rises the head she has danced for, and the lips that would not touch her in life she kisses again and again.

This was a long way from the purity of Dance that Isadora had spent so much time perfecting and campaigning for. In spite of her occasional 'Dionysian' performances, her own dancing was famously non-titillating (partly because she never intended it to be), and to know of this debasement of her Art was galling. More so because the press (and publicists) had at this time whipped up a somewhat spurious 'War of the Dancers', arguing whether the greatest dancer in the world was Maud Allan, Isadora, or the American-based ballerina, Adeline Genée, who was being vigorously promoted by her producer, Florenz Ziegfeld.

Interviewed on the subject of Mlle Genée, Isadora said, 'But *why*? Why put us together? One has respect for Mademoiselle Genée. She has trained for many years and won an honourable place in her profession. She is an excellent acrobat. But if you are speaking of an art ...' Appearing in London for Charles Frohman might do something to let audiences see real Art, and realise what a truly higher and better form of dance hers was.

Frohman of course had his own agenda. He had signed Isadora so that he too would have a famous solo dancer under his wing, and all his publicity for her tended to give the impression that here was a dancer who would out-Allan Allan. Especially as she was billed as 'the Sensation of the Continent' and supported by 'Twenty Parisian Dancers' (everybody in England knew what Continentals were like – especially Parisians).

His attempts at publicising Isadora and her pupils in this way did not really succeed. More high-minded papers, like the London *Times*, might well comment that 'Her dancing is as finely imagined as it was,' and that 'the artist has gained in command of her resources,' but reviews like that were hardly going to pull in the panting punters.

All the same, her London appearances were by no means a disaster. To Craig she reported, 'I have had very nice audiences here, as nice as any place – & it has almost cured the terrible fear I had of London engendered by almost starving to death here 8 years ago.'

To the general public, Isadora's pupils had been even more of a success than she was, dancing with her in *Iphigénie* as her attendants and playmates, and performing German folk songs and dances on their own. The novelist John Galsworthy, after attending a performance, wrote an article about them, calling it 'Delight':

> I was taken by a friend one afternoon to a theatre. When the curtain was raised, the stage was perfectly empty save for tall grey curtains which enclosed it on all sides, and presently through the thick folds of those curtains children came dancing in, singly or in pairs, till a whole troop of ten or twelve were assembled. They were all girls; none, I think, more than fourteen years old, one or two certainly not more than eight. They wore but little clothing, their legs, feet and arms being quite bare. Their hair, too, was unbound; and their faces, grave and smiling, were so utterly dear and joyful, that in looking on them one felt transported to some Garden of Hesperides, where self was not, and the spirit floated in pure ether. Some of these children were fair and rounded, others dark and elf-like; but one and all looked entirely happy, and quite unself-conscious, giving no impression of artifice, though they evidently had the highest and most careful training. Each flight and whirling movement seemed conceived there and then out of the joy of being – dancing had surely never been a labour to them, either in rehearsal or performance. There was no tiptoeing and posturing, no hopeless muscular achievement; all was rhythm, music, light, air, and above all things, happiness. Smiles and love had gone into the fashioning of their performance; and smiles and love shone from every one of their faces and from the clever white turnings of their limbs...

Queen Alexandra, wife of King Edward VII, came twice to see Isadora and the children, and at a private performance at the estate of the Duchess of Manchester, who had suggested the whole London engagement, the children danced for both the King and the Queen.

A highlight for Isadora on this visit to London was that at last she met Craig's mother, and Deirdre's grandmother, the witty and talented Ellen Terry. At the beginning of August she wrote to Craig, 'Meeting your mother has been a great thing. She is so marvelous – so Beautiful so kind – She was like a great Lovely Goddess Angel to me – & the two nights she came to the Theatre I danced like a dream.'

Ellen Terry had even done her bit at one of the performances she attended, springing to her feet and herself haranguing the audience with, 'Do you realise what you are looking at? Do you understand that this is the most incomparably beautiful dancing in the world? Do you appreciate what this woman is doing for you – bringing back the lost beauty of the old world of art?'

Craig was naturally furious to learn of Isadora's friendship with his mother – a friendship between these two women who had done so much to let him down. He was additionally furious to hear from Martin Shaw that her new slate-blue curtains had been taken by some as his work (she had recently increased their height from about six feet to a towering twenty-five). Although clearly this change had been partly inspired by the long conversations she and he had had about staging, Craig was inclined to interpret what she had done as a clear case of piracy.

While in London, Isadora was also able to meet again several old friends, among them Kathleen Bruce, whose recent engagement to Captain Scott she was able to help celebrate.

The London appearances of Isadora and her pupils were proving enough of a success to reassure Charles Frohman about her commercial potential, and on 7th July 1908 he announced that during the following month he would be bringing Isadora to America for a twenty-week tour, beginning in New York. (Unfortunately, her pupils would be unable to perform there as well. Recent child-labour laws, rigorously enforced by a watchdog organisation called the Gerry Society, banned children under sixteen from doing almost anything on stage beyond merely walking on.)

In an interview printed in the *New York Times* on 2nd August, while she was still in London, Isadora commented, 'A mad idea it is, going to America to dance in the middle of August. New York must be a furnace, but Mr Frohman wants to get me there before imitations of my dance are done everywhere. Personally, I can't see what difference it makes.'

Not only were her pupils not making the trip to America with her, neither was Deirdre. This was simply because to take her would make life difficult. Isadora, wishing to keep Craig involved with their daughter, suggested that the three of them should meet in Ostend before she set sail for America, but Craig refused.

As it happened, his mistress, Elena Meo, was shortly to join him in Florence with their three children. She did, but shortly after she and the children arrived there, Craig whizzed off to Moscow where, thanks to Isadora, Stanislavsky wanted him to discuss a proposed production of *Hamlet* at the Arts Theatre. During these discussions, which went on for months, Stanislavsky would suggest that Isadora be cast in the role of

Ophelia, saying that in his opinion she was the performer who could best portray Ophelia's 'stillness', but Craig refused to entertain the idea.

Isadora's pupils (and Deirdre) returned with Elizabeth to the Paris rectory they had been living in, and she herself set off across the Atlantic aboard the *St Louis*. The 1908 Olympics, held in London, had just finished, and the American team was also aboard. An American newspaper reported, 'Miss Duncan was seen every day... With the young men returning from the Marathon races in London. In conversation and whenever they were together, they were talking about feats of strength.'

Frohman's advertising for Isadora in America billed her as 'The Rage of London'. He had initially booked her to appear for three weeks at the Criterion theatre on 43rd Street. She would be the sole performer at every performance, and much of Frohman's publicity leant on this fact, describing her appearance as 'a feat of endurance, never previously seen outside Europe... She will be the first example of a single artist devoting a whole evening to dancing, unrelieved by song, skit, or recitation.'

Maybe the word 'unrelieved' didn't help, but her appearances drew only meagre audiences. As in London, the more cultured critics were sympathetic to her dancing. The notoriously severe Henry Taylor Parker of the *Boston Evening Transcript* (who signed his reviews 'HTP' and was generally known as 'Hard To Please') wrote:

> The captivating quality of Miss Duncan's motion is its innocence... Her joy speaks in every motion of her body, in the play of her arms, in the carriage of her head, in the responsive flow and swirl of her draperies...
>
> ...She moves often in long and lovely sensuous lines across the whole breadth or down the whole depth of the stage. Or she circles it in curves of no less jointless beauty. As she moves her body is steadily and delicately undulating. One motion flows or ripples or sweeps into another... No deliberate crescendo and climax order her movements, rather they come and go in endless flux as if each were creating the next...
>
> It is the custom to speak of absolute music – of music ... that imparts nothing but itself, and that makes its own beauty and its own emotion ... Miss Duncan's dancing is absolute dancing in a still fuller sense. It is peculiar to itself, it knows no rule and it has no customs except for those that she imposes... It accomplishes its ends in seeming spontaneity and innocence... It really achieves them – it is easy to suspect – by calculated, practical and reflective artistry.

But, much more than in London, the general public stayed away, and her performances were not helped, as she had feared, by the August heat. After the first of her three weeks she was obliged by exhaustion to reduce her number of appearances a week from seven to four. Her brother Augustin was with her at this time, but even his calm and constant support was not enough to properly sustain her against the exhausting humidity and her sense of failure.

Mary Fanton Roberts, then editor of the arts magazine *The Touchstone*, went backstage to meet her after one performance and found her weeping in her dressing-room. Augustin, who was there, told Mary that Isadora 'was too unhappy to talk with anyone, that she wanted to break her contract and go back to Europe.'

Mary quite understood Isadora's desire to break her contract, saying, 'This is not her audience. She should never have danced in this theatre.' But she urged Isadora strongly not to consider returning so quickly to Europe.

Her reason for this was that she and her husband, the editor and naturalist William Carman Roberts, were part of a new and growing movement through which America would stop looking so totally to Europe for leadership and guidance in Art, and build with pride a new aesthetic of its own. This movement would involve poets, painters and writers, and Mary had understood instinctively that Isadora almost embodied its aspirations, dancing in a way that, as Isadora well knew and admitted, was not really Ancient Greek, except in its reverent attitude to Art, but originally and distinctively American.

Isadora did attempt to honour her contract with Frohman, but her first appearances after New York, in Philadelphia, were so ill-organised and disastrous that she quit, saying in her memoirs that she did this 'from a feeling of hurt pride and also out of contempt for [Frohman's] lack of sportsmanship.'

Mary was not the only person to urge Isadora to stay a while and perform for more select audiences. After she quit in Philadelphia and returned to New York, a sculptor, George Grey Barnard, urged much the same thing on her. With the result that, as in the old days, she leased a studio. It was in the Beaux-Arts building, overlooking Bryant Park, and in it she laid a carpet, scattered pillows around, hung up her slate-blue curtains, and began giving private performances for the enlightened.

She attracted many admirers. Grey Barnard was of course among them. In his words, 'Miss Duncan is the Light of Tomorrow, a torch that lights the path of progress... She has annihilated whole Louvres of self-consciously built-up art.' Miss Duncan was equally admiring of Grey Barnard, who had, she recalled, 'a beautiful frame'. Going every day to pose for him, she made it clear that she 'longed to become the mobile clay under his sculptor's hands.' But to no avail. He was, she concluded 'one of those men who carried virtue to fanaticism.'

While in New York, she had a stroke of luck. She met a wealthy American lady with an interest in encouraging the arts – Mrs Maybelle Corey. Mrs Corey, the wife of the steel magnate W.E. Corey, owned a château about 40 miles outside Paris, at La Verrière. Called the Château Villegenis, it had once been owned by Jérôme Bonaparte, former King of Westphalia, but at present it was standing empty. She offered it to Isadora to house her pupils, and Isadora at once accepted.

Elizabeth moved the girls there in August 1908, after which she vanished for a while, making some excuse to the girls about looking after Deirdre in Isadora's absence. In fact she went away to give birth to a child she had conceived with Max Merz, who was still heavily involved with both her and the school. Unfortunately the child was stillborn.

In New York, Isadora's studio performances led to a major breakthrough for her. In her disastrous Philadelphia engagement she had danced her interpretation of Beethoven's Seventh Symphony, and among the generally unreceptive audience there had been one man who was bowled over. His name was Walter Damrosch.

Damrosch, then aged forty-six, was a composer, and the conductor of the New York Symphony. He was known as an enthusiastic innovator in music (sixteen years later he would successfully propose to George Gershwin that he write a piano concerto) and of Isadora's dancing to the Seventh Symphony he wrote, 'I have never felt the real "Joy of Life" in an almost primitive innocence and glory as in her dance of the *scherzo...* The *Finale* is a "Bacchanale" of such tremendous intensity that one little dancing figure on the stage is not sufficient. The stage should be filled with twenty Duncans, but alas, so far our age has produced only one.'

In New York, he attended one of her studio performances, at which she danced to a suite of Schubert waltzes, and as a result invited her to perform with the New York Symphony. So on 6th November 1908 she found herself appearing at the Metropolitan Opera, with the house filled to capacity. She was enthusiastically received, and later that month made two more appearances with Damrosch and the New York Symphony – one again at the Met and the next at Carnegie Hall, where she and her family had once had a studio, and where she had appeared with Ethelbert Nevin, nearly ten years previously.

These successful appearances were followed by a triumphant tour, taking in Boston, Philadelphia, Washington, Chicago and St Louis. Everywhere she went she lectured about her school. To the *New York Sun* she said, 'My children! It is of them I love best to talk. How could I help to revive the lost art of dancing without their help? If I should die, if I should become disabled, who else would there be to carry on the work on which I have spent all my years and all my resources?'

On tour in Boston at the end of November, and giving a press conference at the Hotel Touraine, she mentioned people she had seen dancing in the streets and announced that the city had gone 'Bacchic'. The *Boston Sunday Herald* reported:

'Let the women of Boston don their golden sandals and their diaphanous draperies, and go out and dance on Boston Common in the moonlight,' she exhorted the reporters. 'I look forward to the day when I shall lead the maidens of Boston, clothed in white, with dandelions in their hair, round Boston Common in the spring.' When someone asked her if Boston was anything like Athens, she fell over laughing.

'You've got me! You've got me!' Isadora said. 'Well, there is some difference. I can't describe it, but if I were in Athens I'd know it at once from Boston... And it's true. A great wave of dancing, of revelry, has swept over your city. All Boston is dancing.' She turned to her brother Augustin, who came with her on tour. 'What were those people doing, anyway, Gus?'

'The African dodger.'

'Truly Bacchic, anyway,' said Isadora. 'Don't forget to say something about my striking beauty; my features are not classical, but they are – well – oh, yes, and remember that I wore diaphanous draperies. I don't know what I should do if I had an interview where my draperies were not called diaphanous.'

It must have been a blessed relief to her, after so many years of solemn striving after the Ideal, to let her hair down and discover a talent for light-hearted silliness. (It is also possible that she'd had a couple of drinks.)

Back in New York she continued to be joyous. She gave parties at her studio where 'champagne flowed like the brooks in spring', and attended others elsewhere. She recalled, 'I forgot my chagrin and lived in the moment and was careless and happy... My performances bubbled over with renewed vitality and joy.' (She even cast a thoughtful eye on the happily-married Walter Damrosch.)

After completing her tour, she stayed in New York enjoying herself for a month, and might have stayed longer, 'If it had not been for the pulling at my heart-strings to see my baby and my school.' So at the end of 1908, back to Europe she went – to the Château Villegenis at La Verrière, and to her daughter, now two years old.

Chapter Eleven

Enter Lohengrin

As it turned out, the pupils of the school were no longer living in the Château Villegenis itself. Isadora had been wrong in understanding from Mrs Corey that it was empty. Although Mrs Corey herself was not living there, her mother, a Mrs Gilman, was, together with a little girl named Françoise, who was some sort of distant relative.

When the school arrived, Mrs Gilman announced that she did not want girls running about all over the château, scuffing her parquet floors, and ordered Elizabeth to move herself and her staff and pupils into a primitive four-room apartment overlooking the stable courtyard. As there were at the time sixteen pupils, this made their quarters somewhat cramped. Not only that, there was no furniture except a large table and some chairs in the dining-room (it turned out later that Mrs Gilman had hidden a lot of the apartment's furniture in a room there, and locked it). So the girls no longer had their little beds with white muslin curtains, but slept on thin pallets on the floor. Their water, for cooking and washing, came from a pump in the yard.

Everyone was desperately short of money. The girls' clothing was becoming threadbare and the soles of their open sandals, which was the only footwear they had, were wearing through. As the winter of 1908–09 was a particularly cold one in France, they had a miserable time – perpetually freezing and perpetually hungry, surviving on such unappetising meals as pumpkin soup.

Not that everything was misery. The girls found the château and its wooded surroundings romantic and beautiful, and there were enjoyable times when Preston Sturges, now ten and again in Europe, taught the girls French folk songs. He also taught them to ride, on a horse his mother had bought him.

His mother, Mary D'Este, had by now separated from her husband,

Solomon, and decided to base herself in France, where she had taken up with a handsome young French actor, Jacques Grétillat. She had settled in the village of Fleurines, north of Paris, where she had had a house built (disastrously badly) by a local builder, who had also designed it. She also had coops and runs built, intending to breed exotic chickens for the table.

Fleurines was not far from La Verrière, where the château was, and the girls from the school were frequent visitors. Mary had bought two cottages adjoining her land, renting one out (except for its stable, where Preston kept his horse) and allowing the Duncan girls, on their visits, to use the other.

With Isadora so frequently absent, Elizabeth and Max Merz came more and more to consider the school as their school. They had gone about finding funds to support it, and had been considerably more successful and businesslike than Isadora.

Aware that the girls were mostly German, and feeling that thus Germany was where the school should be, they had approached the good-natured Ernst-Ludwig, Grand Duke of Hesse, for support. Of royal blood, he was the son of Queen Victoria's second daughter, Alice, and the great-uncle of Philip, Duke of Edinburgh. He responded warmly to the appeal of Elizabeth and Max, and after some thought offered them a plot of land at Marienhöhe, near Darmstadt, then capital of the grand duchy of Hesse-Darmstadt. Funding from other German sources was raised, sufficient to build a brand-new school and dormitory.

When Isadora returned to the château, in January 1909, she immediately threw everything into confusion by announcing that she had a month's booking in Paris for herself and the girls, and that she and they were to set off into the city at once. It was her intention to build on her success in America by giving similar performances, both private and public, in the major cities of Europe. In pursuit of this she had persuaded the French impresario, Aurélien Lugné-Poë, who was Duse's manager in France, to present herself and her pupils at the Théâtre-Lyrique Municipale de la Gaité (known colloquially as the Gaité-Lyrique) in Montparnasse. (He claimed she had done this by inviting him to her hotel suite and offering herself to him, but whether he accepted the offer is unclear.)

Isadora had already rented for herself a studio/apartment in the Hôtel Biron, at 77 rue de Varenne. This was a celebrated residence for those involved in the arts. Designed by Jacques-Ange Gabriel in the eighteenth century, its structure enclosed a large garden, deliberately left as a wilderness as a reminder of Art's debt to Nature. Among those renting its studios over the years were Rodin, Rilke, Matisse and the young Jean Cocteau, and eventually it became so notorious for the wildness of its celebrations that the owners, who happened to be the French government, shut it down.

As soon as she saw the discomfort her pupils were enduring in the stable-yard, Isadora at once took them away and rented two apartments in rue Danton, on the Left Bank – one for herself and Deirdre, the other for them.

Once they were safely installed in Paris, she had them all sent to the couturier Paul Poiret, who fitted them out in green silk coats, dresses and little green hats. Poiret, then still rising to fame, was a major influence in liberating twentieth century women from the stifling decorum of the century before, so his attitude to what women should wear strongly resembled Isadora's. Among his fashion ideas was the discarding of petticoats and corsets, and he had great success around 1906 with a version of the 'empire line', such as Isadora had taken to wearing when first in London. He even named one of his dresses after her.

The season of dancing that she and the girls were to perform at the Gaité-Lyrique was to be accompanied by the Concerts Lamoureux Orchestra. They opened on 17th January. Every one of the 2,200 seats had been sold out within hours of booking being opened, and their performances were a sensational success from the first night. The American author Edith Wharton, who was present at one, described the whole season as 'a white milestone... It shed a light on every kind of beauty, and showed me for the first time how each flows into the other as music merged with her dancing. All through the immense, rapt audience one felt the rush of her inspiration.' So successful was the season that early in it Isadora and the girls were booked for a second one, at the same theatre, to take place in May and June.

Among the pieces Isadora danced was *Iphigénie* (with the girls), and throughout the two seasons she performed almost her whole repertoire. An outstanding addition to it at this time was her dance *Death and the Maiden*, which she had been performing without music since 1903, but which she now began performing to a Chopin mazurka. It was described towards the end of 1909 by the writer Jeanne Gazeau:

I know of nothing more beautiful than the sudden transformation of this young creature, dancing and laughing at life, who suddenly feels herself seized by death. It is only a shudder, then an effort to shake off the cold embrace, finally a desperate hardening of her whole being and a supreme convulsion, when she seems to shrink into herself like a flower against the blow, and then falls dead. It is the eternal mystery of death in all its anguished simplicity... I am only reporting the facts. I saw people weeping who were laughing when it started.'

Late one morning in February 1909, Isadora was in her dressing-room at the theatre when she had an unexpected visitor. As she recalled in her memoirs, 'I remember I had my hair in curling-papers for the afternoon matinée, and it was covered with a little lace cap. My maid came to me with a visiting card on which I read a well known name, and suddenly there sang in my brain, "Here is my millionaire!" '

'Let him enter!' she said to the maid. The name was Paris Eugene Singer, and like his elder sister Winaretta, who as the Princesse de Polignac had done so much to introduce Isadora's dancing to fashionable Paris on her first visit there, he was an heir to part of the massive (and much fought over) Singer sewing-machine fortune.

He entered Isadora's dressing-room, tall and blond, and with curling hair and beard, and her first thought was that he looked like Wagner's hero, Lohengrin. In fact in her memoirs she refers to him only as Lohengrin (or simply 'L'), never revealing his real name. He was accompanied by his young daughter, also named Winaretta, whom he had brought along to disguise the fact that he had definite designs on Isadora (he had instructed Winaretta to make herself scarce as soon as possible after meeting Isadora, by going off and mingling with the girls from the school).

Almost the youngest of Isaac Singer's twenty-four children, and named Paris after the city where he was born (Isaac's third and last wife, Isabella Boyer, was the daughter of a French tavern-keeper), he had been brought to England by his mother after his father's death, which took place in 1873, when he was seven. The American writer Alva Johnston, in his book about Addison and Wilson Mizner, tells of Singer's early life:

> While still in knee pants, the boy, who was evidently born with a wonderful property sense, went to a British judge with a hunch that his mother was mismanaging his estate, and he was made a ward of the British Court. The Royal Family interested itself in the well-heeled waif, and Paris was practically raised in Buckingham Palace, where he came to look on [the future] Queen Alexandra as his royal stepmother.

206

He received his university education at Cambridge, studying medicine, chemistry and engineering (and also eloped with one of his mother's maids, Henriette Marais, although the marriage was soon annulled). Johnston continues:

As a young man, he was a glittering figure – six feet three inches tall, of fine physique, handsome, highly educated, with a Court of St James's air and a nest-egg of fifteen million dollars. He became a liberal patron of worthy young poets, artists, playwrights and soubrettes. Occasionally ambition seized him, and he hurled himself at professional studies. He steeped himself in architecture until splendid edifices and stately cities ran out of his pen. Dedicating himself to the search for a compound to abolish all diseases, he swallowed a new drug called aspirin in such quantities that for a time his life was despaired of. Deserting art and science for beauty, he became a celebrated international Romeo. Any disappointment in a romantic matter always caused him to console himself with architecture. A tiff was enough to start him on a villa or a harbor improvement. A broken heart inspired a project for a great medical-research institute, but a reconciliation canceled it.

In short, he was a dilettante, too undisciplined to develop any of his undoubted talents into any sort of solid achievement. He was also somewhat highly-strung, given to tantrums and to sulking, and a hypochondriac. And an enthusiastic womaniser.

In 1887, aged nineteen, he had married an Australian, Lillie Graham, and even though they had five children, his incessant stream of amorous encounters never dried up. His daughter Winaretta recalled, 'He was very good looking and women threw themselves at him, and he'd had a great many *affaires* – but when he saw Isadora he fell straight in love with her before she fell in love with him, which was quite the other way around, usually.'

By 1909 his marriage was effectively over. At the time he introduced himself to Isadora, he and his wife had just agreed to separate (although they would not get around to obtaining a divorce for another nine years).

'I admire your art,' he told Isadora, once Winaretta had dutifully gone and they were alone in her dressing-room. 'I admire your courage in the ideal of your school. I have come to help you. What can I do?'

As he spoke, it dawned on Isadora that they had briefly met before. In 1901, when she was first in Paris, his sister Winaretta's husband,

Prince Edmond de Polignac, had died. She had attended the funeral, Paris Singer had been there, and they had been introduced. She was not at all sure that this was a good omen, recalling in her memoirs, 'We had first met in a church before a coffin. No prophecy of happiness, that! Nevertheless, from that moment I realised that this was my millionaire... For whatever fate, it was *Kismet*.'

She latched onto him at once, accepting his overtures. At the end of February, when their first run at the Gaité-Lyrique came to an end, she took the girls (and Deirdre) for a month's holiday, renting a villa in Beaulieu, near Nice. At the same time, Paris booked himself into a hotel in Nice, where his vast steam yacht, the *Lady Evelyn*, was moored. He and Isadora became lovers, and soon she and Deirdre set sail with him on the *Lady Evelyn*, bound for the Mediterranean. In Isadora's account of this interlude, her socialist sympathies surfaced:

> I can see it all as if it were yesterday: the broad deck of the yacht; the table set with crystal and silver for lunch, and Deirdre, in her white tunic, dancing about. Certainly I was in love and happy. And yet all the time I was unpleasantly aware of the stokers, stoking in the engine-room; the fifty sailors on the yacht; the Captain and the Mate – all this immense expenditure for the pleasure of two people... And sometimes I contrasted unfavourably the ease of this life of luxury, the continual feasting, the nonchalant giving up of one's being to pleasure, with the bitter struggle of my early youth. Then quickly I would react to the impression on my body and mind of the glory of the dawn as it melted into the heat of a dazzling noon. My Lohengrin, my Knight of the Grail, should come, too, to share the great idea!

Already she was beginning to realise that, for all his offered generosity to her, and his lavish supporting of the arts, Paris Singer not only had no holy cause of his own, he was unaware of the possibility of being possessed by such a cause. He was, at heart, as down-to-earth and materialistic as his father, devoted to business and the development of machinery.

During this first cruise on the *Lady Evelyn*, Isadora on one occasion tried reading Walt Whitman to him, explaining that Whitman's 'Song of the Open Road', with its line 'Camarado! Give me your hand!' expressed her own attitude to life perfectly. Finishing reading, she looked up to see, as she recalled, Singer's 'handsome face congested with rage.'

'What rot!' he exploded. 'That man could never have earned his living!'
'Can't you see,' said Isadora, 'he had the vision of Free America!'
'Vision be damned,' said Singer.

As Isadora remembered, '...suddenly I realised that his vision of America was that of the dozens of factories which made his fortune for him. But such is the perversity of woman that, after this and similar quarrels, I threw myself into his arms, forgetting everything under the brutality of his caresses.'

One thing was clear. Of all the lovers she had so far had, Paris Singer was by some way the most sensuous and experienced. She wrote:

> For the first time [I learned] what the nerves and sensations can be transformed to. I became a quivering mass of responsive senses in the hands of an expert voluptuary... Like a flock of wild goats cropping the herbage of the soft hillside, so his kisses grazed over my body, and like the earth itself I felt a thousand mouths devouring me...
>
> Like Zeus, he transformed himself into many shapes and forms, and I knew him now as a Bull, now as a Swan, and again as a Golden Shower, and I was by this love carried over the waves, caressed with white wings delicately, and strangely seduced and hallowed in a Golden Cloud.

Returning to Nice, Isadora went to Beaulieu to collect her pupils, and thence to Paris. Then, leaving the pupils and their governess at the apartment in the rue Danton, she set off to make brief appearances in several Russian cities.

As luck would have it, Craig would be in Russia at the same time, again discussing *Hamlet* with Stanislavsky, and when Isadora learned of this she was ecstatic. As she recalled, 'For a short moment I was on the verge of believing that nothing [else] mattered, neither the school, nor Lohengrin, nor anything – but just the joy of seeing him again.'

She arranged for Craig and Stanislavsky to come to her hotel in St Petersburg, where she gave them dinner, the party being made up by her 'very pretty secretary' (remembered only as Miss S).

The dinner turned out to be a somewhat undignified affair. In Craig's recollection, Isadora had rather too much to drink and again began making advances to Stanislavsky. She 'began to kiss him – he objecting most politely all the time – & she refusing to accept his objections.'

In Isadora's recollection, Craig, becoming jealous, 'flew into one of his old-time rages.' He picked up Miss S in his arms, carried her into the next room, and locked its door. 'Stanislavsky,' she recalled, 'was terribly shocked.' He and Isadora knocked on the door for half an hour, begging Craig to unlock it, but he did not. So Stanislavsky went home and Isadora went miserably to bed.

As it happened, Craig and Miss S were no longer in the room. They had sneaked out by another door and gone for a sleigh ride. After which they came back to the hotel and spent the night together in another room.

Late next morning Miss S hurriedly dressed and went to find Isadora only just in time to catch their train to Kiev. Craig, lunching alone, suddenly remembered about the train, and went out into the lobby just in time to catch them leaving for the station. He was smugly pleased with himself, writing in *Book Topsy*:

> As I helped to arrange the rugs [in Isadora's sledge] I could not help saying with polite smiles that I hoped she had passed a pleasant evening anyhow. To this she said neither a yea or a nay but, as was her custom when utterly boulversé, she uttered a brief sermon – said she, 'Try to emulate the virtues of the *good* man with whom we supped last night,' & signing to the coachman to jolly well drive on she drove away. These sudden bursts of damned hypocritical sermonising *rarely* seized her – but when they did one stood staggered & uncertain whether to weep, laugh, howl, or shoot...

Returning to Paris at the end of this brief Russian tour, Isadora was met by Paris Singer, and taken by him to spend the night at his apartment in the Place des Vosges. There he continued to prove more exciting in bed than the self-absorbed Craig or the caring Pim. He also, at around this time, proposed to her, but she, with her firm views on the irrelevance of marriage, turned him down.

On 19th May 1909 an event took place in Paris that took the dancing world by storm. At the Théâtre du Châtelet, Diaghilev's newly-founded Ballets Russes gave its first performance outside Russia. He had transformed the theatre into 'a gigantic salon', his idea being that theatre-going should be a total experience. The seats, carpets and walls were all richly red, the foyers and dress circle crowded with statuary and potted plants.

Among those invited, apart from as many of the most beautiful actresses in Paris as were free (whom Diaghilev conceived of as part of the ambience), and assorted diplomats and dignitaries, there were many artists

– painters, sculptors, composers, musicians, singers, authors, poets –
among them Chaliapin, Fauré, Mirbeau, Rodin, Saint-Saëns, and Isadora
Duncan, who was given a seat in the front row.

The entire programme was choreographed by Michel Fokine, and the
exotic sets and costumes were by Benois and Bakst. The leading ballerinas
were Anna Pavlova and Tamara Karsavina, and the leading male dancers
were the twenty-year-old Vaslav Nijinsky and the slightly older Adolf
Bolm. (Isadora later noted with approval that one of Fokine and Diaghilev's
achievements was to restore the male, after two thousand years, to a
prominent place in the world of dance, but Bolm was equally a part of
this, restoring, in the words of *The Dictionary of Modern Ballet*, 'the
male dancer to his rightful place in the world of ballet as the equal of
the ballerina, not just a *porteur*.')

Nijinsky was noted for his grace and power, and for doing much to
break away from the stylised forms and movements that had characterised
ballet before his time. He had seen Isadora dance in Russia, and she had
been one of his influences. Later he would comment that she had 'dared
to give liberty to movement.' As a measure of his talent and importance,
the American dancer and critic, Roger Pryor Dodge, wrote in 1938,
'The two greatest dancers of our time, Vaslav Nijinsky and Isadora
Duncan ... were not only the greatest artists of their own time but
apparently the two greatest in the past two hundred years and, who
knows, perhaps for many years to come.'

The programme Isadora saw on this historic opening night was *Le
Pavillon d'Armide*, to music by Tcherepnin, the Polovtsian dances from
Borodin's opera *Prince Igor*, and a suite of dances that Diaghilev had
entitled *Le Festin*, which was danced to a medley of themes by various
Russian composers. (Later in its season the Ballets Russes would also
perform a piece that Fokine had choreographed two years before, to
music by Chopin, and called *Chopiniana*, but which had now acquired
its enduring title of *Les Sylphides*.)

Isadora, while retaining her idea that ballet was artificial and more
related to acrobatics than to dancing, was deeply impressed by Nijinsky,
Karsavina and Pavlova, finding them all 'ethereal'. She was less impressed
by the sets they danced against, or among – lavish with greenery and
such props as fountains, against elaborate painted backdrops. This to her,
as to Gordon Craig, was a step backwards, and the enemy of the simplicity
in staging they wished to encourage.

Also in May, Isadora and her girls returned to the Gaîté-Lyrique for
their second season. By this time she had abandoned her studio/apartment

in the Hôtel Biron, and bought a house in the prosperous suburb of Neuilly-sur-Seine, at 68 rue Chauveau.

Set in a shaded park, a little distance from the Seine, it had been built only a dozen or so years before by the painter Henri Gervex. He had been commissioned by Tsar Nicholas II to create a series of giant murals in celebration of his coronation in 1896, and Gervex had built the house as a place where he could work on them. As a result, it had a gigantic studio area, three storeys high and with a floor area of some 100 feet by 66.

This Isadora decorated in her usual style. As her pupil, Irma, remembered, 'Entering [it] was like entering a cathedral. The long blue drapes covering the walls and hanging down from the ceiling in heavy folds suggested a Gothic interior. The soft light filtering through alabaster lamps lent a mystic atmosphere.' She used the studio to give lessons to her pupils, while they continued to live in their Paris apartment.

Isadora of course lived at the house. Her quarters were two floors up, reached via a long staircase terminating in a railed gallery, and these she hired Paul Poiret to decorate. Her own recollection was that he made the main room into 'a veritable domain of Circe. Sable black velvet curtains were reflected on the walls in golden mirrors.' There was 'a black carpet and a divan with cushions of Oriental textures.' The windows were covered, so that no sunlight could enter, and the doors were 'strange, Etruscan tomb-like apertures.' She adored the effect, finding that, 'The little room was beautiful, fascinating, and, at the same time, dangerous.' Her bedroom had red wallpaper covered in lace, and on the golden background of its doors Poiret had designed a double black cross, a conceit she enjoyed as 'bizarre'. Deirdre, with her nurse and Isadora's servants, lived in a small cottage in the grounds.

Isadora's liaison with Paris Singer continued as tempestuous as it would always be, with frequent quarrels and splittings-up and passionate reconciliations. She was hurt by his lack of comprehension of her ideals, and found it difficult herself to comprehend a man who seemed to have no ideals of his own. Or even a proper career. In all their years together she never managed to understand exactly what it was he did in life, beyond imagining that he must have had an office (or offices) somewhere to manage his financial holdings.

Most of the time, apart from leading an active social life, he seemed to hop undecidedly from one wild enthusiasm to another, never finishing anything. As Isadora once recalled in an interview, 'He was the busiest man you ever heard of. At one time he was going to build an Italian castle on Cap Ferrat and on Mondays he would be rushing to Paris, and then rushing back to Cap Ferrat on Wednesdays… All those schemes, and always on the grandiose scale, were his diversions.'

Unfortunately, in Singer's limited understanding, Dance was similarly a diversion to Isadora, and he could never understand how central it was to her whole being. Mentally they were poles apart.

There was one way, however, in which his mind did connect with hers, and influenced her. He introduced her to the good life, especially to the good life of Paris. As she recalled, 'I learned to know all the really good restaurants in the city of Paris, where L. was kowtowed to and treated like a king. All the Maîtres d'Hôtel and all the cooks vied with one another to please him – and no wonder, for he distributed money in a truly royal manner.'

She learned 'the difference between a *poulet cocotte* and a *poulet simple*.' She learned 'the different values of ortolans, truffles, and mushrooms.' She learned the best vintages of wines.

She also began enjoying *haute couture*, beginning with that of Paul Poiret, and, 'fell for the fatal lure of stuffs, colours, form – even hats.' Uneasily aware that she was allowing her sensibility to descend from the aesthetic heights of pure art to the mundane world of clothing design, she attempted inwardly to excuse her behaviour by telling herself that Poiret was a genius. Yet, as she knew and later admitted, 'this was for me the change from sacred to profane art.'

In June 1909 Stanislavsky came to Paris, met Isadora, and found her 'changed beyond recognition', reporting in a letter to his wife that she 'imitates a *Parisienne*.' She took him to a restaurant for dinner with herself and Singer, and the kindly and surprisingly conventional Stanislavsky was further disconcerted that she made no attempt to stop flirting with him, which clearly made Singer jealous. 'All this stupidity,' wrote Stanislavsky to his wife, 'makes me despair.'

Isadora and the children were still appearing at the Gaîté-Lyrique while he was in Paris, and the night after this uncomfortable dinner he went to see the performance, but decided he was too depressed by the change he felt in Isadora to go backstage afterwards and see her. Before he could make his escape from the theatre, however, he was caught by her impresario, Aurélien Lugné-Poë, who had been sent by Isadora to find him.

Taken to her dressing-room, he found her distraught. She explained that, after the dinner the previous night, she and Singer had had a furious row, and he had left her. Stanislavsky was just beginning to make sympathetic noises when, to Isadora's obvious surprise, Singer walked in. Greeting Stanislavsky warmly, he invited him to come next afternoon to Isadora's studio at Neuilly 'for a lecture and demonstration of the principles of her school.'

Stanislavsky, momentarily disconcerted but still admiring of Isadora's ideas, accepted. But he was to regret it. As he wrote to Lev Sulerzhitsky, a colleague at the Moscow Arts Theatre:

> I don't quite understand what she wants – apparently she expects me to help her with the organisation of her school. The point is that a rich man has built a wonderful huge studio for her near Paris [not quite true – it was bought, not built, and Isadora was always proud that she paid for the house herself, out of her American earnings]. I entered it during a lesson for the children. The mysterious semi-darkness, subdued music, dancing children – all this made a great impression on me... But when the dances ended, she took me upstairs to show her own tiny rooms. I was literally scared. These are the rooms not of a Greek goddess, but of a French *demi-mondaine*. When she showed the bedroom, she poked her finger at the lace covering the red wallpaper of a courtesan, saying, 'Mister Singer ordered this.' She suddenly became quite shy. She then went into a long explanation about how ... her sister and some German have signed contracts with all the remaining children and their parents, and there she is with a school but no children, even though she has fed and clothed them for years.

This could not have been exactly true. After all, the children of the school, who now numbered sixteen, were still there dancing with her. But certainly Elizabeth and her colleague Max Merz were making attempts to take them over.

A few weeks earlier, on 7th June, Isadora had sent a circular letter to the parents of all the pupils. It read:

> My dance school no longer exists in Germany because of insufficient support. My own resources are no longer adequate to enable me to carry the expense alone. A group of influential friends, here in France, is now engaged in organizing a dance school under my sole direction, but supported by other funds.
> In this new establishment the pupils will continue as hitherto, to receive an academic, as well as an artistic education. The parents

are requested to agree by contract to leave the children at the school till they have reached the age of eighteen. Having finished their education, the graduated pupils will then be able to obtain dance engagements through the school organization. Half of their fee will then be deducted for repayment of the expenses incurred for their education.

If you should consider leaving your daughter with me under the above stipulated conditions, I beg you to let me know immediately. If otherwise, I shall find myself constrained to return your daughter to you.

Unfortunately, Elizabeth and Max Merz were by now beginning to build their new school in Germany. They had been aware of Isadora's plans for some time, but now that she was involved with the wealthy Paris Singer it was obvious that all their hard work in fund-raising and planning was in danger. So they inserted a notice in the German press, over Elizabeth's name:

With reference to the sojourn of my sister Isadora Duncan and her school in Paris, I beg to state that I have been associated with this school since its foundation in the capacity of both teacher and director. My own activities have been widely recognised in Germany. I therefore declare that I am not taking any part in the re-establishing of a new school in Paris, France. As repeatedly stated, I shall continue my activities in Germany, specifically in Darmstadt, where my own school is now in the process of being built. I beg you not to construe this as going against my sister. I merely continue to pursue my long and successful – if at times difficult – activities in Germany. I shall proceed on my chosen path with the guarantee of the fine support I have received so far for my undertaking.

She and Max Merz were so concerned that they themselves might end up with a school, but no pupils, that one day they went so far as to travel to Paris and turn up at the apartment where the pupils lived. Irma (who did not much like Elizabeth) recalled:

We had not seen her for ages when she appeared one afternoon at our pension all smiles and innocence. Although most of us instinctively scattered like birds, *sauve qui peut*, at her approach, she managed to catch a few of the more trusting ones who had lingered behind. She made an unusually friendly gesture without arousing any suspicion and invited them to have tea in town. The girls accepted with pleasure. The next thing they knew, instead of having tea and cakes at Rumpelmayer's, they were on a train bound for Germany [for Frankfurt].

Isadora, returning to the apartment and learning that five of the pupils had been kidnapped, was outraged, storming, 'How is it possible that my own sister could do a thing like that to me? It is incredible!'

After thinking for a moment, she asked the remaining girls whether they wished to remain with her, and on being assured that they all did (which moved her), she said, 'Very soon I'll have a beautiful new school organized here. Just have a little patience.'

Isadora's encounters with Stanislavsky at this time did not end after his visit to Neuilly (where, incidentally, he was not impressed with her teaching, feeling that she had no talent for it). A day or so later he was back there attending one of her receptions, and described the occasion in a letter:

> You know, I slandered Singer and am sorry now. Yesterday there was a reception at Duncan's. There was a horde of guests there, including the director of the Comédie Française, celebrated writers, artists, political figures. Singer played the host... He looked after the children as a nurse, spread the carpets out, rushed about, entertained the guests, while she, adroitly posing as a grand celebrity, sat in a white costume among admirers, listening to compliments. This time the barometer of my sympathies suddenly turned and I befriended him and helped him to spread out the carpets and do the children's hair before letting them dance for such a choice society... Singer stopped being jealous of me and entrusted me with taking Duncan in a car, and when we sat there, she started kissing [me], while I was trying to impress on her that Singer was a charming fellow. In other words, everything got mixed up.

That night, going to the Gaité-Lyrique, he left a note in her dressing-room, without seeing her. It said:

> You asked my advice... I have understood everything now and am able to say: 1) Run away from Paris. 2) Value freedom above all. 3) Give up your school, if it has to be paid for at such a price.

4) Whatever happens with you – I shall always understand and will sympathise with you from all my heart.

He would, however, see her once more before leaving Paris. Going again to Neuilly, he took a quiet walk in the park surrounding the house, in the company of Isadora and of Deirdre, now almost three. He liked Deirdre, telling a friend, 'A charming child. Craig's temperament and Duncan's grace. I liked her so much that Duncan promised to let me have her if she (Duncan) should die... If she leaves me all her future children, too, I can rest assured that I shall spend my old age surrounded by a numerous family.'

Nonetheless, he felt he had had enough of the new Isadora, reportedly saying of his Paris visit, 'All this makes me ill. I have said goodbye for good to Duncan.'

In June, when their second successful month at the Gaité-Lyrique came to an end, Isadora announced to her pupils that it would be a good thing if they went home for a while to see their parents, which many of them had not done for over four years. While they were away she would continue setting up her new school, and when it was ready she would send for them. Somewhat surprised by the suddenness of this decision, off they went.

But Isadora had lost her hunger. If she had still held the dream of a school that she once did hold, she would have used Paris Singer to the utmost. But her dream was now, at least for the moment, more a reverie than a passion.

She went off with Singer (and Deirdre) to spend the summer aboard the *Lady Evelyn*, stooging around off the coast of Brittany, in the Bay of Biscay. Worried as she was about the school and about the future direction of her work, this holiday, she felt, would give her time to realise what would be best and how best to set about realising it. Which she attempted to do, hampered to some extent by the fact that the Bay of Biscay was frequently so rough that she and Deirdre had to go ashore and follow the yacht from place to place by car (she had become much attached to the motor car as a mode of transport).

At the beginning of autumn, in September, she left Singer and the yacht and went with Deirdre to Venice. There, at a social gathering at the Lido, she encountered Nijinsky. Offstage, he tended to be shy and uncertain, and, according to the recollections of his future wife, Romola de Pulszky, Isadora embarrassed him not only by attempting to dance with him, but by suggesting he give her a child.

As it happened, it was while on this trip to Venice that she realised that she was already bearing another child, by Paris Singer. Her feelings were a mixture of 'joy and disquietude', the disquietude arising from a dread of going through the agonising ordeal that giving birth had been for her before.

She went to Milan to consult Eleanora Duse's doctor about the possibility of having an abortion. He came to see her in her hotel bedroom. They discussed the matter, and eventually she asked him to leave her alone to make her own decision. Which she did. Her belief 'in Life, in Love, in the sanctity of Nature's Law' persuaded her to have the child.

Returning to Paris, she set off almost at once on a second tour of America with Walter Damrosch and the New York Symphony, taking with her her brother Augustin's daughter, Temple, now aged ten.

Augustin and his wife Sarah had by now amiably parted company, and he had successfully resumed his stage career. He had been stage manager for the touring Shakespeare company established by the actor Charles Coburn and his wife (that same Charles Coburn who would go on with great success into old age in a succession of films, including *Gentlemen Prefer Blondes* (Hawks), *The Paradine Case* (Hitchcock) and *The Lady Eve* (Preston Sturges). Augustin had also had a considerable personal success on Broadway in a production of the play *Canterbury Pilgrims*.

Isadora's musical repertoire was much the same as on her previous tour, with the addition of Schubert's *Marche Militaire* (in D major) and a suite of his waltzes. She was also joined onstage during one performance at the Metropolitan Opera by Augustin. Together they performed what were described as 'readings from "Greek Choruses"'.

Her performances were greeted with enthusiasm, although not with quite the same enthusiasm as they had been previously. Most Americans, it seemed, had viewed her as an unusual novelty, without perceiving the depth of her conception, and now the novelty was beginning to wear off. Isadora found it depressing that she seemed to be appreciated more in Europe than in her native land, which she felt was sadly lacking in culture.

Her last performance was on 2nd December 1909, at Carnegie Hall. By now she was four months pregnant, and her costumes, already somewhat inadequate by the standards of the time, were becoming even less concealing. A woman came back stage after the performance and warned her that her condition was perceptible, saying, 'But my dear

Miss Duncan, it's plainly visible from the front row. You can't continue like this.'

Isadora replied, 'Oh, but my dear Mrs [X], that's just what I mean my dancing to express – Love – Woman – Formation – Springtime. Botticelli's picture, you know. The fruitful earth – the three dancing Graces *enceinte* – the Madonna – the Zephyrs *enceinte* also. Everything rustling, promising New Life. That is what my Dance means.' As she recalled in her memoirs, the woman looked 'quizzical'.

Shortly before she left again to return to Paris, her brother Raymond, with his wife Penelope and son Menalkas, now aged four, arrived in New York, with a small entourage. Raymond and Penelope were to tour in a production of their own. It was Sophocles' Elektra, and they intended to perform it in the original Ancient Greek, Penelope playing *Elektra* and Raymond dancing the chorus. He was also to lecture on the art and music of that time.

Preston Sturges, who had often run into Raymond in France and elsewhere, wrote of him in later years:

> In those days Raymond traveled with a rather large group of his disciples, mostly of the opposite sex, often young, sometimes comely, and nearly always with recently born or about-to-be-born babies. This entourage required large quantities of milk, and everybody knows that there is no milk like goat's milk for raising robust babies, so attached to the entourage were a number of goats.

In New York, all Raymond's company continued to wear Ancient Greek costume, which caused something of a sensation and would, the following January, result in Raymond and Penelope being fined, on grounds of neglect, for allowing Menalkas to walk the streets barefoot in winter.

Raymond had continued to go his own way so defiantly, paying no attention to anyone who disagreed with him, that he now not only had a headful of eccentric ideas, but also believed himself nearly omniscient. At a press conference late in December, he announced to the assembled reporters, 'I should like [it] if you will first indicate what you wish me to talk about, for I must say to you that I know almost everything under the sun.' Even to Isadora he was becoming excessive. Two years earlier, in one of her letters to Craig, she had written, 'I am so worried about Ray – Too much Too much.'

Raymond being, as he was, an apostle of the simple life, he followed the *Elektra* tour by taking his company for a while to the Pacific Northwest, where they spent several months among the Klamath Indians, 'studying their music and teaching them to weave.' By which time Isadora had boarded the *Lusitania* and returned to Paris and her lover. With her sailed her brother Augustin and his daughter, Temple. Augustin was returning to Paris to set up home with an actress, Marguerite Sargent, living in an apartment in the Hôtel Champs Élysées.

During all this time Isadora seems to have done little towards re-establishing her school. Having sent the pupils, apart from those removed by Elizabeth, home to their parents to await development, she sent them no word. Eventually, while she was in America, most of them yielded to pressure from Elizabeth and Max Merz to come and be part of their new school at Darmstadt (although its new buildings were not yet completed). After all, for over four years the school had been their home and their fellow-pupils their family.

Temple was among those who returned to the school, but by now, according to Max Merz, she had 'completely rejected being trained as a dancer, and was just as subtly charming as she was indifferent.'

What the pupils did not at once realise was that the school Elizabeth and Max were planning would be subtly different from what it had been before. Max, a pleasant, although somewhat pedantic, man in his middle thirties, had a considerable influence over Elizabeth. As well as being a good musician and a useful organiser, it emerged that he also had a passion for Eugenics. That science, given its name in 1883 by one of its founders, the English Francis Galton, had the intention of improving the quality of the human race, especially in intelligence and fitness, by selective breeding. (It foundered when the Nazis perverted its ideas, which were a bit dubious anyway, into an excuse for exterminating whole sections of humanity in the name of racial purity.)

Eugenics was very much in the air at the time in Europe, and Isadora's pursuit of Stanislavsky (and others, such as Nijinsky) may not have been simply because she fancied him. It seems likely that she had by now conceived the idea of having children by a succession of handsome and talented men, thus conducting her own personal programme of selective breeding.

As a result of Max's passion for Eugenics, the school that he and Elizabeth were planning was not to be primarily based on dance, but on a regime of 'physical culture and racial hygiene'. He also, as he later wrote, 'wanted to protect the school from one danger, from the artistic ambitions of the semi-talented, from the thought that one or the other of the little girls should ever try to become a "little Isadora".' (An ambition that, like Max himself, was thoughtful and responsible, but dull.)

After her return from America Isadora basically took things easy. Paris Singer seemed delighted that she was to bear his child, and in January 1910 he and she set off to Egypt, where they cruised for two months on the Nile. With them of course went Deirdre, and also a cousin of Kathleen Bruce (now Mrs Scott) named Hener Skene. He was a pianist and had been brought along, at Isadora's suggestion, to play 'Beethoven and Bach' on a concert grand, which had also been brought along.

Their cruise started in Alexandria, and continued south, via Luxor and Aswân, to Khartoum. Isadora and Deirdre and Hener did not go with Singer when he went off to inspect this ancient city, but stayed on the boat enjoying what Isadora later recalled as, 'the most peaceful time of my life... Our boat seemed to be rocked by the rhythm of the ages.'

Even so, the approaching birth of her second baby was causing her concern, and the very ancientness of Egypt caused her some foreboding. As she recalled, 'The little life within me seemed to vaguely surmise this journey to the land of darkness and death.'

At this time in her life, the tendency towards mysticism she had always had was showing signs of increasing. A year before she had begun repeating 'a hundred times a day' the phrase 'I must find a millionaire!'. At first, as she admitted, this was as a joke, but quite soon it became in earnest. And her millionaire had duly appeared, in the form of Singer.

When in Milan, discussing the possibility of an abortion with the doctor, she had visited the Cathedral of San Marco and imagined she saw, in the blue and white interior of the dome above her, 'the face of a little boy, but it was also the face of an angel with great blue eyes and an aureole of golden hair.' Which vision convinced her that the child she was carrying would be a blue-eyed little boy with golden curls.

Which indeed it was. After returning from Egypt, she went for her *accouchement* to the very villa in Beaulieu where she had stayed with her pupils when beginning her relationship with Singer. He often visited her there, as did her friend Mary D'Este and her son Preston, and Singer was, by all accounts, as generous to Mary and Preston as he was to Isadora and Deirdre.

The doctor Isadora had in Beaulieu, Dr Emil Bosson, was more skilled than the provinicial Dutch doctor who had presided at Deirdre's birth, and Isadora's son was born, easily and painlessly (and with the aid of morphia), on 1st May 1910. She named him Patrick Augustus, and his

221

birth was registered at Beaulieu town hall. Singer's name did not appear on the birth certificate.

Soon Isadora sent a happy note to her 'dear and Great master', Ernst Haeckel, telling him, 'My baby ... is strong and sweet. I am just about to give him the breast. He takes up every minute of my spare time but when he looks at me with his blue eyes I feel royally repaid.'

Deirdre was enchanted by her new baby brother. By now she was talking fluently, and Isadora remembered her saying, 'Oh, the sweet little boy, Mother; you need not worry about him. I will always hold him in my arms and take care of him.' Isadora was naturally enchanted as well. Writing again to Professor Haeckel, she said, 'He takes up every minute of my time but when he looks at me with his blue eyes I feel richly compensated. This boy will be a monist, and, who knows, there may be some of your great and wonderful spirit in him. We will hope so.'

Chapter Twelve

An Experiment in Domesticity

In the spring of 1910 the most dominant thing in Isadora's life no longer seemed to be her school, or even her dancing, but her two beautiful children and her off-again on-again relationship with Paris Singer. When she returned from Beaulieu to Paris he booked a suite at the Trianon Palace Hotel in Versailles, where the two of them (and the children) could be together.

He again asked her to marry him, and again she refused him. In her memoirs she recalled the conversation that followed, wryly picturing the great gulf in understanding that always lay between them:

> 'How stupid for an artist to be married,' I said, 'and as I must spend my life making tours around the world, how could you spend your life in the stage-box admiring me?'
> 'You would not have to make tours if we were married,' he said.
> 'Then what should we do?'
> 'We should spend our time in my house in London, or at my place in the country.'
> 'And then what should we do?'
> 'Then there is the yacht.'
> 'But then what should we do?'
> L. proposed that we should try the life for six months.
> 'If you don't like it, I shall be much astonished.'

After a little thought, Isadora agreed to try what he suggested, to embark on what she called 'an experiment in domesticity'.

Singer also suggested to her that they throw a party to celebrate her return to Paris – expense no object. Isadora accepted the suggestion eagerly, and set about arranging one. While she did so, he went off to London on business.

223

The party was to be held at her house in Neuilly, and it was planned to go on for hours. At four in the afternoon she received her illustrious guests, Diaghilev and Nijinsky among them. She wore a flame-coloured dress designed by Mario Fortuny in the material for which he was famous, pleated silk.

As she recalled, 'there, in the park were marquees with every sort of refreshment, from caviar and champagne to tea and cakes. After this, on an open space where tents had been erected, the Colonne orchestra ... gave us a programme of the works of Richard Wagner.' Then there was dinner, and after it, as cigars were handed round, the cloth of the dining-tent was rolled back and Isadora, now wearing a white tunic and gold sandals, danced on the grass among the trees, this time to a second orchestra, from Vienna.

The whole occasion was, as one guest recalled, 'noisy and joyful', the enjoyment marred slightly for Isadora by the fact that Singer had not managed to attend. Just before her guests arrived she had had a telegram from him, still in London, telling her 'that he had had a stroke and was too ill to come, but that I was to receive the guests without him.'

Knowing by now that Singer was something of a hypochondriac, Isadora was not unduly alarmed. She was more indignant that he had let her down. But as it happened he had had a stroke, although only a minor one, and he was, for the time being, a semi-invalid, recuperating at the 'place in the country' he had spoken of.

It was in Devon – a vast mansion at Oldway, on the coast near Paignton – and it had belonged to his father Isaac, who always referred to it lightly as his 'wigwam'. When Singer had inherited it, he had set about using his architectural skills to transform it into something resembling the Palace of Versailles. Indeed, he had installed a marble staircase that had originally been commissioned by Louis XIV, and intended for Versailles. He had also hung Gobelin tapestries on the walls of the ballroom, as well as a large canvas depicting the coronation of Napoleon, painted by David.

It was to Oldway that Isadora went, leaving her children still with their governess in Versailles, to begin her three-month 'experiment in domesticity'. It did not turn out a success.

Singer, ill or not, had whole-heartedly embraced the role of invalid. Installed in the house with him were a resident doctor and nurse, who supervised him, for instance when he made use of an electro-therapy device he had bought. Isadora recalled it as 'a sort of cage which had been brought over from Paris, in which he sat while thousands of volts

224

of electricity were turned on him, and he would sit there looking extremely pathetic and saying: "I hope this will do me good."' (At that time it was widely believed that electricity was in some way connected with the 'life force' and that exposure to a magnetic field would increase vitality.) The doctor and nurse gave strict instructions that, in order for their patient to have as much rest and quiet as possible, Isadora should have her room in a distant wing.

Singer did continue to welcome guests, mostly from among the British upper class, and Isadora found them insufferably tedious. Their days revolved around country walks, shooting parties, games of bridge, and formal meals. 'The really important business of the day,' she recalled, '[was] dressing for dinner.' The main amusement she was able to find for herself was going every afternoon for a chauffeur-driven ride in one of Singer's fourteen cars, but even that pleasure was diminished by the fact that it rained incessantly.

After a couple of weeks, feeling she could stand this life no longer, she complained to Singer about her situation. He suggested she use the ballroom to begin dancing again, performing for his guests. She objected that the ornate Gobelins and the David were hardly a suitable background for the simple gestures of her dancing, also that the ballroom had an 'oily, waxed floor'. He suggested that in that case she should send for her blue curtains and for one of the carpets she danced on. 'But I must have a pianist,' she said.

Singer told her that of course she must send for one, and she at once sent a telegram to Paris, to Edouard Colonne, whose orchestra had played at her party. It read: SPENDING SUMMER IN ENGLAND. MUST WORK. SEND PIANIST. He sent his assistant director and first violinist, André Caplet, a talented musician who was a friend of, and collaborator with, Debussy, and a man Isadora had already met. She was not pleased, describing Caplet (although not by name) in her memoirs as, 'a strange-looking man with a very large head, which oscillated on a badly made body... This person was so unsympathetic to me that he gave me a sense of absolute physical revulsion whenever I looked at him or touched his hand.' This reaction of hers at least reassured Singer that he need have no cause for jealousy.

For want of any better occupation, Isadora began practising with Caplet, and sometimes performing to his playing in front of Singer's guests. She made sure, however, that he and his grand piano were safely hidden behind a screen so that she could not see him.

One of the guests rebuked her for this rudeness to her accompanist, and she was sufficiently chastened to make some slight amends by inviting Caplet to come with her on one of her afternoon drives. This did not turn out as she had expected. Before the car had gone far, she felt 'a feeling of such disgust' that, as she remembered:

> I rapped on the glass and told the driver to turn and go home. The country road was full of ruts and, as the car turned, I was thrown into the arms of [Caplet]. He closed his arms around me. I sat back and looked at him, and suddenly felt my whole being going up in flames like a pile of lighted straw. I have never felt anything so violent. And, all of a sudden, as I looked at him, I was aghast. How had I not seen it before? His face was perfectly beautiful, and in his eyes there was a smothered flame of genius. From that moment I knew that he was a great man... How was it possible that from such violent antipathy could be born such violent love?

Arriving back at the mansion they at once made passionate love on the ballroom floor, underneath the grand piano. 'From that day in the auto,' she later told a friend, Victor Seroff, 'we had one obsession, to be alone – in the conservatory, in the garden, even taking long walks in the muddy country lanes.'

After only a few days of this idyll, Singer began to be told about it by his staff. He confirmed the truth of what they said by eavesdropping on conversations between Caplet and Isadora on the house telephone. Sending for her, he angrily accused her. Isadora felt ashamed of herself. It had not been right of her to have an affair under the very roof of the man who was supporting her and was supposed to be her lover, especially as he was in poor health and should not be upset.

She agreed with Caplet that their affair, then ten days old, should end at once (as a matter of fact, she later admitted that, although it had remained 'perfect', it had steadily grown less exciting after that first heady day).

He went back to Paris and, shortly afterwards, so did she. The episode had taught her that she was in no way fitted to be a respectable faithful wife, and she determined 'for the hundredth time ... that hereafter I would give my entire life to Art.' Briefly, she and Singer would part.

She had managed to achieve one thing during her time in Devon. She had begun designing a new extended piece which would develop further the dark and threatening themes she had been working with for almost two years in her dance *Death and the Maiden*. The new piece was to

226

depict the legend of Orpheus, and she would dance it to the music from Gluck's *Orfeo ed Eurydice*, which she had long loved. But this time her dancing would be even more violent and unsettling (perhaps partly reflecting her own loneliness and her growing fear that nothing in life lasts – except maybe Art).

In September 1910 her friend Mary D'Este had moved into the centre of Paris to live, after a summer spent at a resort on the coast of the English Channel. There she had finally fallen out with her lover, Jacques Grétillat. She had first rented a medium-sized apartment at 19 avenue Charles Floquet, then a large one at the same address. When her landlord refused to cancel her lease on the first apartment, she took her revenge by turning it over to Raymond Duncan and his commune, goats and all. The goats, as Preston Sturges' biographer Donald Spoto explained, 'fouled everything and, when tethered on the balcony, also rather nastily surprised pedestrians below. Presently the landlord agreed to cancel the lease.'

Isadora gave the first performance of *Orpheus* at the Théâtre du Châtelet, in Paris, on 18th January 1911, and in the next month presented it in America during her third tour there accompanied by Walter Damrosch. The writer Charles H. Caffin, who saw *Orpheus* in February, shortly afterwards wrote of her 'Dance of the Furies' sequence:

> Here the expression of concentrated venom and malice is carried out with an intensity and detail more dramatic, savage, earthly than in the earlier dances. The muscles harden in the face and limbs, the movements are abrupt, fierce, now bowed and now angular. The carriage of the body is stiff and inflexible, and then quivers and vibrates like a bow-string, loosed from the hand... It goes without saying, after all, that a spirit so sensitive as Miss Duncan's to the diverse moods of joyousness and gaiety cannot fail to respond to the deeper emotions.

As well as depicting Furies, she portrayed doomed souls fated to bear boulders on their backs, the torturers who lunge and claw at them, and frenzied demons. As Gluck's libretto deals with the triumph of love over death, she of course also depicted Blessed Spirits dancing for joy in the Elysian Fields. But, drama being what it is, it was generally agreed that her damned souls in torment were more rewarding to watch.

But this third American tour was to prove much less successful than her previous two. Although her Art was continuing to develop and mature, the taste of the dance-going public of America had also moved on since she had last been there, even though that was little more than a year before. Not only were dancers like Loie Fuller and Adeline Genée still active (and easier to appreciate than Isadora), another had recently arrived on the scene. Anna Pavlova had left the Ballets Russes to strike out on a solo career, stunning audiences everywhere she went with her *Dying Swan* (choreographed by Fokine six years before – shortly after he had seen Isadora – to music by Saint-Saëns).

This bravura piece had given the general public a new idea of what dancing should be – although in truth it was in many ways that same old acrobatic ballet that Isadora had for years been campaigning against. The result was that many people, even some critics, tended to criticise Isadora for not being a real dancer at all. One critic, reviewing her *Liebestod* in the *New York Sun*, wrote, 'There were no long leaps upward and forward about this dance, if it could possibly be described as a dance, since it bore no more relationship to that act than an occasional run backward and forward.'

The press also commented with mild disapproval on the new stylishness of her dress, the *New York Tribune* pointing out that she had 'put behind her all her old ideas about sackcloth and ashes for art's sake', the 'simplicity of the Greek' having given way to 'the frills of the Frank.'

Attendances everywhere were poor. The cold-eyed Boston critic, Henry Taylor Parker, wrote of her appearance there, 'The boxes yawned in emptiness, above stairs and below, the audience was scanty; the social and aesthetic contingents that used to profess the utmost joy in Miss Duncan were lacking; the throng of the merely curious had declined into scattered hundreds of spectators, many of whom were elderly women.' He also noted that Isadora had 'grown somewhat too stout of leg and body.'

Disappointed by her poor reception, it was with relief that, in April 1911, she set off to sail back to France.

There things were at once better. In her memoirs she wrote, 'I shall never forget my return to Paris. I had left my children at Versailles with a governess. When I opened the door, my little boy came running towards me... I had left him a little baby in the cradle.' She decided then and there that in future she would spend more time with her two children, and, indeed, she would not dance professionally again for some six months.

She loved Deirdre and Patrick deeply. Her friend Victor Seroff recalled that 'whenever Isadora mentioned her children in conversation, she invariably left me with an impression of her almost uncanny, physical, animal love for them.'

It was convenient, in the light of Isadora's decision to devote herself to motherhood, that shortly after she came back to Paris her friend Kathleen Bruce, now also a mother, arrived in the city. Kathleen was just back from New Zealand, where she had seen her husband, Captain Scott, set off, aboard the *Terra Nova*, to find the South Pole. She had with her in Paris her own baby son, Peter, who was two, a year older than Patrick and two years younger than Deirdre, and as an officer's wife she was a little disapproving of Isadora's affectionate and casual approach to child-rearing. In her diary she wrote, 'Patrick is just a year, so pretty, but oh! so fragile – such a contrast to mine. They are rearing him all wrong. He wears too many clothes, has hot baths, and is half-starved.'

Craig was also in Paris. Now living in Florence, he had begun publishing a magazine called *The Mask*, to set forth his ideas on staging, and had come to Paris to try and find backing for a French-language version of it. The ebullient Mary D'Este had offered to help him, telling him, he recalled, that 'she could find all the money and support he needed,' and dragging him from salon to salon to introduce him to suitable wealthy art-lovers. (Mary was by now divorced from Solomon Sturges, and proposing to marry her new lover, a tall, handsome, charming Turk named Vely Bey.)

Her efforts on Craig's behalf bore no fruit, and soon he was writing with irritation to a friend in America, George Plank, 'The men are asses, the women are foul. Champagne, the arts of Greece & millionaires are all reconciled under the table... The nicest people seem to become fakes when they get [to] drinking champagne in Paris.'

He did meet Isadora while he was there, but was equally unimpressed by what he felt Paris had done to her, writing that it had 'cooked her & dressed her up – absolute murder of the girl.' Worse, he felt she was 'frivolling' instead of devoting herself to her Art, and indeed was turning into a different person – a fashionable, champagne-swilling gossip. 'I was very fond of Topsy Duncan,' he noted, '... But slowly and surely Topsy grew very vague [and] "Madame Duncan" grew more & more horrific. I'm not sure that this third party wasn't a performance, but anyhow it was a most unpleasant one & a role she really had little sense to assume.'

At around this time Isadora did make her peace with Elizabeth (and Max Merz), and reconciled herself to accepting their school (still not completed) at Darmstadt.

In its own peculiar way, the school was becoming something of a success. In 1911 it was awarded a gold medal at the First International Hygienic Exhibition, held in Dresden. This Exhibition, intended to demonstrate modern healthy living, went on for several months, and while it lasted the girls lived in Dresden, giving demonstrations of their physical fitness to the attending visitors.

It was there that Isadora went to meet again her sister and her pupils. Not having seen her for two years, the girls were astonished by her Parisian style of dress.

She, for her part, was appalled by their 'uncomfortable, unbecoming' school uniforms. There was nothing stylish about either Elizabeth or Max. For dancing, the girls wore a sort of grey woollen underwear. Nor did their dancing in any way resemble what Isadora had taught. It was, pupil Irma recalled, something 'resembling in every respect the stiff drill of soldiers on parade.' Yet those pupils who remembered Isadora, including Irma, had 'kept the spark alive and continued to dance the way Isadora had taught us.'

An arrangement was reached whereby Elizabeth and Max would continue to house and instruct the pupils, while the best of them would go and dance with Isadora whenever she needed them. Of these there were six – Anna, Theresa, Lisa, Gretel, Erika and of course Irma. And before leaving Dresden, Isadora invited Elizabeth to come in July to Ostend, where Paris Singer's yacht would be moored, and to bring with her Irma, now aged fourteen. (Isadora and Singer were by now somewhat raggedly together again.)

Elizabeth and Irma arrived in Ostend late at night, and were met at the railway station by Isadora. She took them by car to the hotel where they were to stay, and Irma found herself ushered into a room where Deirdre and Patrick were fast asleep, watched over by their Scottish nanny, Annie Sim.

'You go and sleep in that bed beside the nurse, darling, and I'll see you in the morning,' said Isadora.

Irma was in heaven. Isadora was to her everything that was wonderful, and, as she recalled, 'Getting into bed beside her sleeping children, I had the sweet sensation of actually being one of her children, too.'

Next morning, waking early from excitement, she rushed to the balcony to look out at the sea, and her movements woke Deirdre, who looked her over carefully and then asked timidly, 'Who are you?'

'I am your new playmate,' answered Irma. 'I hope we shall be friends.'

'Have you seen my little brother?' Deirdre asked, pulling Irma over to his crib. 'His name is Patrick and he is twelve months old.'

Irma found Deirdre enchanting, remembering her years later as 'such a beautiful child, so exquisitely made.'

The party did the usual seaside things, paddling in the sea, making sand castles, and sitting in deckchairs listening to the band. And Irma was delighted when Isadora suggested she teach Deirdre some dancing steps. 'I had never taught anyone,' Irma wrote in her memoirs, 'and so Deirdre, Isadora's little girl, became my first pupil. She also suggested I teach her some simple piece of poetry like William Blake's "Little Lamb, who made thee?"' Isadora herself had not had much success in teaching her daughter this poem. Deirdre tended to get stuck after the first line, and Isadora's over-eagerness that her daughter should be bright led her to become insistent, which reduced the child to tears.

Eventually everybody boarded the yacht, and it sailed round the coast to Boulogne, where they were all booked into another hotel. Isadora had invited Kathleen to come to Boulogne, when the yacht arrived there. She came, bringing her infant son Peter, and an old friend of hers and her husband's, a Captain Sykes. When their train arrived, Kathleen wrote in her diary, '[Isadora and Deirdre] came in a big motorcar to meet us, both dressed in Poiret gowns looking perfectly beautiful.'

Unfortunately, not everything was beautiful. The yacht remained moored at Boulogne for a week, during which, Kathleen remembered, Isadora and Singer fought, and made up, and fought again, several times. Much of the trouble was caused by Isadora flirting with every man in sight – the sailors, the officers, and Captain Sykes, who warded off her advances with gentlemanly charm.

After a particularly bad quarrel, which ended with Isadora and Singer both in their hotel rooms, each too proud to open the connecting door, Isadora fled back to Paris. But not for long. A day or so later she was back again, and the quarrels resumed.

During one of their quieter moments, Isadora suggested to Singer that, as Kathleen and Peter were due to go back to England anyway, they should take her there on the yacht. After one abortive attempt, when a rough sea caused everybody to be seasick, beginning with baby Patrick, they eventually made it, landing in Devon. Isadora and her children, Elizabeth, Irma and Singer then all motored to his mansion at Oldway.

But their stay did not last long. Around the middle of August, Patrick developed a fever and Isadora insisted she take him at once to the doctor she now most trusted, the doctor who had delivered him, Dr Bosson in Nice.

They returned to Paris. Isadora saw Elizabeth and Irma off back to Germany on a train from the Gare du Nord, stunning Irma by saying to her, quite casually, 'Goodbye, dear. I'll see you next winter in Egypt.'

She took Patrick to Nice, to Dr Bosson, and as soon as he was well again, carried on with her children to Venice, a city she always felt congenial when wishing to work out new ideas. And new ideas she certainly needed. She was still unhappy about her relationship with Singer, feeling that, 'This human life [of his] seemed so heavy beside my dreams of Art.' And she was dissatisfied with her Art itself, feeling that, to some extent, she was stagnating.

A way out of her creative stagnation presented itself after she returned to Paris in September. Her brother Augustin was still living there, with his mistress Marguerite Sargent, and they by now had a baby son, Angus. Augustin called on Isadora and explained that he was planning to set up a theatre company of his own. He asked whether she would become involved.

She would, and on 1st October 1911 they signed a preliminary contract. He would head the company, and she would 'devote her genius for a period of three years', directing 'the plastic movements, dances and stage deportment of the principals and chorus' and dancing herself 'in such of these productions as it shall be mutually agreed upon lend themselves to her purpose.' (Augustin also attempted to interest Craig in the project, but Craig was having none of it.)

Together that month Isadora and Augustin went to London, staying at Paris Singer's house, and from there visited Oxford to talk to the eminent classical scholar Gilbert Murray. Then in his forties, he was the Regius Professor of Greek at New College, and the Duncans wanted to discuss with him the possibility of their using his translations in performing the works of Euripides.

October 11th that year was Mary D'Este's fortieth birthday, and she decided to celebrate it by joining Isadora in London and throwing a party at the Savoy Hotel. Isadora and Augustin attended, and so did the poet, mountaineer and practitioner of black magick, Aleister Crowley, also known at various times in his life by such names as Frater Perdurabo, the Master Therion and the Great Beast 666.

Reacting against an upbringing among fanatical Plymouth Brethren, he had developed for himself a pagan religion based loosely on cults of pre-Christian times, astrology and the mocking rituals of the eighteenth-century Hell-Fire Club. Its ceremonies made heavy use of sex and drugs, and he was of course its High Priest.

It has never been entirely clear whether Crowley took his wizardry seriously, or whether he found it a rewarding dream-world to inhabit, but he was then a man of considerable sexual magnetism. He was four years younger than Mary, and on meeting him at her birthday party, she fell for him at once. He was equally attracted to her, finding her (he later wrote) 'a most powerful personality [with] terrific magnetism which instantly attracted my own. We forgot everything. I sat on the floor like a Chinese god, exchanging electricity with her.'

Instantly forgetting the man she proposed to marry, the Turkish Vely Bey, Mary set off almost at once with Crowley, first to Paris and then for a winter holiday in Switzerland. She was, according to Crowley, 'a voluptuous and passionate woman of the world, an amorous ... lioness ... quick-tempered and impulsive, always eager to act with reckless enthusiasm.'

Back in Paris herself by November, Isadora danced for a season at the Théâtre du Châtelet, accompanied by her six star pupils from the school. She was prevented from presenting her version of the Bacchanal from *Tannhäuser* by the Paris Opéra, who had held the rights to it since Wagner presented his 'Paris version' there in 1861. But she did present an extended version of her *Iphigenia*, giving the girls larger roles and employing an actor, Jean Mounet-Sully, to deliver verse interludes. Although this sounds like something of a throwback to her early days, she was in fact moving towards an ambition she now had to present dancers and actors on the stage at the same time.

Unfortunately, this season at the Châtelet was dogged by prudishness. First, there was the old problem of the girls' costumes. The police received complaints about 'the commercial exploitation in Parisian theatres of young children, parading around in skimpy costumes and baring their naked legs.' (It probably didn't help that a couple of years before the French poet Fernand Divoire had given the girls the nymphettish nickname 'Les Isadorables'.)

Complaints about her harmful exploitation of her girls caused Isadora to deliver one of her harangues from the stage. 'Look at these children,' she exhorted the audience. 'They are healthy and robust; eyes are clear and no one is tired or weakened. To the contrary, listen as they breathe freely. Do you think it is wrong for them to dance?'

Worse, during one of her own dances something in her tunic slipped or came unstitched, and a breast (or, according to some authorities, two) came into view. She was outraged when, the next night, police were posted in the theatre to make sure that there were no further offences against decency, and even more so when she learned they were considering investigating her past for similar offences. Angrily she told Jean Mounet-Sully that if this went on she would give up performing. 'If they annoy me about this,' she told him, 'I will dance in the forest naked, naked, naked ... with the song of birds and elemental noises for an orchestra.'

Of course, that was spoken in the heat of the moment. She had no intention whatever of giving up performing. And even if she had, that intention would soon have vanished, because, not long afterwards, Paris Singer announced that he was intending to build her a theatre of her very own. There she would be able to work with her pupils and with Augustin, and provide, as she hoped, 'a meeting place and haven for all the great Artists of the world.'

In January 1912, before getting down to serious planning, Isadora and Singer made the Egyptian trip she had mentioned briefly to Irma. Isadora was by now deeply enamoured of Egypt, and Singer liked it too. He had bought a villa in Alexandria and both of them frequently spoke of living in it permanently.

With them as they sailed again to Alexandria and then up the Nile, were a number of guests. As well as Irma and Elizabeth (whose school had at last been built), there were Deirdre and Patrick. There were the painter Jean Grandjouan, a French count and countess romantically named Tristan and Isolde de Bérault, and the young pianist, Hener Skene.

Hener had been with Isadora and Singer on their previous trip up the Nile, and he and Isadora had grown close. He was, Isadora would recall, 'my best friend and comforter in those days. He adored my Art, and was only happy when playing for me. He had the most extraordinary admiration for me of anyone I have ever met.' Their relationship does not seem to have been a sexual one, although some sources suggest that he was somewhat sexually active himself, and possibly for a time a member of Aleister Crowley's cult of sex and drugs (which may explain how Crowley happened to turn up at Mary D'Este's birthday party).

The trip was a pleasant one, although Irma had a rather unnerving experience that showed her a harder side of her beloved Isadora's character. They had docked at the temple of Horus, at Kôm Ombo, between Luxor and Aswân. Isadora and Singer and their guests were ashore, sitting on and among the broken columns and stone slabs of the temple. Irma was alone on deck, looking at its moonlit stones and dreaming of 'forgotten centuries', while from it wafted the sound of Hener Skene playing the *Moonlight Sonata*.

Suddenly Elizabeth appeared and told her that Isadora wanted her to dance for everybody. Irma was appalled. She had never danced alone in public, and, as she recalled years later, 'I dreaded the outcome and, hoping I would be let off, I said quite truthfully that I had not brought my tunic.'

Elizabeth, who of course knew this, was prepared. She handed Irma a silk nightgown, saying, 'Here, wear that.'

Irma protested, but to no avail, and, wearing the nightgown, was led by Elizabeth to the temple. 'Ah, here she is,' said Isadora. 'Are you going to dance for us, my dear?'

To Irma's relief, she saw that Hener Skene seemed to have vanished. Grasping at straws, she said, 'I don't know what to dance, without music and everything...'

Isadora went into poetic mode. 'On such a wonderful moonlit night, in this beautiful temple, surely inspiration should not be lacking. Dance anything you fancy, whatever comes to mind.'

But nothing whatever was coming to Irma's mind, which seemed to have ceased to function. Suppressing an urge to simply run away, she did a few turns and sways and leaps, until, she recalled, 'my sense of utter inadequacy struck me dead in my tracks.'

There was a silence, then Isadora rose with the majestic, pale, inexorable speed of boiling milk. 'Have you noticed,' she asked the guests, 'how entirely unrelated her dance movements were to these extraordinary surroundings? She seemed to be completely unaware of them. What she did just consisted of some pretty little dance gestures she had learned – very nice, very lighthearted, but not in the slightest degree in harmony with the almost awesome sense of mystery that pervades this place and of which you are all, I am sure, deeply aware.'

Then she herself began to dance, in and out of the massive columns, and when she at last stopped the guests cried, '*C'était magnifique, magnifique!*'

Irma had heard the voice of the Artistic Conscience speaking with undiluted power, and she was not only mortified by her own inadequacy, but awed.

Back in Paris, Isadora set about planning her theatre – 'Le Théâtre du Beau', Singer would call it. Her plan was that it should be round, like an amphitheatre, with tiers of seats rising around a central stage. It was also to be democratic, with reduced prices for artists and students, and nothing to specially attract the 'over-fed rich'.

Singer, who had involved himself in the project with an energy and enthusiasm that surprised Isadora, hired the architect Louis Sue to design the building, and chose a site for it in the rue de Berri, off the Champs-Élysées, in the wealthy eighth *arrondissement*. Their joint involvement in the project brought Isadora and himself closer together than perhaps they had ever been, albeit now with the slightly tired warmness of a couple in an old imperfect marriage. (Her friend Kathleen, observing their quarrels and reconciliations on holiday the year before had observed that they were 'more married than most married people I ever knew.')

During the whole of 1912 Isadora would perform only for two brief seasons – one in London and one in Rome. This was partly because of her concentration on building her theatre, and partly because for some reason she was again feeling tired and out of condition. Nonetheless, she continued to practise her dancing in every spare moment, and to develop new items for her repertoire, usually with Hener Skene as her accompanist.

She practised in her studio at Neuilly, which was also often the scene of the lavish costume parties that Singer delighted in giving (although his attitude to them while they were happening was oddly remote – the American architect Addison Mizner once noted that 'although his costumes were wonderfully done, he never seemed to enter into the gaiety, but stood in the background looking on.') Often, Isadora recalled, 'the vast studio was turned into a tropical garden or a Spanish Palace, and there came all the artists and celebrated people of Paris.'

Her friend Mary D'Este had returned to Paris, her brief liaison with Aleister Crowley having worn itself out. For a while she had entered enthusiastically into his world of magick, even to the extent of having prophetic visons herself, while possessed of a spirit called Abuldiz. Abuldiz, while they were in Switzerland, had urged Crowley to go to southern Italy (oddly, Mary liked southern Italy) and write a book about his system of belief. Obeying this injunction, they had settled in Posilippo, near Naples, where he dictated his book and Mary wrote it down. It was called *Book Four* (there being no books one to three).

Her son Preston had come from boarding school to join them just after they got to Posilippo, but found Crowley, 'a sinister buffoon ... depraved, vicious and revolting ... [he had] the unappetizing habit of taking out a penknife and adding a small fresh slice to ... his forearm ... each time my poor mother had so far forgotten his teachings as to begin a sentence with "I".'

Soon Mary had had enough of this sort of thing, and in the spring of 1912 she had returned to Paris and to her Turk, Vely Bey, moving in with him at his apartment on the avenue Charles Floquet, and in a short while marrying him. (Preston was not sent back to boarding school, but to a nearby tutor as a live-in student.)

Vely Bey was well-connected. His father, Ilias Pasha, had been personal physician to the Sultan of Constantinople, Abdülhamid II. When the Sultan was deposed, Vely Bey and his mother and father were among a number of aristocratic Turks who were exiled (or exiled themselves) to Paris.

It was through Vely Bey that Mary began a new business that quickly supplanted any such previous ideas as rearing exotic chickens, and would have a great influence in her life. His physician father, Ilias Pasha, owned a vast assortment of perfumes, potions and pomades, and one day, when Mary developed a rash on her face, he treated it with a lotion that, he explained to her, was used by all the major harems in Turkey.

It worked like a charm, and Mary at once hit on the idea of marketing it as 'Le Secret du Harem'. And it wasn't long before she developed this idea further by deciding to sell a whole range of products and, in short, become a cosmetician and *parfumier*. Renting a small mezzanine space at 4 rue de la Paix, she established a beauty institute she named Maison D'Este. This name brought her immediate trouble when it was objected to by the aristocratic French family whose name really was 'D'Este'. Mary overcame this by changing both the name of her business and her own name permanently to 'Desti'.

Craig was also for the moment back in Paris, with his long-time mistress Elena Meo, working on an illustrated edition of *Hamlet*. His production of *Hamlet* for the Moscow Arts Theatre had at last opened, in January 1912, to tremendous acclaim, making him even more of a celebrity than his book *The Art of Theatre* had done. As a result he had attracted patronage from the queen of the Parisian upper *monde*, the Countess Elisabeth de Greffulhe, who hoped he might become as much of an influence on the French stage as he had been on the Russian.

Knowing of the closeness there was between Craig's ideas of theatre and Isadora's, Singer approached him to collaborate with Louis Sue on the design of the stage and lighting for the Théâtre du Beau, persuading him to join the project with an offer of fifty thousand francs.

Craig did join the project, but he was still wary of interference from the new Isadora, writing to Singer in July, 'In the planning and execution of your scheme I would earnestly urge you to exclude from your counsels all and every *performer*.' (Possibly he was also smarting from his experience on Duse's *Rosmersholm*.) Singer reassured him that the theatre was being planned, and paid for, solely by him, Paris Singer.

Now involved, Craig could hardly avoid meeting Isadora, and thus meeting his daughter Deirdre. They met at Neuilly, and he was shocked that she seemed to have no memory of him, or instinctive feeling for him, remembering years later in a letter to Irma, 'With all my children, especially the dear little girls, *all understanding* has ever been between us

– always – and somehow little Deirdre seemed frozen … no tender leap towards me – no eager smile… Can you imagine what that meant to me?'

He remained involved from July till October, when he quit the project, annoyed because it became too obvious to him that in Singer's mind the theatre was Isadora's, and hers alone. In his letter of resignation to Singer he wrote, 'Now although anyone might be honoured to build a theatre for Miss Duncan I have made it one of my rules lately to work for no performer however gifted or eminent, & I cannot break it. This therefore will make it impossible for me to go on with the idea. I am very sorry – & I had hoped things would have been different.' Shortly afterwards he returned to Florence, muttering angrily in his notebooks about 'Isadora & her millionaire'.

Cast down by the loss of Craig from her project, and his disappearance again from her life, Isadora attempted to cheer herself up by throwing a costume party at her studio, all paid for by Singer, and with plenty of champagne. But she was in a strange, unsettled mood, which made her mischievous. For a start she amused herself by stirring up dissension between married couples. As she recalled, 'By this time I was somewhat initiated into the different intrigues of Paris, so I was able to put together couples who I knew wished it, thus causing tears on the part of some of the wives.'

One wife she upset was Paul Poiret's, this by plying him with kisses herself. Nor was he the only man she flirted with. Her behaviour eventually became so outrageous that Singer angrily left her studio, complaining that there was no room for him in it. Poiret noted that she bade him goodnight 'with considerable affectation'. 'Then,' he recalled, 'everyone danced, and above all, She danced, magnificently, marvellously, divinely, as only She knew how.'

The party was still going on at three in the morning, when Singer, having calmed down, returned. Unfortunately, at the time Isadora was in her bedroom with the playwright Henri Bataille. There may have been nothing in it, although rumour had it that he was kissing her foot.

Singer was furious. Isadora swore to him that Bataille was simply an old friend, 'like a brother', but Singer raged and swore. 'His curses fell on my ears,' remembered Isadora, 'with the empty clanging of demon bells. The world seemed suddenly transformed into an obscene Hell.' He stormed out of the house, shouting that he was through with her and with her theatre too. And that was the end of the Théâtre du Beau.

Chapter Thirteen

Darkness Descends

Having lost both Paris Singer and her hope of having her own theatre at one blow, Isadora immersed herself in work, beginning by accepting an offer she had had to make a six-week tour of Russia. As her accompanist she took Hener Skene.

Her performances were successful, but her success did nothing to relieve her unhappiness. She wrote, for instance, to Louis Sue, the proposed architect for the theatre, telling him she was 'desolate' and 'disconsolate'. 'I'm living here like a *monk*,' she told him, 'and apart from moments of exaltation and ecstasy it's very *depressing*... What a joy it will be to see my Patrick and Deirdre again. I am homesick... My soul is drying up.'

She also wrote to Singer at his villa in Alexandria (where he had gone with another woman), but received no reply.

Suffering from depression and tiredness, she was during the whole tour prone to morbid imaginings. In January 1913, for instance, when she and Hener got off their train at Kiev in the early morning, and she was still groggy from sleep, they took a sleigh over the snow-covered roads to their hotel. As they drove along, Isadora had the sudden hallucination that the piled-up snow either side of the road formed two rows of children's coffins. She clutched Hener's arm, telling him this, and he did his best to reassure her. Not entirely successfully, for in her suggestible state she became convinced that what she had imagined was a warning of her own approaching end.

In a sleeping-carriage on another train, she imagined all night that she could hear Chopin's *March Funèbre* (from his second piano sonata), which so impressed itself on her that in her performance the next evening she improvised a dance to it, totally without rehearsal.

In St Petersburg, coming down with a fever, she felt such foreboding that she made out her will. But fortunately not all in her trip was so negative. In Moscow, on 22nd February, she was delighted to catch one of the last performances of Craig's *Hamlet*. After it she dined with Stanislavsky and the Moscow Arts Theatre company.

Finishing her Russian tour, she went on at once to Berlin, where she was met by Elizabeth and the school's six prize pupils, and with them she gave three performances (including again in one of them the *Marche Funèbre*).

Her hallucinations continued. After returning to Paris from Berlin, she was one day at her studio in Neuilly and imagined she saw 'great black birds flying about'. Having dinner one evening with Oscar Wilde's friend, Lord Alfred Douglas, at her apartment at Versailles, she thought she saw three black cats run across the room in front of a curtain, and told him of it, saying that she was afraid she was losing her mind.

In spite of suffering from stress and disappointment, she continued to press forward with the ideas she had intended to carry out at the Théâtre du Beau, in particular by incorporating in her performances other mediums than dance – there would be poetry, singing, and even short introductory lectures. Looking for a future project, she chose Euripedes *The Bacchae*, and asked the classicist Mario Meunier, who happened at the time to be working as Rodin's secretary, to prepare a new translation for her (presumably the discussion that she and Augustin had had with Gilbert Murray had not worked out well).

In March, the six pupils were to dance with her again in Paris, at the Trocadéro. Max Merz was not so happy about this as he had been to have them dancing in Berlin. He was afraid that Isadora might kidnap them (emulating what he and Elizabeth had done). So he insisted that Elizabeth accompany them as a guardian. She in turn insisted that Isadora bill them in all her advertising as 'Students of the School of Dance at Darmstadt'.

At the Trocadéro Isadora presented *Orpheus*. Each performance began with a lecture by the poet and playwright Joséphin Sar Péladan. The actor Jean Mounet-Sully again read poems, and the tenor Rodolphe Plamondon sang arias from Gluck.

Her success continued. The poet Fernand Divoire (he who had invented the word 'Isadorables'), reporting on *Orpheus*, again commented with approval on the pupils – 'six slender young girls in rose-coloured scarves and crowned with flowers... They are grown up now. Tall, supple and graceful, they combine their erstwhile naïve gaiety with all the charm of young girls... Isadora dances with them and is part of them. And the delighted audience applauds and applauds, freed of all everyday worries and care, left with no other thoughts but those of grace and youth eternal.'

Similar acclaim followed her and her pupils when, on 9th April, they opened at the Théâtre du Châtelet, presenting *Iphigenia*. But her hallucinations were continuing. One day, in the bedroom at her studio, she imagined at the foot of her bed 'a moving figure, draped in black', gazing at her 'with pitiful eyes', and the black crosses that Poiret had designed on her golden doors now seemed to her more threatening than amusingly bizarre.

A new theatre opened later that month in Paris. Named the Théâtre des Champs-Élysées, its décor was inspired by her dancing, with bas-reliefs of her on its walls and a sculpted fresco of her above its entrance (all by the sculptor Emile-Antoine Bourdelle). But even this did little to lift her spirits.

Worrying about her exhausted mental state, she telephoned Dr Bosson in Nice, who diagnosed that her nerves were 'overstrained' and ordered her to rest.

This she sensibly did. She decided to put behind her the disappointments that were dragging her down and to concentrate on the one thing in her life (beside her dancing) that brought her joy, her children. To spend more time with them, she moved them at once from Neuilly to her apartment at the Trianon Palace Hotel in Versailles. There, although for the moment she would continue dancing at the Châtelet in the evenings, at once she felt better.

Next day her old friend Rodin came to tea, bringing with him his secretary, Mario Meunier. To Isadora's delight, Mary D'Este (now Desti) could spare time from her beauty salon, Maison Desti, and was able to be there as well. Mary would later recall that she had 'never seen Isadora so happy or tender.'

Dancing that night, Isadora already felt restored. As she recalled in her memoirs:

> I remember that evening so well, for I danced as never before. I was no longer a woman, but a flame of joy – a fire – the sparks that rose, the smoke whirling from the hearts of the public – And, as a farewell, after a dozen encores, I danced last of all the 'Moment Musicale', and as I danced, it seemed to me that something sang within my heart, 'Life and Love – the Highest Ecstasy – and all are mine to give – are mine to give to those who need them.' And

suddenly it seemed as if Deirdre were sitting on one of my shoulders and Patrick on the other, perfectly balanced, in perfect joy, and as I looked from one side to another in my dance, I met their laughing, bright baby faces – baby smiles – and my feet were never tired.

What made her evening even better was that, just as she was getting ready to leave the theatre, accompanied by Mary Desti, into her dressing-room walked Paris Singer. As she would recall, 'He seemed deeply affected by my dancing that evening, and by our meeting, and proposed to join us at supper at Augustin's apartment in the Champs Élysées Hotel.'

As it turned out, he didn't make it to the supper, which left Isadora 'bitterly disappointed', but next morning early, while she was still in her dressing-gown, he phoned her and asked would she meet him for lunch and bring the children. Of course she would. Quite apart from being delighted to see him again, she wanted to show him the son he had not seen for nearly five months, to let him see how 'strong and beautiful' Patrick had grown. Also it would be convenient, because she had to be in Paris anyway, as she was to rehearse with her girls in her studio. The date was Saturday, 19th April 1913.

Isadora had rented a car and chauffeur, and she and Mary and the children (and the children's Scottish nurse/governess, Annie Sim) set off for Neuilly. Fortunately the car, a somewhat old-fashioned Renault, was a closed one, because by the time they reached Paris it was pelting with rain.

Her students arrived at Neuilly shortly after Isadora, as did the pianist Hener Skene. They were delighted to find Deirdre and Patrick there, and their governess egged Patrick on to do an imitation of Isadora acknowledging audience applause. The girls laughed, and Isadora, coming in, laughed too. Then she and the girls rehearsed for a couple of hours, after which she took them with the children (and their governess) to the nearby Italian restaurant where she had agreed to meet Singer. Augustin joined them, but Mary did not, feeling she should go and cast an eye on Maison Desti.

The lunch was a warm and joyous affair, in spite of the grey wet day outside. Singer was in an expansive mood, and it seemed that all his quarrels with Isadora were forgotten. He even spoke of resuming work on the Théâtre du Beau.

'It will be Isadora's Theatre,' he said.

'No,' insisted Isadora. 'It will be Patrick's Theatre, for Patrick is the Great Composer, who will create the Dance to the Music of the Future.'

Singer was so enjoying himself that he suggested the whole party make an afternoon trip to the Salon des Humoristes, but Isadora had to decline. The girls were due back at their pension for their daily music lesson, and Annie Sim felt that Deirdre and Patrick were getting tired and should be taken back to Versailles for a nap.

At the studio, Isadora helped the children into the hired Renault, covered their legs with lap rugs, and kissed them. She kissed Deirdre again through the glass of the closed window, and then the car drove away. Isadora waved goodbye and then went into the house, where she reclined on a couch to rest for an hour or so. Later she was expecting to welcome the Queen of Naples for tea.

There was a box of bon-bons there, and she ate one, feeling that, after all, she was happy. Perhaps, she felt, the happiest woman in the world, with her Art, her success, her money, her children, and again, it seemed, her lover.

The next thing she knew, her lover, Paris Singer, came staggering into the room. At first she thought he was drunk. He collapsed to his knees and said, 'The children – the children are dead!'

They were. The Renault had driven only a short distance along the rue Chauveau, where the studio was, to the T-junction at its end, where it met the boulevard Bourdon. There the chauffeur, whose name was Paul Morverand, had braked sharply to avoid a collision with a vehicle travelling along the boulevard.

Unfortunately, he stalled his engine, and the car came to a halt facing across the boulevard, on the far side of which was the river Seine. Morverand got out, as was necessary in those days, to crank the engine with the starting handle, and when he turned the handle the car leapt forward, shot across the boulevard, over the pavement and down the steep grassy slope into the Seine, disappearing below the surface.

Morverand had chased after it, and even managed to reach the running board, but was knocked to the ground before the car went down the slope. He stood on the pavement, beating his head madly, crying, '*Ah! Quel malheur! Quel malheur!*', and swearing that he had put the car in neutral and applied the hand-brake.

A crowd quickly gathered and, as the London *Times* reported next day:

> A number of workmen, who were drinking on the terrace of a neighbouring café, had witnessed the accident, and they behaved with great promptness and courage. One of them dived several times

into the water, but was unable to locate the submerged car. Others of them ran to the nearest fire station and alarmed the fire brigades of Neuilly and Levallois, who were quickly on the scene, followed at short intervals by men of the Paris brigade, and by M. Hennion, the new Prefect of Police. M. Hennion telephoned for divers from the station of the Island of Saint Louis. A large motor boat was also soon requisitioned and its crew were the first to succeed in locating the submerged car in the bed of the river. Strenuous and indeed desperate efforts were made to get it to the bank, but an hour and a half elapsed before the crew of the motor boat by means of ropes and anchors finally managed to haul it ashore.

When the car's door was opened, the bodies of Deirdre and Patrick were revealed, clinging desperately to the body of Annie Sim. All three faces were stricken with terror.

Augustin, who had been drawn to the scene by the wail of sirens, arrived there in time to see the bodies removed from the car – first Annie Sim, then Deirdre, then Patrick. Realising what had happened, his first reaction was to attack Paul Morverand, who was still standing there weeping. He started beating him around the face, screaming, and had to be restrained by police.

The bodies were taken to a tobacco shop on the other side of the boulevard, and shortly afterwards to the morgue of the American Hospital in Neuilly, not far from Isadora's studio. Augustin, having partially recovered himself, felt that the man to tell her what had happened should be Singer, so he phoned to tell him the sad news.

When Singer told Isadora, she was instantly so in shock that she could not take in the tragedy. She tried to calm Singer, reassuring him that it could not be true.

This state of shocked calm mercifully stayed with her for a while. She did not weep, and as people began assembling at the studio, and as she realised the truth of what had occurred, her instinct still was to console others.

Mary Desti's apartment was of course telephoned, and when she arrived back there from Maison Desti in the late afternoon, her secretary told her she was needed urgently at Isadora's, and they had been phoning from there like mad for half an hour.

Mary's understandable reaction was that this was a piece of Isadora dramatics, and told her secretary that she was tired out and Isadora would have to wait. Almost at once, the phone rang again. The secretary answered. It was Elizabeth, with the message that Mme Desti must come at once. That it was most urgent.

Mary, with a sigh, set off. Even friends can be exasperating. By now she had decided that this must be to do with the visit of the Queen of Naples, so she stopped on the way to buy Isadora a bunch of flowers. Arriving at the studio she found outside a huge excited crowd, including policemen, and thought that Isadora must be having a terrific party. But when she made her way inside she found it didn't feel like a party at all. Isadora was standing in the middle of her studio, and Singer was standing by her, his arms around her.

Isadora, seeing Mary, reached out her hands to her and said, 'Mary, tell me it isn't true, it isn't true. My children are not dead.'

Mary, who knew something of the hallucinations her friend had been having, said, 'Of course they're not.'

'Don't lie to her,' said Singer. 'It is not the time for that.'

'Oh,' said Isadora, 'Mary doesn't know. Doesn't know what happened.'

At which point Elizabeth came up and gently took Mary aside, into the hall. 'Mary,' she said, 'for God's sake, don't lose your head... The babies are drowned, Mary; in the Seine.' (Singer himself was in such a state of emotional collapse that for the next few nights he had himself admitted to a clinic.)

It was Mary, of all those present, who made her way to the hospital morgue to see the bodies. When she returned she 'found Isadora sitting like one in a trance, giving orders unconsciously about everything... She asked me if I had seen the babies and was there any hope and I told her, "No, none."'

She asked Isadora if she wanted the children's bodies brought to the studio, and Isadora said she did. But this proved a problem. The deaths, being accidental, would need to be investigated, and in such cases the Paris police usually insisted that bodies remain in a morgue. But among the dozens of friends and acquaintances who had by now rushed to Isadora's side was the editor of *Le Figaro*, Gaston Calmette, and he agreed to see what could be done.

Meanwhile, Augustin had rushed through the rain to the pension where Isadora's pupils were staying. His daughter, Temple, was among them, and rushing into the room where they were, he hugged her tightly, his clothes dripping wet. He seemed so frantic that Temple was alarmed and asked him what was the matter. He told her, and the others, that Isadora's children were dead, and that their teacher, Elizabeth, would be spending the night with her sister.

Isadora, still in her state of shocked calm – of almost statue-like calm – sent a telegram to Craig in Florence. It said: OUR LITTLE GIRL DEIRDRE TAKEN FROM US TODAY WITHOUT SUFFERING. MY BOY PATRICK IS TAKEN WITH HER. THIS SORROW IS BEYOND ANY WORDS. I SEND YOU MY ETERNAL UNDYING LOVE = ISADORA.

Even for Calmette, arranging the claiming of the bodies was difficult, but after pulling a great many strings, he succeeded in getting permission, and at eleven at night they were brought to the studio, to a library on the ground floor, where Mary Desti had readied a sofa. On it, she recalled, 'I arranged and dressed [the children], combing and curling their golden locks.' She arranged them so that Deirdre's arm was protectively around Patrick, and their heads were turned towards each other, touching.

Isadora by now was upstairs in her room, and Mary went up and asked if she would like to see them. She would and, still numbed by shock, not even weeping, was shepherded down the long staircase by Augustin on one side and Mary on the other. Mary recalled, 'as we entered the library, oh, so gently, so gently, she knelt beside them, taking their little hands in hers, and with a cry that has pierced my heart ever since, whispered, "My children, my poor little children."'

For three days she would neither sleep nor change her clothes, nor would she accept any of the sedatives being urged on her by the two doctors she now had in attendance (one of them had been among those making efforts to rescue her children from the submerged car). On the first of those three days – Sunday, 20th April – students from the École des Beaux-Arts had arrived before dawn and covered the garden and trees around the studio with hundreds of white blossoms. Not only all Paris, but all the world seemed to be in mourning for her.

A reply to her telegram came from Craig, who found himself as bereft of words as she was. 'No, I can't say anything,' he wrote, 'not one word. I've said a million written and written – thought & thought – & all useless – all of no use. Only I can repeat my dear my dear many million times. Hear that continually.'

That same day, Mary Desti had gone in the morning to the students in their pension. She told them how the accident had happened, and that they must pack up their things as they were to return to Darmstadt that day. Before leaving, however, they were to go to the studio and see Isadora. Her two doctors hoped that the sight of her pupils might do something to jolt her out of her frozen shock.

Arriving at Neuilly, the girls found her sitting in her darkened studio, in a tall chair, as Irma recalled, 'immobile, like a statue, tears streaming down her face.' (Seeing the girls, she was for first time able to weep.) Irma, crying also, as were all the girls, stood close to her, and Isadora took her in her arms and said gently to all of them, 'You must be my children now.'

Hundreds of people, many of them bitterly upset, came to offer condolences, and Isadora, shocked and inconsolable, found herself consoling them. One was the sculptor Bourdelle, who had depicted her on the walls of the newly-opened Théâtre des Champs-Élysées. Brought to Isadora by Mary Desti, he fell to his knees and laid his head on her lap, weeping. As Mary recalled, 'She looked at him as the Mother of God might have looked. I can't explain just what it was. She was in the most exalted state, as though some great spirit of pity had taken possession of her and she was sorry for the whole world.'

Word reached her the next day that the chauffeur, Morverand, had been arrested. The charge was 'culpable homicide'. Isadora immediately sent a letter to the Paris public Prosecutor, requesting his release. She wrote, 'I wish to assure you that I do not bear him ill will. He is a father, and I need to know that he has been released to his family before I can regain some measure of calm... It is for the peace of my soul that I make this appeal for pity.' Morverand was released at once.

She also received a second, longer, letter from Craig. It said:

> Isadora, my dear – not I alone but all of us, feel we claim some share of your sorrow – and take it.
> Dear – dear —
> You are bearing all the grief that would have been theirs – then dry your eyes for them
>
> Be sure the Gods are looking at you now
> & I am sure you are bearing yourself nobly.
> And as all their little griefs fall to your share now, so also does all their pride & splendour become yours again by right.
> Dear and Great Isadora now is your time.
> To say I love you would not cover the whole.
> I take your fingers your hands in mine & I pray a great prayer.

To this she at once replied, by telegram: YOUR WORDS AS THEY HAVE ALWAYS DONE BRING ME COMFORT AND IF THERE IS COURAGE FOR A GRIEF LIKE THIS I WILL TRY AND FIND IT. LOVE TO YOU AND YOURS = ISADORA.

247

It was on that day too that the last of her siblings arrived at the studio. Raymond and his entourage had been in Bulgaria helping refugees from the First Balkan War, which had broken out the previous year between Bulgaria, Serbia, Greece and Montenegro on the one side, and Turkey on the other. He had seized this opportunity to set up refugee camps, thus at once giving valuable aid to the homeless and finding for himself vast ready-made communes in which to practise the simple life. His arrival back in Paris, still of course wearing his Ancient Greek costume, added to the newspaper stories.

Isadora, for all her stony calm, was not up to arranging the funeral. All she could do was insist that the bodies be cremated, 'not put in the earth to be devoured by worms' and 'that this horrible accident be transformed into beauty'. (She did, however, working on pure instinct, manage to repulse a priest who arrived offering spiritual comfort. She told him, 'I am a pagan. It is not in your heaven that I shall see my children again... I don't want a church; a mother's heart is deeper than all temples.')

Augustin, Elizabeth, Raymond and Mary Desti handled everything. They built a huge mound of flowers in the studio and brought in the Colonne orchestra to play a selection of pieces, including the lament from Gluck's *Orfeo ed Eurydice*.

The next day – 22nd April – the funeral took place. The bodies of Deirdre and Patrick, in open coffins, were brought from the library into the studio, where they were placed on a catafalque among the flowers. Annie Sim's body was brought there too, but her coffin was not open – her face was covered by a sheet because the undertakers had been unable to remove from it her look of agonised horror.

The *New York Times* reported:

> Very early more wreaths began to arrive to swell the masses of flowers already covering the coffins. A little before 10 o'clock men and women famous in the artistic and literary life of Paris began to assemble, and by 10 A.M., when the funeral ceremony began, the studio was thronged with about seven hundred people.

Among the throng was the actress Cécile Sorel, star of the Comédie Française, who would recall in her memoirs how Isadora, with her brothers and sister round her, 'passed before us like a shadow on the way to the room that held the coffins. Then she seemed suddenly stricken by the reality of what had happened. Her knees gave way, she reeled, collapsing into the folds of a grey curtain. Then, slowly, as if the slightest sudden movement would cause her to fall again, she raised herself.' After a short moment of farewell to her children, she ascended the stairs to the gallery behind which were her private rooms, surrounded by her family. There again her legs gave way, and she collapsed for a moment against the gallery railing.

Count Harry Kessler was there, asked by Craig to attend as his representative, and next day he reported to Craig:

> Yesterday, the poor little creatures were laid to rest. There was a most beautiful, moving ceremony in the studio, *the most moving ceremony I have ever been to.* Nothing but exquisite music, Grieg's 'Death of Aase', then a piece of Mozart, that seemed to embody the tripping of light, childish feet on soft grass and flowers, and a wailing, infinitely moving melody of Bach. I thought my heart would break. Poor Isadora behaved splendidly. She knelt behind her sister and two brothers on the balcony. Then the coffins were carried out, through the gardens all strewn with white daisies and jessamin, the white hearses drawn by white horses, everything most admirable in taste and *restraint.* I haven't spoken to Isadora since the tragedy; but her brother Augustin tells me, that she bears up wonderfully; and others, who have seen her, tell me she is really *heroic, encouraging* the others, saying *there is no death,* really great in her terrible grief... Everyone in Paris is moved to the depths of their hearts.

The ceremony was too much for Paris Singer, who threw himself on the catafalque, sobbing that he loved both children as his own. After it, when the hearses took the coffins to the famous cemetery of Père-Lachaise, he felt unable to follow. Isadora did, tightly holding the hand of Mary Desti during the ride and steeling herself not to weep.

To arrange for the bodies to be cremated had not been any easier than having them removed from the morgue to the studio, since the law laid down that no-one could be cremated who had not requested it. But again Gaston Calmette had managed to arrange things, and at Père-Lachaise, after a service in the crematorium, the coffins were committed to the flames. This was almost too much for Isadora, who had not expected to witness the actual immolation. As soon as it was over, she was, Mary Desti recalled, so 'weak and pathetic' that she had to be helped to the car that was waiting for her.

The children's ashes were eventually placed in niches side by side in the columbarium at Père-Lachaise, simply labelled 'Deirdre' and 'Patrick'. Annie Sim's ashes were sent to her family in Britain.

Everyone was concerned about Isadora's state of mind – concerned even that she might harm herself. In London, Mrs Patrick Campbell wrote to Bernard Shaw:

> I open the paper to read of Isadora Duncan's heart rending sorrow – poor Singer – poor Ellen Terry, poor Gordon Craig – poor all of us that have hearts to ache. It is as though one must go to her these first awful days and try to keep her from going mad – She can never dance again – love to her will mean death – and the sight of little children will always break her heart – she loved them and defied the world with their loveliness – it's pitiable ... if only I could do – or say something to help her.

Leaving the funeral, Mary invited Isadora to come to her apartment and rest, rather than return to the studio. But Isadora now began to take firm charge of her own recovery, telling Mary, 'I have a great mission to do.'

In her studio, she sat down, and remained seated and silent for hours. Although silent, she now appeared agitated, and Mary, who remained near her, drew Raymond aside and told him that, if Isadora insisted on going out, she would go with her, but that he should unobtrusively follow them.

Towards midnight, Isadora decisively stood up, put on a cloak, and made for the front door. Mary begged to go with her, wherever she was going. 'I would die if you left me,' she said.

Isadora looked at her. 'Very well, then, Mary,' she said, 'come, but you must let me decide for myself.'

Mary walked beside her (Raymond following) as Isadora went to the end of rue Chauveau, crossed the boulevard Bourdon, and gazed down into the waters of the Seine where her children and their governess had died. She gazed for a long time, silently, then began to walk. She walked nowhere in particular, just up and down the streets, and as Mary said, 'at a terrific pace.' She walked for some two hours, then stopped. 'Mary,' she said. 'I've decided to see it through. Nothing matters to me now but maybe I can help others.'

Mary accompanied her back to the studio and together they lay on Isadora's bed. Mary put her arm under her friend's head, and Isadora, after weeping softly for a while, fell asleep for the first time in three days.

After a few hours, at around five in the morning, Mary heard footsteps approaching up the gravel drive of the house. Quietly getting up, she set off down the stairs, meeting Paris Singer coming up. He seemed to have recovered himself and looked calm and collected. Mary, relieved, went back to her apartment, leaving it to him to assume the task of consolation.

As it turned out, he was not so good at it as he might have been. Never good at coping with emotion, even his own, he was unable to involve himself with the depth of Isadora's need. While she was grateful he was there, he did not, she reflected years later, 'respond to my call.'

It turned out to be Raymond who offered Isadora the best immediate way to cope with her misery. In his work for refugees from the Balkan Wars he had set up a base on Corfu, the most northerly of the major islands in the Ionian Sea, just across a narrow strait from the southern end of Albania, where Albania has its border with the Greek province of Epirus.

Thousands of starving refugees had gathered in the southern Albanian port of Agii Saranta, and Raymond's plan was to set up communes in Epirus, where he would teach the inhabitants to weave, and then sell their work in London, thus providing money for food, tools, and the wool for further weaving. (This would turn out to work surprisingly well.)

He urged Isadora to come back there with him, to help feed the children and comfort the women, and she numbly agreed to go, aware that wherever she was, her suffering would be the same. Augustin and Elizabeth agreed to go as well.

Before leaving, Isadora issued a letter of grateful thanks to the people of Paris, which was widely published, in which she said, 'My friends have helped me to realize what alone could comfort me. That all men are my brothers, all women are my sisters, and all little children on earth are my children.'

From Corfu, on 14th May, while waiting to cross to Epirus, she wrote (in rather halting French) to the architect of the Théâtre du Beau, Louis Sue, telling him of her situation and her mental state:

We are here in a villa overlooking the sea – completely isolated – one can walk for miles among the olive trees without meeting *anybody*.

I have spent two very difficult weeks – it is so difficult sometimes. Horror itself conquers me and in spite of all my efforts I fall into emptiness – in a sort of hell – it is terrible... I try to wear myself out with long walks – but night comes always when I cannot read any more or think and I fall prey to tortures. What is surprising is that the body still lives...

It is so beautiful here ... I can see right to the mountains on the opposite side which seem to float in the azure between earth and heaven – like a vision of a promised land... Sometimes I feel that maybe I'm dead with my children and have entered Paradise – and I feel them close to me – and then comes again the cruel physical suffering – my eyes will never see them, my hands never touch them again, and I see once more the poor little things waving their little hands – in the automobile driving off – and I want to scream.

After Raymond took her across the water to Agii Santara, she cut off her hair as a symbolic gesture of mourning and, going to the seashore, cast it into the sea. Then she began helping the refugees. At the end of May, writing to Craig, she told something of her experiences:

We have bought tents and provisions and are going back to erect shelters for the children. It is terrible to see the results of war – no one trying to help these poor people – If we can save some hundreds of little children I will say Deirdre & Patrick are doing it for me – We live while there on a little boat as there are no houses – and I lie all night looking up at the stars – Sometimes towards morning I see a marvelous liquid shining one – I think myself is there – what is left of me here – only a poor shadow.

She might have written less open-heartedly to him if she had known that in the private musings of his notebooks he was blaming her bitterly, saying, for instance, 'Never need she have lost her loved children had she realised that to have children entails having obligations. *Someone* must care for them – & that someone is always MOTHER. This truth she never seems to have faced up to... Never could they have died as they did die with their MOTHER watching.' (Craig never escaped from his feeling that the duty of women in the world was not to try and become artists, but to look after children like himself.)

A little later, in July, after several weeks of walking 'fifty miles a day' carrying bread and blankets through the mountainous country of Epirus, she wrote to him again, saying, 'To help those poor starving mites over there does something to keep me from dying in my desolation and despair ... anyway what else can I do.'

252

Not long afterwards she received a polite letter of condolence from Craig's mistress, Elena Meo, and to her Isadora replied heart-brokenly, 'What shall I do with it – all my life gone – and my work too – for how shall I ever *dance* again – how stretch out my arms except in desolation. If I had only been with them, but the nurse had my place.'

She was beginning to comfort herself with the mystical belief that maybe life on earth is an illusion, writing, in another letter to Craig, that perhaps it was 'only a bad dream, a mirage ... This abominable bad dream of matter ... These infernal appearances that are *Shams*.'

During July, Singer came to Corfu to see how she was faring, and again was unable to give her the enveloping depth of love she craved. Not only that, when she told him that she hoped to conceive another child, he was shocked by the suggestion, later telling Louis Sue that he found it 'frivolous and inappropriate'. After a few days he left the island, Isadora remembered, 'abruptly, without warning... I saw the steamer receding over the blue waters, and I was left once more alone.'

Towards the end of July, she began to feel oppressed by the misery round her, and to long for surroundings more peaceful and contemplative. She decided to make a trip to Constantinople. Raymond's Greek wife Penelope accompanied her.

In Constantinople she consulted a fortune-teller, and was told that 'after many wanderings,' she would, at the end of her life, 'build temples all over the world... All these temples will be dedicated to Beauty and Joy because you are a daughter of the Sun.'

Gradually, in spite of what she had written to Elena Meo, she was beginning tentatively to think again of dancing – of using her tragedy, through Art, to give comfort and support. Going back to Corfu, she returned Penelope to Raymond and set off, via Trieste, back to Paris. There she sent a note to Hener Skene asking him to find for her 'a chorale or hymn by Bach or Palestrina', explaining, 'I completely despair of life, but perhaps I could make some thing beautiful of movement in the midst of a *requiem* – which might comfort some people on Earth such as myself – Please search for me.'

But she was not yet ready to actually dance – she was too unsettled. The emptiness of her studio at Neuilly she found unbearable, often dissolving in tears and often imagining she could hear the voices of Deirdre and Patrick in the garden. So she began to wander.

In September she went to England to stay with Ellen Terry at her house in Kent. From there she wrote to Craig, 'I am half mad with grief

253

and pain, and I wanted to feel your Mother's arms around me – as I used to dream they were before Deirdre was born.'

At the time, Craig was in London, accompanied by Elena, and at his suggestion Isadora went there to meet her, but in her tender state she came away bruised bruised when it turned out that Elena had no real concern for anything in the world but Craig. After leaving, she wrote to him crossly, 'Your *own* Nellie has no place in her heart except her all-absorbing ferocious & jealous love for you. I am sorry if you don't understand... Think of the morning Deirdre was born and perhaps you will – and if you can't understand at least pity me.'

She returned to Paris, and there, in November, hired a car in which to tour Italy. Totally alone, driving herself, she crossed the Alps and made her way to Milan, Venice, Rimini, Florence, and from there west to Viareggio, on the coast of Tuscany. Fast driving seemed to help (she had long adored cars), and as she remembered, 'Only when I was in the car and going at seventy or eighty kilometres an hour could I get any relief from the indescribable anguish of the days and nights.'

In Viareggio she renewed contact with Eleanora Duse, and later would always credit Duse for being the one who really helped her return to some semblance of life. Duse, who had been in retirement from the stage herself for several years, from a mixture of poor health, lack of capital, and reticence, was understanding. 'She never said,' Isadora recalled, ' "Cease to grieve," but grieved with me, and, for the first time since [the children's] death, I felt I was not alone.'

They either met or corresponded every day, and Duse would give her such advice as, '*Ne perdez pas la bonne douleur* (Do not lose this healthy sorrow).' Isadora began regaining hope, which, she reflected, is 'a hard plant to kill and, no matter how many branches are knocked off and destroyed, it will always put forward new shoots.'

All the same, working through her grief was at times bitterly hard. She still sometimes feared she was losing her mind. One afternoon, walking on the seashore, she imagined she saw Deirdre and Patrick walking a little way off. She ran after them, and, as she recalled:

> I followed – called – and suddenly they disappeared in the mist of the sea-spray... I had for some moments the distinct feeling that I was then with one foot over the line which divides madness from sanity. I saw before me the asylum – the life of dreary monotony – and in bitter despair I fell upon my face and cried aloud.

I don't know how long I had lain there when I felt a pitying hand on my head. I looked up and saw what I thought to be one of the beautiful contemplation figures of the Sistine Chapel. He stood there, just come from the sea, and said:

'Why are you always weeping? Is there nothing I can do for you – to help you?'

I looked up.

'Yes,' I replied, 'Save me – save more than my life – my reason. Give me a child.'

That is how Isadora told it, but in fact she had met the young man before, and may have recognised him. His name was Romano Romanelli. The son of a prominent Florentine family, he was a sculptor who had been to Paris and known Rodin.

Whether she remembered him or not, they at once became lovers, which helped her healing. As she recalled, 'When I felt his strong youthful arms around me and his lips on mine, when all his Italian passion descended on me, I felt that I was rescued from grief and death, brought back to light – to love again.'

He also sculpted a bust of her, and she began to see him as 'a second Michelangelo'. With the result that when, in December, she found herself pregnant, she felt sure that the child she was bearing would be either Deirdre or Patrick reincarnated.

Duse, learning her joyful news, was horrified. In a letter to the Paris impresario, Aurélien Lugne-Poë, she wrote, 'Nothing of that which is irreparable is understood by this magnificent and dangerous creature! ... What courage, what strength, what folly.' The situation caused a certain coolness between herself and Isadora, Isadora writing to the Spanish-born author Mercedes de Acosta, 'I could never have imagined that such a supreme artist as Duse could be so narrow-minded.'

But Isadora was in such a state of euphoria as she lifted out of her depression that it did not even bother her greatly when Romano, who was already engaged to be married, ended their affair. 'I felt he had saved my reason,' she recalled, 'and then I knew I was no longer alone.'

Reinvigorated, she summoned Hener Skene to come and help her compose new dances, and, once he had arrived in Viareggio, danced, to his accompaniment, in a private performance for Duse. She danced the adagio from Beethoven's *Sonata Pathétique*, and it was the first time she had danced since 19th April.

With Skene, she went to Rome. There she would have her first Christmas without her children, which was painful for her, but, as she recalled years later, 'Rome is a wonderful city for a sorrowful soul. I was a ghost who had walked the Appian Way for a thousand years, with the great spaces of the Campagna and the great arch of Raphael's sky above. Sometimes I lifted my arms to the sky and danced along – a tragic figure between the rows of tombs.'

In spite of her sadness, she worked steadily with Hener, reflecting philosophically that at least she was not in 'the tomb or the madhouse'. Until a telegram arrived from Singer, begging her to come back to Paris. At once she went, joining him in a suite he had booked at the Hôtel Crillon.

She told him at once about her pregnancy, at which, she recalled, 'he hid his face in his hands.' But soon he rallied, and explained to her that he had been thinking. In 1912 he had bought the Hôtel Paillard, intending to endow it as a hospital, but now had decided that a better use for it would be as a new school for her, and he was giving it to her as a present.

She was not the first woman to get it as a present. It had originally been built by Louis XV as a house for Madame Pompadour. After a chequered history, including being sacked during the French Revolution, it had been turned into a hotel in the late 1890s.

Situated in Bellevue, it stood on high ground, overlooking the Seine. Singer took Isadora to see it. She was delighted with the idea of a school, but found the decor 'rather banal'. Paul Poiret and Louis Sue were set to work to correct this, and soon had the two dining-rooms converted into dance studios. The larger one, now to be called the *salon bleu*, would be decorated in Isadora's known style, and used for performances, lectures and receptions. The smaller, now the *salon blanc*, would be decorated with depictions of the frieze of the Parthenon, and used as a practice room by her students. In it, as well as a statuette of Isadora dancing (created by Walter Schott in Berlin in 1903), was Louis Sue's model for the proposed Théâtre du Beau.

The school was planned to cater for fifty students, and Isadora at once advertised for candidates, this time offering places for boys as well as girls, none to be under the age of six. Tuition and board would again be free, as at Grunewald, but instead of Elizabeth being the director and main dance-tutor, Isadora would be the director and the dance tuition would be provided by her six star pupils – she was in any case tired of having to import them from Darmstadt every time she wanted them to perform with her.

It was Augustin who got the job of inviting the six to accept Isadora's offer of leaving Darmstadt and joining her school. Naturally they accepted. Elizabeth gave them her blessing, but Max Merz was furious, shouting at her, 'You don't know what you're doing! This is ruin for us!' and (according to Anna) threatening to throw himself out of a window.

The six girls started commuting to the new school in January 1914, and moved there full time in March. The school was to be called *Dionysion* (the god Dionysus, although most well known for instructing man in the cultivation of the vine, was also said to have travelled through Asia, teaching the elements of civilisation).

Isadora had her own room there, again decorated by Paul Poiret. In it hung a painting by her (and Rodin's) old friend Eugène Carrière, showing a mother gathering to her breast the spirits of her lost children. She had several paintings by Carrière, but it was said that she valued this one more than any other possession she ever had.

In April, in pursuit of pupils, Augustin led a party to Russia. It consisted of Marguerite Sargent (by now his wife), Hener Skene, and four of the new young instructors – Irma, Anna, Lisa and Theresa. From there, from France, from Poland and from Italy, by June the school had assembled twenty students – of which, as it turned out, only one was a boy – a Parisian named Jean, aged eight (for a few months it also had as a student a seven-year-old English girl, Elsa Lanchester, who would become a considerable supporting actress on stage and film, and marry the actor Charles Laughton). Isadora, increasingly pregnant, turned over not only most of the tuition, but most of the auditioning, to her six star pupils, restricting her own activities mostly to delivering inspirational harangues.

Nonetheless, in a surprisingly short time the school was a lively success. Every Friday the pupils would give a performance to a selected audience, after which the members of the audience would socialise. On Saturdays, painters and sculptors were invited, and the children would dance, either indoors or out, while the artists made sketches and models of them. The ageing Rodin was overheard saying that he wished he had had such models in his youth.

Among Isadora's Friday guests at various times, as well as the nobility and gentry, were the playwright Maeterlinck, the philosopher Bergson, and the poet-artist-writer-filmmaker Jean Cocteau.

Ellen Terry came, as did Duse. And Duse's ex-lover, the poet and playwright Gabriele D'Annunzio (who had written the play *La Gioconda* for her back in 1898). Isadora had first met him in 1912, when he showed up unannounced at her studio at Neuilly, clearly intending to seduce her. 'This,' as Isadora recalled, 'was no compliment, as D'Annunzio wanted to make love to every well-known woman in the world and string them round his waist as the Indian strings his scalps.' Somewhat to her own surprise, she had resisted him, and he left the studio unfulfilled (although he continued unsuccessfully trying, sending her notes like '*Douce amie*, would you like me to come pay you a little visit? I am only a spirit. D'Annunzio.')

All the same, she liked him, and now, at *Dionysion*, he was close enough to her (and brave enough) to tell her that the death of her children was 'the most fortunate thing that could have happened to her as an artist.' Isadora would have none of it. 'Grief,' she told him, 'clogs the spirit, numbs the soul; there is no impulse to self-expression in sorrow – only a desire to keep still and be let alone.'

On 26th June 1914 her new students (led by her six experienced students) gave their first public performance – a three-hour dance recital at the Trocadéro. In one item, to the music of a Schubert *Marche Héroïque*, Anna took the lead in what was described as a dance of grieving women, seen as Isadora's tribute to her children.

She herself, now well advanced in her pregnancy, did not dance (to the disappointment of the audience) or even appear, watching the performance hidden in a private box. Partly this was to reassure herself that her type of dancing would be able to survive her, and she was satisfied enough with what she saw to remark, 'In two years, it will be quite good.'

Two days later, on 28th June, the Archduke Franz Ferdinand of Habsburg-Este, heir apparent to the throne of the Austro-Hungarian Empire, was shot dead on a state visit to Sarajevo, along with his morganatic wife Sophie, Duchess of Hohenberg. Within two weeks, as Isadora awaited the birth of her third child, the Great War started.

Suddenly the whole of Europe seemed thrown into nightmare. In March, the editor of *Le Figaro*, Gaston Calmette, who had been such a staunch friend to Isadora after her children's death, was shot dead in his office by the wife of Joseph Caillaux, the French minister of finance (Calmette had repeatedly denounced Caillaux in print for his efforts to sustain peace between France and Germany, calling him, among other things, 'Germany's man'.)

Now, in July, Mme Caillaux was on trial, which kept the incident in the forefront of the news. (She was eventually acquitted, largely because evidence implied that Calmette had been involved in what was seen, in the climate of the time, to be anti-French propaganda.)

Wanting solitude for herself, Isadora sent all her students for a summer holiday at Singer's mansion in Devon, and remained almost alone at *Dionysion*. She was concerned about the child she was carrying, feeling that somehow its movements were weaker than those of her previous babies.

She had also sent many of her staff on holiday, and several of those remaining fled the city as rumours of war increased. On 1st August it arrived, when Germany declared war on France. Paris became chaotic. Mary Desti recalled, 'Our bookkeepers, doormen, and other men employed around the place [the Maison Desti] ran out shouting, stuffing razors in their pockets, and five minutes afterwards, down the street, they were handed bundles of military uniform, fitting them in any haphazard way. Such joyous shouting, shrieking and hurrahs.' In those innocent days almost everyone thought that the war would be over by Christmas.

On 3rd August Germany invaded Belgium, and immediately there were rumours that the Germans were almost at the gates of Paris (the Franco-Prussian war, during which the city had been occupied, had happened only forty-four years before, and memories persisted). Soldiers were ordered to tear up the pavements and use the stones to build barricades.

Isadora repaired to the Crillon to have her baby. Dr Emil Bosson, her physician, had been summoned from Nice and had been booked a room there as well. But just as she went into labour, he too received his call-up papers, effective immediately.

Desperately, accompanied by Mary, Isadora tried clinic after clinic. But, fearful of repeating her experience in Holland, she found fault with the doctor at each one. Eventually, at the last minute, a highly-respected Parisian specialist was found. He came to Isadora at the Crillon, accompanied by a nurse. But again delivery was not easy. Isadora recalled it vividly:

> The doctor kept on saying, 'Courage, madame.' Why say 'Courage' to a poor creature torn with horrible pain? It would have been much better if he had said to me, 'Forget that you are a woman and that you should bear pain nobly, and all that sort of rot; forget everything, scream, howl, yell –' or, better still, if he had been humane enough to give me some champagne. But this doctor had his system, which was to say, 'Courage, madame.' The nurse was upset and kept on saying, 'Madame, c'est la guerre – c'est la guerre.' . . .

259

Finally I heard the baby's cry – he cried – he lived. Great as had been my fear and horror in that terrible year, it was now all gone in one great shock of joy... Outside my window and door was a running to and fro and voices – the weeping of women – calls – discussions as to the mobilisation, but I held my child and dared, in the face of this general disaster, to feel gloriously happy, borne up to the Heavens with the transcendental joy of again holding my own child in my arms.

This joy was to last only hours. The child had difficulty breathing. Suddenly he started choking for breath. Isadora shouted for the nurse, who took him away. An agonising hour went by while oxygen was fetched, but by nightfall the baby was dead. He never had a name.

'I believe in that moment,' Isadora said, towards the end of her life, 'I reached the height of any suffering that can come to me on earth.'

Chapter Fourteen

The War to End Wars

Within a few days of the war beginning, Isadora's school in Paris closed down. Swept up herself by the general feeling of mobilisation, and losing for the moment her belief that Art was greater than life, she turned over the building that housed it to the Dames de France, to be used as a hospital for wounded soldiers. Her studio at Neuilly she made available as lodgings for French refugees who had fled the German advance.

Recuperating from her ill-fated pregnancy, she was still at the school herself when the first casualties arrived, and going to greet them in what had been her *salon bleu* she was saddened to see that on the walls where her blue curtains had hung there were now 'cheap effigies of a black Christ on a golden cross.' 'I felt,' she later wrote, 'that Dionysus had been completely defeated... My temple of Art was turned into a Calvary of Martyrdom and, in the end, into a charnel-house of bloody wounds and death.'

It would in any case have been impossible for her to have kept her school running as it had been. Most of her six older pupils held German passports, and most of her thirteen new pupils held French ones, and these countries were now on opposite sides.

What was to be done with them? Paris Singer, who had also turned his mansion in Devon into a military hospital, had decided to settle in England for the duration. But Britain had signed a treaty obliging it to defend Belgium in the event of that country being attacked, and so had duly declared war on Germany on 4th August. So the German pupils could not move to Britain. He decided that the best place to send Isadora's pupils was America, and arranged for them all, old and new, to travel to New York.

Elizabeth and Max Merz shortly afterwards followed his example. With the help of Kathleen Bruce (since 1912 the widow of Captain Scott), they moved their pupils and themselves from Darmstadt and went to New York as well.

Isadora, when she was sufficiently recovered to travel, went with Mary Desti for a few weeks' recuperation in the coastal resort of Deauville, on the English Channel, staying in a suite at the Hôtel Normandie.

Deauville had long been a fashionable resort for both British and Continental visitors. Mary had even opened a branch of Maison Desti there, with her son Preston, now sixteen, as manager. But now the town was sadly changed. At the Casino, now a hastily-equipped hospital, Mary would recall, 'where but two weeks before all the beauty and grace of Europe had gathered to gamble, dance, or dine,' the gaming tables had been removed and replaced by camp beds, 'each containing a broken piece of humanity, with terrible, sorrowful eyes wondering what it was all about.'

Mary, who had nursing training, briefly worked there. Isadora, who of course had not, did what she could for the wounded men, 'writing letters home, reading and doing the countless little things that bring cheer.'

Still needing to recover strength herself, she found the sight of so much suffering disturbing. Death seemed to be hovering all around her. With a shock she recognised the chief physician, 'a short man with a black beard', as the doctor who had been part of the attempt to rescue her children from the Seine, and who had then attended her. 'I looked,' she recalled. 'The mist cleared away. I gave a cry. I remembered. That terrible day. The doctor who came to bid me hope.' In a confusion of emotions she embarked on a violent affair with him, but it became for her too terrible and intense and soon she broke it off, saying later, 'I could find no relief either in Art, the rebirth of a child, or in love. In every effort to escape, I found only destruction, agony, death.'

Deciding that she was now well enough to join her pupils in New York, she asked the staff at her school, now a hospital, to send her a trunk she had packed with winter clothes. Someone sent her by mistake a trunk full of clothes that had belonged to Deirdre and Patrick. Opening it shocked her so much that she fainted.

Sailing for New York on the *Franconia*, she arrived on 24th November 1914. She rented a studio at 311 Fourth Avenue and, as always hung it with her big blue curtains, keeping out the daylight to create her own personal atmosphere. It was, in a way, her refuge, and she took to referring to it as 'the Ark'.

Mary Desti, as it happened, had preceded her. The previous summer she had opened a branch of Maison Desti in New York, installing as manager a stout gin-swilling lesbian named Daisy Andrews. But Daisy had let the business go to pieces, so Mary now removed her and decided that she and her son Preston would try and get it back on its feet.

When Isadora arrived, booking herself into the Hotel Ritz, she invited Mary to move in with her. Which Mary did, installing Preston in the less prestigious Hotel Irving, on Gramercy Park.

Isadora, by this time in her life, was becoming more flamboyant in her manner and appearance. In the year and a half since Deirdre and Patrick had died, her hair had turned white, although she was still only thirty-seven, and, since cutting it in Agii Santara, she had kept it quite short (around earlobe length), and had taken to dying it red, often rather crudely, with pure henna. She had also taken to wrapping herself in great cloaks or mantles, often in striking colours, such as violet.

The impression she gave was well described by the American stage designer Robert Edmond Jones, who saw her in 1915:

> My first impression of her is one of violence. There is a suggestion of fierce movement about her, an atmosphere of storm... All other images fade away before the sheer intensity of the grief that is in her eyes. I am face to face with ruin, with unending bitterness, with woe beyond description... Then I hear her voice. It is unexpectedly light in quality, allusive, not sharp, and oddly *absent*. It is an American voice, an Irish voice, and in some curious way a humorous voice.

When she arrived, her pupils were living at the Simeon Ford estate in Rye, on Long Island Sound, and she was indignant to learn that on their arrival in America the younger children had been detained at the immigrant clearing-house, Ellis Island, for four days, because they had no proper guardianship papers. This was one of the first of the many things she would find to dislike in her native country as she set about attempting to re-establish Dionysion. Another, having witnessed herself the first wounded men of the Great War, was America's isolationist indifference to the suffering in Europe. Once again, mainstream America seemed to her to be money-grubbing and self-absorbed.

Partly to try and drum up financial support for her school, and partly to reassure America that her girls were not 'German spies' (as had been rumoured), she arranged for them to perform, without her, at Carnegie Hall, accompanied by the New York Symphony. The performance took place on 3rd December 1914, and was well received. Anna wrote to her father, 'We had quite a big success for America, and Isadora, who sat in the loge, was very pleased with us, that's the main thing.'

The biggest problem for Isadora was that she ran head-on into the great change in Art that took place all over the western world at around the turn of the Twentieth Century. To disciples of the Aesthetic Movement, whose ideas were so dominant in England and America in her childhood, Art was regarded as the pursuit of Beauty. By this, people such as Isadora did not simply mean the pursuit of the aesthetically pleasing. They aimed to find that ideal Beauty that lies behind the surface of things, and their quest was without ego – it had something of the feel of a believer seeking to become united with God.

During the later nineteenth century Art became more individualistic. It was an artist's personal vision that counted, and seeking Beauty was regarded as less important than portraying Reality. The new Art would even prove capable of expressing Ugliness.

An important figure at this time (among many important figures) was the philosopher-artist Marcel Duchamp. In February 1913 his famous '*Nu Descendant un Escalier*' (Nude Descending a Staircase), which had been rejected for showing by the Salon des Indépendants in Paris, was exhibited at the International Exhibition of Modern Art at the Sixty-ninth Regiment Armory in Manhattan, and caused a furore. Described by him as 'an expression of time and space through the abstract presentation of motion', it was both determinedly non-realistic and an attempt to investigate human perception. The pursuit of Beauty, as previous generations understood it, was completely absent.

What is significant is that the picture was first shown in America, having been being rejected by an avant-garde Salon in Paris. America was growing in cultural confidence and, though well-informed about new artistic developments in Europe, was no longer looking to Europe to show it the way.

In Isadora's own medium, Dance – or at least in social dancing – it was already beginning to show the world the way. America and the world were about to go dance crazy. This came about because the syncopated new music of ragtime was so exciting. As early as 1910 the sheet-music publishers of popular songs had begun insisting that new tunes should be 'danceable'. New steps were invented, and for a brief while there was a craze for dances that mimicked the movements of animals – the turkey trot, the buzzard lope, the camel walk, and countless others.

These types of dance originated among the inhabitants of the southern and south-western states, chiefly among Blacks, and they were regarded in polite society as crude and vulgar. But from 1911 a young married couple, Vernon and Irene Castle, tidied up and smoothed out such dances, educating the country with such advice as, 'Do not wriggle the shoulders. Do not shake the hips. Do not twist the body. Do not flounce the elbows. Do not pump the arms.'

Their aim was elegance, and their style caught on. It was once estimated that between 1912 and 1914 over one hundred new ballroom dances were invented, and the two most popular, which swept America and the world during 1913, were the tango and the fox trot (which, confusingly, was not an 'animal' dance – its name came from a vaudeville performer called Harry Fox).

Isadora hated this new dancing. However much she'd been amused by the 'African dodger' being danced on the streets of Boston late in 1908, now, returning to America more permanently, she was outspokenly against what she saw, partly because she saw it as a profanation of the Art she had dedicated her life to, and partly because she found it too openly and unsubtly sexual. Not, she was careful to explain, that she was against sex (which was an outspoken thing for anyone, let alone a woman, to say at the time). Sex was to her 'a fine thing'.

In an article she wrote, 'Dancing in Relation to Religion and Love', she warned that: 'Very little is known of the magic that resides in movement, and the potency of certain gestures.' She felt it would be less dangerous for American girls to attend 'a real orgy, which after all, might not be so harmful to them – since a real orgy might, like a real storm, clear the atmosphere for purer things... For we are no longer in the state of the primitive savage, but the whole expression of our life must be created through culture and the transformation of intuition and instinct into art.'

Here again she was out-of-step with the artistic drive of the period. This was a time when many leading young artists, such as Ernst and Picasso, feeling that European art had become over-civilised, were beginning to look to savage cultures to teach them something richer and more intuitive.

Isadora soon found that she was in a paradoxical situation. Although she detested the new attitudes to Art, and although the new styles of dancing that were to be seen everywhere, at social dances and on the vaudeville stage, were making her own style look dated, she was regarded by the New York avant-garde as almost their symbol.

Centred in Greenwich Village, the young radicals of the time believed in the two gods of Art and Socialism (in varying proportions), and the most long-lasting legacy of their time was in the work they did towards emancipating women. The New Woman (as she had been called since the 1890s) believed in her rights to vote, practise free love, use contraception, marry or not marry, and keep custody of her children.

The influential magazine of the place and time was *The Masses*, founded in 1911, and whose editor since 1912 had been the socialist and poet Max Eastman, now aged thirty. In his opinion, Isadora 'was the extreme outpost of the movement for women's emancipation.' This was more for the way she had conducted her life than for any philosophy she had worked out. Eastman later wrote of 'the admirable force of character with which Isadora insisted on being half-baked.'

By coincidence, one of the signals announcing membership of the female avant-garde was wearing short hair – not by any means as short as women's hair would become in the Twenties, but around earlobe-length, like Isadora's. This helped her to be seen as a figurehead. Another sign of membership was openly smoking cigarettes, which she did only occasionally.

All the same, she did feel a political kinship with these young people. It was not long afterwards in her life that she would begin referring to herself as a 'red' or a 'Bolshevik', although it must be said that she was at heart more of an anarchist than a socialist – Art for her had always been, and would always be, such a supreme authority that beside it the demands of any state dwindled in importance to nothing.

It wasn't long before Isadora met the woman whose salon was its centre – Mabel Dodge, recently returned herself from a decade in Europe. Mabel's house at 23 Fifth Avenue, just north of Washington Square, was a meeting place, as she herself recalled, for 'Socialists, Trade-Unionists, Anarchists, Suffragists, Poets, Relations, Lawyers, Murderers, "Old Friends", Psychoanalysts, I.W.W.'s, Single Taxers, Birth Controlists, Newspapermen, Artists, Modern-Artists, Club-women, Women's-Place-is-in-the-Home Women, Clergymen, and just plain men.'

It was Mabel Dodge who had helped Elizabeth and Max to re-established their school, at Croton-on-Hudson. Now she would be influential in trying to help Isadora too, when a group of Isadora's friends set up the Committee for the Furtherance of Isadora Duncan's Work in America. This group included the sculptor George Grey Barnard and Mary Roberts (who in 1908 had introduced her, after her abortive Frohman tour, to her true New York audience of 'poets, painters, writers'), and the committee it set up, eventually numbering more than fifty, came to include such as Max Eastman, the author Theodore Dreiser, the future political philosopher Walter Lippmann, the pioneering social worker John Collier, and Ellen Terry (who conveniently happened at the time to be lecturing New Yorkers about Shakespeare's heroines).

In January 1915, Mabel Dodge wrote to her friend Gertrude Stein in Paris:

> I am up to my neck in Duncans this winter. John Collier & I got a school started for one of them, & for Isadora we are engaged in the maddest project of getting her the Armory, where she can teach a thousand unemployed poor people's poor children to *dance* & feed & clothe them & charge rich people sums to come in & see her teach 'em. And we're going to get up some great out of door festivals for her in the Stadium at Cambridge & in New Haven's *Bowl!* We're perfectly insane in our plans but sometimes insanity works!

Not this time it didn't. The man who had the power to allow Isadora the use of the Armory was New York's boyish mayor John Purroy Mitchel (he was thirty-seven), and Mabel's plan was that John Collier would bring him to Isadora's studio, where her six star pupils would dance while she did all she could to charm him. Mabel even got Walter Lippman to attend the meeting. Though only twenty-five he already had gravitas, and she felt his presence would lend weight to the proceedings. She asked several other eminent men as well, and their wives, for the same reason.

Mabel recalled:

> The place was large and dim and romantic-looking, with a few shaded lamps burning. It was a contrast to the hard, bright city streets we had left, and Isadora in a flowing Greek dress, ample and at ease, made us look and feel dingy and utilitarian. Particularly the men, as they stood beside her, appeared stupid, inexpressive and as though cut out of wood, there was such a radiance about her compared with other mortals. I could see Isadora appraising them as she glanced them over. Others came forward: Augustin Duncan, with his round, candid forehead and tip-tilted Irish nose, [Margherita] Duncan, his wife, a tall, adequately Grecian type with pale gold hair and flowing draperies, and some of her young girls: Anna, Lisa, Theresa, Irma... They were lovely, with bodies like cream and roses, and faces unreal with beauty whose eyes were like blind statues, as

267

though they had never looked upon anything in any way sordid or ordinary... I felt myself to be shorter and more square than I had ever been in my life, and my gloves suddenly ceased to fit my hands.

Isadora was at her most flamboyant. She gushed to the mayor about how young he looked ('I thought you would be an old, old man with a long white beard!'), and tried to seat him on one of her low divans. Which caused him to make a dash for the safety of the piano stool, nearly falling off it as it spun.

Isadora reclined on a divan, her students grouped around her, and began to harangue the mayor about releasing a woman recently indicted for poisoning her two children ('How do you suppose she feels shut up in there? How can *anyone* be certain that she did it? How can anyone believe a woman would or could kill her children?')

John Collier managed to stem her flow by pointing out that the mayor had no authority in the case, and suggested Isadora tell him about her methods of teaching. 'Oh,' she said airily, 'my methods of teaching are probably very different from anything *he* has ever known!' She indicated the students round her. '*These* children have always had a *beautiful* life. Look at them! *They* don't have to get up in the morning and go down to breakfast with their cross fathers and mothers! *They* don't have to go to school with horrid dirty books in satchels! *They* don't have to go to church on Sunday and listen to stuffy old men in ugly buildings!' (At which point, Mabel remembered, her dress briefly slipped off one shoulder, exposing a breast.)

As she went on to reminisce about her lovers, some of those present, embarrassed, began to talk among themselves in a far corner. Noticing them, Isadora's voice rose: 'Who are these people? What do they know of Art or what can they understand of my work? Who are these women? Wives with feathers?'

The mayor asked whether the children would dance. 'Oh,' said Isadora, 'I do not think the children feel like dancing this afternoon.' She reclined further on her divan, stretching herself languidly across its cushions and giving a soft contented laugh.

And that was that. Lippman was furious. Although he was lending some of his gravitas to Isadora, being involved in her affairs might in return taint him with frivolity. Next day he wrote to Mabel, saying, 'If this is Greece and Joy and the Aegean Isle and the Influence of Music, I don't want anything to do with it. It's a nasty, absurd mess, and she is obviously the last person who ought to be running a school. I want you to let me off the committee! You can tell the others I'm too busy... I should have known better than to be dazzled into a shortcut to perfection – there are none and Isadora is not the person to show the way...'

Shortly after this meeting, still in January, Isadora made her own first onstage appearance since returning to America. From now on, from all her personal sorrow and her sorrow at the suffering that the war was bringing the world, her dancing would take on a different character. It would lose its great lightness and acquire a stark, monumental quality – her gestures would be slower and stronger, and her performance would often use sombre religious themes.

This appearance took place at the Metropolitan Opera House. Isadora was accompanied by an orchestra conducted by Edward Falck, and with her were the soprano Marguerite Namara and her brother Augustin, who read passages from the Bible – among them the one from Christ's Sermon on the Mount beginning 'Blessed are they that mourn.' (Audiences found him depressing and doleful.) The heart of Isadora's performance was a dance to Schubert's 'Ave Maria'. This she had conceived as a tribute to Deirdre and Patrick, and it would remain in her repertoire all her life. Sometimes she danced it alone, as now, and sometimes with her pupils, portraying angels. At the end of the evening, as so often in her life, she addressed the audience, asking them to help fund her school and to send her prospective students.

The performance was generally panned. The perceptive but severe Henry Taylor Parker, writing in the *Boston Evening Transcript*, said, 'Miss Duncan seems to have experienced a change of faith as to the purely artistic purpose of her performances. They are sicklied over now with the pale cast of some very immature and hasty thought of some kind. It is a most disheartening and amateurish mixture of music and recited literature, from the Bible, and other sources entirely unsuited to any such purpose.'

It was now that Americans started pointing out how much Isadora seemed to have lost touch with the times she was living in. For instance, one of the Greenwich Village feminists, Henrietta Rodman, having attended a gathering at Isadora's studio, was dubious about how blindly devoted her students were to her attitudes and ideals. She felt that 'the one weakness of their education [was] their lack of contact with the harsh and ugly realities of our present-day life.' Making some such comment to Isadora, Henrietta found herself sternly rebuked – 'I am preparing them to be priestesses of beauty, not factory girls,' Isadora told her.

Not that Isadora despised the labouring classes. Indeed, in 1915 America they seemed to her to be the only worthwhile people. When people criticised her high-mindedness as being out of touch, telling her that 'If you play a symphony of Schubert on the East Side the people will not care for it,' she at once arranged for her students and herself to give a free concert on the poverty-stricken East Side, at Jacob Adler's Grand Theater. It worked, and she was proudly able to tell her next audience at the Met, when she returned there in February, 'Well, we gave a free performance – in a theatre without a box office – so refreshing! – and the people sat there transfixed, with tears rolling down their cheeks; that is how they cared for it.' She went on to castigate 'the rich' for being 'crude, vulgar, heartless, barren and inartistic.'

Somehow this castigating of her paying audiences for the moment won her sympathy. After announcing that she found America so unsympathetic that she was 'going to an island in the Greek Archipelago to live on bread and onions and worship beauty,' she gave two more concerts at the Met that were billed as 'farewell' concerts. At the first of these, on 25th February, her dancing earned her twenty-seven curtain calls and her speech after them was wildly applauded. Sylvester Rawling, writing in the *New York World*, reported:

> Miss Duncan excused her berating of Americans for their ignorance of Art on the score that she was born in America and that, like the man who poured invectives upon the woman who had rejected him, she loves us. She was taking herself and her school away to a foreign land, she said, to give it the proper atmosphere
> 'Stay with us!' yelled an enthusiast.
> 'Build me an opera house on the east side and I will,' she replied. 'Give me an auditorium that will seat 2000 people free, 2000 people for ten cents a chair and 2000 people for twenty-five cents a chair. It is a crime to force art-loving people to sit suffocating up under the eaves of a great house like this!'
> 'Right you are, Ma'am!' yelled a man who was one of the suffocating victims.

As it turned out, by the time she played her 'farewell' concerts they had ceased to be anything of the sort. At this first one she was also able to announce that she and her pupils had been offered the use for a season of the Century Theater on Central Park West at 62nd Street, by one of its directors, Otto Kahn.

270

Otto Kahn was a rich man Isadora could appreciate. German-Jewish by birth, he was a broker, art-lover and bon vivant who supported liberal causes and did a great deal to finance, and find finance for, shows of all sorts – from musicals to the avant-garde. When it was arranged that he come to her studio to meet her, Isadora was on her best behaviour, recognising that she had behaved foolishly when meeting the mayor. She told Otto Kahn of her ambition to create a unified theatre, using all the performing arts, explaining, 'As the Greek dances were the forerunner of the Greek drama, so we believe we are laying the foundation for the development of a great universal art.'

Her season at the Century, organised in only a few weeks, and beginning on 25th March, was by far the most ambitious presentation she had ever planned. It would run through April, and contain, as well as her regular dance programmes, solo concerts by herself, 'religious offerings' during the Easter period, and three Greek tragedies, staged in collaboration with her brother Augustin (she would direct the movements of the crowds and chorus). There would be on hand throughout an eighty-piece orchestra and a choir of a hundred, under the direction of Edward Falck. Mary Desti's son Preston could not escape being hired as an assistant director, but was let go after making a hash of the lighting cues at one performance. (Mary herself was too busy at her shop to become involved.)

Isadora made considerable alterations to the auditorium. She removed the first fifteen rows of the seats in the orchestra stalls, so as to extend an apron stage out beyond the proscenium arch, and, in a spirit of democracy, hung the walls of the auditorium with blue curtains similar to those she used on-stage, thus covering and abolishing the private boxes. She decreed that the price of the remaining seats in the orchestra stalls should be two dollars each, but that the seats in the upper balcony should each cost ten cents, so that 'the people' could afford them.

The season was a failure. People complained that they felt no connection between her dancing and the plays, which seemed hastily-planned and stodgy. In the same way, the readings interspersed between her dances felt as if they were simply stuck in, so that the evening had no coherent pattern. Worst, the prevailing feeling of moral uplift was simply tedious. At one matinee, when Isadora danced to a set of mazurkas and waltzes by Chopin, a woman in the audience shouted, 'That's what we want! We don't go to the theatre to be made sorrowful, but to be made happy!' Which, while understandable, was hardly a demand for high Art.

Isadora quickly became discouraged, and this made her dictatorial and emotionally unpredictable. It was understandable that she refused to rehearse with the pianist George Copeland, who was to play Chopin for her, explaining, 'You don't understand. It's the *music* which is important. Play as if I were not there, as if you were simply playing a recital alone, and it will be all right.' But when Augustin gave her pupil Irma a speaking role in the chorus of *Iphigenia* she was incensed, yelling, 'What is this, Gus? She can't do that; take her away!' The fact that Augustin succeeded in getting his way upset her even further.

For one of her concerts she demanded that Frederick Toye, a new manager she had acquired, should cover two altars placed at either side of the stage with 'masses of roses'. By now her money was running desperately short (Paris Singer seems to have stopped subsidising her, although this time there had been no obvious breach between them), and Toye bought all the roses the budget would stand. Isadora, seeing them, was cross. 'Do you call that "masses of roses"?' she demanded. 'We can't afford masses,' said Toye. 'Since you had most of the orchestra seats removed, even with capacity business we have a deficit of three thousand dollars a week. Do you want to add to our deficit?' Isadora became sarcastic. 'How wonderful,' she said. 'You always know what everything costs! I just know what I want.' He bought more roses.

Her miserable season ended miserably, and a week early. She had been saving money by letting some of her pupils sleep in the theatre, which was against the law. The authorities found out, and on the night of 23rd April they were evicted, the older girls shepherding the younger ones to spend the night at the Empire Hotel on Broadway.

Isadora was furious, and took her revenge on the world by failing to appear for either of the two performances she was to give the next day. Instead she began packing, announcing that she and her girls intended to leave New York to its 'philistine darkness' at once.

Even that wasn't easy. Her season at the Century had lost her over $12,000. She had unpaid debts (to performers, musicians, backstage staff and to various merchants), and against these debts U.S. Customs threatened to confiscate the trunk that held her carpets and curtains. She appealed for help in all directions, and eventually was bailed out through the united efforts of Mabel Dodge's committee, the banker Frank Vanderlip, the newspaper publisher Ogden Reid, and Paris Singer. They settled her most pressing debts, and over a period merchants eventually wrote off some 80 per cent of what was still owed.

As to the fare back to Europe for herself and her pupils, that was paid for out of the blue by a rich woman who admired Isadora's dancing. Her name was Ruth Mitchell, and all she asked in return for the favour was

Isadora's friendship. Which she got, although the girls would always be a little wary of her, fearing she enjoyed stirring up dissension between themselves and Isadora.

Mabel Dodge was inclined to attribute much of Isadora's erratic behaviour at this period to drink, saying years later, 'Calling it Dionysian to quaff great goblets of wine did not lessen its evil influence upon her... No one could stop her or control her, ever... Lovers – lovers – and wine – with nothing allaying that hunger and thirst in her, and no way of understanding it, no realization... Like all tragedies, Isadora's came from not knowing.'

She and her pupils set off for Italy on 9th May 1915, aboard the *Dante Alighieri* (just at around the time that a sketch of her, dancing her *Marche Militaire* and drawn by John Sloan, appeared on the cover of Max Eastman's *The Masses*). Mary Desti and Preston came to the pier to see her off. She was distraught, 'crying into her handkerchief', and at the last moment she called out, 'Mary! If you don't come with me I don't know what I'll do!'

Mary, crying herself, at once rushed up the gangplank, shouting back to Preston, 'Do the best you can, darling. Keep things going. I'll send you some money as soon as I can!' She sailed with no money and no luggage – without even an overcoat.

Preston recalled, 'At the rail, Mother and Isadora started laughing, and it turned out that what they were laughing at was the face of the purser when he discovered that not only *Mother* didn't have any money for her ticket, but Isadora didn't have a dime either.' By the time the boat pulled out into the Hudson River, Isadora and Mary, with the girls alongside them, were cheerfully singing the *Marseillaise*.

It was a somewhat nerve-racking time to be sailing the Atlantic. By now it was quite obvious to everyone that the war being waged in Europe was much bigger than anyone had feared. Only two days before, on 7th May, the Cunard liner *Lusitania*, sailing from New York to Liverpool, had been torpedoed off the south coast of Ireland by a German U-boat. 1,198 died, including 124 Americans, among them Isadora's one-time producer, Charles Frohman. This incident would be a major factor in changing America's attitude from one of isolationism (which Isadora so disliked) to eventual involvement in the war. The captain of the *Dante Alighieri*, to keep his ship as safe as possible, deliberately steered a more southerly course, staying away from the dangerous waters around the British Isles and northern Europe.

Isadora's plan was to go, after landing, from Italy to Athens, and to camp out on the hilltop at Kopanos, which the Duncans still owned, and where Raymond's temple remained unfinished. She had left instructions with her manager, Frederick Toye, to arrange a tour for her and her pupils in South America, which seemed sufficiently distant from warfare. But during the voyage she was furious at getting a telegram from him saying that he had managed to arrange such a tour, but for the girls only, not her.

That was the end of her association with Frederick Toye. She dismissed him, and sent from the ship an angry cablegram to Mary Roberts: DISCOVERED TOYE'S COMPLETE DISHONESTY. GIRLS TRAITORS.

In fact the girls had known nothing about the proposed tour, and had been no part of arranging it. But there was already bad feeling between them and Isadora. Now in their late teens (Anna and Theresa were twenty) they were of an age to assert themselves, even against their beloved teacher, and they had flatly refused to go with her to Greece. It was worrying enough for girls with German passports to be going to Italy, which was already threatening to enter the war on the side of the Allies. But there was the possibility that Greece might also become involved. So, as Irma, then eighteen, remembered later, 'we put our collective foot down... But it took a real mutiny on her pupils' part before [Isadora] would change her mind.' By the time the *Dante Alighieri* docked at Naples, they and Isadora were barely on speaking terms.

She was still responsible for them, however, and managed, with some difficulty, to get her pupils, young and old, safely installed in a boarding-school that was also a finishing-school in Switzerland. It was in Geneva and was called Les Hirondelles. At this time, too, she got each of the six girls to sign a contract with her, pledging themselves to remain her students until they reached the age of twenty-one, after which point they could remain with her, or leave, as they chose. If anyone did leave, however, she would be barred from publicising herself as one of Isadora's students.

After safely settling the girls, in a desperate attempt to raise some cash, Isadora travelled with Mary to Paris, mortgaged her studio at Neuilly (still filled with refugees), borrowed heavily from moneylenders (at the exorbitant interest rate of fifty per cent), and returned to Switzerland to live for the moment in a hotel on Lake Geneva.

She stayed there till October, socialising mostly with a group of gay (and cheerful) Polish draft dodgers, before persuading one of them to drive her to Athens. Mary, having found a new investor for her business, disappeared to attend to it. Isadora, on reaching Athens, rather than join Raymond and his commune, who had by now moved from the Albanian border back to Kopanos, booked herself into the Hotel Grande Bretagne.

Greece, as it turned out, would not join in the war on either side. In spite of emerging successfully from the Balkan Wars of 1912–13, having gained a substantial amount of territory, mainly in Macedonia, the country was torn between supporting the Kaiser and supporting the Allies. The royal family, with King Constantine I at its head, supported the Kaiser (his wife was, after all, the Kaiser's sister, and he himself held the honorary rank of field marshal in the Prussian army). The prime minister, Eleuthérios Venizelos, was a populist and, like the people of Greece, tended to support the Allies. In spite of Venizelos having a substantial parliamentary majority, the day after Isadora arrived in Athens King Constantine removed him from office.

Isadora began to campaign for Greece's entry into the war on the Allied side. Dining at her hotel with a group of guests, all of whom happened to be royalists, she heard a group of German officers at a nearby table toasting victory. Defiantly she rose to her feet and cried, 'Vive la France!' Later that night, going out into Syntagma Square, she gathered a crowd, urged them into singing the 'Marseillaise', and led them in procession to the house where Venizelos lived, attempting, as she said, 'to dance the Athenians into a sense of their responsibilities.' It didn't do much good. Venizelos refused to show himself, although he did later send a dozen roses to her in grateful appreciation.

In December she returned to France. Her house at Neuilly and her school both being occupied, she booked herself into the Hôtel Meurice, where she suffered an attack of typhoid fever. On her recovery, she moved to a house at 23 avenue de Messine. It was rather dark inside, with a studio and a large reception hall, and there, from January 1916 for several months, she held what was in effect a continuous party.

In the sea of despair that was now her life – having lost children, lovers and pupils, and with the world she had functioned in made ugly by battle, she still pursued her Art, although now almost as a reflex. She depended more and more on the twin distractions of sex and drink – the one diverting her from her sorrow, the other numbing it. As she later wrote herself:

The most terrible part of a great sorrow is not the beginning, when the shock of grief throws one into a state of exaltation which is almost anaesthetic in its effects, but afterwards, long afterwards, when people say, 'Oh, she has got over it' – or 'She is all right now, she outlived it'; when one is, perhaps, at what might be considered a merry dinner party to feel Grief with one icy hand oppressing the heart, or clutching at one's throat with the other burning claw – Ice and Fire, Hell and Despair, overcoming all – and, lifting the glass of champagne, one endeavours to stifle this misery in whatever forgetfulness – possible or impossible.

But her parties were not only to distract herself. Although they were attended by artists, politicians and journalists, by far the most numerous of her guests were soldiers on leave from the trenches. Soldiers of all ranks, 'from private to general'. She entertained them lavishly, providing vast quantities of food and wine.

As the weeks passed, and word of her hospitality reached the front line, she became regarded by the French army as a national heroine. As to the matter of cost, she told Maurice Dumesnil, who was among those soldiers who came to her house on leave, 'Money, money, what does it matter after all! You see, I've had a long career already, and there was never a moment when I wasn't worried financially... We must be confident that things can be arranged. They always arrange themselves.'

Of course financial affairs don't always arrange themselves, and by April 1916 not only was Isadora deeply in debt, but both she and her pupils in Geneva were being threatened with eviction. There was nothing for it but for her to begin dancing again.

Dumesnil, as it happened, was on the verge of ceasing to be a soldier. As an officer of the 'automobile service' of the Thirteenth Artillery Service, he had been suffering from complications following a bout of pneumonia (physically he was somewhat delicate), and in February 1916 was given an honourable discharge. This was fortunate for Isadora, because he was also a talented musician, a student and disciple of Debussy.

She would begin by presenting 'a great programme' at the Trocadéro, produced by the French Ministry of Fine Arts, and all the proceeds would go to war relief (earning for herself could come later). Dumesnil would be her musical director, and she began rehearsing, accompanied by his piano, at eleven every morning. For these rehearsals she paid him herself, out of her dwindling funds. They were supposed to last for two hours, but often went on for four or more, and as far as Dumesnil was concerned could have gone on for ever.

As soon as her Trocadéro concert was announced, it sold out, most of the audience being soldiers on leave from the trenches. At it she danced three of the great set pieces of her mature years – César Franck's haunting piece, *Rédemption*; Tchaikovsky's *Sixth Symphony* (*The Pathétique*); and at the end, unannounced, *La Marseillaise*.

The Pathétique, presented by Isadora as 'the story of the present world struggle' was a triumph. She began with its second movement, transforming a dance of careless charm into 'a battle charge ... totally unbridled, a plunging, tearing at the enemy, a fury not to be stopped,' and ended with its final *adagio lamentoso*, depicting 'supreme sorrow and complete hopelessness' in mourning the fallen. When she ended this, lying motionless on the ground, the dying chords of the music suggesting a beating heart, the audience applauded rapturously. Rodin, who was among them, Dumesnil recalled, became 'wild with excitement. His arms went through the air like the wings of a windmill, and he seemed to shriek, although his voice was lost among the general shouting.'

La Marseillaise, which Isadora claimed to have danced first in one of her concerts at the New York Met in 1915, would become the great *tour de force* of her career. She was able to pour into it all the dramatic force at her command, basing much of it on poses she copied from François Rude's sculpted *Marseillaise* on the Arc de Triomphe. For her final pose she stood with one breast bared, evoking the famous Delacroix painting, *Liberty Leading the People*.

Her Trocadéro audience, not having expected the piece, 'wept unashamedly', and sang the words of their anthem as she, in the words of a later writer, Allan Ross Macdougall, 'imperiously, with proud, wide gestures, beckoned to a great, unseen army that seemed to fill the stage at her magnetic command.'

When encores were demanded, she danced to Chopin – to his waltzes, mazurkas and preludes – and so great was the audience enthusiasm that these encores went on for an hour. In her dressing-room afterwards, lying exhausted while her maid wiped perspiration from her body with a sponge, she said, 'I did my very best. I think I've given the best performance of my life.' It quite possibly was – for the first time she was expressing, not Greek myths nor generalised emotions, but an aspect of the times she was living in.

She had been such a success that a second similar concert at the Trocadéro was hastily scheduled, to take place at the end of the month, on 29th April. While waiting for that she got on with earning for herself, going to Geneva with Maurice Dumesnil and giving two performances with her star pupils at the Grand Theatre.

Although she made enough money from these appearances to pay her pupils' school fees, the trip was not a happy one. The girls, having done little for months but sit sewing and knitting under the eye of the headmistress, Madame Dourouze, were less than welcoming to her. And the Swiss audiences were markedly less enthusiastic than her French ones. For one thing the Swiss had little experience of watching dance, and for another they were not at war, and thus were less responsive to patriotic fervour.

After her disappointing first performance, Isadora went with a party, which included Dumesnil and the poet-playwright René Fauchois, to have dinner in a restaurant on the shore of Lake Geneva. There she got so drunk that after the meal she refused to get into the car that was to take her to her hotel. Instead, Dumesnil remembered, she 'wanted to go to the garden, dance in the moonlight and descend to bathe her feet in the clear waters of the lake.'

He and Fauchois got her home somehow, although in the hotel lobby she fell over, refusing to be helped up from the floor by insisting, 'You are drunk! And besides, *vous êtes des mouches* (you are flies)!' (This was an expression she had by now become excessively fond of, and would use again and again.)

Returning to Paris, she discovered that her landlord had impounded all her possessions for non-payment of rent, and that he was preparing to padlock the premises. Fortunately, Dumesnil was able to get in for long enough to retrieve five of Isadora's cherished Carrière paintings, lowering them down the side of the building to Fauchois and to the writer Fernand Divoire.

It was lucky for Isadora that the trunks containing her stage equipment – mostly her curtains and her carpets – were still backstage at the Trocadéro, so she was able to fulfil her return engagement there.

This made up for much. It was as great a success as the first had been, and at the end of her performance she announced to the cheering audience that she was off to dance the *Marseillaise* 'all over South America.' Which she was. A tour had been arranged, at her request, by the Argentine impresario Walter Mocchi. It would have overtones of wartime propaganda, she being an artist from one of the Allied countries dancing in countries that were neutral. And Maurice Dumesnil would go with her, as her musical director, conductor and pianist (although he would not be paid until she received the receipts from her first performance, in Buenos Aires). He would not become her lover. On the contrary, being somewhat fastidious by nature, he would be rather shocked by her goings-on.

They left Paris by train for Bordeaux from the Gare d'Orsay on 13th

May 1916, Isadora wearing, Dumesnil recalled, 'an entirely green outfit: a long gown, a soft felt hat, and a scarf... No jewelry, except a magnificent large emerald worn on the front of her dress.' On the train she encountered a man she knew – the violinist Jacques Thibaud – and on arrival at Bordeaux she disappeared with him for several hours, almost missing the boat and explaining to Dumesnil that he was 'divine ... ravishing'.

The boat they sailed on was the *Lafayette*. It left at midnight, under cover of darkness, to reduce the risk of enemy attack. Arriving safely in New York, they stayed for several weeks at the Plaza while the next leg of their journey, to Argentina, was arranged. In spite of her continuing contempt for most Americans – 'a flock of sheep,' she told Dumesnil – she had quite a good time.

On 21st May she took part, unannounced, in the inaugural pageant of *Caliban of the Golden Sands*, a vast festival organised by Percy MacKaye to mark the 300th anniversary of the death of Shakespeare. It was held at the Lewissohn Stadium, the vast outdoor concert-hall, seating up to fifteen thousand, that stood on 138th Street in Manhattan and had been given to the city only the year before by mining millionaire Adolph Lewissohn. Built entirely of concrete, it was intended to be reminiscent of a semi-circular Roman amphitheatre, surrounded by a pillared arcade. Unfortunately, according to some, it more resembled a municipal sewage plant.

More than fifteen hundred actors, singers and dancers joined a Broadway cast 'with songs, hobbyhorses and maypoles' in what the *New York Times* reported as 'the biggest dramatic entertainment ever presented within the limits of the city.' During the programme Isadora appeared in 'a great beam of white light'. With her arms raised, she moved slowly across the giant field to a reading of MacKaye's own translation of Sophocles' 'Many are the wonders of time, but the mightiest wonder is man', with musical accompaniment.

During her stay at the Plaza she discovered the Manhattan cocktail, preferring it very dry (she was also enjoying Sauternes, red Burgundy and champagne). She went out a great deal, having had many invitations from old friends, and rarely returned to the hotel until well after dawn. Dumesnil encountered her one early morning in the elevator, with a male friend still in evening dress. Asked later about the man, she simply said, 'Oh! ... he is divine ... ravishing.' 'Like Thibaud?' he asked. 'Oh, yes. But ... so different.'

When they eventually set sail for Argentina, in the second week of June, it was aboard a decrepit British liner called the *Byron*, so slow-moving that the journey would take three weeks. With them was brother Augustin. In New York Isadora had persuaded him to resume the role of her business manager, telling him, 'I'm tired of taking care of my own affairs. An artist cannot be a businesswoman at the same time.'

On board the *Byron*, Isadora suddenly felt the need to get into better physical condition. As there were no proper facilities to exercise, she did the best she could by spending hours each day walking around the deck. In this she was accompanied by a fellow-traveller, a Spanish painter called Ernesto Valls. 'He is an extraordinary genius,' she told Dumesnil. Which meant the usual thing.

Unfortunately for Valls, who suffered from jealousy, also on board was a group of New York boxers, headed for Brazil to engage in a competition. Isadora, watching them sparring, remarked, 'In ancient Greece, they could have been an inspiration to the artists.' They inspired her sufficiently for at least two to be seen slipping surreptitiously out of her cabin.

Within a few days she had consumed almost the ship's entire stock of champagne. Augustin tried to rein her in, but she told him, 'Why worry? The ocean is beautiful. We have peace. No wires, no letters, no lawyers, no creditors. No trouble of any kind. We are alone with the water and the sky.' Enjoying herself, she even tried smoking cigarettes.

As they crossed the equator, the heat became oppressive. One morning Dumesnil happened on a half-dressed stoker hurrying away from Isadora's cabin. Later in the day he asked her, 'How did you sleep, Isadora, on such a stifling night?'

'Oh,' she said. 'I had a perfectly glorious night.'

When Dumesnil protested that for lord's sake the man was only a stoker, he got a socialist lecture – 'Think of those poor men down by the furnace, and the hours of toil and labour they have to put in. Here we are on deck and lying comfortably on soft cushions... No one ever thinks of the inferno below. It seems to me that at least one of these poor fellows should be given a little happiness. I had one last bottle of champagne and I shared it with him... And you know, he had the legs of an Apollo!'

They docked at Buenos Aires on 1st July 1916, and immediately there was a problem. Isadora's curtains, costumes and musical scores had been shipped separately by a cargo ship, and they had not arrived. Because of wartime security, the cargo ship could not be traced, and her opening night was only a week away. At her hotel, the Plaza, she met her impresario's assistant, Renato Salvati, who strove to reassure her that the scores were no problem. They could be obtained from the library of the city's opera. And she could buy new curtains 'at one of the London furniture houses', which were represented in the city.

The biggest problem for Isadora was that her impresario, Walter Mocchi, was not there himself to receive her, being, Salvati explained to her, 'too busy with the operatic season ... To concern himself with minor details of management.' This set her against Argentina from the start. When she was asked by Mocchi's office to supply a complete list of her programmes and the dates on which she would dance them (she was expected to dance three times a week, but could choose her own dates), she exploded to Dumesnil, 'What's the idea! I'm not in the habit of preparing my programmes like an opera season.' She could not possibly say what she would feel like dancing after her premiere. She might not feel like dancing at all. 'I'm an artist,' she complained, 'not a machine.'

Saying similar things to Mocchi's secretary, she was told straight out that the organisation couldn't work with temperamental women. Which seemed to bother her not at all. Who were bothered were Augustin, who had been appalled at having to go to the Maples store and buy two thousand dollars-worth of 'inferior' blue curtains (to be paid for out of the receipts), and Dumesnil, who kept finding her surrounded by new hordes of male admirers.

Isadora herself was past caring. At an afternoon tea at the Plaza she learnt, and danced for the first time, the tango. 'From my first timid steps,' she remembered, 'I felt my pulses respond to the enticing, langourous rhythm of this voluptuous dance, sweet as a long caress, intoxicating as love under southern skies, cruel and dangerous as the allurement of a tropical forest.'

She even tried attending a pornographic film show, in the city's red light district, but found the experience so upsetting that she ran out, next day complaining about the degradation of simple-minded girls, and saying that the criminals who carried on such a trade ought to be 'shot, hanged or guillotined.'

On the night before her opening, she went with Dumesnil to 'the best known night club in Buenos Aires', the Pigall, where she danced the tango with a succession of gigolos, drinking from each of their glasses in turn. By three in the morning she was sufficiently drunk to announce, 'I will now interpret for you the national anthem of this great country. Long live Argentina!' And she did. As Dumesnil recalled, 'The audience did not know what to think. The more distinguished portion, seated in the boxes, seemed to be shocked beyond words.' Finishing her dance,

281

she tossed one of her sandals to an admirer. Some of the audience laughed at her, and she threw her other sandal at them, in anger.

This performance led to unexpected trouble. Firstly, representatives of the Mocchi office showed up at her hotel early the next morning complaining that performing in public without their permission was a breach of her contract. That, with Dumesnil's help, she managed to talk her way out of. But worse was that she had offended the respectable residents of the city – those very people who would provide the majority of her audience – thus forfeiting any indulgence they might have had for a form of dancing that was foreign to them.

The audience for her first night were, in Dumesnil's words, 'cold and indifferent' and the papers next day panned her performance. Her second performance fared no better, and her third did even worse, mainly because its music was to be entirely by Wagner and Dumesnil refused to conduct it on the grounds that Wagner was a German, and thus against the propagandising aspect of the tour. The hastily-hired substitute conductor was under-rehearsed, the auditorium was only half-filled, and those who did attend turned up late and chattered. Isadora stopped the orchestra in mid-performance and harangued the audience, telling them that she had been warned about Argentinians being unable to appreciate her Art, and that the people who warned her had been right. Shortly afterwards Mocchi cancelled the rest of her engagement, refused to pay her, and confiscated her new curtains as collateral. Isadora, desolate, wrote to Fernand Divoire in Paris, 'If you knew how tired and unhappy I am ... Oh! I want to come home.' Broke, she even thought of sending a telegram to Paris Singer, begging him for help. But she had no idea where he was.

She was also concerned about her pupils in Geneva, who again were being threatened with eviction, and immediately after Mocchi cancelled her tour she sent Augustin to Switzerland to try and make some arrangement (she also insisted he discourage the older girls from trying to return to America, which they had expressed a desire to do). Meanwhile, she was lucky enough to find another impresario, Cesare Giulietti, who offered to book her to make appearances in Montevideo, Rio de Janeiro and São Paulo. An offer she gladly accepted.

But to leave for Montevideo she had first somehow to cover her bill at the Buenos Aires Plaza, which amounted to some $4,000. This she managed to do only by leaving behind as security an ermine coat she had, plus her magnificent emerald. She was also lucky in that Walter Mocchi at the last moment relented and allowed her to reclaim her curtains. This he did as a favour to Dumesnil, knowing that he had as yet received no payment.

Somehow the curtains failed to arrive in Montevideo, but Isadora was so relieved to have escaped from Buenos Aires that she shrugged the problem off, saying, 'I feel that I could even dance without any decoration at all. I could dance right here in the public square.'

This time her confidence was justified. Her performances in Montevideo were highly successful, a fact Dumesnil was inclined to attribute to the traditional rivalry between Uruguay and Argentina. Unfortunately she made little money. As impresario Giulietti explained after her first performance, 'We split sixty-forty with the theatre. What remains we split fifty-fifty with the benefit society which sponsored the concert. Out of our share, I take my commission of fifteen per cent.'

For that one she got three hundred dollars. For her second she got just over two hundred, and for her third even less. Giulietti explained that unfortunately he had had to paper the house. It was obvious to Dumesnil that he was cheating her, but she brushed his suspicions aside. She liked Giulietti because he treated her courteously, unlike the arrogant Walter Mocchi.

In Rio de Janeiro, her Brazilian audiences were even more appreciative. They erupted with enthusiasm, and the local critics joined in to swell the applause, hailing her as, 'a cosmic expression ... original, unexpected, more sensed than understood.' At her last concert there she received more than thirty curtain calls. While she was still onstage, poets and students read out tributes to her, causing her to weep openly. Financially, too, she did better. She left the city sufficiently in funds to be able to send money to Buenos Aires and redeem her ermine coat and her emerald.

All in all, she managed to leave South America out of debt, but still broke. She had also had disturbing news from Augustin in Geneva. Just before he arrived there, her six star pupils, tired of sitting around waiting, had accepted the suggestion of composer Ernst Bloch that they make a dancing tour of Switzerland on their own. Augustin had agreed to act as their manager. And as the most sensible course of action, he had arranged to send the younger pupils back home to their parents. Isadora's school had ceased to exist.

Dumesnil she paid off, giving him four months' pay and leaving him to make his own way back to France. For some reason she had grown displeased with him, and as she gave him his cheque she told him he was nothing but a fly, and worse than Mocchi. She herself set sail back to New York on a boat called the *Vestris*, which, coincidentally, was also carrying the same group of boxers she had socialised with on the way to Argentina. But they were not enough to keep her from feeling 'sad and lonely' during most of the voyage.

On the morning she arrived in New York, flat broke, to her dismay there was no one at the pier to meet her. A cable she had sent ahead to friends had apparently gone astray, and for a moment she was at a loss. In desperation she phoned a man she knew only slightly, the photographer Arnold Genthe. But it wasn't Genthe who picked up the phone. It was Paris Singer.

Chapter Fifteen

Patriotism and Despair

Isadora was both relieved and delighted to meet Singer again. Hearing of her plight, he at once came and collected her, taking her and her luggage back to an apartment he was renting on West 57th Street. He was, Isadora later recollected, 'in one of his kindest and most generous moods.'

By the end of that evening he had hired the Metropolitan Opera House for her, so that she could give a benefit concert in aid of the families of French artists impoverished by the war. It was to be held on 21st November 1916, and Isadora would dance essentially the same programme she had performed at the Trocadéro in April, with the orchestra this time conducted by Oscar Spirescu. The audience would all be there by invitation only. Mary Roberts, who was one of the organisers, later recalled, 'It was a tremendous undertaking, and when we neared the day of the performance we were offered as high as a hundred dollars a ticket, but none were sold.' Among the invitees were Anna Pavlova, Otto Kahn, and the mayor, John Purroy Mitchel.

The concert was a triumph. Isadora received a standing ovation, and afterwards joined Singer and several of their friends for dinner at Sherry's. Among these friends was Arnold Genthe, who later recalled being taken aside by Singer before Isadora arrived:

'I have placed you next to her,' he said. 'You know she never eats before a performance – she's had nothing all day but a cup of coffee at breakfast. I want you to see that she doesn't drink anything until she has had some solid food.'

Isadora had scarcely sat down when she said, 'I'm dying of thirst. I just have to have a sip of champagne.'

I have never seen her in better form than she was during the dinner. As a rule, she paid very little attention to clothes. And she cared nothing at all for jewelry. But that evening, to please Singer, she wore an exquisite white chiffon frock and a diamond necklace which he had just given her.

She was clearly happy to be back with Singer. Not just for the financial protection he gave her, but for the feeling of emotional security. Here was someone who loved her, who was dependable (in spite of their quarrels), and who supported her Art, even if he did not always appreciate it. But somehow, once safe back with him, there rose in her a definite desire to make mischief, like a young girl wanting to reassure herself that her father will still love her no matter how she misbehaves. After the meal, it had been arranged that about a hundred further guests would join the party for dancing. Genthe reported:

> All went well until the dancing began. I was talking to Isadora when all of a sudden her face lit up. 'Do you see,' she said to me, 'that dark, handsome young man over there? ... I want you to go over and bring him here.'
> I did as she asked and they proceeded to dance a tango that astonished the guests by something more than mere grace and rhythm.

Max Eastman, who was also there, takes up the story:

> They danced with so little restraint that [Singer] finally got up... Lifted the slender swain by the pants and collar, and carried him through the door. When [he] returned, Isadora was standing in flames of ice, if for her sake there can be such things, in the center of the floor.
> 'If you don't like my friends,' she cried, 'I don't want your jewelry!'
> She ripped off the fabulous necklace and, with a gesture between Mars God of War and Zeus the Rain-bringer, scattered the flashing gems in every corner of the room, and marched out in the wake of the beautiful tango dancer. Arnold Genthe was standing near the door, and as she passed him she murmured, without turning her head: 'Pick them up.'

It is no wonder that Singer once said to her, when she asked him, late in her life, why he kept returning to her, 'You are the one woman in my life who never bored me. Ever.'

This time he had no need to return, because their quarrel was quickly resolved, and Singer remained in a warm and generous mood. He did, however, complain. The American poet Witter Bynner witnessed a conversation between them at this time, which went:

Singer: If you could only cease making these public scandals, there's nothing I wouldn't give you.
Isadora: What would you give me?
Singer: Madison Square Garden.
Isadora: What are your conditions?
Singer: That you always behave yourself with dignity in public.
Isadora: I'm not sure that I can meet your conditions.

Bynner was a friend of the young man who was currently Singer's secretary, enjoying a salary of a thousand dollars a week. He also had ambitions to be a poet, and his name was Allan Ross Macdougall. He was also gay, which was why Singer was quite happy to send him and Isadora off for a Christmas holiday in Cuba during December – Macdougall (who became Isadora's first biographer), was to act as a sort of chaperone.

She enjoyed herself, although maybe not always with dignity, dancing on deck during the voyage to Havana to a portable gramophone she had brought along. (She was unexpectedly at home with new mechanical gadgets as they came into being, such as cars, telephones and gramophones, none of which existed when she was born.) She danced the hula, wrote Macdougall to Bynner, 'with a very boisterous drunk man', and followed it up by calling for silence, donning a green velvet cloak, and dancing an allegory of the birth of Christ to the 'Air' from Bach's Suite no. 3 in D – the celebrated 'Air on the G String'.

Isadora herself recalled performing, at New Year, in a Havana bar, 'the dance of Christ crucified' in front of 'the usual collection of morphimaniacs, cocainists, opium smokers, alcoholists, and other derelicts of life.'

In January, she and Macdougall sailed to Florida, staying at The Breakers in Palm Beach, where they were shortly joined by Singer himself. Also there was a man whose name has passed into the language – Kid McCoy, who in 1899, when a successful boxer, was tagged 'the real McCoy' by a San Francisco sport (who based the expression on an earlier one from the world of the Scottish clans – 'the real McKay').

McCoy, whose real name was Norman Selby, was a flamboyant and much-married character, about four years older than Isadora. After retiring from boxing he had gone on to have a useful career as a road-company actor, but by the beginning of 1917 he had arrived in Palm Beach to take on the job of physical instructor at Gus's Baths. (Which was not quite the comedown it sounds – the man handing out the towels there was an authentic Italian count.)

The story goes that Singer left Palm Beach for a few days on a business trip and returned to find Isadora either in Kid McCoy's arms, or else throwing lavish champagne parties (for which Singer was of course paying) in McCoy's honour. Either way, they had another row.

Again they made up and, early in 1917, after they returned to New York, he paid for her six star pupils to be brought there from Switzerland. Clearly Isadora had changed her mind about discouraging them from returning to America, because when they arrived she welcomed them with delight. She also announced her intention of legally adopting all six of them, saying, 'I should have done this long ago.' Unfortunately, because of the war, the necessary papers from Germany (such as their birth certificates) could not be obtained, so instead of being adopted the girls all settled for making legal application to change their last names to 'Duncan'.

At the beginning of March 1917 Singer threw a small dinner-party at the Plaza Hotel for Isadora and several of her family and friends. Among those present were Augustin and his wife Margherita, Elizabeth, Mary Desti (back in New York), Arnold Genthe, and the sculptor George Grey Barnard.

Singer had not only remembered his light-hearted promise of rewarding her for behaving with dignity in public, he had acted on it, putting down $100,000 as a deposit towards buying Madison Square Garden. This was the original Madison Square Garden, completed by architect Stanford White in 1890. Occupying an entire block, and built in an ornate 'Spanish Renaissance' style, it was immense. Its main auditorium could hold as many as 17,000 for a boxing match (although only 8,000 for a horse show), and it also included a second theatre seating 1,200, the largest restaurant in New York, a third (open-air) theatre on the roof for use in the summer months, surrounded by eight domed cupolas and a vast tower rising to 300 feet, with a statue of Diana on the top that revolved as a weather-vane.

At the dinner party Singer announced what he had done, and offered to give Madison Square Garden to Isadora as a home for a new school.

This was such an outlandish suggestion that Isadora was instantly furious. 'What do you think I am?' she shouted. 'A circus? I suppose you want me to advertise prize fights with my dancing!'

Maybe Singer's choice of building had been inappropriate, but nobody there could ever remember him being more upset than he was at her response. As Mary recalled, 'Singer turned absolutely livid. His lips were quivering and his hands were shaking. He got up from the table without saying a word and left the room.'

'He'll come back,' said Isadora. 'He always does.'

But this time he didn't. As the days passed she heard nothing from him, except indirectly that all his financial support for her had stopped. He even accepted the loss of his $100,000 deposit on Madison Square Garden. She sent him letters, but received no answer. She sent others to try and make peace with him – Augustin and his wife, Mary Desti, even some of her pupils. All to no avail. Wanting his life cleansed of anything to do with her, Singer even fired his secretary, Macdougall.

Isadora, short of funds, had reluctantly to move from the Ritz, where she had a suite, to a cheaper hotel, the Woolcott, on the west side of town. As she was unable to pay rent for her girls, they were forced to find temporary homes with friends and relations – except Irma, temperamentally perhaps the closest of her pupils, who was taken by Isadora to keep her company at the Woolcott.

That was the final breach with Singer. In 1918, having finally divorced the wife from whom he had separated nine years earlier, he would marry Joan Balsh, the nurse who was running the wartime hospital at his mansion in Devon, and together they would spend most of their time in Florida, doing more than anyone else to turn its swampland into the wealthy enclave it became.

On 6th March Isadora and her six girls gave the first of a series of performances at the Metropolitan Opera House, again dancing a version of the programme she had developed in Paris, which she had now entitled *The Spirit of a Nation Drawn into War*. As America was now on the verge of entering the war, and the prevailing mood of the country was warlike, her programme received rapturous applause. People could understand patriotic fervour.

The *New York Sun*, describing her opening piece, *Rédemption*, wrote:

Miss Duncan was discovered upon the deep shadowed stage, utterly prostrate, her white robes draped down upon her huddled figure as upon a thing grotesquely useless and inert. Then slowly, laboriously, the stir of life came; one could see it only in the trembling fingers at first, then along the uplifting arms. Then to knees, then to full height – and the figure could stride and assert itself in broad, deliberate motion. It was all a cycle of slow gestures, unalterably slow and stern, every inward impulse of it seeming to find fight and oppression from the unseen force without. And when, in the end, self-mastery came, with head high and face gladdened, with the pride of peace, it was as if a great battle of humanity unlimited had been enacted through one strong, transparent soul.

She ended, of course, with the *Marseillaise*, which she again danced alone, and the writer Carl Van Vechten described it in the *New York Herald*:

> In a robe the color of blood, she stands enfolded; she sees the enemy advance; she feels the enemy as it grasps her by the throat; she kisses her flag; she tastes blood; she is all but crushed under the weight of the attack; and then she rises triumphant with the terrible cry, *Aux armes, citoyens* [unspoken of course] but the hideous din of a hundred raucous voices seems to ring in our ears.

Again she received a standing ovation. As the *New York Sun* reported:

> The heavy golden curtains had to swing back many times in order that Miss Duncan could acknowledge the cheers which sometimes reached the height of pandemonium... And when at the end, it was encored, and the American anthem trumpeted in behind it, [she] had only to tear off her outer skirtlet and discover herself in the Stars and Stripes. It was daring – but the audience, not entirely unacquainted with that sort of thing in other sorts of entertainments, seemed to like it.

Her speech at the end of her performance, as she stood draped in the American flag, showed clearly how her attitude had changed. In it she said, 'This is no time for art and artists. Men should want to serve in the trenches and women should nurse the soldiers.' She announced her intention of staying in America until the war was won, saying, 'I feel that America is on the brink of a great awakening and that now it is going to be a really interesting country to live in.' As she said good night, she kissed the flag around her, unleashing a further torrent of applause.

It was early in this series of performances, which would go on into April, that an event took place that shook the world. On 12th March the Russian Revolution erupted, and on 15th March Tsar Nicholas II was forced to abdicate. Isadora was ecstatic. 'On the night of the Russian Revolution,' she recalled in her memoirs, 'I danced with a terrible fierce joy.' The Russians had been fighting on the Allied side, and for the rest of the war their contribution would falter and then fail. But the fall of the Tsar did much to reassure Americans that it would be right to join the Allies, as the war was now much more clearly seen as a fight for democracy against autocracy, as personified in the German, Austro-Hungarian and Ottoman Empires.

At a concert on 28th March, Isadora dedicated her programme to the new Russia, for the moment being run by a moderate provisional government, and on 6th April America did declare war on Germany. Isadora drove to Washington to hear the official proclamation. After it, working 'at white heat', she created a dance in praise of the Revolution, to the music of Tchaikovsky's *Marche Slave*. On 11th April she added it to her repertoire, again dancing it alone. Carl Van Vechten described it:

> Groping, stumbling … she struggles forward, clad only in a short red garment that barely covers her thighs. With furtive glances of extreme despair she peers above and ahead. When the strains of 'God Save the Tsar' are first heard in the orchestra she falls to her knees and you see the peasant shuddering under the blows of the knout. The picture is a tragic one, cumulative in its horrific details. Finally comes the moment of release and here Isadora makes one of her great effects. She does not spread her arms apart with a wide gesture. She brings them forward slowly and we observe with horror that they have practically forgotten how to move at all. They are crushed, these hands, crushed and bleeding after their long serfdom; they are not hands at all but claws, broken, twisted, piteous claws! The expression of frightened, almost uncomprehending, joy with which Isadora concludes the march is another stroke of her vivid imaginative genius.

It was a stroke of genius indeed to choose *Marche Slave* as her music. A brassy and imperialistic piece, it made a telling counterpoint to the crushed serfdom, rising to hope, of her dancing. And although many of her friends and fans among the socialist avant-garde were dubious – they felt that the war was basically between capitalist governments, and that the working-class of all nations should unite with each other and have nothing to do with it – even they found themselves carried along by the strength of her performance. Carl Van Vechten described this strength in a letter to Gertrude Stein: 'People – this includes me – get on their chairs and yell. It is very exciting to see American patriotism thoroughly awakened – I tell you she drives 'em mad; the recruiting stations are full of her converts.'

That was undoubtedly so, but now that America was in the war, there was a quite predictable, although somewhat hysterical, public concern about enemy aliens. Although Isadora's pupils now all bore the surname 'Duncan', it was common knowledge that most of them were originally German. It was also known to the authorities that, in spite of her new-found patriotic fervour, she had continued, while in New York, to welcome dignitaries and diplomats from Germany (as well as from other countries, such as Russia) to her open-house parties. For this reason, late in 1917, she was investigated by the U.S. Government.

As were Elizabeth and Max Merz. The staff at their school consisted almost entirely of Germans, and Max himself had continued to lecture the students about 'racial purity'. But the school now had a number of American pupils, and one of these complained about being subjected to 'propaganda'. The fact that the investigation revealed that one of the pupils was seven months pregnant did not help, but eventually no further action was taken. Nor was it against Isadora.

By this time she was having increasing troubles with her own girls, whose ages now ranged from sixteen to twenty-two. Although all six still worshipped her, and although they were grateful for the adventurous life she had given them, they wished more and more to achieve a measure of independence, both financial and artistic. But Isadora would have none of it, insisting that their dancing was not yet perfect 'or as near perfect as possible', and that until it was she would not have them dancing independently of her. Her attitude, Irma recalled, 'became a constant source of friction and contention between us.'

Nonetheless, they all still hung together. In the summer of 1917, with her funds exhausted, Isadora rented a cottage for them all on the Atlantic coast of Long Island, paying for everything by selling the ermine coat and emerald that she had had in South America, and by pawning the diamond necklace that Singer had given her (and which she had retrieved after flinging it aside). In her own words: 'As I was now practically penniless, it would, no doubt, have been wiser to have invested the proceeds ... in solid stocks and bonds, but of course this never occurred to me, and we spent a pleasant enough summer... We had no studio, but danced on the beach.'

And as usual she received a constant procession of guests, including such celebrities as Sarah Bernhardt, then in her seventies, composer Edgard Varèse, the violinists Fritz Kreisler and Eugène Ysaÿe, and the leaders of the Dadaist movement in New York, Marcel Duchamp and Francis Picabia. Mary Desti was also there for almost the whole summer, as was the social-climbing San Franciscan Elsa Maxwell, who would eventually make a living by devoting most of her life to hosting celebrity parties.

There too came the writer Mercedes de Acosta, then in her mid-twenties and later described by actress-writer-photographer Jean Howard as 'a little blackbird of a woman, strange and mysterious, and to many irresistible.' The daughter of Cuban aristocrats, and with a sister, Rita de Acosta Lybig, who was a celebrated society beauty, Mercedes had already embarked on a career of mingling with the leading lights of the artistic world, in both Europe and America, and knew Gertrude Stein, Mrs Patrick Campbell and Eleanora Duse. With a lively and curious mind, she was part Buddhist and part Spiritualist, a vegetarian and an active bisexual (although predominantly lesbian).

'Always go barefooted whenever you can,' Isadora advised her as they walked on the seashore. 'With your bare feet free your whole body assumes a natural grace. Contacting the earth barefooted revitalizes brain and body. It is a wonderful health cure... Let me see how you move your body. Come, let's run.' They ran, and when they stopped, out of breath, Isadora said, 'Not bad – not bad. I wish I could have trained you when you were four years old. I could have made a dancer of you.'

Summing up her impression of Isadora, the perceptive Mercedes wrote:

> I approached Isadora altogether differently from any other person in my life. I not only approached her differently but I also evaluated her differently and, in a manner of speaking, I saw her differently. I am quite sure of this... In after years when many people were critical of her, I was always tolerant – tolerant of her violence, her recklessness, of all her wild and uncontrolled love affairs. I understood all these passions in her as I could say I understand thunder, or a hurricane, or, in the case of her love affairs, as I understood a great cosmic maternal urge. She wanted ceaselessly to give of herself to all her loves as a mother gives to her child. And she gave herself indiscriminately because mothers, of which she was the supreme one, do not discriminate among their children.

Since her breach with Singer, Isadora's love life had again become as wild and uncontrolled as it had been when without him in South America. And the wildest lover she ever had in America was the Dadaist, Francis Picabia. Cuban-French by birth, Picabia was a short wealthy man, manic, hypersexed, and addicted to drink and opium. Unlike Isadora, he had a cheerful contempt for anybody foolish enough to become involved in the war, and had come to New York from France in 1915 in order to evade it (ostensibly he was on an official mission to Cuba to buy molasses for the troops).

The Dadists' opinion of the war was that it had been caused by men being out of touch with the anarchic forces lurking in their subconscious, a condition brought about by an excessively cerebral and mechanistic civilisation. Thus they rejected the Victorian belief in progress, the belief that man's nature could in any meaningful way be tamed and civilised, and that man is a rational animal. And they believed that art of any kind was a dangerous mystification, making the ephemeral seem stable, and giving the illusion that man is the centre of the universe. In Picabia's own words, 'Art is useless and impossible to justify.'

Although by this time Isadora was more involved in raising enthusiasm for the war than in Art, one would have thought that such an attitude would conflict so much with her own that a relationship between them would be impossible, but paradoxically Dada had the effect of clearing the ground for Art to start anew – after all, Picabia himself was a prolific painter – so even if she found new attitudes to Art somewhat strange and unsettling, and even if Picabia would have rejected the label 'artist', it was obvious that he and Isadora shared ideals of a similar nature.

What also formed a spiritual bond between them was that he too had a fascination with death (as did most Dadaists – it was once observed that almost all of them would have committed suicide, but were saved by their shared sense of humour). And of course he was fascinated by sex. 'There is nothing modern about making love;' Picabia once said, 'however, it's what I like to do best.'

Isadora's six pupils too had at last begun to form romantic attachments. The days were gone, Theresa recalled, 'when we lived like ensorcelled virgins in the depths of the woods, hidden away from the world that might claim our hearts.' They and Isadora moved from their summer cottage in September, renting a studio in the recently-completed Hôtel des Artistes on West 67th Street, in Manhattan, and for the next couple of months lived an uneasy and distracted sort of life. They had no money, no bookings to perform, and perpetual arguments, mostly about the girls' increasing desire for independence, both professionally and in their personal lives. But this was one argument Isadora could not totally win. By November 1917 five out of the six had a regular admirer.

At the end of the first week in November there had been further developments in Russia. The first part of the Revolution, when the Tsar was deposed and the moderate wing of the Social Democratic Party (the Mensheviks) took power, was succeeded by the second and greater part, when the hard-line wing of the party, the Bolsheviks, led by Trotsky and Lenin, swept them aside and established what would become the Soviet Union. Isadora welcomed the news with enthusiasm, saying a few years later, 'Here at last is a frame mighty enough to work in... Here one feels that perhaps for the second time in the world's history a great force has arisen to give capitalism, which stands for monstrous greed and villainy, one great blow.'

In mid-November Isadora set off alone for California, to give a performance that she hoped would be the first of a nationwide tour, arriving in San Francisco on the 19th, just in time to read the saddening news that her old friend Rodin had died two days before in Paris, aged seventy-seven.

Although the local papers welcomed her home with lavish headlines – OAKLAND GIRL IS BACK HOME WITH WREATH OF FAME, read one – she found her homecoming something of a strain. It was an ordeal to go and visit her mother, who had remained estranged from her for ten years, and all she recorded in her memoirs of their meeting was the disheartened reflection that she 'looked very old and careworn... I could not help contrasting my sad face and the haggard looks of my mother with the two adventurous spirits who had set out nearly twenty-two years ago with such high hopes to seek fame and fortune. Both had been found – why was the result so tragic?'

She was also saddened by seeing for the first time the changes wrought in the city by the earthquake and fire of 1906. By now a new city had arisen on the ruins of the old, and there was little sign of devastation left, but all eight of the downtown theatres she had known no longer existed, and at the site of the house where she had been born, on the corner of Geary and Taylor Streets, nothing remained but 'an empty place of rubble and sand, some weeds and nothing more.'

The theatre she was to perform at was a new one, part of the rebuilt town. Still surviving today, and now called The Geary, in 1917 it still bore its original name, The Columbia. She gave four matinees there, performing in turn almost all her major pieces – *Iphigenia*, Tchaikovsky's Sixth Symphony, Beethoven's Seventh Symphony, Chopin and Brahms, and at each performance, to finish, the *Marseillaise*. Here, as in New

York, the patriotic fervour she aroused was immense. A man sitting next to the music critic for the *San Francisco Examiner*, Redfern Mason, turned to him, saying, 'That'll get recruits!'

While she was in California, Mason became her lover. As did pianist Harold Bauer. Bauer, who had seen her dance in a salon years before, when he was a music student in Paris, told her that seeing her had changed his life. He had, he explained, been having trouble with his piano technique. Watching Isadora, he recalled, 'Her movements fascinated me with their beauty and rhythm... As I watched her carefully the idea crept into my mind that this process might conceivably be ... a reversible one... As long as a loud tone brought forth a vigorous gesture, and a soft tone a delicate gesture, why in playing the piano should not a vigorous gesture bring forth a loud tone and a delicate gesture a soft tone? The fact that this was precisely what had always taken place (in piano playing) did not occur to me.' Naturally his respect and admiration for Isadora aroused her affection.

The tour she believed she was beginning never materialised. It seems most likely that while she was in California her tour manager absconded with the takings. Whatever happened, suddenly she was flat broke. To make some money, she and Bauer arranged to give a joint Chopin recital, again at the Columbia Theater. It took place on 3rd January 1918, and Redfern Mason reported that their performances merged perfectly.

Isadora frequently referred to Bauer as 'my musical twin soul'. He was impressed by her musicianship. Listening to him play Chopin's Étude in A flat, Opus 25, No. 1 in rehearsal, she objected that one phrase, 'a tremendous crescendo followed by a diminuendo,' had a wrong dynamic, that the crescendo should continue to the end. He showed her the expression marks in his music. 'It cannot be done that way,' Isadora persisted, 'because if it were I would have nothing to do with my arms.' Later, Bauer managed to see Chopin's original manuscript, and found out she was right. Printers had erred.

Shortly after their joint performance, Bauer's wife arrived in San Francisco, and their love-making abruptly ended. Isadora went back to Mason, who complained of having been jealous. She wrote him a gentle chiding note: 'Do you want me to be walking on my bare knees on broken glass? Aren't you glad I can still dance a Bacchanal & that sometimes in a quiet landscape I wish for a Faun to part the bushes and leap forth and seize a not unwilling nymph?'

Meanwhile, back in New York, there was trouble of another kind. Isadora's students had continued to chafe at their continued lack of dancing activity, and by her apparent intention to keep them as simply her students for life. They confided their frustration to the gentle and sympathetic Augustin – 'Uncle Gus' to them – and, defying his sister's wishes, he arranged with his former employer, Charles Coburn, for them to perform together for a short season at the Liberty Theater. Augustin naturally informed Isadora of the engagement, with the result that after the girls had performed for only a few nights, he received a telegram from her in Los Angeles: I FORBID IT. THE GIRLS ARE NOT YET READY FOR PERFORMANCES OF THEIR OWN IN NEW YORK. Because of the contract they had signed with Isadora, and as they were using her name and dancing her dances, the girls had no option but to cancel the rest of their run.

This incident caused lasting ill-feeling between Isadora and her brother, he having negotiated the girls' contract with Coburn. And it caused ill-feeling on the part of her pupils too. As Irma later wrote, recalling the time, 'If she did not consider us ready now, at the age of twenty, she probably never would, we told ourselves.'

Dancing in Los Angeles, at a matinee at the Mason Opera House, Isadora unknowingly influenced another young dancer – the eight-year-old Agnes De Mille, niece of the famous film producer Cecil B. De Mille, and in years to come an innovative and influential choreographer, her works including *Rodeo* and *Fall River Legend* (on the stage), *Oklahoma!* and *Carousel* (on stage and film), and *An American in Paris* (on film).

Writing in the late 1980s, towards the end of her life, Agnes remembered:

> Children were taken as to a shrine. What they saw, alas, was a prematurely aged and bloated woman, coarsened by terrible trials, laboring through gossamer steps and classical evocation. [At the end, after the *Marseillaise*, for which the audience stood] Everyone wept for various reasons. I became aware that this audience was reacting quite differently from any other theater or moving-picture audience I had ever before experienced. Nothing was happening onstage that seemed to me worthy of tears, yet they wept. Isadora wore a blood-red robe which she threw over her shoulder as she stamped to the footlights and raised her arms in the great Duncan salute... This was heroic and I never forgot it. No one who saw Isadora ever forgot her.

In 1963, writing her encyclopaedic *The Book of the Dance*, Agnes gave the frontispiece to Isadora.

Still in California, Isadora hoped to give a performance at the Greek Theater in Berkeley, but when officials denied her permission she was stunned, especially as the dancer Ruth St Denis had appeared there only a few months before. (Ruth St Denis, with her husband Ted Shawn, had founded the influential Denishawn School of Dancing and Related Arts in Los Angeles in 1915.) A great flood of disappointment came over her, not just with her native state, but with the whole of America, and she decided that it was time she returned to Paris. Maybe there she could raise money to continue working with her students.

Back in New York, in February 1918, she told her students, 'I am going back to France because I find conditions here more than I can bear. My struggles to establish a permanent school here have been to no avail. I feel utterly disheartened and much too discouraged to continue. Perhaps in France, where I have certain properties left, I may be able to raise some money and return in the fall.'

The girls were by now becoming resentful that she seemed determined to keep them dependent on her, and would not let them make their own way and support themselves. They asked what they were supposed to do while she was off in France, and were stunned when she suggested they rejoin Elizabeth's school, which was now under the patronage of Mabel Dodge and had moved to new premises in Tarrytown. They refused outright to consider putting themselves back under Elizabeth's thumband, after a bitter argument, walked out on her. This so upset Isadora that for the next few weeks, until she left New York, she made no attempt to contact them, even to say goodbye. She attempted to solace herself by running up a huge hotel bill she had no hope of being able to pay.

She was only able to afford a passage to London through the friendship and help of Mary Desti, who managed to talk the department-store magnate, Gordon Selfridge, into buying her a one-way ticket on a ship he himself would be sailing on. (Mary's business, Maison Desti, was now doing extremely well, partly because her son Preston, now serving in the U.S. Army Air Corps, had invented a kiss-proof lipstick, calling it 'Red Red Rouge'. This had been a huge success.)

Isadora, meeting Gordon Selfridge, had reminded him of the previous time he had helped her out, when he was working at Marshall Field's in Chicago in 1895 and 'a hungry little girl asked him for credit for a frock to dance in.' But their voyage together turned out something of a letdown, because the first night out Isadora accidentally 'fell down an opening in the deck, a drop of about fifteen feet.' She sprained her hip, and while

Selfridge gallantly lent her his cabin to recuperate in, she was confined to bed for the rest of the voyage.

In London, Kathleen Bruce found her rooms to rent in Duke Street, in fashionable St James's, not far from Piccadilly Circus, but in general Isadora found few old friends, and life there was miserable. She recalled:

> I spent some terrible and gloomy weeks in that melancholy lodging, completely stranded. Alone and ill, without a cent, my school destroyed and the war appearing to go on interminably, I used to sit at a dark window at night and watch the air raids, and wish that a bomb might land on me and end my troubles. Suicide is so tempting. I have often thought of it, but something always holds me back. Certainly if suicide pellets were sold in drug stores as plainly as some preventatives, I think the intelligentsia of all countries would doubtless disappear overnight in conquered agony.

Some of the few people she met socially during this dismal period were, as it happened, intelligentsia, to whom she was introduced by Kathleen Bruce. One was Bernard Shaw, of whom Kathleen had recently sculpted a bust. Shaw remembered Isadora being 'clothed in drapery.' He also remarked that her 'face looked as if it had been made of sugar and someone had licked it ... rather like a piece of battered confectionery.' By now, partly in dramatic defiance of convention, and partly to hide the signs of advancing age, Isadora had taken to wearing (in addition to her hennaed hair) heavy make-up – dark red lipstick and heavy eye-shadow. She got on flirtatiously well with Shaw, joking to him, 'Though I may not be much to look at I'm very good to feel.'

Her flirtatiousness was less well received when Kathleen introduced her to some members of the Bloomsbury group, and Isadora, somewhat drunk, hurled herself unsuccessfully at the critic Clive Bell (brother-in-law of Virginia Woolf), crying, '*Je ne suis pas une femme! Je suis une génie!*' Kathleen began to avoid her.

Desperate to move on from London, Isadora managed to drum up enough money to get herself to Paris by selling the last of her jewellery. Getting there, she took out another mortgage on her studio at Neuilly, and booked herself into the Hôtel Palais d'Orsay.

It was better for her here than in London. Paris might be woken early in the morning by the distant booming of trench artillery, but there were still one or two of her old friends in evidence, such as the poet Fernand Divoire and the actress Cécile Sorel. It was sad, however, that so many people now seemed to have vanished from her life. Even, for the moment, Mary Desti. She wrote several times to Mary, on one occasion asking her desperately if she could persuade Paris Singer to send her a thousand dollars. But for the moment Mary did not reply. In April Isadora was writing to her, 'Still not a word from anyone... *Please* write me news... What is Augustin doing – and the girls? ... I am living here on Hope.'

When she did hear about the girls, from Elizabeth, the news was disquieting. They, being broke, had at last decided that, Isadora or not, they would try and drum up work. They conferred with Augustin, and he sensibly suggested that the first thing they should do would be to move into Elizabeth's school. Not as students – he knew how they felt about that – but simply as paying guests. This would be less expensive, and in the meantime he would see what he could arrange in the way of dance engagements. The girls were willing to try this, so he spoke to Elizabeth. She was amenable, and into her school at Tarrytown they moved.

Elizabeth wrote to tell Isadora, who replied:

Dearest Elizabeth:
    The first letter I received from any of you was April 20th – so you see I was more than two months without news. If the girls had only told me that they would go to Tarrytown we could have enjoyed four weeks of pleasant work. But human beings, contrary and cussed – and such a pity. It would have been such a comfort to know.

The engagement Augustin found for the girls amused him. Although they had all applied for American citizenship, their papers had not yet been processed, so technically they were still 'enemy aliens', and the tour he had arranged for them (with the full approval of the War Department Commission on Training Camp Activities) was to a series of army camps.

They were delighted. At last they would be giving performances they had arranged themselves. They would be making money and it was in a good cause. So although their dancing was not the sort of dancing that soldiers were particularly anxious to see, with the result that they played to half-empty houses, they enjoyed the tour. Irma recalled, 'we girls, on our way to becoming full-fledged citizens, got a great kick out of it and a wonderful sense of belonging.'

Their music during the tour was provided by pianist George Copeland,

and when Isadora heard this she was concerned. She had given a series of performances with him in New York in 1915, when he played Chopin for her, but she also knew that he was an enthusiastic interpreter of what was then modern music, especially Debussy, and she at once leapt to the erroneous conclusion that it was his music they were dancing to. Completely forgiving the girls for embarking on an independent career, she wrote them jointly a heartfelt letter, a loving outpouring of her deepest feelings, that they would all treasure:

Please don't let anyone persuade you to dance to Debussy. It is only music of the *Senses* and has no message to the Spirit. And then the gesture of Debussy is all inward – and has no outward or upward. I want you to dance only that music which goes from the soul in mounting circles. Why not study the Suite in D of Bach? Do you remember my dancing it? Please also continue always your studies of the Beethoven Seventh and the Schubert Seventh; and why not dance with Copeland the seven minuets of Beethoven that we studied in Fourth Avenue? And the Symphony in G of Mozart. There is a whole world of Mozart that you might study.

Plunge your soul in divine unconscious *Giving* deep within it, until it gives your soul its *Secret*. That is how I have always tried to express music. My soul should become one with it, and the dance born from that embrace. Music has been in all my life the great Inspiration and will perhaps some day be the Consolation, for I have gone through such terrible years. No one has understood since I lost Deirdre and Patrick how pain has caused me at times to live in almost a delirium. In fact my poor brain has more often been crazed than anyone can know. Sometimes quite recently I feel as if I were awakening from a long fever. When you think of these years, think of the Funeral March of Schubert, the *Ave Maria*, the *Redemption*, and forget the times when my poor distracted soul trying to escape from suffering may well have given you all the appearance of madness.

I have reached such high peaks flooded with light, but my soul has no strength to live there – and no one has realised the horrible torture from which I have tried to escape. Some day if you understand sorrow you will understand too all I have lived through, and then you will only think of the light towards which I have pointed and you will know the *real* Isadora is there. In the meantime work and create Beauty and Harmony. The poor world has need of it, and with your six spirits going with one will, you can create a Beauty and Inspiration for a new Life.

I am so happy that you are working and that you love it. Nourish your spirit from Plato and Dante, from Goethe and Schiller, Shakespeare and Nietzsche (don't forget that the *Birth of Tragedy* and the *Spirit of Music* are my Bible). With these to guide you, and the greatest music, you may go far.

Dear children, I take you in my arms... Let us pray that this separation will only bring us nearer and closer in a higher communion...

After their tour of the army camps, the girls were soon able to get bookings at more prestigious venues. It was not long before they could afford to move away from Tarrytown, subletting a large studio on the top floor of the annexe to Carnegie Hall, and on 27th June were performing in the Hall itself. The *New York Globe* headlined its review of their performance: DUNCAN DANCERS ON THEIR OWN AT LAST.

Meanwhile, in Paris, Isadora was taking her mind off her misery by having a brief affair with one of France's most famous flying aces, Roland Garros. Garros was famous, not only for his success in shooting down German planes, but for having been the first to invent (in 1914) a way of firing his machine-gun forward through his plane's propeller (which meant that in effect his whole plane itself became a gun, which could be aimed directly at the enemy).

Garros was on leave from active service and, like most long-serving pilots of the Great War, living day after day and week after week in the expectation of death, had acquired a haunted, faraway look. One night, as he and Isadora were on their way home from a party, they saw a zeppelin dropping bombs on the (fortunately empty) place de la Concorde. Isadora began wildly dancing to the crashing of the bombs, and Garros began applauding her, his eyes, she remembered, 'lit up by the fire that fell and exploded quite near us. He told me that night that he only saw and wished for death.'

He would get his wish in October, a month before the Armistice. By which time Isadora had met the next great love of her life, the pianist and composer Walter Morse Rummel.

302

Chapter Sixteen

The Archangel

She met Walter Rummel in July 1918, introduced to him by the painter Christine Dalliès, then working as her secretary. Rummel, although he had been raised in Berlin, was technically an American citizen, his mother, Leila, being the daughter of the famous Samuel Morse, the American painter who turned to invention and became a pioneer of telegraphy and designer of the Morse code.

Aged thirty-one when Isadora met him, Walter had moved to Paris in 1908 and become one of Europe's foremost concert pianists. He had arranged choral works by Bach and Vivaldi for the piano, and, having a deep interest in early music, including plainsong, had already published two anthologies of it. His interest in plainsong had gained him the friendship of Debussy, who had died only the previous March. They had even collaborated on some compositions. But above all he was a pianist – both a gifted technician and a sensitive interpreter. Bernard Shaw, hearing him play in London, had told him, 'You make Chopin stand out ten times bigger than he is.' And Debussy, who generally loathed the way pianists performed his works, was lavish in praise of Rummel, for instance writing to him in 1917, 'One does not congratulate a sunset, nor does one congratulate the sea for being more beautiful than a cathedral! You are a force of nature.'

Isadora, meeting this tall, slender, blue-eyed man, was even more bowled over, recalling:

> When he entered I thought he was the picture of a youthful Liszt ... so tall, slight, with a burnished lock over the high forehead, and his eyes like clear wells of shining light. He played for me. I called him my Archangel... And during the booms of the Big Bertha, and amidst the echoes of the war news, he played for me

Liszt's 'Thoughts of God in the Wilderness,' St Francis speaking to the birds, and I composed new dances to the inspiration of his playing, dances all composed of prayer and sweetness and light, and once more my spirit came to light, drawn back by the heavenly melodies which sang beneath the touch of his fingers. This was the beginning of the most hallowed and ethereal love of my life.

Her love was returned by Walter, who was a gentle and kindly man. With him she found something of the peace of mind that had long eluded her. Not only did they become lovers, they deeply enjoyed working together, he playing and she dancing. In fact they enjoyed this so much that at first they did it for the sheer love of it, with no thought of performing in public. They spent hours developing dances, working in a studio on avenue de Montespan which had been kindly lent to them by the great actress Réjane, then in her early eighties.

Walter was a fervent disciple, as was his mother, of the Austrian mystic and educationist Rudolf Steiner. Steiner, born in 1861, had been influenced by the theosophy movement of Madame Blavatsky, who held that the truth about the world could not be learned through science, but through mystical study and contemplation. He called his system anthroposophy, and the educational system he developed leant heavily on the arts, and on developing the whole human being – mind, body and spirit. All this was naturally congenial to Isadora, who since the death of her children had tended more and more to accept fringe beliefs like spiritualism and astrology.

In the summer of 1918 she and Walter moved south, to Cap Ferrat, on the Riviera (Isadora always loved the sea). Writing to Mary Roberts in New York, she admitted she was 'finally out of breath from this unequal battle with Destiny... Dionysos has been a too Strenuous God to follow – *Je me repose.*' In her memoirs she reflected, 'Now and then we issued from our retreat to give a benefit for the unfortunate or a concert for the wounded, but mostly we were alone, and through music and love, through love and music, my soul dwelt in the heights of bliss.'

It did not bother her at all that Walter was ten years younger than she was, writing of their relationship, 'What nonsense to sing always of love and spring alone. The colours of autumn are more glorious, more varied, and the joys of autumn are more powerful, terrible, beautiful... I was the timid prey, then the aggressive Bacchante, but now I close over my lover like the sea over a bold swimmer, enclosing, swirling, encircling him in waves of cloud and fire.'

But in spite of the boldness and fire of his music, as a lover Walter was somewhat restrained – one of those men who find the physical act of sex somewhat distasteful. 'He did not,' as she put it, 'give way to passion with the spontaneous ardour of youth.' She formed the definite impression that he spent his nights at Cap Ferrat in his separate bedroom physically communing with himself. From early in their relationship she realised that she must not be too aggressive with such a man, saying later, 'To love such a man is as dangerous as it is difficult. Loathing of love can easily turn to hatred against the aggressor.'

She did not need to concern herself that technically he was married. As had been the case with Singer, his marriage was already effectively over when they met, and soon he would divorce his wife, the respected musician Thérèse Chaugneau – an act that disturbed Thérèse so deeply that not long afterwards she was admitted to a Swiss mental asylum from which she was never to be released.

Walter and Isadora's musical collaboration flourished. To his playing she again began to dance to the music of Wagner, whom she had for some time rather neglected, using piano transcriptions of *Tristan*, *Tannhäuser* and *Parsifal*, several of them made by Liszt. With Walter she developed her large repertory of Chopin dances into an allegory of the peace that now looked as if it was at last on the way. The three sections of this she called *Poland Tragic*, *Poland Heroic* and *Poland Languorous and Gay*.

In October 1918 they set off to give a series of performances together. They performed in Marseilles, Bordeaux, Nantes and Geneva, after which their tour had to be curtailed because Europe had been overtaken by the great influenza pandemic that swept the world from April to November of 1918, killing over 21 million people (many more than were killed in the war).

On 11th November the Armistice was declared, and the war ended. Shortly afterwards Isadora and Walter returned to Paris (although they would continue to visit Cap Ferrat), and she again took a suite at the Hôtel Palais d'Orsay. It was their intention, now that her school would no longer be needed as a hospital, to reopen it, not only as a school but as a centre for good music. It would, however, take several months for the building, by now being used by the American Army, to be returned to her.

It was at this optimistic time in Isadora's life that she received a visit at the Hôtel Palais d'Orsay from Paris Singer's former secretary, Allan Ross Macdougall. He had joined up when America entered the war, and was still in army uniform. Isadora and Walter invited him to lunch, and before lunch walked with him in the gardens of the Tuileries. Macdougall recalled:

> I can still remember her sprightly step, her high good humour and her jokes about the classical statues that sprout all over the gardens. I still recall, too, the excitement of the lunch served in Isadora's salon. There was the dancer's favourite Pommery Sec to celebrate our reunion and a special sole dish. After the first taste of the sole she asked the waiter if he were sure the fish was fresh. Turning to me, she said, 'How does it taste to you, Dougie?' I could only say that for me, after months of slumgullion and cheerless chow, it was ambrosia. But Isadora, with a grand wave of her hand and a backward toss of her short auburn hair told the hovering waiter to remove it. 'The poor boy,' she said to him in French, 'The poor boy is an American *poilu* whose taste has been dulled by his terrible war experience!'
>
> During the rest of the regal meal I remember ... Isadora telling me that the American Army had taken over her big Bellevue house outside Paris... There was a laughing promise that when they were all cleared out and I, too, was demobilized, we would all – including the six 'Isadorables' – be installed there in an idyllic, arcadian existence, where nothing else would matter but the Dance, Music and Art.

Unfortunately, when the school was cleared, she and Walter found it in a ruinous condition. Part of it had been shelled, another part had suffered a fire. But in the new optimism of peace, they decided to set about rebuilding it, and set about trying to attract sponsorship.

They had no luck in finding backers, and decided to give a fund-raising joint recital at the school itself, in what had been the *salon bleu*, charging a hundred francs a ticket. At it Isadora for the first time performed her Chopin allegory for Poland. But fewer people came than expected, and they raised only a fraction of the money that would be needed. On top of this she sprained an ankle while dancing, causing her to say to the Paris correspondent of the London *Times*, Sisley Huddleston, 'It's not money that's needed, it's a miracle.'

In October 1919, in one of her letters to her six students, who were still successfully touring America, she attempted to sound out whether, after two years performing without her, they would be willing to consider returning to Paris and rejoining the school. She wrote, 'Perhaps you would all like to come in the spring? But tell me frankly your ideas and wishes... If you were here we would study the 9th Symphony to celebrate the Peace.'

But the Peace was not proving to be all she had hoped. A year after the Armistice it was clear that the world would never be what it had been before. From the great loss of life, and the shattering of the old certainties, with civilisation no longer seeming to have a solid footing, cities like Paris had acquired a hectic irresponsible gaiety. Music and the other arts had a new and frantic feel, questioning all that had gone before, and the deep reflective spirituality of Isadora's dancing was increasingly out of tune with the times.

America too had changed. There the mood was one of reckless confidence. At last, because America's entry into the war had turned the tide in favour of the Allies, and because President Woodrow Wilson had been so dominant in arranging the terms of the Armistice, the country had realised gleefully that it was now a fully-fledged world power. As its losses had been less and its success great, the feeling was of high celebration. This the government marked in 1919 by passing the 18th Amendment, prohibiting the sale or consumption of alcohol ('It was put over on our boys while they were overseas,' was the prevailing attitude.)

Many Americans had visited Paris while on active service in Europe, and now wanted to see it as civilians, and many others had heard about it from those who had seen it, so from the end of the war through the Twenties Paris was thronged with visiting Americans, rich and poor. (The fact that it was possible to drink legally in Paris did something to help too.) In 1919 the flood was already beginning.

Back in Paris by 1919 was Isadora's brother Raymond. His wife, Penelope, had died of tuberculosis two years before, in Switzerland, and he now had a new companion, Aia Bertrand. He also had an entourage of around thirty followers, and a developed philosophy which he called 'actionalism'. This was based on the idea that it wasn't love of money that was the root of all evil, but industrialisation, and he had developed his passion for hand-crafting into a system. Opening a shop on the Right Bank, he sold the goods that he and his followers made to tourists, mainly Americans, who flocked to buy from him. Isadora was not entirely happy about this, describing his activities, her student Irma recalled, as 'the chamber of commerce in Greek disguise.' Irma herself commented, 'A sack of beans and goat's cheese go a long way, [and] he had cleverly invested in real estate.'

All the same, Isadora remained fond of her 'little brother', no matter how exasperating he could be (her friends tended to avoid him because of his fondness for lecturing everybody against such evils as drinking, smoking and eating meat). She wouldn't hear a word against him from anyone but herself.

The Clan Duncan had by now almost totally disintegrated. Isadora was still estranged from her mother in San Francisco. Her brother Augustin, and her sister Elizabeth were still in New York, and neither had bothered to reply to her letters for many months. Elizabeth and Max Merz were still running their school, and Augustin, after quarter of a century of acting, had at last come into his own. After having considerable success on Broadway in the play *John Ferguson*, written by the Ulster-born St John Ervine, and originally presented at the Abbey Theatre in Dublin, he had become one of the founding directors of the Theatre Guild.

This was actually a re-founding, because the Guild had grown out of a group of semi-professionals – aspiring playwrights, actors, directors and producers – who had banded together in 1915, calling themselves the Washington Square Players. This group closed down in 1917 when America entered the war. Reformed in 1919, with Augustin among the directors, their shows were mounted to professional standards, and had, as their basic audience, a group of Guild members who subscribed enough to guarantee each production a four-week run. They were helped to get going by Otto Kahn, who lent them the Garrick Theatre rent-free to mount their first production, a play by Jacinto Benavente called *The Bonds of Interest*. This did outstandingly well because during its run there was a strike by Actors' Equity, which closed down all the companies playing on Broadway except the Theatre Guild. They, being a co-operative, were deemed exempt.

The money the Guild made from *The Bonds of Interest* established it fairly firmly. It settled down to a string of highly-regarded plays by such as Shaw and Strindberg, and from now on Augustin would be more involved in its doings than in anything else. Having organised the American tours of Isadora's students since 1918, he now turned their management over to the Russian-born Sol Hurok, then in his early thirties and just beginning his career as an impresario. Hurok would go on to become one of the greatest presenters of dance and music in America, his clients over the years including Pavlova, the singer Marian Anderson, the violinist Isaac Stern, and Isadora herself.

At around this time Isadora met again the man who had partnered Gordon Craig in the agency business, not altogether successfully, years ago in Berlin – Maurice Magnus. With his help, she and Walter arranged a month-long tour, beginning in Switzerland and going on from there to the Arab-speaking countries of North Africa. With them went Isadora's secretary, Christine Dalliès – the woman who had introduced her to Walter.

The tour turned out an enjoyable one. In North Africa, all three delighted in wearing Arab costume, and Isadora even pursued the possibility of establishing her school there. As Walter wrote to their friend Fernand Divoire, 'In the sun at last – a marvellous chance to open the School here, many Negro pupils, government backing with big subsidy and a splendid site... Isadora enthusiastic. Sees the future of the dance in Africa.' What became of this project is unknown. Possibly it was a case of hasty over-enthusiasm on the parts of all concerned. For whatever reason, no more was heard of it.

Returning through Rome, and knowing that Craig was there, Isadora sent him a note: 'I should love to see you if you are free – telephone tomorrow – or send me a word – Isadora.'

In spite of the loving and creative relationship she had with Walter, it would always be Craig who was her deepest and dearest love, and undoubtedly at this time she for a moment entertained the hope that perhaps he and she could again come together. It could not be, of course. Craig had by now left Florence and was living in a villa near Rapallo, sometimes with Elena Meo, sometimes with some other woman. Both their lives had moved on too far.

Craig described their brief meeting in his private notebooks:

> We came together again for a brief moment in Rome ... the night of December 12, Friday ... This to a day was 15 years after we had first met... We walked & walked arms linked in the darkest Rome (it was as we passed an occasional shaded lamp, for the lights were dimmed in Rome, that I turned my head to see her dear face.) – we talked of nothings as we walked & again our hearts SANG – we were weeping as we walked but we walked all that away & ended smiling. Just to stand together was to us supreme intoxication.

The next day Isadora wrote him a note, saying, 'For so long I have only turned my head looking back & weeping for the past. Now when I see you Life seems again full of Hope & Joy & Enthusiasm, & everything seems possible, Even a Future!'

Craig wrote in reply:

Don't forget – you are a great being – Act as you have always done – greatly – my beloved – & when in doubt – go one better... 'The past' – 'the present' – 'the future' ... All these are words which have some meaning when used in speaking of most people – *they have nothing whatever to do with you* – They have not touched you, nor can they... Dear dear dear Isadora... All the days and years with their sorrows of regret dance with me at this moment with LOVE... You are one of the greatest of beings comparable only with – no one.

Isadora, revitalised by Walter (and Craig), was by 1920 performing regularly. Her new programme was called *Festival of Music and Dance*, and that year she performed it in Paris, at the Trocadéro, during March and April. In May she toured Holland and appeared in Brussels. There she danced her Chopin trilogy, renaming its sections *Belgium Tragic, Belgium Heroic* and *Belgium Languorous and Gay*. It was received with great enthusiasm.

In June she was back in Paris at the Champs-Élysées. But time was catching up with her. Now forty-three, she was no longer as fit as she had been. As Sisley Huddlestone would write:

She was slower, heavier, more deliberate in her movements, and indeed had reduced her movements to a minimum. She employed fewer and fewer gestures, stood stationary in the centre of the stage. She was at times a mere point which held the eye while one listened to the music... With all her great gifts, it is necessary to remind her that the Greek dance had its roots in popular feeling and popular understanding, and it is putting too great a strain upon her admirers to ask them to be satisfied with witnessing the faint stirring of an arm from time to time.

In one of her printed programmes of the time she deplored the popular feeling of 1920 Paris, regretting that in its post-war mood it was full of 'profane music' and shiny amusements, and warning the public that 'distraction can lead to destruction.'

Another aspect of the post-war mood was that the French, no longer needing her dancing of the *Marseillaise* to encourage fervour, were looking at her performance more coldly, and journalists were beginning to attack her for dancing it, calling her 'impious', 'disrespectful' and 'an affront to the public!' One suggested she should instead 'botch the work of foreign composers.'

In April 1920 she again wrote to her six students in America, asking them if they would come and work with her again. They were not unanimous in their response. Theresa would be happy to leave for France immediately, but Anna wrote to her parents, 'She says we can meet anywhere. What she means by that I don't know... My place is now here, and I really can't – none of us can wait around Isadora any longer without working until she actually feels like teaching us something. If we dance with her in Paris it will be in only one or two numbers. I'm sorry to have to say this, but it is true.'

Erika, the youngest member, had become keen on painting (and on her painting teacher, Winhold Reiss), and had already decided that she was going to leave the group. The next youngest two, Lisa and Gretel (who had by now changed her name to 'Margot'), wanted the three older girls to decide. And Irma, aware, like the rest, that their producer Sol Hurok had already booked them into Carnegie Hall in October, refused to come to Isadora unless Isadora sent them a written guarantee that they would be released to make the engagement. Surprising all of them, Isadora sent such a release, but as Irma remembered, 'once I held it in my hands I instantly realized the futility of this gesture. It was just a piece of paper.' Nonetheless, the girls (except Erika) finally agreed to come. They would arrive in Paris in June, and stay until the autumn.

Before that, in May 1920, Isadora had been unsuccessfully taken to court by her increasingly business-minded brother Raymond, in an attempt to stop the girls from using the name 'Duncan'. They never would, he said, understand the gift that Isadora had given them, or that it was a gift she herself, the youngest of the family, had received from its older members, including him. The girls were, he declared, '*vampires, vipères et cochonnes.*'

He need not have worried. In the middle of May the girls learnt from the bureaucracy of the U.S. Government that their application to legally change their last names to 'Duncan' had failed. It failed because Isadora had omitted to send in her written consent, and after this the application faded away. Three of the girls – Anna, Irma and Lisa – simply adopted the name 'Duncan' without formal approval, and used it for the rest of their lives.

When the girls arrived in Paris, they were a little taken aback to discover that Isadora had grown disillusioned with the city, and that she wanted them all to go to Kopanos (now for the moment abandoned by Raymond). 'Let us all go to Athens,' she declaimed, 'and look upon the Acropolis, for we may yet found a School in Greece.'

Things had changed in Greece since Isadora had last been there, early in the war. Venizelos, the prime minister who had just been deposed by King Constantine when she arrived there, had gone back to his native Crete and formed a rebel Greek government. That government had declared war on Bulgaria and Germany, and, with the Allies victorious, had secured the abdication of Constantine, exiling him and most of his family (including his wife, the Kaiser's sister).

To replace him, Venizelos, back in power in Greece, had declared Constantine's second son, Alexander, king, although all knew that he was merely an amenable puppet. Isadora wrote to Venizelos, asking his help to found a national gymnasium of Duncan Dance in Greece, and he replied enthusiastically, offering her the Zappeion Exhibition Hall, in Athens, to rehearse in. Her hope, she recalled, was to train 'a thousand children for great Dionysian festivals in the Stadium.'

She, Walter, Christine Dalliès and the girls prepared to leave Paris in July. But unfortunately, before they could set off, Anna developed appendicitis. Hastily they revised their plans. They had arranged to travel to Greece from Venice, and Isadora sent Theresa, Irma, Lisa and Margot there, with Christine Dalliès, to stay at the Lido while she and Walter stayed behind to look after Anna.

The gentle and reserved Walter had been enchanted by meeting the girls. Unfortunately, now left for several weeks helping to care for Anna, this enchantment developed into something else. As Isadora would recall:

> My Archangel, among this bevy of flower-crowned maidens, resembled Parsifal in Kundry's garden, only I began to notice a new expression in his eyes, which spoke more of earth than of Heaven. I had imagined our love so strong in its intellectual and spiritual fastness that it was some time before the truth dawned on me.

Walter had fallen for Anna, who was almost exactly as different from him in age as Isadora was, only in the other direction. On Anna's side, at this early stage, their affair was merely a flirtation (or so she later claimed), but Isadora spotted exactly how Walter's feelings were running, and they had a serious row.

Irma, still with the others in Venice, wrote in her diary on Sunday, 8th August, 'They came today... Isadora invited me for a gondola ride... She seems to be in a state of shock. Very taciturn and morose. It seems she and the Archangel had a serious quarrel.'

Isadora tried bravely to fight down her feelings of jealousy. Lord knows she had had enough practice with Craig and with Singer. She kept telling herself things like, 'One can't argue about these things. Either one is in love or one isn't.' She told herself that if she simply hung on, all would be well – that Walter was more interested in music than in women – that, after all, she was Isadora and Anna was only one of her 'little pupils' (even if she was small and delicate and white, with dark, almond eyes and an attractive husky voice). And anyway, was she (Isadora) not an emancipated woman who believed in free love.

None of it worked. Seeing 'a meeting of their eyes, flaming with equal ardour in the scarlet sundown', she felt bitterly jealous, later saying:

> All my experience availed me nothing, and this was a terrible shock to me. From then on, an uneasy, terrible pain possessed me, and in spite of myself I began to watch the indications of their growing love with feelings which, to my horror, sometimes awakened a demon akin to murder... Never to such a degree had I been possessed by such a terrible passion as I now felt. I loved, and, at the same time, hated them both... I cannot understand such a possession now, but, at the time, it enmeshed me and was as impossible to escape as scarlet-fever or small-pox.

It was not easy for Walter or for Anna either. Walter tended to retreat into his music, feeling guilty about his feelings. Anna, as she became more emotionally involved, simply gritted her teeth and told herself to hang on until the girls' summer with Isadora was over.

While in Venice, waiting for their passage to Greece, Isadora happened to meet the famous American photographer, Edward Steichen. Two years younger than she was, for some years before the war he had lived in Paris, photographing Rodin among others, and she knew him well. He had come to Venice to recover after separating from his wife, Clara, and Isadora seized on the idea of using him to try and excite jealousy in Walter. So she inveigled Steichen into coming to Greece with them, using the lure that, once there, she would permit him to take moving pictures of her dancing among the ruins of the Parthenon.

All her life she had resisted, and would continue to resist, being filmed dancing. Partly this is explicable on the grounds that her music was inseparable from what she danced, and to film her without sound, which was all that could be done up to 1927, would be ludicrous. But partly it was also an attempt to mythologise herself – to make sure that when she was gone she would be a legend, her dancing living on only through her hoped-for myriads of pupils.

On 17th August 1920 the whole party, Steichen included, sailed for Athens. At the last minute Anna had tried to withdraw, sending a note to Isadora saying it would be better for everybody if she simply went back to Paris. But Isadora had sent her a note in return, saying, 'Be sensible. In any case I will not start out for Greece with Walter unless you come – he would simply be sad & miserable all the way and no possibility of work or pleasure either... All these things are too important to let personal feelings interfere – I beseech you be reasonable and you will not regret it.' Anna saw reason, and the whole party arrived in Athens on 22nd August, taking rooms in the Hôtel d'Angleterre.

Raymond's temple at Kopanos had been neither well-built nor completed. 'We found it a ruin,' Isadora would recall, 'inhabited by shepherds and their flocks of mountain goats.' The shepherds and their goats were requested to leave, Isadora hired an architect to build a new roof, and the five girls were set to work sweeping and shovelling, after which Isadora installed her curtains, carpet and piano. The work took weeks. Raymond had never succeeded in finding water, so fetching that from the bottom of the hill was added to the girls' duties.

Every day, however, they did make time to visit the Acropolis. 'It was for me,' wrote Isadora, 'an intensely touching sight to see the youthful forms of my pupils... Realising a part, at least, of the dream that I had had there sixteen years before.'

Attempting to build the groundwork for her proposed school, Isadora appeared at a rally in support of prime minister Venizelos, held in the Athens Olympic stadium. Addressing the crowd of fifty thousand, she pledged to create 'a thousand magnificent dancers' and was crowned with a wreath of laurel. Also in the interests of the school, she tried to divert her girls from resuming their career in America by encouraging them to find Athenian young men for themselves. It didn't work, and in two cases it had no hope of working. Anna was falling ever-deeper in love with Walter, and Theresa had quickly embarked on an affair with the recently-separated Steichen.

With Steichen, Isadora became evasive. Whenever he suggested filming her against the Parthenon, she demurred. 'She always said she was so completely overwhelmed by what she felt there that she could not pose,' he recalled. There was truth in what she said, but finally he did manage to catch her in a more co-operative mood. She agreed she would pose for him, but only for still photographs, not for filming. Not having expected to take stills, he had no camera with him, but managed to borrow an inexpensive one, a Brownie, and together they went to the Parthenon. He recalled:

> The camera was set up far enough away to include the whole portal wall. The idea was that she should do her most beautiful single gesture, the slow raising of her arms until they seemed to encompass the whole sky. She stood there for perhaps fifteen minutes, saying, 'Edward, I can't. I can't do it. I can't do it here.' But finally, after several tries, I saw the arms going up. I waited to catch a particular instant near the apex of the movement. Then we went around to the portico with its line of columns. She removed her cloak and stood there in her Greek tunic. And here she contributed what only an artist like Isadora could contribute. She made a gesture completely related to the columns... She was a part of Greece, and she took Greece as a part of herself.

These pictures of her, published later in 1920 in the American magazine *Vanity Fair*, became and remained enormously popular, reproduced again and again in books of the best of art photography.

After a pleasant August things began to get difficult. Isadora, under pressure from her hopes and struggling to contain her jealousy of Anna, became increasingly tetchy, and all the girls seemed to have some ailment. Margot (the former Gretel) had always had fragile health (eventually it would turn out she had incipient tuberculosis). Theresa got severe sunstroke, Anna got a blood infection, Irma got a throat infection, and Lisa caught a cold. As a result, the atmosphere became increasingly fraught, and the tension increased when one day in mid-September Isadora announced straight out that she was opposed to the girls returning to the States. 'I told you so,' Irma told the other girls when they were alone. They were expected back in New York by Sol Hurok in two weeks' time.

Because of their work on the temple, and later the procession of ailments, Isadora and the girls only began to work together seriously on 25th September. In the Zappeion Exhibition Hall they began practising Beethoven's Seventh Symphony and the Scherzo from Tchaikovsky's Sixth.

A few days later, when the girls failed to show up in New York, they received a telegram from Hurok, threatening them with a suit for breach of contract and heavy costs. To try and salvage the situation, Irma and

Lisa wired back to say that they were prepared to come to him at once, but he would have none of it. He wanted the whole troupe.

The girls laid the matter before Isadora, Irma suggesting that the right thing to do would be for all the girls to go back and make their contracted appearance at Carnegie Hall, then return to Isadora. But Isadora refused to entertain the idea, saying, 'I did not bring you up and teach you my Art, only to have you exploited by theatrical managers,' and a huge argument erupted. Irma lost her temper, and Isadora told her that she had an ugly Broadway spirit, and if that was the way she felt she had better go back to America right away. Irma stormed out and headed straight for the steamship office to enquire about a passage. She was told that there was a very good boat sailing for New York on 10th October.

Fortunately, by the time she got back to the Hôtel d'Angleterre she had cooled off somewhat, and the upshot of the whole affair was that Irma and Isadora made somewhat grudging apologies to each other. Irma would stay on, as would the other girls, though she and Isadora agreed it would be best if the two of them did not speak to each other.

But as things turned out, Isadora's whole idea of a school in Greece would soon collapse. On 2nd October, the puppet king, Alexander, was walking in a garden of the royal domain of Totoi, when his dog was attacked by a monkey. He attempted to separate them and, while he was doing so, another monkey attacked him. It bit him in the legs and stomach. The wounds were not at first thought to be serious, but they caused blood poisoning, of which he died on 25th October.

This weakened the position of prime minister Venizelos, who was already losing favour with the electorate for having provoked a further war with his old enemy, Turkey, and almost at once he was voted out of office. The right wing was back in power, and Isadora's hopes were dashed.

Abandoning Greece and Kopanos, she and Walter and the five girls returned to Paris. The girls rented a furnished flat in rue de la Pompe, not far from Isadora's house. All were downhearted – Isadora because of her failure in Greece, the girls because she had now firmly robbed them of their American career. The contract Irma had got her to sign, agreeing to release them in October, was torn up as so much waste paper. Unsure what would happen next, they also dismayed Sol Hurok by backing out of a tour he had proposed for the spring as well.

As it happened, by this time Isadora's sister Elizabeth (and Max Merz) had managed to bring their school back from New York to Germany. It was now installed in one of the ex-Kaiser's former palaces, at Wild Park, near the Prussian city of Potsdam.

In November, a few weeks after Isadora returned with Walter and her girls from Greece, they were appalled to discover that she had just approached Hurok on her own account, hoping he could arrange an American tour for her. Or rather, that she had acquired a new American manager, Norman Harle (a friend of Mary Desti's), and he had, at her request, approached Hurok. But Hurok was not interested. As her brother Augustin wrote at the time in a letter to Harle, no American producer would risk money on Isadora 'as confidence in her likelihood of fulfilling a contract, once made, is down to zero.'

In Paris, however, she could still get work, and she and her girls began appearing together at the Trocadéro that same November. Their bookings there continued into December, and drew packed houses. Isadora presented Wagner evenings (in spite of the fact that in post-war Paris nobody else was allowed to present Wagner), she presented a reworking of her *Orpheus*, and she presented lighter evenings of Chopin, Schubert and Brahms.

After her shows, Isadora now had the habit, almost the trademark of fashionable Paris in the Twenties, of going to a nightclub, or *bôite*, and dancing through the night. What she liked to dance socially was now, of course, the tango, and her favourite club became El Garron, in Montmartre, where the music was provided by strapping Argentinian accordionists. She also re-involved herself in the world of Paris fashion, buying cocktail dresses and evening gowns from couturiers like Paul Poiret and Lucile, as well as from one new to her, Coco Chanel. She also, now that her relationship with Walter was failing, took lovers, among them her old producer, Aurélien Lugné-Poë.

At the end of 1920, Margot, whose weak health had not yet quite recovered from the rigours of the Greek summer, felt she had to take a break from dancing. So when Isadora began a short season at the Champs-Élysées in January 1921, it was with only four girls – Anna, Irma, Therese and Lisa. But feeling between her and them was still not good. Still fretting over the continuing affair between Anna and Walter, and aware that, while she was approaching middle-age, they were still young, she tended to aim her resentment at all four, giving them little to do on-stage and belittling their abilities. As Anna would recall:

> I realized that none of my best intentions and efforts ... was of any use. I knew she used the situation between Walter and myself as an excuse to cover the real reason for her resentment towards us. Her exaggerated assertions, that we were absolutely incapable of performing her art and work to her artistic satisfaction, [were] too hurtful.

317

Soon the pressure became too much for the weak-willed Walter. Without warning, he left and went to ground in Monte Carlo, giving up both Anna and Isadora, and writing spinelessly to the latter, 'Oh, I know I gave the initial blow. I now give up all hope. I was ready to do everything, all, not with a spirit of sacrifice, no but from my heart – But I see that it is all over... Everything is breaking down... Well, let it break, break and crash.'

It took little time for Isadora to prevail on him to return. But when he did, Anna, who had steeled herself to his leaving, and now found herself having to adjust to having him around again, found the emotional pressure too much, and left in her turn. As she later told it:

> I came to the conclusion, after thoughtful deliberation, to eliminate myself from this emotional upheaval... I gave up the man I loved more than anyone else in the world for the sake of the future of [Isadora's] school.
>
> I went to tell her of my decision. It was to be the last talk we had together. During the two hours discussion she destroyed a large bouquet of red roses, by breaking off the petals in a very nervous way and throwing them all over the floor and on her bed, on which she was reclining. I could not help but think of the times I had watched her strewing white petals so exquisitely in her lovely 'Musette' from *Iphigenia*, or when she danced an improvised encore how gracefully she would throw some flowers to the orchestra for their beautiful playing. But this treatment of the roses was evidently consonant of her inner struggle of the last months.

In a last note to Isadora, written on 29th March 1921, Anna wrote, 'Keep to the heights where the gods have put you, and don't sink to the human depths. Anna tells you this, your grateful and heartbroken pupil, who for sixteen years stood by you in sorrow and joy.'

In April 1921, Isadora went with Walter to London, where Norman Harle had arranged for them to appear with the London Symphony Orchestra for a two-week season at the Prince of Wales Theatre. The season was a success, both commercially and critically. The somewhat over-intellectual critic Ernest Newman, praising her in *The Times*, gave one of the best-ever descriptions of her later dancing style, saying:

> She has overcome criticism, and in these days her genius is realised. She found dancing an art: she will leave it a language.

It is not as a dancer that she stands out among her contemporaries...
What she gives us is a sort of sculpture in transition. Imagine a
dozen statues expressive, say, of the cardinal phases of despair – the
poses and gestures and facial expressions of the moment in which
each of these phases reaches the maximum of intensity. Then imagine
some hundreds of statues that represent, in faultless beauty, every
one of the moments of slow transition between these cardinal phases,
and you get the art of Isadora Duncan. The soul becomes drunk
with this endless succession of beautiful lines and groupings.

The muscular control they imply is itself wonderful enough, but
more wonderful still must be the brain that can conceive and realise
all these faultless harmonies of form. She seems to transfer her magic
even to the fabrics she works with; no one who has ever seen it can
ever forget the beauty of the slow sinking of cloth to earth in one
of her dances; the ripples in it move the spirit like a series of soft,
mysterious modulations in music.

Her secret, as far as we can penetrate to it, is apparently in the
marvellous cooperation of every cell in her brain and every movement
of her face and limbs... The most wonderful illustration we had of
this was at a certain moment in her miming of the 'Ride of the
Valkyries', when, in dead immobility, she gave us an incredible
suggestion of the very ecstasy of movement, something in the rapt
face, I imagine, carried on the previous joy of the wild flight through
the air. The sudden cessation of physical motion had the overwhelming
effect that Beethoven and Wagner now and then make, not with
their music, but by a pause in it.

While she was in London her four remaining students – Irma, Theresa,
Lisa and Margot – were left idle and increasingly hard up in Paris. As
the only way they knew of making money was to dance, they were
pleased when a Paris promoter offered them a French tour. Naturally
they wrote to Isadora for her permission, which she gave them, but with
a number of grudging provisos. They were to pay her one-third of what
they earned (less expenses), they were to dance only to pieces of music
they had already rehearsed with her (she suggested *Iphigenia*, Schubert
waltzes, and the *Marche Militaire*), and they were to dance to no modern
music nor to Chopin.

As Chopin was the composer they had been dancing to with most
success all over America, this last suggestion in particular did not go
down well. Angry with Isadora, frustrated at the obstacles she seemed to

319

be putting in their way, and with no-one else to turn to for advice, they confided their grievances to Mary Desti, who was then in Paris, and to another of Isadora's acquaintances, the wife of a Russian timpanist, Dolly Votichenko. (Mary, having decided that her Turkish husband, Vely Bey, had died during the Great War – which he hadn't – had just married an English ex-army officer, Howard Perch, known as 'Punch'.)

Naturally both Mary and Dolly relayed the girls' grievances at once to Isadora, who wrote to them angrily from London, saying, 'If you could only learn a bit of discretion. I assure you that this can do you no good and my patience is almost at an end... Please work & live simply – read & study – and either be true to me or leave me on your own names & your own responsibility.'

Isadora's *Marche Slave* was seen in London by the Russian diplomat Leonid Krassin, described as one of the most cultured and charming of the Bolshevik leaders. In a conversation with her after the performance, they discussed in a light-hearted and somewhat bantering manner the possibility of her founding a great school of dance in Russia. Eventually Krassin promised, quite seriously, that he would do all in his power to further the scheme.

Isadora leapt into action. Only a few days later she sent a letter to the Soviet commissar for education and the arts, Anatoly Vassilievitch Lunarcharsky, in Moscow, which in 1918 had replaced St Petersburg (renamed Petrograd in 1914) as capital of what was now the RSFSR (the Russian Soviet Federated Social Republic). In the letter she laid down firmly her conditions for running a school, sounding like a true Bolshevik and saying:

I shall never hear of money in exchange for my work. I want a studio-workshop, a house for myself and pupils, simple food, simple tunics, and the opportunity to give our best work. I am sick of bourgeois, commercial art... I am sick of the modern theatre, which resembles a house of prostitution more than a temple of art, where artists who should occupy the place of high priests are reduced to the maneuvers of shop-keepers selling their tears and their very souls for so much a night. I want to dance for the masses, for the working people who need my art and have never had the money to come and see me. And I want to dance for them for nothing, knowing that they have not been brought to me by clever publicity, but because they really want to have what I can give them. If you accept me on these terms, I will come and work for the future of the Russian Republic and its children.

In a very short while she received Lunarcharsky's answer, by telegram: COME TO MOSCOW. WE WILL GIVE YOU SCHOOL AND A THOUSAND CHILDREN. YOU MAY CARRY OUT YOUR IDEA ON A BIG SCALE.

Isadora's reply was even prompter: ACCEPT YOUR INVITATION. WILL BE READY TO SAIL FROM LONDON JULY 1.

Completing their London run, she and Walter went on to Brussels. The situation between herself and the girls was continuing to smoulder. There was no way she was going to permit them to grow up and become independent. From Brussels she wrote to them again:

> Dolly ... says that the way you all speak of me made her think I was possibly some sort of Monster. And in fact she repeated to me word for word what Mary had already told me. This is really too much and my patience is at an end. That you should speak of me in this way is simply disgusting... And to crown this you tell Dolly that I am *jealous* of you as an Artist – really my poor children I think you have all taken leave of your senses... In the meantime I beg you not to tell every stupid little idea in your heads to strangers... Your present attitude toward me seems to make further relations very difficult. I am, as Harle says, 'fed up'.

Nonetheless, she was still prepared to take them to Russia with Walter and herself. But she was taken aback when Walter refused to go.

He was still trying to resume his love-affair with Anna, who for the moment was of course still in Paris, but, out of self-protection, not letting him know where she was. He had to write to her via Christine Dalliès. Beseechingly he wrote, 'I am tired, tired, and want to rest with you. Dear Baby, I am very sad and quite at the end of my strength. There is no use in speaking of it all, and talking will only complicate matters and bring more misunderstanding... Isadora wants to go to Russia... Maybe it's for the best; perhaps there they will better understand her wild, disorganized nature.'

After Brussels, Isadora would not see him again. Returning to Paris, he managed to persuade Anna out of hiding and into a relationship.

Chapter Seventeen

The Russian Temperament

Of Isadora's six star pupils, Erika had stayed in America, Margot was in poor health, and Anna had gone off with Walter, so Isadora, returning from London to Paris, now had only three left – Lisa, Theresa and Irma. She asked them, 'Who wants to go to Russia with me?' Irma said, 'I'll go wherever you want me to go.' Theresa and Lisa hung back, silent. 'I knew I could count on you,' Isadora said to Irma, glaring a little at the other two. But it was no wonder they held back. In the early Twenties there were all sorts of rumours reaching the West about what was going on in the new communist Russia. Foreigners were being shot on sight, or raped. There was cannibalism. You might buy a bowl of soup and find human fingers floating in it. Young babies, slaughtered, were to be seen hanging up in the windows of butchers' shops. Lisa admitted she was 'simply plain scared of the Bolshies.'

Isadora told the three that she would give them a little while to think it over. But when she eventually did go, only Irma went with her. Her leaving was delayed a little because she learned that her mother, by then in her early seventies, was in failing health. She wanted to be in Europe, where most of her children were, and Raymond had agreed to take care of her. As a result, her mother was en route from San Francisco to Paris. But the boat was delayed. Isadora remained in Paris until 3rd June 1921, when, reluctantly, she had to leave for England, partly because it was from there she was to set sail for Russia, and partly because she was engaged to perform there. Her mother arrived in Paris the day after she left.

In London, she danced for the last time with Irma, Lisa and Theresa, at the Queen's Hall. They were accompanied by the London Symphony Orchestra, conducted by Désiré Defauw. After the performance, Ellen Terry, who was present, said, 'I never saw true tragedy before.' Ellen,

323

who had been hurt, although not so much as Isadora, by the death of her grand-daughter Deirdre, came to Isadora's dressing-room to bid her farewell, later sending her a note saying, 'Oh, Lord – it is a queer world. Well, well! – or rather ill, ill – We must cheer up. We'll soon be dead.'

Lisa and Theresa, having chosen not to go to Russia, decided that instead they would return to the USA and attempt to resume their dancing careers there, possibly with Margot, when her health improved. They asked Irma to help them tell Isadora of their plan. But as Irma recalled, 'It turned out exactly as we had feared; grand hysterics on [Isadora's] part and a flood of tears on theirs. "Ingrates," she called them.'

Irma accompanied Lisa and Theresa to catch their train to Paris, then returned to the hotel where she and Isadora were staying. Isadora, dressed in a tea-gown of white lace, was hosting a cheerful party for her friends. When Irma walked in, one called out, 'Here comes the *school!*' Isadora raised her glass of champagne, saying, 'I propose a toast to Irma. Here is to the school! God bless her!'

She and Irma sailed for Tallinn, the capital of Estonia, on 13th July 1921, aboard the *Baltanic*. In spite of an understandable nervousness, their hearts were high. Isadora, an Idealist in politics as she was in Art, worshipped what she had heard of the Soviet system, believing that she was entering a brave and high-minded new society, where passionate clear-eyed revolutionaries would fight for a world where money did not exist, and where food and art would be freely available to all, from the highest to the lowest (except that everybody would be equal).

In London they had spoken with Leonid Krassin, who had promised they would have a thousand pupils, and to teach them in and to house them she would be given a palace that had belonged to the late Tsar Nicholas (he and his family having been shot in 1918). It was near Yalta, in the Crimea, high on a rock overlooking the Black Sea, and in the Second World War would be the scene of the famous Yalta Conference.

Boarding the boat with them were Isadora's French maid and dresser, an attractive Frenchwoman called Jeanne, and Isadora's New York friend and admirer Ruth Mitchell, who would simply sail to Tallinn, then return. Mary Desti came to see them all off, resisting Isadora's pleas that she come with them.

At Tallinn they were welcomed by the English-born Ivy Litvinov, wife of the Assistant Secretary for Foreign Affairs. Which disappointed the romantic Isadora somewhat – she had expected to be greeted by a 'Bolshevik with red flannel shirt, black beard, and a knife between his teeth.' Nor was the courier who accompanied them on the train to

Moscow any better – a timid, bespectacled young man, who, however, had the useful ability to speak English (none of Isadora, Irma and Jeanne spoke any Russian).

Isadora's disappointments continued. Stopping off in Petrograd (formerly St Petersburg), which she had not seen since she was there with Hener Skene early in 1913, it first dawned on her that some things in Russia might have changed for the worse. Taking a walk alongside the river Neva, she was saddened to see the deserted shell-torn palaces along its banks, saying things like, 'This one was a present from the Grand Duke to the ballerina Kschessinska.'

After many delays, their train finally arrived in Moscow at four in the morning on Sunday, 24th July. Isadora, her lipstick and eyeliner freshened, draped in scarves and wearing a bright red cape, prepared herself to be welcomed. In the words of Mary Desti:

> She waited a few minutes to give the reception committee a chance to be sure she had arrived. Then, her feet scarcely touching the earth, she stepped from the train, expecting to be engulfed in the embraces of countless comrades and children. She had visions of them all in red shirts, waving red flags, and welcoming her to their midst, but no one paid the slightest attention to them but the guard, who looked at them most suspiciously. How different it all seemed from what Isadora had imagined! Soldiers everywhere. She seemed to be thrown back into the midst of war. Everyone looked at the other with suspicion. Courtesy and politeness had dropped from the world.

What on earth had happened? She had sent a telegram to Lunacharsky, the Commissar for Arts and Education, telling him when she would be arriving. Had he perhaps not received it?

The young courier did the best he could by hiring a taxi and taking them to the Foreign Office, housed since the revolution in what had been the Metropol Hotel. He went in to make enquiries, while they waited in the taxi, and things took a turn for the better when at its window appeared a familiar face – Count Florinsky, whom Isadora and Irma had met in New York when he was attached to the Imperial Russian Legation there.

Lunacharsky being nowhere to be found, Count Florinsky took Isadora, Irma and Jeanne to the hotel where he was living, cooked them an omelette, and found them a room, the last one available. There they spent an uncomfortable night, with an absence of sheets and pillows, and the presence of occasional huge rats and hordes of flies. Next morning, Isadora went down to the hotel restaurant wearing 'a Callot Soeurs creation' that she realised at once looked badly out of place.

Fortunately, however, Lunacharsky was now in his office. When Isadora went to see him, he admitted he had gone to the country on holiday, not believing that the famous Isadora Duncan would truly come to Soviet Russia. Indeed, no preparations for her arrival had been made at all.

Lunacharsky, who was homosexual, was an amiable man. A Bolshevik of long standing, and a close friend of Lenin (which gave him considerable power), he was also a journalist, historian, playwright and critic. He sent for his deputy, Ilya Ilyich Schneider, to sort out the situation, and Schneider soon had them installed in the apartment of a friend of his, Ekaterina Geltser, a leading dancer in the Bolshoi Ballet who was currently away touring southern Russia (he was shocked when Isadora asked who Ekaterina Geltser was, feeling that so great a dancer should know her contemporaries).

Schneider would become a mainstay of Isadora's Russian life. As well as acting as her interpreter (including translating her articles and letters into Russian), he would help establish her school. Also, from the moment he laid eyes on Irma – 'a very slim girl in a long, silk peignoir' – he was besotted. As was she. By the end of the year they would be engaged.

The first visitor Isadora had at the Geltser apartment was Stanislavsky. He seemed to have aged since she last met him (when she saw Craig's *Hamlet* in early 1913 and dined with the Arts Theatre company afterwards), and he was not happy with the new Soviet regime. Surprisingly few Russians were card-carrying party members at the time of the Revolution, and actors and artists were even less politically-minded than the general public – Schneider once estimated that in Moscow there were then about three thousand of them, of whom about eighteen were in the party. Isadora took it on herself to give Stanislavsky a firm lecture, telling him, '*Cher, grand artiste*: you are faced with this dilemma; either you must consider your career at an end and commit suicide, or you must begin a new life by becoming a communist.'

She herself was a fervent, if unreflecting, communist. On 30th July she and Irma attended a party being given in what had been, until the Revolution, the palace of Russia's wealthy 'sugar king', Pavel Kharitonenko. Wearing a red dress and turban, Isadora entered the room. It was over-decorated, in the style of Louis XIV – somewhat reminiscent of Paris Singer's mansion in Dorset – with gilt furniture, a painted ceiling, and

Gobelin tapestries on the walls. The guests were listening to a young soprano, singing French country songs to piano accompaniment, and dressed as a shepherdess.

Isadora erupted. 'What do you mean by throwing out the bourgeoisie only to take their places?' she lectured all those present. '*Plus ça change, plus c'est la même chose!* ... You are not revolutionists. You are bourgeois in disguise. Usurpers!' As Lunacharsky wrote, in a piece about her in the newspaper *Izvestia*, 'Comrade Duncan is going through a phase of rather militant communism that sometimes, involuntarily, makes us smile.'

It was Lunacharsky who took her, in August, to visit an orphanage outside Moscow. There she asked the children to dance their 'peasant dances' and, when they did, was again outraged, crying, 'These are the dances of slaves you have danced! All the movements go down to earth. You must learn to dance the dance of Free People. You must hold your heads high and throw out your arms, wide, as though you would embrace the whole world in a great fraternal gesture!'

She was introduced to Nikolai Podvoysky, the man who had helped Leon Trotsky organise the Red Army, and who had himself led the attack on Petrograd's Winter Palace. Podvoysky, now teaching physical education to 'a small army' of young Russians, invited her to spend the rest of the summer in a log cabin in the country, attending a course he was giving, and away from the bourgeois atmosphere of Ekaterina Geltser's apartment.

He was just the sort of Bolshevik that Isadora had hoped to meet. He lectured her in the way she was prone to lecture others, telling her, 'In your life you have known great theatres with applauding publics. That is all false. You have known trains de luxe and expensive hotels. That is all false. Ovations – false. All false... Dance your dances in little barns in the winter, in open fields in the summer. Teach the people the meaning of your dances. Teach the children. Don't ask for thanks!'

Isadora found him, as she wrote in an article she sold to the London *Daily Herald*, 'a God-like man.' She went to the log cabin with him, but it was not a success. The Russian summer proved cold and wet. In the cabin she had to sleep on the floor, and the sanitary arrangements were primitive. Also, Podvoysky turned out to be respectably and definitely married. She stood the simple life for a week, bored, uncomfortable and frustrated, then headed back into Moscow. She was beginning to realise just what a pampered life she had been living, and that a real communist, as she later said, 'is indifferent to heat or cold or hunger or any material sufferings.'

She wasn't, and her discomfort and frustration led her to start making indignant demands for the school and pupils she had been promised. It happened surprisingly quickly. As Podvoysky knew, but did not tell her, Lenin himself had 'given instructions' to those around him regarding her. What he had said was, 'Duncan did not appear with us accidentally... If she does something in excess, let us correct her by advice, but the more attention we pay to what she is doing the better the results will be.'

At the end of August she moved, with Irma, Jeanne and Schneider, into Prechistenka 20, which was a palatial rococo mansion in what had been a fashionable district of Moscow. It had been built in the Eighteenth Century for the prosperous Smirnov family, of vodka fame, but had quite recently belonged to another ballerina, now fled to France, Alexandra Balashova. By coincidence, Balashova, on arriving in Paris, had expressed interest in renting Isadora's house on the rue de la Pompe (eventually rejecting it for not having a proper dining-room). And now here was Isadora in *her* former house. The coincidence amused her.

The house had been badly looted by its previous occupant, the Hungarian communist, Béla Kun, who in March 1919, after returning to his native Hungary, had established a Soviet republic there (it was overthrown the following August). Kun, according to Irma, had 'filched everything, including the bric-a-brac. He had even stripped the silk damask from the walls.' Nonetheless, the building itself was in reasonably good condition. It had tall, plate-glass windows, two ballrooms either side of a large entry hall, and a marble staircase with a rosewood balustrade leading to the upper floors. The upstairs rooms bore names reflecting their decor, such as the Blue Room, the Oriental Room, the Turkish Room, and the Empire Room.

A small problem was that various peasant families and government dependants were squatting there, and clearing them out took several weeks. Bedding and crockery were brought in for the pupils. Unfortunately, the new Russian state was having difficulty making ends meet, and Isadora was depressed to learn from Lunacharsky that far from being able to give her a thousand pupils, the state could afford to fund only forty or fifty, in the beginning at any rate.

It was arranged that the academic teaching staff would be provided by the state. Curiously, the mansion still retained a service staff of sixty – porters, maids, chefs and typists – and these would be retained. Food would be state-provided as well. Every two weeks Jeanne would go to the Kremlin and collect the extra rations allotted to 'brain workers' – white flour, sugar, tea and caviar. The staple food, food in Russia being desperately short, would be potatoes.

In one of the ballrooms, the Napoleon Ballroom, Isadora hung her blue curtains, hammering nails into the elegant woodwork, and laid her carpeting on the floor. This was to be the children's rehearsal studio, and by October she was finally ready to hold auditions.

Late in September, Schneider got official permission to advertise the opening of the school in *The Workers' Moscow*. The advert stated that it would be 'for children of either sex between the ages of four and ten.' This differed from Isadora's school at Grunewald, which had accepted only girls, and from the age of six.

Auditions began early in October, and hundreds of children showed up. From them, over a few days, Isadora and Irma chose a short-list of one hundred. The plan was to work with these all through October and November, and at the end of that time choose the forty or so that the school could afford. Isadora would teach them for only two hours a day, from five to seven in the evening. Irma would guide them through the long, hard hours of basic training, which gave her, as she put it, 'the strenuous, physical effort and exertions required to whip a solid mass of untrained humanity into a semblance of agility and grace.'

About half way through this period of selective training, on 7th November 1921, Isadora and Irma and their young pupils gave a Tchaikovsky programme at the Bolshoi Theatre. It could hold three thousand, but ten times that number showed up to try and get in, with quite a few of the extra ones forcing their way in through the police cordon, so that every inch of standing-room was taken. Among her audience for this special show were many of the Bolshevik hierarchy, including Lenin himself.

The show went splendidly, although there were gasps from the audience when this flame-haired, plump woman made her entrance, with 'massive' legs, and wearing a nearly-transparent chiton that would from time to time, slip to disclose a 'wobbling' breast (which she would replace, noted the actor and choreographer Alexander Rumnev, 'with a gesture full of chastity and grace').

The audience was agog to see how she would interpret the *Marche Slave*, the papers having discussed for days the propriety of using this Imperialist piece. During it, as she portrayed an oppressed slave liberated from bondage, an observer noted that Lenin, who had so far been absorbed by every nuance of her performance, leant forward in his seat and gripped the balustrade in front of him. When the piece ended, he stood up and, joining in the cheers of applause, shouted, '*Brava, brava,* Miss Duncan!'

The performance ended triumphantly when Isadora, instead of concluding with her now-traditional *Marseillaise*, danced to the music of Soviet Russia's new national anthem, the *Internationale*. Draped in red, she mimed the overthrow of the old order and the coming of the new. The audience stood and began to sing the words – 'Arise, ye starvelings from your slumbers! Arise, ye criminals of want! For reason in revolt now thunders, and at last ends the age of cant!'

After that first verse, Irma entered, leading a little child by the hand. The child's right hand held the left hand of another, who in the same way held another, and another, till there were a hundred red-clad children circling the stage against the blue curtains, and at last stretching out their arms towards the great teacher in their centre, erect, proud and undefeated.

One thing that Isadora was discovering was that the Soviet system had a growing and politically-based bureaucracy. This was not yet anything like the great bureaucratic machine that would eventually help to stifle it, but the embryo was there. While her school was being readied, she had received from Lunarcharsky's office a detailed plan for the instruction of her students, 'reduced,' she recalled, 'almost to the rules and regulations of a ballet school.' This was so foolish, and indeed presumptuous, that she simply scrawled at the top of it, in red ink, '*Idiot!*'

Similarly, on the day before her performance at the Bolshoi, Lunarcharsky had insisted on seeing a rehearsal of the *Marche Slave*, 'to see if [her] interpretation of the music had anything treasonable about it.' To her, Bolshevism meant increased freedom for everyone, but she was now beginning to realise that to the Soviet government it too often meant restriction.

Even more disappointing to her was the announcement by Lenin in November 1921 of his New Economic Policy. Till then, ever since the 1917 Revolution, the Russian Soviet Federated Social Republic had been trying to operate (internally at least) on a non-monetary system. It wasn't working – food was scarce, and agriculture and industry were struggling. So Lenin's policy introduced a limited form of private enterprise (although the government would continue to control major industries). For instance, shops would be permitted, and the state, rather than requisitioning all agricultural produce and distributing it, in future would take only part, allowing the peasants who produced it to retain the rest and make money by selling it.

As far as Isadora was concerned, it meant that theatres would no longer be free, but would charge admission, and that she would be able to charge a fee for performing. Lunacharsky came to explain to her that, although she could continue to use the mansion on Prechistenka for her school, there were no longer state funds available to subsidise it. However, she would be able to subsidise it herself by performing.

Isadora was stunned. In Irma's words, 'her idealism was blown sky high.' In *Izvestia*, on 23rd November, she complained, 'I have left Europe and Art that was too tightly bound with commercialism, and it will be against all my convictions and desires if I shall have to give again paid performances for the bourgeois public... No government has yet understood that through music it can inspire the masses with the might and power of its ideals and convictions.'

Nonetheless, she pressed ahead. At the end of November she chose her forty resident students, to the bitter despair of those who were rejected (for several days angry and desperate parents besieged Schneider's office at the school, although he could do nothing). Those chosen, whom Isadora nicknamed 'Dunclings', were issued with tunics such as the students at Grunewald had had.

Unfortunately, just after she had admitted them, the Russian winter struck, and Isadora, having no money to heat the school, and little enough for food, was forced for the moment to send all her students home.

In December, she began a series of performances for money, appearing at the Zimin Theatre, which could hold even more than the Bolshoi. Again she danced mostly to Tchaikovsky, and the performances were well-attended. Soon she was able to invite her students back.

At Christmas she was able to give a performance at the Zimin that was more in accordance with her own idea of a communist utopia, when she was invited by Ivy Litvinov to repeat her programme at a free concert for workers and peasants.

A few weeks earlier, escorted by Schneider, she had attended a party given by the painter and designer George Yakulov. For the occasion she had dressed as if she were still in fashionable Paris – all in red (as she later told Mary Desti, she wanted to look devilish). Already present when she and Schneider arrived was the young poet, Sergei Alexandrovich Esenin, famous all over the Republic as 'the poet of the revolution'. His best friend, fellow-poet, and probably lover, Anatoly Mariengof, later recalled Isadora's entrance:

> She advanced slowly, with grace. She looked round the room with eyes that seemed like saucers in blue delft, and her gaze was

stopped by the sight of Esenin. Her mouth, small and delicate, smiled at him. Isadora then reclined on the couch, and Esenin came and sat at her feet. She ran her fingers through his curly hair and said, '*Solotaia golova!* (Golden head!)

We were surprised to hear her say these two words, she who knew only about a dozen Russian words all told. Then she kissed him on the lips, and again from her mouth, small and red like a bullet-wound, came with pleasant caressing accent, a Russian word, '*Anguel!*' (Angel!)

She kissed him again and said, '*Tschort!*' (Devil!)

At four o'clock in the morning, Isadora Duncan and Esenin left.

It was generally agreed among all present that Isadora, who had immediately been attracted by Esenin, made all the initial running in their relationship. Which was among the worst mistakes of her life.

Esenin, who at this time was twenty-six, was a handsome, blue-eyed young man, who looked sometimes 'cherubic' and sometimes 'depraved'. He was not tall, and much of his attraction for her was his blond curly hair, which at once reminded her of her lost son. As she later said to Mary Desti, 'I couldn't bear to have a hair on his head hurt. Can't you see the resemblance? He's the image of little Patrick. Patrick would look like that one day, and could I allow him to be hurt?'

Of working-class parents, Esenin had been born in the small town of Konstantinov (later renamed Esenino in his honour) in 1895. At the age of two he was sent to his grandparents to be raised, his grandfather, a miller, being reasonably prosperous.

His family intended him to become a schoolteacher, and he was sent to the parish school for teachers, but on graduating at sixteen he announced his intention of becoming a poet. The next year he went to Moscow, where he enrolled himself for night courses at the university and joined a literary-revolutionary society, supporting himself by a succession of casual jobs.

During one of these jobs (as proofreader at the Sytin Printing Press), he made love to a fellow-worker, Anna Izryadnova. Their son, Yury, was born at around the end of 1914, but a couple of months later, early in 1915, Esenin abandoned both mother and son to go to the capital city of St Petersburg and pursue his literary career. There he attached himself to members of the Symbolist movement, that late-Victorian group whose members included Verlaine, Mallarmé and Rimbaud, and whose poems used words symbolically rather than with straightforward accuracy.

The St Petersburg poet Riurik Ivnev described him at this time:

> ...he was thin, frail, indeed tender... He had a very modest
> calm mien... It seemed as if he did not value himself. But it only
> seemed this way until you noticed his eyes. It was worth it to meet
> him eye to eye, for his secret was revealed: in his eyes little devils
> jumped about. His nostrils dilated. The glorious steed was intoxicated
> by the smell of glory and was already tearing ahead into the lead.
> And his modesty was a fine cover under which beat a greedy,
> unsatiated striving to conquer everyone with his poems, to subjugate,
> to trample.

In his poetry he used the cadences and images of peasant speech and
folk-verse, and his first book of poems, *Radunitsa*, was published in 1916.
In the same year, being twenty-one, he was called up for military service,
and while in the army was already famous enough to be invited to read
his poems before the Tsarina Alexandra. When she commented that they
were very beautiful, but very sad, he replied, 'So is all of Russia.'

In 1917 he married Zinaida Raikh (although they separated in March
1918, and later divorced), and as the Revolution approached, his poems
reflected the feeling of the times. On one occasion he pledged 'to
overthrow everything, to change the structure of the universe.'

Once the Revolution began, he deserted from the army and joined the
revolutionaries. But his actual understanding of the real world of
revolutionary Russia was as unformed as Isadora's (by the time she met
him he was already as disillusioned with the way it was turning out as
she was).

At the end of 1918, along with his friend and fellow-writer Mariengof,
he had initiated a movement he called the Imaginists. He flaunted himself
as their leader, dressing like a dandy in top hat and patent-leather shoes.
As his contemporary, Nikolai Poletaev, commented, he was, 'playing the
part of leader of a kind of "golden youth" in impoverished, hungry, cold
Moscow ... charming the public, showering them with pretty images
and then suddenly shocking them with some obscenity.' (The Imaginists
had recently distinguished themselves by going round Moscow urinating
on convent walls – an act that delighted Bolsheviks, whose party line
included atheism, and gratifyingly shocked older and more conventional
Russians.)

Esenin and the other Imaginists co-owned a raffish night-club, the
Stable of Pegasus, and Walter Duranty, Moscow correspondent of the

New York Times, described Esenin reading one of his poems there: 'The poem was raw and brutal but alive and true... Line after shattering line banged the consciousness of that motley crowd... When he stopped there was not a sound. Everyone – cab men, speculators, prostitutes, poets, drunkards – all sat frozen with pale faces, opened mouths, and anguished eyes.'

His personal charm and the vital, aggressive music of his verses were his best qualities. When he drank – and he drank in amounts that amazed even hard-drinking Russians – he was a violent manic-depressive, his emotions veering wildly from almost hysterical glee to (more often) rage and violence. Coarse in his feelings and manners, his self-understanding was almost nil. While revelling in his celebrity (which was partly why he allied himself so readily to the famous Isadora), inwardly he loathed himself as much as he loathed and despised almost everything else.

But Isadora doted on him. Quite apart from fancying him, she had an urge to mother him. After all, was he not a poet, and at heart a needy child, even if a spoiled one.

The morning after the party, his friend Mariengof came to Isadora's room at the school to find him. Speaking a little French, he was able to act as Isadora's interpreter. He recalled:

> On a little table by the bed stood a big picture of Gordon Craig. Esenin took the photograph, looked at it attentively, and then asked, 'Your *mouge*?'
>
> 'What is *mouge*?'
>
> 'Husband: spouse.'
>
> 'Yes, he is my husband; but bad husband. He work and write all the time. Craig is a genius.'
>
> Esenin pointed his finger to his chest, saying, 'I also genius. Esenin genius – Craig nothing.'
>
> He then slipped Craig's photograph under a pile of old newspapers, saying, '*Adieu!*' to it.
>
> Isadora was enchanted, and repeated, '*Adieu!*' making a gesture of farewell toward the picture.
>
> 'Now, Isadora,' said Esenin, 'dance! Dance for us.' He felt like Herod calling for the dance of Salome.

Three days later he saw her dance again. As Irma recalled, she was holding one of her evening salons, and the tranquil mood 'was shattered by a dozen feet pounding on the stairs and half-a-dozen drunken voices lifted in raucous laughter and vinous wit.' Into the room came Esenin and several friends.

Isadora, taking in the situation quickly, said, 'I'm going to dance for you!' She danced a Chopin mazurka, then a waltz, which she danced with 'rapturous joy and seductive grace'. When she finished, 'her eyes radiant,' she reached out her arms to Esenin and asked him how he liked it. Schneider translated the question for Esenin, who made a deliberate point of knowing no language but Russian. 'Esenin said something coarse and brutal that brought howls of . . . laughter from his drunken friends.'

Schneider haltingly translated for Isadora. 'He says it was – awful, and that he can do better than that himself.' At which Esenin began to leap around the room – jumping, kicking and waving his arms at Isadora, who was 'crestfallen and humiliated.'

The erratic unpredictability of his behaviour was almost consciously designed to manipulate her. The poet Ivan Startsev would recall:

> At times he seemed to love her as much as he could, never leaving her side for a moment. At other times he would stay by himself, turning to her from time to time, cruelly, coarsely, even striking her and cursing her with the most vile street language. At such moments, Isadora would be especially patient and tender, attempting to calm Esenin by any means.

From the moment they met, Isadora and Esenin were together for part of almost every day. He moved into the school to live with her. As he refused to learn any language but Russian, she even made an effort to learn some Russian herself, taking lessons from the English teacher at her school. Eventually she managed a vocabulary of about four hundred words (although very little grammar). She and he would continue to communicate largely by mime and gesture.

Often Esenin would wander off on some mysterious errand, and if he was gone too long she would become frantically worried, imagining him lying in an alley with his throat cut. He was so often afraid of being late for whatever rendezvous he had to make that Isadora bought him an elegant slim gold watch, inserting into its case her passport photograph. Not long after, in a rage, he smashed it angrily against a wall. The only thing salvageable was the photo.

Sometimes, when they had a row, he would pack up his few clothes in a bundle and head off to his friend Mariengof (who had offended him earlier in the year by getting married). Hand-delivered notes from Isadora would start to arrive, begging him to return. Then it would be Schneider, bearing the same plea. Then Isadora herself would arrive, weeping, and eventually, when she had begged long enough, Esenin would take up his bundle and go back with her.

On the many evenings when she was left alone at the school, she would throw herself into rehearsing, dancing alone to Scriabin, to Liszt, or to Beethoven (especially his Fifth Symphony).

The school, substantially managed by Irma and Schneider, but overseen by Isadora, was now running successfully. The pupils were often taken to performances by such as the Moscow Symphony or Stanislavsky's Arts Theatre. But never to the ballet. Schneider, somewhat surprised by this, once asked Isadora why not. Her answer contained her mature assessment of ballet. 'They will be enticed by those fairy-tale spectacles,' she told him. 'They are not yet able to distinguish between spectacular and natural, beautiful movement.'

In February 1922, when she went to Petrograd to give several concerts at the Maryinsky Theatre, she naturally took Esenin with her. They stayed at the Hôtel d'Angleterre, which, among other things, was famous for its cellars, containing unimaginable amounts of pre-revolutionary (and indeed, pre-war) vintage wines and spirits. Esenin made the most of this, and more than once was seen running naked through the public passages of the hotel, and had to be escorted back to his room.

Isadora's performances in Petrograd were received ecstatically by press and public, although at one of them, on 13th February, she ran into her old problem with the orchestra. They objected to her dancing to the classical pieces they respected, and deliberately played badly, playing out of tune and out of tempo, and out of sync with each other. This was a problem that Isadora encountered now and then, all the time she was in Russia.

One night at the Maryinsky she gave a special performance for Russian sailors (Petrograd being an important port). Half way through it, the electricity failed. Unable to dance in the dark, she asked for a lantern and, when one was produced, held it above her head for over an hour while the audience sang revolutionary songs. The effect was enthralling, and when Schneider remarked afterwards that it was a climax that 'even the most talented producer' could not have planned, she replied, 'When masses sing it is always beautiful. I shall never forget what I have heard tonight.'

Esenin came to her dressing-room after the concert, and as she recalled,

'He looked as if he were in a trance, or still seeing some kind of vision. I have never seen him look as beautiful. When he put his arms around me and repeated several times, "Sidora... Sidora..." I felt for the first time that he really loved me.'

By March 1922 Isadora was beginning to chafe somewhat at being in Russia, feeling that she needed a break from it. Furthermore, she felt that exposing Esenin to the culture of the rest of Europe might help his creativity, as well as widening his fame beyond the Russian Republic. (She was also worried that his heavy drinking might be damaging his health, and wanted him examined, and maybe treated, by a better doctor than she could find in Russia.)

In March, having all this already in mind, she formally transferred artistic direction of the school to Irma, as years ago in Germany she had done to sister Elizabeth. (Irma and Schneider had by now formally announced their engagement, and he was named as the school's headmaster.)

As it happened, the greatest spur to Isadora's decision to leave Russia came in the form of a subtly vindictive letter from Elizabeth, herself now back in Germany. Dated 11th April 1922, it gave Isadora the news that their mother was dying, and it said:

> Called to Paris by three telegrams from Raymond. I arrived within forty-eight hours to find our mother waiting with a shining face and a great beauty of expression for the final parting with her children. That she made this long journey from California for this purpose I know – otherwise she would never have had the strength... I am surprised to find us, her children, so small. We are so small beside her simply heroic lines... We should all be here with her together – It is my great regret that we are not big enough – She passes on as ever The Leader. All Love Elizabeth Duncan.

On 12th April, before Isadora received that letter, Dora Duncan died. Within a week Isadora had sent a cable to Sol Hurok in New York, saying, PROPOSE TOURNEE TWELVE WEEKS OR MORE MYSELF IRMA GREAT RUSSIAN POET ESENIN AND TWENTY PUPILS... Hurok took a deep breath and offered to pay all expenses and to guarantee her a fee of forty thousand dollars, for a tour to take place in October.

Isadora accepted, but was now too on edge to wait till October. She and Esenin would leave as soon as possible. By now an air service had been established between Moscow and Berlin, although it was so prohibitively expensive that only people on government expenses were

337

able to use it. Isadora decided that, expensive or not, that was how she and Esenin would leave Russia, even if, she said, 'it was the last act of my life.'

Urged by colleagues at the school to make a will before flying, she wrote one on a page of Schneider's notebook, willing everything she had to Esenin, and if they both died, then to Augustin. Dated 9th May, it was witnessed by Schneider and Irma.

She also decided that before leaving she would give a party at the school, at which the children could demonstrate what they had learned. The theme of the dancing was to be a Gypsy cabaret. There would be songs, and she would dance herself. Many people, including Esenin, tried to dissuade her from this 'Gypsy' idea. In Russia the word was associated with riotousness and heavy drinking. But she would not be dissuaded, and had posters printed to advertise the event.

These resulted in a stern letter from Commissar for Arts and Education Lunacharsky – 'The notices you have issued have met with an unfavourable reception by our Party leaders. I must warn you that everything you do should be kept within the limits of the strictest decorum.'

But Isadora was not to be lectured by mere politicians. She replied, 'Dear Comrade, the words "within the limits of the strictest decorum" do not exist in my vocabulary. Will you, please, explain what you mean?' Soviet Russia, not yet the brutally repressive power it would become, said no more.

She also had to apply to Lunacharsky for permission for Esenin to leave Russia with her. He gave it, but advised her to marry him first, so that he would be protected by her name. Surprisingly, in flat contradiction of her lifelong beliefs, she agreed. Possibly this was because she had heard of the hounding another great Russian writer, Maxim Gorki, got, when touring America in 1906, because he had with him his common-law wife. Possibly, too, she found it easier to accept the loose ties of marriage in Soviet Russia, where a married couple were bound by neither legal contract nor financial obligation, and where they could simply end the union at any time by mutual consent. And it would undoubtedly help them in their travels. As she later told a reporter, 'I was forced into marriage by the silly laws of the lands I had to travel through as an artist. I married my husband to get him past the customs officers... That's why I married and that's only why.'

In spite of her need to escape Russia for a while, her feelings for Bolshevism remained strong and hopeful. On 1st May, the annual holiday in celebration of the workers, her heart was lifted by seeing the streets of Moscow 'like crimson roses. Thousands of men, women and children, with red handkerchiefs about their heads and red flags in their hands, swept by singing the *Internationale*.' The next day she and Esenin were married at the Registry of Civil Statistics. Afterwards, at the school, they held a party at which both got deeply drunk.

A few days later, Isadora, rather shyly, brought her newly-issued Russian passport to Schneider, asking him if he would alter her date of birth on it. 'It's for Esenin,' she said. 'We don't feel the difference of fifteen years in our ages [actually it was eighteen], but when it's written down here and we hand our passports to strangers, it may make him feel uncomfortable.' Schneider obligingly altered her year of birth from 1877 to 1884.

After a rough flight from Moscow to Berlin, with buffeting winds, she and Esenin (and her maid, Jeanne) checked into the Hotel Adlon on 11th May 1922. The Adlon was the finest and most expensive hotel in the city, much patronised by American foreign correspondents, and Isadora was able to afford it thanks to a payment she had received for her former school at Grunewald, which had been compulsorily purchased during the war. The sum she got – 90,000 marks – was derisory, but it was something. She intended to spend several weeks in Germany, then move on with Esenin to Paris.

Isadora's aim was, according to Mary Desti, 'to show the beauties of the world to her young poet... she was his Virgil and would lead him through the world, opening his eyes to all the precious beauties in art.' But the immature Esenin, being able to afford for the first time the luxuries of a major European city, wanted them all. He wanted rings, watches, perfumes, toiletries and fine clothes – 'costumes, boots, caps, overcoats, silk shirts, pyjamas,' recalled Mary.

One of the American reporters at the Adlon, Joe Milward, made the acquaintance of Isadora and Esenin in the bar. She was feeding Esenin from her plate. 'I keep him eating steak tartare to keep him interested,' she told Milward. 'Do you think he may get bored?'

Milward got the impression she was grateful for the chance to talk to someone who spoke English, being unable properly to talk to her husband. Esenin, she explained to Milward, would speak only Russian. Milward wrote:

He had vehement reasons for this decision. He said that Russia was alive, that he was a genius of Russia and that he could not permit his genius to be contaminated by the use of languages of dead cultures. He stuck to his guns with the exception of two words:

genius and *kaputt*. When he talked about himself he used the word *genius*. When he talked about the people, the arts, or the culture outside Russia he used the word *kaputt* and defined it first by slashing his throat with his finger followed by a gleeful pop of his tongue...

I never saw him sit with either a book or a pencil in his hand, and seldom without a glass of cognac or a bottle of vodka. Day after day he was surrounded by hours of talk in languages he refused to understand... One day after lunch, in the middle of a violent show of rage, he grabbed a carving knife from the table, turned, winked at me, and drove the other luncheon guests out of the house. Years of training as a roughneck enabled him to act out very exhausting performances. If this expenditure of energy were not sufficient he would rush down to the street and disappear into a bar.

These wild disappearances into a city that was strange to him, and in which he did not speak the language, drove Isadora frantic with worry. Life with Esenin was proving to be a wild emotional roller-coaster ride, which she tended to excuse because of his talent. 'Like all geniuses, he's cracked,' she once told Schneider. 'Mad as a hatter, strong, full of vitality. Poetic!'

She hired a five-seater Buick convertible so they could tour the city. Together they visited the Russian House of Arts, at the Café Leon in Nollendorfplatz. This was the central meeting-place for Russian émigrés of all backgrounds and all shades of political opinion. In 1922, before the Soviet government banned travel abroad, Russian citizens could travel there and meet others who had been driven into exile.

It even had a house magazine, *On the Eve*, and within days of Esenin's arrival in Berlin it published two of his poems. Friday evening poetry readings were held there, and he and Isadora went to one so that he could recite some of his poems. He did, but as he finished Isadora swept onto the stage in a blaze of red silk and proposed everyone sing the *Internationale*. She and Esenin led the singing, but many White Russians objected, and tried to break up the anthem by whistling. The whole occasion turned into a drunken altercation.

The night-life of post-war Berlin was even more hectic and nihilistic than that of Paris. There were the cabarets, with their world-weary cynical songs and sketches, and there were numerous clubs featuring sexual deviation (as it was then known). There were clubs for sado-masochists, fetichists, transvestites, and homosexuals of both sexes. The American writer Ben Hecht recalled visiting 'the Officer Clubs, where aristocratic perverts gathered to exchange data and addresses' and 'macabre parties where Lesbians beat up college boys and bemedaled colonels sat with painted children in their laps.'

At the House of Arts Isadora and Esenin had made the acquaintance of composer Nicolas Nabokov, and he recalled the night Esenin insisted taking Isadora to a homosexual nightclub. 'Men get undressed there and bugger each other on the stage,' he said. 'I want to see it.'

At the club, they found themselves seated at the table next to Craig's old patron, Count Harry Kessler, and, as Nabokov recalled, Esenin soon took a violent dislike to him, feeling that Kessler was eyeing him up. He began shouting (fortunately in Russian), 'I never saw so many *Tyotki* [Aunties] in one place!... Oh, shit. Tell him to stop ogling or I'll smash his...'

'Will you stop, Sergei!' said Isadora. 'Stop being obscene!' Eventually, angry and drunk herself, she tried to hit him with a vodka bottle.

She was becoming as unpredictable as he was. On another occasion, when she could not stop him from drunkenly smashing everything in their room at the Adlon, she joined in and gleefully began to hurl crockery at the walls. At once Esenin became petrified and fell to his knees before her, begging her to stop. 'For a while the trick worked,' Isadora recalled, with a certain satisfaction.

But it was not in her ever to be as cruel as he was. One night, when they were dining at the house of the writer Alexei Tolstoy, Esenin read a poem he had written in 1919. Maxim Gorki, who was one of the guests, recalled to a friend that the poem was 'about a dog: the dog's puppies are drowned, she sees this happen, and then she runs about, howling as she goes, for it seems to her that the moon in the sky is her puppy.'

Isadora was overwhelmed. 'I wept, and when he finished I asked him, "Now Sergei, tell me what would you say if such a thing had happened to a woman?"'

'To a woman? A woman?' said Esenin. He spat derisively on the floor. 'A woman is a piece of shit! But a *dog!* Ah! a dog!'

At times his contempt for her, and for himself for loving her, seemed bottomless. Isadora's friend and first biographer, Allan Ross Macdougall wrote:

What a rare lyric confession this roughneck could have made of that day in Berlin when, coming into the hotel room and finding his wife weeping over an album containing portraits of her unforgettable Deirdre and Patrick, he ruthlessly tore it from her and, throwing it into the fire, cried in a drunken rage, as he held her back from saving her precious memorial: 'You spend too much time thinking of these —— children!'

No-one can be as bitterly jealous of a child as another child.

Isadora had hoped they would be in Paris by the end of June, but difficulties began to arise. First, under American law she had lost her U.S. citizenship by marrying a foreign national. So the only nationality she now had was Russian, and there were not many countries in 1922 who had agreed to recognise the Soviet Republic. As Joe Milward recalled:

> In desperation she and Esenin called on the French consul, who refused to grant a visa for them because Esenin was a citizen of a government which had not yet been recognized by France. Into the middle of this muddle a letter arrived from Isadora's bank in Paris returning a cheque she had cashed on her arrival in Berlin, on which payment had been refused, explaining that a number of creditors had attached her bank account and that none of her funds in the bank could be used until said creditors had been satisfied.

In Paris she owed banks, moneylenders and tradesmen a total of almost fifty thousand francs. To sort out her situation she gave Joe Milward her power of attorney and asked him to go there. He was to pay off as many creditors as possible from whatever money she had in the bank. Furthermore, she produced from a trunk a bolt of red velvet about ten feet by three, heavily embroidered, and studded with pearls, rubies, emeralds and amethysts. It had been, she told Milward, the train of a court dress belonging to the Tsarina Alexandra, looted from the palace during the Revolution. He was to take it to Cécile Sorel in Paris for her to raise what she could on it. Also he was to ask Cécile, who was the 'favourite' of the ex-President of France, Raymond Poincaré, to exert what influence she could to enable Isadora and her husband to enter France.

Before Milward set off, he did Isadora one other service. He hired her a Russian interpreter, a twenty-three-year-old Polish writer called Lola Kinel, so that she could speak directly to her husband.

Kinel and Esenin didn't hit it off. Worried at last about the amount he was drinking, Esenin had for the moment gone on the wagon, and so was less violent, but he could still be truculent. Once he gave Lola this message for Isadora: 'Tell her,' he said, 'I want absolute freedom – other women if I like. If she wants my company I shall stay in her house, but I don't want any interference.'

Lola protested. 'I can't tell her that, Sergei Alexandrovich. Please!'

'You have to,' insisted Esenin. 'It's your job.' But she refused.

On another occasion, with Isadora present, he asked Lola to translate his poems into English. Lola was 'a bit frightened and a bit shocked... I knew that it was a sacrilege and an impossibility both. Esenin's poetry is almost purely lyrical: it is music expressed in terms of Russian words, of Russian phonetics, and so could never be rendered into any other language.'

But Esenin insisted, desperate to be as famous as his wife in the English-speaking world. After attempting to work out with Lola the world's English-speaking readership, he mockingly told Isadora, 'A dancer can never become very great because her fame doesn't last. It is gone the moment she dies.'

'No,' Isadora protested, 'for a dancer, if she is great, can give to the people something that they will carry with them forever. They can never forget it, and it has changed them, though they may not know it.'

'But when they are gone, Isadora?... People may come and admire you – even cry. But after you are dead no one will remember. Within a few years all your fame will be gone... No Isadora!'

Lola's account continues:

All this he said in Russian, for me to translate, but the last two words he said in the English intonation, straight into Isadora's face, with a very expressive, mocking, motion of his hands, as if he had waved the remnants of the mortal Isadora to the four winds... 'But poets live,' he continued, still smiling. 'I, Esenin, shall leave my poems behind me. And poems live. Poems like mine live forever.'

Beneath the obvious mockery and teasing tone there was something extraordinarily cruel. A shadow passed over Isadora's face as I translated what he said. Suddenly she turned to me, her voice very serious: –

'Tell him he is wrong, tell him he is wrong. I have given people beauty. I have given them my very soul when I danced. And this beauty does not die. It exists somewhere...' Suddenly she had tears in her eyes and she added in her pitiful, childish Russian, *'Krasota nie umiray.'* (Beauty not dies.) ... With a characteristic gesture, he pulled Isadora's curly head towards him and patted her on the back, saying mockingly, '*Ekh*, Duncan.' ... Isadora smiled. All was forgiven.

Milward returned from Paris. He had paid off bankers, lawyers, and the bill at the Swiss sanatorium where Raymond's wife Penelope had died. He had also paid off a damages claim from the painter Sylvestre Bonnard, who had briefly rented Isadora's studio at Neuilly, where a water-pipe had burst, causing a wall and ceiling to collapse. (He had sued her for the inconvenience and been awarded ten thousand francs damages by the court.) When all was paid off, and with what the Tsarina's train had fetched, he was able to bring to Isadora forty thousand francs.

He also brought her a sensible suggestion from Cécile Sorel. She had no influence in Germany to get Isadora and Esenin French visas, but if they could get themselves that little bit further, to Belgium, she might be able to help.

Isadora hastily arranged, with the help of her old friend Eugène Ysaÿe, to make some appearances at the Théätre Galéries in Brussels, and using those bookings was able to get a transit visa, as a touring performer. Esenin got a visa by swearing an affidavit that he was her manager.

In the few weeks before they were to set off for Belgium, Isadora decided that her husband should be got away from the excitements of Berlin. He and she, accompanied by Lola, Milward, and her maid Jeanne, would first drive in the Buick to her sister Elizabeth's school in Potsdam (where she had been driven with Craig on the first night they met). There they would spend a quiet week, after which they would go on a motoring tour of the Rhine.

Surprisingly, the week at Elizabeth's school passed peacefully. Esenin was in a quiet mood. When they began their tour, he wrote to Irma's fiancé, Schneider, in Moscow, saying:

> The atmosphere in Berlin made me go to pieces. My nerves are so on edge I can hardly walk... I don't drink anymore and am starting to work. If only Isadora were not so crazy and would allow me to settle down somewhere, I could make a lot of money... [Her] affairs are in a terrible mess... As if nothing were the matter she rushes by car now to Lübeck, now to Leipzig, now to Frankfurt, now to Weimar. I follow her in silent agreement for she becomes hysterical whenever I disagree with her.

Writing to his friend Mariengof a little later, his gloom was deeper:

How I would like to leave this nightmarish Europe... It is an endless graveyard. These people who move faster than lizards are not people, but worms who eat their dead, their houses are coffins and the Continent is the grave. Those who live here died long ago.'

Cécile's stratagem to get them to Paris worked perfectly. Isadora's performances in Brussels were a financial success, as a result of which she was offered a run of ten concerts at the Trocadéro in Paris, with her Russian pupils, if she could get them into France.

Her pupils were also expected to appear with her (and Irma) on Sol Hurok's American tour in October, so it was a blow for Isadora when, in response to a query she sent to Schneider about the possibility of them coming to France, he cabled back that the Kremlin would not permit them to leave Russia. Which meant, of course, that Irma would have to stay with them too (which didn't bother Irma too much as, in Isadora's absence, she had been trying to establish a solo dancing career for herself in Moscow). The booking at the Trocadéro never materialised, but fortunately, as far as Isadora was concerned, Hurok agreed to her touring alone.

Getting to Paris, Isadora and her party found that the house she still owned on rue de la Pompe was in chaos. She had let it, complete with servants, to a rich American who had absconded without paying the rent, and taking with him her best carpets. Her servants, now having the house to themselves, were feeding their friends every night in the kitchen, at her expense.

She did not feel up to putting her foot down and stopping this. Instead, she simply headed off with Esenin and Lola and Jeanne for a month in Venice, where they booked into the Hotel Excelsior, on the Lido. There Isadora and Lola became close, as together they tried to keep Esenin, who had started drinking again, from harming himself. But after a couple of weeks Isadora was forced to let Lola go. Esenin, in a drunken stupor, had dictated two telegrams to Moscow which Lola refused to send – whether because they were abusive, obscene or politically undiplomatic is unclear. He demanded of Isadora that Lola be sacked for insubordination, and she had no choice but to accede, apologising to Lola as she did so.

Back in Paris, still unable to cope with life among her chaotic staff at rue de la Pompe, Isadora spent many nights with Esenin at the Hotel Crillon. When she proved unable to pay her bill there, they moved on to try the Majestic. But the management there demanded payment in advance. Offended and desperate, she took a taxi to Versailles, to the Trianon Palace, where she had shared an apartment with Paris Singer, and where she had spent her last night with her children. The management there remembered her with kindness, and agreed to send her bill on to her later. Also to pay the taxi, which she had no money to do.

When another friend of Esenin's, Vladimir Vetlugin, turned up in Paris, Isadora, aware that a Russian interpreter would make life easier for her husband in America, asked him to come on tour with them as her secretary. Vetlugin agreed, and after a time in Paris that was much less tumultuous than their time in Berlin, they set sail from Le Havre to New York, aboard the luxurious S.S. *Paris*, during the last week in September. Isadora and her husband of course sailed in a *suite de luxe*, she showing the purser her signed contract and explaining that her manager, Mr Hurok, would pay.

Esenin, who had never been to sea, was astounded by the open Atlantic, roaring with delighted laughter at the sight of it. But he was even more astounded by the S.S. *Paris*, which had been launched only three years before. He was amazed at the sheer size of it, as well as the luxury, marvelling that it took him five minutes to walk from his *suite de luxe* to the dining saloon. He admired the grand staircase in the A deck foyer, and the fact that the ship had libraries, movie theatres, swimming pools, bars and dance-halls. As he later wrote, 'The world I had previously inhabited struck me as terribly comic and absurd . . . From this moment I stopped loving beggarly Russia.'

During the voyage, Isadora, feeling she was on a mission, wrote out a statement entitled 'Greetings to the American People', and when the ship docked at New York, on 1st October 1922, she handed it to the press. It began, 'We are the representatives of young Russia. We are not mixing in political questions. We believe the soul of Russia and the soul of America are about to understand each other.'

She could not have been more wrong. America was still strongly in the grip of its first wave of anti-Soviet feeling. This had arisen immediately the Great War was over and the country had leisure to turn its attention to other things.

The Russian Revolution had shocked and scared many ordinary Americans. The image in people's minds was of a violent and ignorant underclass rising to tear down all the hard-won trappings of civilised living – the idle and shiftless enviously tearing down all that hard work and respectability had achieved. Isadora, later in her tour, would remind reporters that America too had been born out of a revolution, but the

American Revolution had been different. The Russian Revolution, like the French before it, had been risings of the have-nots against the haves, in each case initiated by thoughtful well-meaning intellectuals. In America, the revolution had been led by a prosperous middle-class, angry at having their profits reduced by taxes and trade restrictions (America, when a British colony, had been barred from exporting goods to anywhere but Britain).

Fearing a Red Revolution in America, from 1919 many suspected socialists, anarchists and immigrants were simply deported without trial. And now here was this dancer – this notorious dancer – who had abandoned U.S. citizenship to become a Russian, with her husband, the hero-poet of the Revolution, preaching that the Communist system was a good thing.

What made it extremely uncomfortable for her impresario, Sol Hurok, was that he himself, although now a U.S. citizen, was originally Russian, and thus liable to come under suspicion. He came to meet Isadora and Esenin as the ship docked, and found that, although their passports and visas were in order, they had been forbidden to leave the ship by Customs officials. No explanation was given.

He came on board and to the first class lounge, where Isadora was quite cheerfully chatting to reporters and reassuring Esenin by keeping her arm around him, from time to time whispering, '*Sois tranquille.*' The captain of the S.S. *Paris* gallantly invited the pair to be his guests aboard that night, thus saving them from having to sleep in dormitories in America's famous immigrant clearing-house, Ellis Island. Hurok, on leaving the ship, found himself being strip-searched by the recently-formed FBI. Edgar Hoover's men were searching his body for 'invisible writing'.

Next day, after Isadora had visited Ellis Island and undergone a two-hour interview, and their luggage had been minutely searched (especially any poems in Russian and sheet music), they were allowed to enter America. According to Hurok, 'A statement was issued later that she had been held by the Department of Justice because of her long residence in Moscow, and because there was some supicion that she and her husband might be acting as "friendly couriers" for the Soviet Government, carrying secret documents.'

The publicity all this gained her did Isadora no harm. Her first three concerts, to be held at Carnegie Hall, sold out in a day.

She opened there on Saturday, 7th October, dancing her Tchaikovsky programme. She was well received, and some reviewers even commented that she had lost a little weight (no doubt partly a result of the severe food shortages in Russia).

After Carnegie Hall, the touring began, and as Hurok ruefully remembered, 'From that day never a phone rang but I trembled to answer it.'

In Boston, her first stop after New York, Esenin caused an uproar on her first night by hanging a Soviet flag out of an upstairs window at Symphony Hall. When a crowd gathered, he cried out, 'Long live Bolshevism!' Isadora reassured Hurok over the phone that he'd had a drink or two, but it wouldn't happen again.

Her reviews in Boston were less kind than in New York. When the papers came out next day they mocked her size, her legs, and her dyed hair, and called the Wagner interpretations she had danced 'tedious'. Which caused her at her next performance, a Saturday matinee, to harangue the audience, saying, 'Thank God the Boston critics don't like me. If they did, I should feel I was hopeless... I give you something from the heart. I bring you something real.'

Having gone on to dance the *Pathétique*, she ended it by waving her red Liberty shawl above her head and crying, 'This is red! So am I! ... You were once wild here! Don't let them tame you!' (Her remark about wildness being a deliberate reference to the beginnings of the American Revolution in Boston, this was not perhaps the most diplomatic thing she could have said.)

What happened a little later is clear, although how it happened is not. Once again, the top of her costume slipped, revealing her breasts. Whether this occurred as she brandished her red shawl aloft, or as she reached to congratulate her conductor, or as she ripped her tunic top down deliberately (all of which have been claimed), the result was clear. Proper Bostonians (and Boston could be very proper) were outraged. The press reported the affair gleefully all across America.

Soon, Boston's Irish mayor, James M. Curley, announced that 'No further licenses to perform' would be issued to Miss Duncan. She was banned, and her Boston season came to an abrupt end.

Hurok begged her to stop making speeches from the stage. With the result that in Chicago she announced to her audience, 'My manager tells me that if I make more speeches the tour is dead. Very well, the tour is dead. I will go back to Moscow where there is vodka, music, poetry and dancing... Oh, yes, and Freedom!'

Cancellations began pouring into Hurok's office from around the Midwest, 'punctuated,' as he recalled, 'by the indignations of mayors and leading citizens.' Isadora, on-stage, continued to defend her attitudes and her costume. In Cleveland, in a performance at the Public Hall, she harangued her audience, 'And this is the little red dress which frightened Boston! I've worn this dress for twenty years. Is it so shocking? Is Cleveland more hardboiled than Boston?'

As she continued speaking, she was hissed and booed, and many of the audience walked out. One who did not was the young Ohio poet Hart Crane, who gave the following description of her Tchaikovsky programme:

It was glorious beyond words, and sad beyond words, too, from the rude and careless reception she got here. It was like a wave of life, a flaming gale that passed over the heads of the nine thousand in the audience without evoking response other than silence and some maddening cat-calls. After the first movement of the *Pathétique* she came to the forefront of the stage, her hands extended. Silence – the most awful silence! I started clapping furiously until she disappeared behind the draperies. At least one tiny sound should follow her from that vast audience. She continued through the performance with utter indifference to the audience and with such intensity of gesture and such plastique grace as I have never seen, though the music was sometimes drowned out by the noises in the hall. I felt like rushing to the stage, but I was stimulated almost beyond the power to walk straight.

In November 1922 Isadora briefly ceased touring and returned to New York, where she gave two more performances at Carnegie Hall. After the first of these she addressed the audience, saying again that she had been warned not to make speeches, but wanted to make just this little one. 'I preach only love,' she said. 'The love of mother for her children; of lover for wife – of my own for the top gallery!' She went on to speak about Soviet Russia, and the audience cheered her. When she spoke of her school in Russia, and asked for contributions, a rain of dollar bills descended from the gallery and the boxes. Esenin dashed round picking it up.

Then it was off on the road again, followed everywhere by lurid reporting in the press. In Indianapolis four policemen were stationed in the auditorium while she danced, to ensure that she stayed fully clad. In Louisville, Kentucky, her next stop, there were no policemen, and at times her upper costume did slip.

From there she went on to Kansas City, St Louis, Memphis, Milwaukee, Detroit, Toronto, Baltimore and Philadelphia. At every city, the moment

349

she arrived, she sent Hurok, if he was there, or if not, his representative, out to find a bootlegger. As Hurok ruefully remarked, 'Never was a woman more generous in supplying her enemies the ammunition with which to destroy her.'

Then it was back to New York, where, on Christmas Eve, she was to deliver a lay sermon at St Mark's-in-the-Bouwerie Episcopal Church in Lower Manhattan. Her subject was to be 'The Moralizing Effect of Dancing on the Human Soul'. But this never happened. So many letters of protest had been sent to Episcopal archbishop William T. Manning that he cancelled her booking.

On Christmas Night she did appear, dancing at the Academy of Music in Brooklyn, where her music was provided by the pianist Max Rabinovitch. But that night, rarely for her, she was drunk on stage, having got drunk after learning that Sarah Bernhardt was dying. The performance descended into chaos. She decided on the spur of the moment that she would like to improvise a funeral dirge for the great actress, which led to such a disagreement with Rabinovitch that he stalked off the stage.

Left alone, Isadora decided she would provide her own music. She began to hum Brahms's 'Waltz in A Flat'. As Joseph Kaye reported in *Dance Magazine*: 'To this accompaniment she began dancing and continued for a short time. But the effect was so grotesque and eerie that she realized she would be better not to go through with it.' Later she told reporters that her condition was due to terrible bootleg liquor, which, she said 'would kill an elephant', and had made both herself and her husband ill. (Also it turned out that Sarah Bernhardt was not yet dying. She was well enough the following year to begin work on a film. During the making of it, on 21st March 1923, she collapsed, dying three days later.)

Esenin had not been with Isadora during most of her touring. Much of the time he had stayed in New York, with his friend and interpreter Vetlugin (who had turned out to be a hopeless secretary). America was doing terrible things to Esenin's self-confidence. There he was not recognised as a poet. Two years later he wrote:

Once I saw a newspaper-seller on a corner, and my face was in every newspaper. My heart gave a leap. There's real fame for you!...
I bought a good dozen papers from him, and rushed home, thinking
– I must send this to so-and-so and to what's-his-name. And I asked someone to translate the words beneath my picture. And they did so. 'Sergei Esenin, the Russian peasant, husband of the famous, incomparable, enchanting dancer – Isadora Duncan – whose immortal

talent...' etc. etc. I was so furious that I tore the paper to shreds...
So that's fame for you! That evening I went down to the restaurant
and, as I recall, I got really drunk. I drank and wept.

Nor could he stand it when Americans asked him what he did. If he
said he was a poet, he always got the same reply: 'But that's not a job!
What do you do?' He became more and more angry, drunken, violent
and self-destructive. More and more frequently he would attack Isadora
physically, and once he told her, 'I am thinking of making the Woolworth
Building my tombstone, by jumping down from its tower ... carrying
the last poem I am going to write.'

He and Isadora were staying at the Waldorf, and one night at about
three in the morning Hurok got a panic-stricken phone-call from Isadora
there. 'Come quickly!' she begged. 'He's killing me!' Hurok hurried to
the Waldorf, and to their suite, where he found both Isadora and Esenin
passed out cold on their bed. Soon after this, Waldorf himself requested
they leave. They moved into the Brevoort, on lower Fifth Avenue.

Isadora's last two American concerts took place at Carnegie Hall in
January 1923, and she sailed away, on 2nd February, feeling she would
never see the native country that had disappointed her so much, ever
again. In spite of the many performances she had given on her tour, she
had ended it flat broke, without even money for boat fare. Mary Desti
later alleged that once again, as so often, the long-suffering Paris Singer
had provided it. In a final press interview, sounding tired and disillusioned,
Isadora told the reporters, 'I really ought not to say a word to you
newspapermen... You newspapermen wrecked my career... I'm going
back to Russia. I'd rather live on black bread and vodka there than on
the best you've got in the United States... If I didn't get out of this
country soon I'd be killed by the liquor anyhow.'

The boat was the American liner *George Washington*, which she had
chosen deliberately because, like America itself, it was alcohol-free. She
hoped that this would at least give Esenin a break from drinking. But
of course the ship held as much bootleg liquor as America itself, and
after it docked at Cherbourg, and they took a train to Paris, Esenin had
to be helped off the train, wrapped in a bundle of furs.

From the boat, Isadora had sent a wire to Mary Desti, saying: IF
YOU WOULD SAVE MY LIFE AND REASON MEET ME IN PARIS.
When the faithful Mary did, Isadora, who may have been a little drunk
herself, said, 'Mary, Mary, oh, Mary, at last you have come to save me...
Promise, Mary, never to leave me again.'

She and Esenin checked into the Crillon (which apparently had forgiven them), but she was appalled to discover, while there, that he had been systematically robbing her. In his trunks he had secreted, along with his own extravagant new wardrobe, many of Isadora's clothes and seven or eight thousand dollars in cash. 'My God,' she said to Mary, using the language of the old melodrama, 'can it be possible that I have been harbouring a viper in my bosom.'

On their second night at the Crillon, Esenin went into such a frenzy of violence that Isadora left the hotel, afraid for her life. Esenin completely wrecked their suite. As Mary recalled, 'The beds were broken, the springs on the floor, the sheets torn into shreds, every bit of mirror or glass broken in bits – really, it looked like a house after a bomb had hit it.' The hotel called the police, and it took six of them to haul him off to jail.

Isadora went off with Mary to hide in the suburb of Versailles, although the press soon tracked her down to get her statement. 'I never believed in marriage,' was one of the things she told them sadly, 'and now I believe in it less than ever.' She begged the reporters to allow her peace and privacy.

Eventually the police agreed to release Esenin, but only on condition he leave France at once. Isadora used the last of the money she had borrowed from Singer to transport him to Berlin, where one of his Moscow poet friends, Alexander Kusikov, still was. From there, the Soviet consul could arrange his transport back to Moscow. Isadora's maid, Jeanne, accompanied him, and as they were setting off he went out of his way to tell reporters that he was off to Russia, 'to see my two children by a former wife.'

From stress and exhaustion, Isadora became ill. Still at Versailles with Mary, she ran a high temperature. Her condition over the next days was not improved by a series of wounding statements Esenin gave to the Berlin press. 'Russia is vast,' he said in one of them, 'and I will always find a place where this terrible woman cannot reach me.' And in another, speaking of their marriage, 'It was hell which I bore for six months, but then I could not stand it any longer. I fled, and now I feel well again for the first time since my wedding day, as a free man, dependent on no one.'

It was not long, however, before he found himself desperately missing Isadora, and began bombarding her with telegrams, 'five or six a day,' remembered Mary, 'all of which kept Isadora's temperature soaring. The doctor could do nothing to make her sleep.'

The telegrams were, if anything, more disturbing to her than his insults. She loved Esenin, and began to fear he would harm himself if she were not with him. Eventually she said, 'Mary, dear, if you are really my friend, find a way to take me to Sergei or I will die. I can't live without him. I don't care what he has done... Find out where we can get a car to take us to Berlin.'

Thus began one of the most chaotic periods of even Isadora's life. They hired a car that took them to Strasbourg, on the German border, but there the driver refused to enter Germany. They hired another, which promptly crashed into a bridge and broke down. A third, and a fourth, and a fifth broke down without crashing into anything. Isadora, anxious as she was to be with Esenin, insisted on making a detour to Bayreuth. There she left a hundred roses for Cosima Wagner, and there they were lucky enough to meet 'a very charming young man' who was prepared to drive them on to Leipzig.

Eventually they reached Berlin, where they were met by Esenin and his friend Alexander Kusikov. Mary recalled:

> As we drove up in front of the Hotel Adlon ... a flying leap landed Sergei in our car, he having bounded straight on to the engine, over the chauffeur's head into Isadora's arms... There he was in flesh and bone, his golden hair waving in the electric lights. He had thrown his cap away as he sprang – an expensive but beautiful gesture. For what did he now need a hat? His love, his darling, his Isadora was here, so away with the hat. He would just as quickly have thrown his coat and boots after it.
>
> This was not posing; these two *exaltés* were beyond the consciousness of their surroundings. The police finally disbanded the onlookers, and by a little urging we persuaded the lovers to descend; but as to which hotel they wished to go to, or whether the poets had engaged rooms for us, we could get no answer of any kind.

Isadora eventually took command. 'When in doubt,' she said, 'always go to the best hotel.' So she and Esenin and Mary and several of Esenin's friends checked into the Palace, Isadora grandly declaring, 'Rooms for all. They are my party.'

That night there was a reunion celebration in Isadora and Esenin's apartment, at which endless champagne and vodka was consumed. Esenin, drunk, began, as was his habit, to throw crockery, and his friends joined in. As Mary told it:

Before we quite knew what had happened, there wasn't a thing left in the whole apartment. Sergei meanwhile hurled abuse at Isadora and myself, which mattered not to me, as I didn't understand a word of it. Three or four of his friends tried to hold him down. They might as well have tried to stop the waves of the ocean... The morning after, we got a very polite note from the management, saying the suite was engaged for that afternoon, and would we please be out of it by twelve noon.

Isadora and Esenin and Mary began touring, in a series of hired cars. They went to Weimar, then to Strasbourg, and everywhere they went there were similar scenes. Mary began begging Isadora to come back to Paris, or maybe to go back to Moscow and seriously work. But whatever it was, she must, for her own sake, leave Esenin.

Isadora would have none of it. It would, she said, be like abandoning a sick child. Somehow she managed to talk the French authorities into letting Esenin back into France. But their first attempt to get there misfired when the only car they could hire was a closed saloon. Isadora, remembering her children, was terrified of such vehicles, and although Mary and Esenin succeeded in talking her into getting into it, so great was her panic that as soon as they set off she began beating frantically on the windows. They were forced to abandon the trip.

They all did manage to get back to Paris in mid-May, but there Isadora and Esenin were asked to leave three hotels in three days. At last, in desperation, they moved back into Isadora's house on the rue de la Pompe, living there in poverty by selling what remained of the furniture. Esenin continued to have violent outbursts every few days, till at last Isadora admitted to Mary that she was at the end of her tether. They must find some money, perhaps by renting or selling the house, and send Esenin back to Russia. Finally she managed to arrange two concerts at the Trocadéro. They were scheduled for 27th May and 3rd June.

As it happened, two of her former students were also in Paris at the time. Lisa, who, as hard up as Isadora, was dancing with a male partner in a music hall for fifty francs a night, and Anna. Anna's relationship with Rummel had ended some months before. He let her know he had left her in a letter, in which he coldly said, 'I do not miss you and have decided to live quite alone and to be alone. You must make your own life, do not count on me.' Anna would never get over him.

In February 1923, a few weeks after Rummel's rejection of her, Anna was dancing in Nice when she received another letter, this time from

Isadora. It came via her lawyers, and it demanded she take Isadora's name off her posters at once. She didn't, but when she, Lisa and Margot got together later in the year to tour America, they felt forced to issue a joint statement to the American press 'disavowing Isadora Duncan's political beliefs and making it clear to the general public that they have no connection whatever with this woman.'

Isadora's first appearance at the Trocadéro went well, and after it she was joined onstage by her brother Raymond, by the artist Kees van Dongen, and by the Russian-born French deputy and socialist leader, Charles Rappoport. Isadora embarked on a speech to the audience. She asked them whether she looked like a Bolshevik, and was rewarded with shouts of 'No! No!' She asked for money for her school and, as at Carnegie Hall, notes rained down. She went on, 'When I was a little child I dreamed of smashing the bourgeois mould and remaking the world. Do you understand?... I was the first communist. At present—' At which point the socialist Rappoport started laughing. 'If she continues to talk about sociology,' he told the audience, 'I'm going to dance.' The audience, and Isadora, broke into laughter and cheers.

Afterwards, at rue de la Pompe, Isadora held a reception. Esenin went to bed before it ended, but when it was still going on at three in the morning he came flying down the stairs, screaming (in Russian) 'Band of bloated fish, mangy sleigh rugs, bellies of carrion, grub for soldiers, you awoke me!' He grabbed a candelabrum and smashed a mirror with it. The police were called, and he was hauled off again, and next day Isadora arranged for him to be committed to a sanatorium at Saint-Mandé. After three days he was released, sober and apologetic, but Isadora hired two strong male nurses to keep an eye on him for as long as they were in Paris.

Isadora's second Trocadéro concert, a Wagner programme, seemed more subdued than her first, although her Bacchanal from *Tannhäuser*, Lisa thought 'was wilder than ever.'

So was Esenin. The two strong nurses were not strong enough. One day, at rue de la Pompe, he was observed running stark naked down the stairs brandishing a five foot length of two by four, studded with protruding nails. He had disabled one of the nurses by kicking him in the groin, and was now being followed, at a cautious distance, by the other. His expressed intention was to find Isadora and kill her.

Somehow he was discouraged from doing this, but another run-in with the police not long after landed him back in jail. On 11th July the authorities gave him twenty-four hours to leave the country. He tried to obey, getting as far as the Belgian frontier, where he was turned back for having no visa. Returning to Paris, Mary recalled, '[he threw] himself on his knees before Isadora and said he could not live without his adorable wife... He would never be separated from her again.'

Isadora helped him sort out his visa, and, impelled by having received a telegram from Schneider insisting she return to her school, set off with Esenin back to Moscow. Mary accompanied them as far as Berlin, then went back to Paris and booked herself into a rest-home.

Chapter Eighteen

A Wild Ride

The reason why Schneider had sent his urgent message insisting Isadora return to the school was that it was becoming desperately short of funds, and its only hope of getting more would be for Isadora to return to what was now (since 1922) calling itself the Union of Soviet Socialist Republics, and give some performances.

During her fifteen-month absence, he and Irma had made certain changes to the school, in the course of which they had many bitter fights with the Soviet bureaucracy, such as over the question of whether the school was an institution for social education or an institution for professional training. The authorities liked things to be cut and dried.

He and Irma had reduced the number of professional staff, and had admitted a number of fee-paying students. Their fees were used to fund classes for more advanced students, and during the summer these advanced students helped Irma teach hundreds of children to dance in Moscow's open-air stadiums. There was rather more emphasis on physical health than there had been, and the school's motto was now 'A Free Spirit in a Healthy Body'.

It had also ceased to accept boys as students, the expense of providing separate dormitories for boys and girls having proved too much for its slender finances.

Isadora and Esenin arrived back on 5th August 1924. Their train pulled in to Nikolaev Station, and Schneider remembered meeting them:

> As she descended from the train she looked harassed and worried. She was in reality very glad that she had finally arrived at the end of an extremely tiring task; she had brought back her poet, as she had promised herself she would, to the place where he belonged.
>
> The object of her solicitous care stumbled down the steps of the

357

coach. He was inebriated ... as much, perhaps, from the overpowering emotional excitement of being back again in Russia as from the effects of the continual stream of vodka that had poured down his patriotic throat... And in his riotous joy he had smashed all the windows of the coach.

In German, Isadora hissed to Schneider, 'I'm bringing this child back to his homeland, but I want nothing more to do with him.' Nonetheless, she did not get rid of Esenin at once. The children of the school, thanks to Schneider's influential connections, were enjoying a summer holiday at what had been someone's country estate at Litvinovo, outside Moscow. There they played and swam and studied French and English, as well as tending a garden which would provide extra food for the winter.

Isadora and Esenin, the first night they were back, hired a car to drive there. Although it broke down, and they had to walk the last three miles in the dark, Isadora's meeting with the children was a joyful one. Several had been sent out with lanterns to look for her, and once they found her they gleefully danced her up to the house.

But her stay there would not be long. It rained, and Esenin soon became bored and insisted they return to the city. Once there, he moved into her room at the school with her, but almost at once went off to his old riotous life with his fellow-poets, and that first night did not return.

Isadora worried. 'Something must have happened to him,' she told Irma. 'He's been hurt. He's had an accident. He's ill somewhere.' Irma, understanding Isadora's exhausted state, told her firmly that she should go for rest and maybe medical treatment at a spa. Somewhat to her surprise, Isadora meekly agreed.

Irma booked her into the resort spa of Kislovodsk, 700 miles south of Moscow, in the Caucasian mountains, and famous for the health-giving powers of its Narzan water. On the day she was to set off there, Esenin returned to the school, after being missing for three days. Although Irma had tried to ensure that he be kept away from Isadora, he insisted, and going to her room, where she lay on a couch, bent down and caressed her face, saying, 'I love you very much, Isadora. I love you very much.'

But Isadora was at last beginning to run out of patience. In her halting Russian she told him that if he ever went away again without telling her where he was going or for how long, that would be the end. She also told him that she herself was leaving Moscow that night for a rest-cure.

He left the room laughing, not having believed her, but somehow managed to find out which station she would be leaving from – it was Kazan Station – and turned up there that evening just before her train pulled out. As Irma, who was accompanying her, reported, he was sober and smiling, and this so touched Isadora that she tried to talk him into joining her on the train, telling him that a rest-cure would do him good as well.

He refused, but promised to join her later in the week, coming with Schneider, who was due to go and visit her. Before the train's leaving-bell rang, they embraced tenderly, and as it pulled out, Isadora waved her scarf in goodbye until he was out of her sight. She would receive no news of him for a couple of weeks.

Getting off the train at Kislovodsk, by an amazing coincidence the first person she encountered was the American writer Max Eastman. He was in the town because he was working on a biography of Leon Trotsky, the Soviet second-in-command, and Trotsky happened also to be there taking a rest-cure. Eastman was at the station buying milk, and later described meeting Isadora, who greeted him affectionately. He walked her and Irma to their hotel, the Grand Hotel (which turned out to be run-down and vermin-infested).

Isadora was, Eastman recalled, in splendid form, predicting the triumph of communism everywhere, and insisting that Esenin was the finest poet since Pushkin, Whitman and Poe. He came to the conclusion that her continuing 'mad passion' for her poet was 'not purely masochistic' but 'a gesture towards her childish notion of the sublime.'

Isadora rested at Kislovodsk for two weeks, towards the end of which time she at last heard from Esenin. He sent her a letter which said, 'Dear Isadora! I am very busy with literary matters and cannot come to you... Things are going splendidly for me ... and I am now being offered a lot of money for a publishing venture. I wish you success and health and that you should drink less... Love, S. Esenin.' She at once sent him a telegram, dated 22 August: DARLING VERY SAD WITHOUT YOU COME HERE SOON I LOVE YOU FOREVER ISADORA.

Feeling refreshed, she decided she should be doing something, and arranged to give a performance in Kislovodsk. Unfortunately, at an early-morning rehearsal with the orchestra she had hired, which took place outdoors, their playing of the *Marche Slave* was overheard by the members of the Cheka – the much-feared secret police. Before the rehearsal of the piece was over, during its third run-through, the conductor was faced by an angry Cheka official, demanding to know what he meant by playing a Tsarist hymn. Isadora tried to explain, but that night, before her performance, she was told that if she performed the piece she would be arrested.

Facing her audience, with the help of a translator in the front row, she explained the situation, that there were police waiting backstage to arrest her, but that she intended to dance *Marche Slave* anyway, that jail could not be much worse than her room at the Grand Hotel. This drew much laughter from the audience and, as it subsided, her interpreter said to her, 'You need not worry, Tovarisch Duncan. You can begin your performance. As President of the Soviet Ispolkom I give you permission to dance the Tchaikovsky march.'

She did, and it was well-received, as was her whole programme, but the Cheka felt vengeful. Schneider, now with her in Kislovodsk, had fallen from a horse and sprained his leg. The evening after her performance, as he was lying in his bed resting it, three Cheka officers came to arrest him for 'counterrevolutionary activity'. Isadora, dining at the *Kursaal*, was immediately told, and hurried angrily back to the hotel.

Rushing into Schneider's room, and finding him under armed guard, she hurled at the guard the lowest word in Russian she could think of. '*Svoloch!* (Bastard!),' she cried. 'Yes, *Svoloch! Svoloch!*' Then she had an inspiration. Eastman had told her where Trotsky was staying, and, commandeering a hotel porter and a lantern, she hastened to the great man's villa.

It was guarded by two more Cheka officers, who would not let her in, but she pencilled a note and they agreed to take that to Trotsky. Back came the reply that she could return to the hotel, that everything would be all right. Which it was, except that the Cheka, as revenge for her having insulted their guard, had ransacked Schneider's room, searching every trunk and drawer. They were still there when she delivered Trotsky's message, and as they left they warned her that they would have further revenge. '*Svoloch!*' shouted Isadora.

All the same, she felt it might be safer for her and her friends to move away from Kislovodsk, and embarked on a short tour of the Causasus. She performed in Baku, on the Caspian Sea, and also, while there, gave a free concert for workers in the Caspian oil-fields. Then she went on to give several performances in Tbilisi, the capital of the Soviet Republic of Georgia. These were so well-received that she was asked to give several more.

While in Tbilisi, on 10 September, she received a disturbing reply to her telegram of three weeks before. It said: DON'T SEND ANY MORE

LETTERS TELEGRAMS ESENIN HE IS WITH ME… YOU MUST COUNT ON HIS NOT RETURNING TO YOU. GALINA BENISLAVSKAYA. Galina Benislavskaya, known as 'Galya', who was a decorated Heroine of the Revolution, was an old friend of Esenin's, who had long yearned for him but had never, until now, held any hope of getting him.

In Schneider's opinion, 'Isadora was crushed by that telegram, but she pretended only to be hurt.' She at once sent a telegram to Esenin, saying: I'VE RECEIVED TELEGRAM EVIDENTLY FROM YOUR SERVANT BENISLAVSKAYA. HAVE YOU CHANGED ADDRESS I ASK YOU EXPLAIN, and this rather unsatisfactory exchange of telegrams continued for some time, even with Esenin sending such messages as: I LOVE ANOTHER AM MARRIED AND HAPPY. As Galya would recall, Isadora's 'telegrams harassed him and got on his nerves dreadfully.'

Isadora's short tour ended in Batum, also in Georgia and on the shores of the Black Sea, where she was lent a villa to stay in by the regional Soviet. It was still a hot late summer when she arrived there, and Isadora, looking out at the palms, cypresses and magnolias, exclaimed, 'The tropics! How wonderful it is here!' After which it set in to rain non-stop. Looking out at the dripping cypresses, she said to Schneider, 'I hate them. They are the trees of the dead.'

That night she went into the town and two days later was found by Irma installed in the apartment of a handsome young Georgian poet. He was one of a group of poets and 'black-eyed Ganymedes' who had elected her their Muse. Irma could only hope that this brief affair would do something to ease her grieved longing for Esenin.

When Isadora and her party returned to Moscow at the end of September 1924, she hoped to see him, but he, having heard of her impending arrival, had fled to Petrograd.

A few weeks afterwards, however, he did return, and even came to the school to see Isadora, but caused such a scene that Schneider felt obliged to send him a letter saying, 'Don't you think it's in bad taste to scream in Isadora's room in front of people about your love for another woman? I see only shame and lies coming from you, and after the scandal of last night, I can only tell you that I do not want to see you again.'

Nevertheless, Esenin had to return to the school a little later, when he was to be presented with a wooden bust of himself, carved by the sculptor Sergei Konenov. But he did not stay long, arriving drunk and leaving as soon as the presentation was over, dropping the sculpture several times and cursing.

361

But gradually, it seemed Isadora was steeling herself to get over him. On 22nd November he and three fellow-Imaginists were arrested in a bar for making 'anti-Semitic remarks' about various Bolshevik leaders. After they were released, a day later, he told reporters that he was 'finished with Duncan', and that if she wanted a divorce she could get it herself.

Isadora, commenting on this to the Moscow correspondent of the *New York Times*, Walter Duranty, said 'He really is too impossible. If it were only women I wouldn't mind so much, but Sergei's trouble comes out of the bottle... It was bad enough in America, but here his crazy goings on interfere with the work of my school, which I won't have.'

In January 1924, Esenin entered a sanatorium, and from around that time, Schneider observed, 'She shut herself up in her shell, never mentioned Esenin's name, did not attempt to arrange any meeting with him, and outwardly seemed absolutely calm. She devoted herself entirely to her work with the children and seemed to be interested only in the problems of the future of her school.'

During November and December of 1923 she had danced several times at the Bolshoi to make money, getting enough from one performance to pay for wood for the winter, and from another to buy flour and potatoes and other foodstuffs. But money was also necessary for such things as electricity and clothing. She wrote to her brother Augustin:

> The children at the school are simply a Miracle. The first school nothing in comparison, but – *Hélas* – How shall we feed them – The Government gives nothing... We do not know from day to day when the school will cease & it will be a crime, for such beauty of movement and Expression I have never imagined could come true... It is a wonder that it still exists. Our only hope is that they may send us help from America.

But she found writing fund-raising letters to America discouraging, as, she said, 'nobody answers.' But she carried on working. Many of the dances she composed for her students she based on songs of the Russian workers. Probably her best-known is *Warshavianca*, based on a revolutionary song from 1905 about the heroic endurance of the proletariat. As she created it, it depicts wave after wave of workers advancing with a banner held high. As each wave is gunned down, another seizes the banner, holds it high, and continues the advance.

One of her students recalled her being unsatisfied with the way they were dying. 'Don't you know how people die?' she asked. 'She then

362

collapsed in perfect unison with the music, only to rise slowly and resolutely when coming back to life in order to join her comrades and pick up the banner from their hands.'

Towards the end of January 1924 she was scheduled to make a tour of the Ukraine, but this was delayed for several weeks owing to the death, on 21st January, of Lenin, aged only fifty-three. His death would mark the beginning of a protracted struggle for power between Trotsky, who felt that socialism could never properly be established in the USSR until there had been revolution in Western Europe, and Stalin, who felt that it would be best to establish the USSR as a strong socialist state, and from that base fight to expand communism elsewhere. Stalin would win, but not until 1927.

Deeply moved by Lenin's death, Isadora went and stood in line, 'with millions of other people', outside the House of Soviets in Moscow, in sub-zero temperatures. And on her Ukrainian tour, which eventually took place in February, she danced two revolutionary funeral songs in his memory at every performance. She danced them in Kharkov, Rostov, Krasnodar, Ekaterinoslav, Kiev, Vinitza and Odessa, and performed with such passion that during the tour she lost thirty pounds.

When it was over, she went on to Leningrad (as Petrograd had now been renamed) and booked herself into the Hotel Europa, where she proceeded to spend more in a month than she had earned for the school in a year. Schneider, in his capacity as headmaster, was irritated, and felt he must find some way to deny her access to the school's bank account.

In May she began another fund-raising tour, but was dogged by misfortune. Having danced at Vitsyebsk, she had to travel 350 miles to reach Leningrad. Her car had got about half way, to Pskov, when it broke in two. The front half, containing the driver, turned a somersault, and the rear, containing Isadora, hurtled into a ditch. Thrown out, she hit her head, but by good luck landed in a puddle, which helped to cushion the blow, so that she was not badly hurt. Getting to Leningrad, she again stayed (briefly) at the Europa, but this time did not pay her bill.

On her return to Moscow, she at once arranged another tour of the Ukraine, this time with Irma and some of her pupils. But at their first stop, Kiev, there was such a heat-wave that during the two weeks they performed there they played to very poor houses. They barely covered their expenses, so Isadora sent Irma and the girls back to Moscow and soldiered on alone, also dismissing her orchestra, apart from the pianist, Mark Meichik.

363

Travelling east, towards the Ural mountains, by 28th July she was in the city of Ekaterinburg, and wrote from there to Irma, saying:

> Perhaps the killing here of a *certain* family in a cellar has cast a sort of Edgar Allan Poe gloom over the place, or perhaps it was always like that... You can't imagine anything more fearful.
>
> We arrived here more dead than alive after 5 nights on the r.r., twice changing trains & waiting all day in villages without hotels... The tournée is one calamity after another, for although I dance to large publics of communists & workmen no one has money to buy tickets except the new bourgeoisie & they cordially detest me. When we have a little money Meichik takes it all on the pretext that he will not play unless he receives all the money at once & after that he calmly sits by & watches us starve. He is a wonderful Tovarisch and ought to be sent to [Siberia].

Working her way back towards Moscow, she wrote again to Irma, on 12th August, from Vyatka:

> We were twelve days in that awful Ekaterinburg. You have no idea what a living nightmare is until you see [that] town ... no restaurant ... no coiffeur. The only remaining fossil of that name, while burning my hair off with trembling fingers, assured me that there was not one '*Dame*' left ... they shot 'em all.
>
> In Perm we did not make expenses – and arrive here without a kopeck. This is a village with awful hotel – bed bugs mice and other agreements... It is too awful. I haven't had a bottle of eau de cologne no soap no tooth paste since a month. The beds are made of boards and populated. The halls are splashed with the filth of ages & blood stains & pistol shots in the mirrors... My hair is quite white from lack of a Henna champoo – & I feel extremely *kaputt.*

Fortunately, at the end of August she made it back to Moscow, where she was uplifted by being welcomed back to the school by five hundred cheering children in red tunics. At once she got down to helping Irma with her summer dance lessons in Red Stadium, writing resiliently on 2nd September to her old friend Allan Ross Macdougall, 'Everyone can say what they please, in spite of the catastrophe and suffering and all, the *idea* of the New World is born here, and nothing can kill it.'

364

In this confident mood, she happily signed a contract to tour Germany, which had been arranged for her through Irma while she was away. Before leaving, she gave several 'farewell' performances at Moscow's Kamerny Theatre, and a last one at the Bolshoi, on 29th September. This had been organised by the wife of Mikhail Kalinin, President of the Politburo. It was attended by many Party leaders and by four thousand 'young Pioneers and Communist youths'. The next day she left for Berlin, telling Irma and Schneider that she wouldn't be away long. She would perform the tour, collect some things she had in store in Berlin, and be back for the better weather in the spring.

Her journey began badly. Her plane from Moscow to Berlin crash-landed twice – once on takeoff and again at its stopover in Kaliningrad in Lithuania. But Isadora took these mishaps in her stride. Arriving in Berlin, she took rooms at the Hotel Eden (feeling it would perhaps be better to give the Hotel Adlon a miss this time). But again she was on a tour where everything seemed to go wrong. In Twenties Germany, her dancing was not appreciated. She was seen as overweight and passé and politically contentious. Managers she signed contracts with hadn't enough money to pay her, or at times even the money for train tickets. She was more alone than she had ever been in her life, without family, friends or pupils, and early in October she wrote to Irma:

It seems my fate in 1924 to be tragically stranded. I am still waiting here for something – God knows what – Berlin is simply fearful. Better to sell matches on the streets of Moscow. Here is no spirit; everything congested with *Patriotismus* and fatherland. It is awful... I danced two evenings *without receiving a penny*... Altogether it is Hell!!! And I spend my time wondering which poison doesn't hurt the most. I don't want to take any of the fearful kind... Write to me what is happening. If you can fix the contract for Siberia I will come. Love to you and to all the dear children. Love – Isadora. *Poor thing*. Love to you all. Maybe I die tonight.

She was also concerned about the legacy of dance she hoped to leave the world, expressed through her pupils, and was distressed that her ex-pupil Lisa was still dancing in Paris nightclubs, and using her adopted surname of Duncan. On 13th October, in a letter to Irma, Isadora complained, 'If she wishes to go to such filth she ought at least to take her own name. When she knows what I have suffered and gone through to keep my name from the music hall, and then she drags it there.'

At the end of October, unable to afford the Hotel Eden, she got herself to her sister Elizabeth's school in Potsdam, but was told by Max Merz that Elizabeth was away in Vienna. She told him that she was broke and had nowhere to stay. That, he said, was her own fault, and turned her away.

Back in Berlin, she booked herself into a cheap hotel called the Central, near the Friedrichstrasse station. There she had one stroke of luck in meeting a young American, Allan Coe, who was studying to be a pianist and had a small allowance. He was there with his boyfriend, a singer named Martin, and for a while the three of them rubbed along on Allan's allowance, he bringing Isadora small amounts of food, such as a slice of roast beef. Then word got back to America that he was leading 'a wild, debauched life' in Berlin, and his allowance was cut off. By the end of November, Isadora, in another letter to Irma, was saying:

> I was ill for two weeks with bronchitis, and now, to cap the climax, an ulcerated tooth. I have telegraphed Raymond, but he is in Nice, and apparently *can't* or *won't* do anything. Germany is the limit, simply fearful. I don't know what's going to happen next... Yours in a dying stage, Isadora.

Allan Coe sent a letter to Allan Ross Macdougall, in Paris, saying, 'We boys have given our last cent, and we all three are broke – stranded! Honest to God!' and Isadora wrote on the back, 'Where is Raymond? ... Perhaps if you asked Walter he would do something – or his dear brother, who really is my friend – Frank – *Pour l'Amour de Dieu sauvez-moi.*'

She had met a respected American journalist, George Seldes, who was working for the *Chicago Tribune*. In his 14th December report to the *Tribune* he wrote:

> Isadora Duncan is at the end of her rope and does not know how to pay her rent or where her meals are to come from next week, she told the correspondent today. Two courses are open to her, she said. The first is to sell her houses in Paris, which is difficult, because France will not give her a visa to visit Paris, and the second, to publish 1,000 love letters received in her prime.

Two days later, she was writing to Irma:

> Why don't you answer my telegrams and letters? Since six weeks

I am without any word from you... Are you ill? Does the school still exist? I can obtain no passport here from the Russian Embassy. Please do whatever is necessary to obtain this passport for me and also a divorce from Sergei Alexandrovitch – God bless him, but he is no good for a husband.

I may have to return to Moscow, as here my allowance to stay expires in a week. *Every country has refused me a visa* on account of my '*political connections.*' Where are my political connections, I would like to know? I am utterly stranded and lost here in a very hostile city.

Irma claimed, believably, that she had been away with some of the students, on a tour of the Volga, and did not know of Isadora's letters until it was too late to help her.

The *Tribune* sent Seldes a telegram authorising him to buy Isadora's autobiography – 'containing love letters' – for five thousand dollars (to be paid on delivery). He approached her about collaborating with him on writing it, and she agreed to begin provided he would buy her a quart of gin. She was in tears as she asked for it, but insisted, 'No gin, no deal.' He bought her the gin, and hired an English shorthand-typist, and at her hotel she began dictating what Seldes would describe as 'a strange and not too sober jumble of opinions, anecdotes, childhood reminiscences, mentions of her notable lovers, family life in San Francisco, art, love, and passion.' She also touched on Lenin, Christ, Buddha, children and dancing. When he asked her if she was a Bolshevik, she replied, 'No, I am not a Bolshevik. All I did was work for the starving children... Men have loved me, but my only love has been children.'

After only one day the shorthand-typist quit, saying, 'I don't like her ideas, and I can't permit myself to work for a woman who drinks gin.' Finding another was not easy, but Seldes managed it. However, when he returned to the Central Hotel a few days later, he found a different Isadora.

His article in the *Tribune* had caused some of her friends and acquaintances to rally round. In particular, another American newspaperman, the Russian-born Isaac Don Levine, had paid off her debts in Berlin and arranged for her to get a visa to travel to Paris. He had also told her that selling the contents of her love letters for money was beneath her, so when Seldes arrived, to find her packing to set off for a rest-cure at Spa, she told him that she had no intention of continuing with her memoirs, saying, 'What do you think I am? An old woman? Am I dead?

367

Only the dead publish memoirs. I'll have time enough when I am dead to write them... Life is changed... Life begins again.'

She reached Paris late in January 1925, and on 2nd February was writing to Irma, 'At last I have arrived here. I am hardly alive, just gasping.' It was on that day, she soon learned, that her ex-pupil Margot had died of her TB, aged only twenty-six, in a Paris hospital. Isadora, although knowing she was there, had not gone to see her, and so was doubly depressed by the news.

Paris Singer, still in Florida developing the land boom, had not heard of Isadora's troubles in Berlin, but he did hear of the death of Margot, and how hard up Isadora was. He at once telegraphed his Agent in Paris, telling him to send Isadora money without letting her know the source. However much he sent, she soon went through it.

She now embarked on a lengthy period of inactivity, poverty and general lack of direction, wandering restlessly from place to place, mostly dividing her time between Nice and Paris. By now, nearing fifty and somewhat overweight, she was by no means the dancer she had once been, even though her years of experience did much to counteract her loss of youthful litheness.

Also, she had to a large extent lost her drive to innovate. Indeed, in a sense she had lost it for some years – her innovative approach to dance had reached its perfect state by the end of the Great War. All that her years in Russia had given her was a range of new emotions and attitudes to express in dance – her basic technique and approach remained the same. It was as if in her mind she had arrived at a perfect understanding of dance, and felt there was nothing more that could be learned, beyond creating another dance in similar style to a new piece of music.

All of which left her somewhat at sea. She found in Western Europe during the Twenties no great cause that she could understand and embrace. So she drifted, solacing herself with drink and with handsome young men.

At first she did try. Early in March she was driven to Nice by her brother Raymond, who himself had tired of the cynical post-war Paris and, while maintaining his Parisian shop, had opened another in Nice. One critic, typical of others, had written, 'Paris is weary of men who disguise themselves as carnival-time Athenians, and walk the streets with bare legs and dirty feet so that they can sell rugs of doubtful quality at high prices.'

He offered Isadora the use of an apartment over his Nice shop, and she tried it for a while, but it was furnished in the Spartan Raymond manner, and after several weeks of sleeping on wooden benches, she began to look elsewhere. Fortunately she soon found a place, through the writer Georges Maurevert, whom she had known in Paris from almost the first day she arrived there. He persuaded the most expensive hotel in Nice, the Hôtel Negresco, to rent her a small room with bath at a much-reduced rent – a not-unknown arrangement in cultured France, and referred to as *tarif d'artiste*.

She also, at the end of March, found a studio she could rent, a converted garage at 343 promenade des Anglais, facing the water at Henri Plage, on the western edge of the city. Its rent would be paid for her at first by her brother Augustin, and later by her staunch American friend, Ruth Mitchell. At once she wrote to Mary Desti in New York, telling her about it and saying that she was 'stranded as usual and have no money to fix it up – on receiving this if you can telegraph me $200 I could get my carpet from Paris & piano – & work again.'

In the same letter she spoke of her ex-pupils Anna and Theresa, still touring America. She said, 'Couldn't you hint delicately to Theresa & Anna that they might at least pay me the usual 10% *Author's* rights – in using my work – as they are doing!!!'

Presumably Mary sent the $200, but in early April, before Isadora could get her carpet and piano, and start work, she went sunbathing and was stung on the arm by a hornet. The arm began to swell dangerously, and soon she was writing in haste to Mary:

> All the calamities of the Universe seem to fall on my poor head. I was poisoned by a demon in shape of a fly and had to be rushed to hospital for operation to save my arm. I am getting well now but very shaky. I was about to sign a contract for a tournée of France. I have a wonderful little Theatre by the Sea... If you and Augustin could see your way to send me $50 a week until I can work again I will be able to refund it all in October when I have a prospect of a great deal of money for a contract – France and Spain.

Isadora's experience of trying to set down her memoirs with George Seldes, even though abortive, had put the idea in her mind. This too she had mentioned to Mary, who in New York had contacted the publisher Horace Liveright, of Boni & Liveright, who expressed interest. So on 18th April she sent a telegram to Mary, who had been considering coming to France: BRING CONTRACT BOOK ISADORA. But for the moment Boni & Liveright did not offer her a contract, nor did Mary come to Europe.

Recovered from her hornet sting, Isadora continued to divide her time between Paris and Nice. But socially the France she now found herself in was different from the country she had known before the war. More and more often, the people she met were Americans, many connected with the arts. Nice, even more than Paris, had a carefree, almost carnival atmosphere, and it was there, in the summer of 1925, that she met Scott and Zelda Fitzgerald.

Zelda, already in her twenties, was obsessed with becoming a ballet dancer, and so was inclined to be ill-disposed towards Isadora for her contempt of it. Describing meeting Isadora, she wrote, 'She had got too old and fat to care whether people accepted her theories of life and art, and she gallantly toasted the world's obliviousness in lukewarm champagne.' And when Scott and Isadora began to flirt, although it is probable that what Isadora really wanted from him was advice about writing her memoirs, Zelda hurled herself down a stone staircase, badly grazing her knees.

At the Victorine film studios in Nice she met the Dublin-born American director Rex Ingram, most famous for directing Rudolf Valentino in *The Four Horsemen of the Apocalypse*. He was there making a film called *Mare Nostrum*, and through him she met such cinema celebrities as Douglas Fairbanks and Mary Pickford, Anita Loos, Harpo Marx, Chaplin, and Valentino himself.

The Rumanian Jean Negulesco, then in his early twenties, who years later would become a workmanlike Hollywood director, remembered her giving a private dance recital at her studio (her curtains and carpets by now having arrived). He wrote:

> The people invited that night were Jean Cocteau, Richard Le Gallienne, Marie Laurencin, Picasso, Marguerite Jamois, Rex Ingram, Walter Shaw ... my fiancée Winifred, and I. On a platform a few steps higher than the floor, all of us were seated on enormous, comfortable cushions of the same color as the draperies.
>
> Some twenty tall church candlesticks with heavy unlighted candles were spaced around the walls and front (furnished by Rex Ingram, courtesy of Metro-Goldwyn-Mayer).
>
> The décor was majestic in its simplicity. It was in complete darkness. A Bach sonata on a record player weighed heavily on us. It was Isadora's way to embarrass us into silence with heavy, almost

funereal music. By the last note we were enormously moved – quiet, relaxed.

Then on the waves of a new record Isadora appeared suddenly between two curtains holding a single lighted candle, dressed in a simple white classical toga, barefooted, hair free, not moving, still. It looked as if she listened only to the music... She was there but not with us. She was there not to dance, but to listen, to be still. She was like a stopped frame in a film, stopped in motion, not moving, just projecting. She moved. Or did she move? How long before she was in front of the first candlestick giving light? Her bare feet did not move; there was no moving of her toga; she was ahead of the music. You felt that in her motionless attitude – completely oblivious of her surroundings – she was trying to convey the very essence of music and dance.

Later that evening, Negulesco recalled, Rex Ingram took a number of those present in his big sedan for a midnight bouillabaisse in a waterfront restaurant. The group consisted of Isadora, Negulesco and his fiancée, Cocteau, and Walter Shaw (a pianist friend of Cocteau, who at the time was also supposed to be helping Isadora begin her memoirs).

The restaurant was full of young sailors, and Walter Shaw picked one up and brought him to their table, handsome and blushing. At which point an argument began between Cocteau and Isadora over which of them should have him. Cocteau seemed to be winning the argument when Isadora, pleading like a child, said, 'Sweetest Cocteau, you had the one last night. Let me have this one.' She appealed to the others, 'Make him realise how unfair he is.' The group backed her up, and Cocteau reluctantly gave in, saying, 'She can have him. But this is the last time.'

When visiting Paris, she lived in a succession of hotels and apartments, paid for by friends. On one of her 1925 visits she went with Walter Shaw to a salon given in Montmartre by a Mrs Marvin. When she entered a young Russian pianist, Victor Seroff, was playing. As he recalled:

She came up to the piano after I had finished... One noticed at once her lovely arms, with their fine small hands, and the line of her neck and shoulders was magnificent. Her whole body moved beautifully as she came across the room. She wore a simple, loose suit, and on her head was a shapeless felt hat, with a rather large brim, which seemed to express her personality. Her voice was low and gentle, and it had a tone which gave her whole character a quality of naivete. Her face was tired and looked as if she had rouged without looking in the mirror, and around her eyes ... she had streaks of black and blue make-up, which did not quite hide the small wrinkles under the eyelids.

She asked him to play the piece again, as she had come in in the middle of it. He did, and as he played she listened, rapt, totally absorbed in the music. When he finished, she said to the room, 'He's a genius. Doesn't anybody know he's a genius? I have a nose for genius.' She turned to Mrs Marvin. 'Is he your lover?'

'Why, no, Miss Duncan,' Mrs Marvin said. 'He's my guest.'

'He must be somebody's lover.' Isadora looked round the room. 'Well, he is nobody's lover, then I will take him for myself. I always take genius for myself. Genius needs me.' Borrowing a piece of paper from Walter Shaw, she gave Seroff her phone number at the Hôtel Palais D'Orsay, and before long they became lovers. Aged twenty-five, he was small, dark-eyed, with black curly hair and (according to Mary Desti) 'the merriest smile in the world.'

He became her accompanist (although in truth he was not one of her best), and she spent many hours in the seclusion of his studio, which was in the Bois de Boulogne, in a private estate surrounded by high walls. There she felt safe from the agents of her creditors, who increasingly pursued her. She took to referring to it, Seroff recalled, as 'the home of Alice in Wonderland'.

On her visits to Paris she persevered in trying to persuade the French Communist Party to either subsidise her school in Moscow or, even better, to bring her best Russian pupils to Paris, find an additional thousand French pupils, and re-establish it there.

At the end of 1925 she was in Nice, and it was there, on 28th December, while she was getting ready to go to a party, that the phone rang. There were by now so many Americans on the Riviera that the *Chicago Tribune* published a slim edition there every day, and on the phone was a *Tribune* reporter. His name was James Thurber, then aged thirty and on the brink of becoming one of America's greatest and funniest writers.

Thurber asked her if she had any comment to make on the death of Esenin. Isadora had not heard her husband was dead, and her anguished response of 'No, no, no, no!' shook Thurber as much as his news shook her. But bravely, like a good reporter, he persevered. As he recalled, 'She was asked several other questions, including one as to whether she had ever thought he would end his life violently, but she held the phone without response. After nearly a minute, she silently hung up the receiver.'

Esenin's life had continued to be as emotionally chaotic as ever. His affair with Galya had soon ended, and he had then (bigamously) married Sofia Tolstoy, grand-daughter of the great writer. But they too had separated, and at the age of thirty Esenin had hanged himself from a heating pipe in the Hôtel d'Angleterre in Moscow. The day before he had romantically made a cut in his wrist and written a last poem rather messily in his own blood. It is called 'Goodbye, My Friend, Goodbye' and contains the lines: 'In this life there's nothing new in dying, but nor, of course, is living any newer.'

Towards the end of 1926, the Russian courts would decide that Isadora, as Esenin's legal wife, should inherit his estate, which had grown to a considerable sum, owing to the vastly increased sales of his poetry after his death. She refused to accept it, and turned the money over to his mother and sisters.

After his death, she remained in Nice for several months, her life sad and directionless. She told a reporter, 'It's so terrible to think that God has given me the secret of beauty, which he gives to so few of us, and yet I've no longer the power to give it to the world. It's all there inside me; there, there, waiting to come out.'

In her anger and despair, by now nothing mattered to her, and her behaviour became more and more outrageous. Through Cocteau she met the high-born English painter, Francis Rose. Then only sixteen, it was he who would later become the inspiration for Gertrude Stein's famous line, 'Rose is a rose is a rose is a rose,' and she would become an enthusiastic collector of his paintings. Later he described himself at this time as 'a precious, spoilt youth.'

He turned seventeen in the spring of 1926, and his mother, Lady Rose, arranged a birthday party for him at the Hôtel Welcome in Villefranche-sur-Mer, just outside Nice. Cocteau, who was present, recalled the occasion:

Lady Rose had invited only English officers and their wives. Around eight o'clock, a strange procession appeared on the road that leads down to the harbour. Crowned with roses, Francis Rose supported on his arm Madame Isadora Duncan in a Greek tunic. She was very fat, slightly drunk, and escorted by an American girl, a pianist, and some people picked up along the way. The astonishment of Lady Rose's guests, her anger, the entrance of the procession, the fishermen pressing their faces against the window, Isadora kissing me. Francis very proud of his crown – that was how the birthday party began. A deathly silence turned the guests to statuary. Isadora laughed, draped herself over Francis. She even stood up and dragged him into the window recess. It was then that Captain Williams, a friend of the family, played his part... He strode across the dining room, approached the window, and shouting in a tremendous voice, 'All right, old lady, let go of that child!' he brought his cane down on the dancer's head. She fainted.

Francis Rose, in his 1961 memoirs, gave a slightly different version of the same incident. According to him, Isadora had taken him out through the window onto a balcony, and she certainly did not faint. His account continues:

> Suddenly a terrible cry rang out from one of the balconies and through the window the Captain's watch came flying into the room. Isadora, with a torn toga, then appeared on the threshold with the beginnings of a beautiful black eye. She cried out that the Captain had struck her. When one of the 'pigeons' protested at this scene and told her that her black eye was only mascara and green eye-shadow paint badly smeared, she seized a lobster covered with mayonnaise and threw it at him. Luckily, or unluckily, it missed and landed in Lady McCarthy's lap. 'For God's sake, stop those lobsters screaming,' Isadora said.

She was still occasionally dancing. To raise money to pay her studio's quarterly rent, due on 15 April 1926, she presented a progamme of sacred music and dance there on Good Friday (2 April). She reported to Irma a few days later that it was 'a great success. A hundred tickets were sold at [a] hundred francs a ticket and great *Stimmung* (atmosphere) and enthusiasm. The studio was lovely with alabaster lamps, candles, incense, heaps of white lilies, and lilacs. Quite like the Archangel's times.'

The money soon went. Having paid her studio rent (and her pianist and florist), she relinquished her room at the Hôtel Negresco and returned to Paris, booking into the Hôtel Lutétia, on the Left Bank. She hired a Mathis touring car, and drove north in it to meet the Soviet Envoy to France, Christian Radovsky. He had always been enthusiastic about transferring her Moscow school to Paris, but as usual had regretfully to explain that the USSR had no money to effect such a transfer. This was the last attempt she made, through either the French or the Russian communist party, to bring her school to France. After this, her beloved idea of founding a great proletarian dancing institute, which would serve as a model for the entire world, collapsed.

In mid-June her old acquaintance Mercedes de Acosta arrived in Paris from America. As Mercedes recalled, one evening she 'ran into a man who said, "I know you are a friend of Isadora Duncan's. I hear she's behaved so badly that everyone has abandoned her. I am told she's in a hotel on the Left Bank, practically starving."'

Mercedes rushed to the Lutétia, where she found Isadora sitting up in bed in her darkened room. Isadora was delighted to see her, and Mercedes at once took charge. Learning that she now owed money at the hotel, and that the management were refusing her any further credit, she asked Isadora why her friends hadn't helped her.

'I have spent their money and not repaid them,' said Isadora.

'Did they ever think you would repay them?'

'That's just it. I spent their money which is just what they should have expected me to do. What else is money for but spending?'

Mecedes laughed, and Isadora said, 'Please don't scold me. I am hungry.' Mercedes paid for a leisurely dinner of roast chicken, strawberries and wine. They ate and drank and talked until dawn. Observing the light in the sky, Isadora called down to the garage to get out her Mathis, and drove Mercedes to Longchamps in the morning sunlight.

They had breakfast together, and then drove to the Guaranty Trust Company, where Mercedes drew out enough money for Isadora to settle her hotel bill, with something over for the future.

That whole day Isadora begged Mercedes not to leave her. They went together to Mercedes' hotel, where Mercedes lectured her about her life, saying she must absolutely stop squandering it and pull herself together and begin to dance again, but Isadora persisted that those days were done. Mercedes reassured her, saying, 'You will be given Divine Energy, if you will only call upon it,' and Isadora took her hands and replied, 'Your hands are strong. You are strong. Do you know that you are giving me new life? ... Deep down, in the inmost part of my soul, I believe every word you say.'

They began spending much time together. A couple of weeks after they met, Isadora sent Mercedes a photograph of herself, inscribed, 'Mercedes, lead me with your little strong hand and I will follow you – / To the top of a Mountain / To the end of the world / Wherever you wish – Isadora.'

They became lovers. A note from Isadora reads, 'Dear, Will you ride with me in the Bois from 3–4 –? At 4 I go to Lawyers – but then am free.' Then, in a quick scrawl, 'All night the crystal clearness of your eyes...'

Trying lesbian love was a new and alarming experience for Isadora, as is clear from a note to Mercedes (addressed to '*Adorée*'):

I have played with your flames and been horribly burned. I thought I knew already every mortal suffering, but now I see the worst was still in store for me – I suffer *fearfully* – but I accept it because the source is *so beautiful*... But how to live with this passion in my veins... I beg you not to make fun of me. I may die from it. I'm horrified to learn that only now have I known love for *the first time*. Don't laugh ... a little word... If there is any pity in your heart for me. Respect my secret – I am tortured and ready to cry Mercy. Isadora.

Mercedes also encouraged her to work on her memoirs, with a view to attracting a publishing contract. She had made a beginning in Nice, and had been struggling on at the Lutétia, but found writing a difficult and alien art. As she wrote in the book's introduction, 'It has taken me years of struggle, hard work and research to learn to make one simple gesture, and I know enough about the Art of writing to realise that it would take me again just so many years of concentrated effort to write one simple, beautiful sentence.'

With Mercedes' help – and Mercedes always swore that she herself took no part in the actual writing, that the sentences were all Isadora's own – she finished the first few chapters, and Mercedes neatly typed them out. When she had to leave Paris and return to America, she took a copy of the manuscript with her, intending to submit it to various publishers and see whether she could secure for Isadora a contract and an advance.

With Mercedes gone, Isadora was lucky that Ruth Mitchell arrived from America at almost the same time, so she had, while not a lover, another wealthy encourager.

Ruth also did her best to take Isadora in hand, although with limited success. Her problem was that Mercedes was a vital, intelligent, strong-minded woman, whereas she, to Isadora, was simply an adoring fan, who got, in return for her money, the privilege of being in the presence of genius.

Nonetheless, she did Isadora good. Insisting that both the Lutétia and the rented Mathis were a waste of money, she got rid of both, buying a second-hand Renault and driving Isadora back to Nice in it. Which wasn't as straightforward as it might have been, owing to Isadora's insistence on making long detours to expensive restaurants, vineyards and country inns. At all of which Ruth, of course, paid.

Reaching Juan-les-Pins, a few miles west along the coast from Nice, she insisted on stopping for several days to swim and sunbathe. Here, as Mary Desti learned, 'The sea acted on Isadora like an elixir. She became quite another person, so gentle, so tender… She began seriously to want to dance.' Arriving at last in Nice, Ruth paid for her to rent an apartment next door to her studio. Francis Rose, who went there to sketch her and to gossip about their acquaintances, gives this description:

> She lived … In a tall 1900 apartment building that was so thin and high that it seemed to be only a façade of shutters and balconies for a film set. Her flat was on the first floor, furnished with fake Louis XV furniture from the Galeries Lafayette, aspidistras in pots from oriental bazaars, and dyed bulrushes in fake Sèvres vases. There were crochet-work antimacassars, curtains, and tablecloths in all the rooms. The walls of her untidy bedroom were covered with photographs of her innumerable lovers: famous writers, negro boxers, millionaires, sailors in uniform, and a few royal princes. Her bed was festooned with grubby mosquito-nets, and the old-fashioned bath-tub in her dressing-room was filled with oddments that had to be moved constantly by the 'pigeons.'… They were men of a type that can look after a beautiful, aging woman, and they fought hard to prevent her from drinking anything she could lay her hands on. I remember her mixing a cocktail … out of eau-de-Cologne, Pernod, brandy, and the dregs from nearly empty wine bottles, which she had kept hidden in her bidet.

On 10th September 1926, at her studio, she gave a joint recital with Jean Cocteau, he reading from his poem *Orphée*, and she performing a programme of Liszt, dancing by candlelight. Praised for her dancing, she replied, 'Well, I don't know, can't tell… When I was a lovely young woman I danced like a lovely young woman; when I was a mother, I danced like a mother, and now I dance I suppose like heaven knows what.' All the same, four days later she gave a similar recital, this time participating with Jean Cocteau and the actor Marcel Herrand, who would go on to a successful career on the French stage and in such films as *Les Enfants du Paradis*.

As the days went by, Ruth hovered over her, encouraging her to perform, and attempting, with limited success, to keep her on some sort of diet. 'Poor Ruthie,' Isadora said to a new friend, the British journalist and playwright Sewell Stokes, 'it's really a shame. She's so good to me and I behave so badly... But I love potatoes – and young men. That's my trouble!'

She still owned her old studio at Neuilly, although she would never set foot in it, and had not for years, because of its association with Deirdre and Patrick. It was still heavily mortgaged, and in 1925 she had offered actress Lotte Yorksa, whom she had met long years before at Eugène Carrière's studio, twenty per cent of the profit if she could find a buyer for it. Nothing had come of that, but in November, as she also owed 10,000 francs to moneylenders, a Paris court ordered that it be sold at auction to repay her debts.

To try and deal with the situation, Isadora drove back to Paris in the second-hand Renault with Ruth, Walter Shaw and Marcel Herrand. From there, Ruth returned to New York, giving Isadora the Renault. Isadora again booked herself into the Lutétia (a hotel she by now referred to as the 'Lusitania').

In Paris, she acquired for herself a literary agent, William Bradley, an American she had met on the Riviera, and gave him a copy of her unfinished manuscript. Mercedes, in New York, had meanwhile submitted it to a friend of hers, T.R. ('Tommy') Smith, who happened to be editor in chief at the firm of Boni & Liveright. Bradley too approached them.

Considering the craft of writing, Isadora also she tried her hand at a love story that might be made into a silent film. She read it to her friend Sewell Stokes, who thought it 'a very excellent piece of work.' 'Somehow,' he later wrote, 'Isadora had managed, after her infrequent visits to the cinema, to derive a perfect conception of what the mass of the public will always like; and had at the same time preserved her own intelligence.'

She gave it to him, and asked him to try and get some producer to accept it, saying that she herself would be agreeable to playing the part of the vampire in it, Madame Romananini. Unfortunately, nothing came of this interesting project.

Meanwhile, the Paris newspapers had reported at length on her plight with her studio, and a committee, chaired by Lotte Yorska, was formed to try and raise funds to bail her out. Victor Seroff, who was still her lover at the time, later recalled, 'to everyone's surprise painters and sculptors donated their works to be sold for Isadora's benefit, actors and actresses, music hall performers, and scores of art students generously contributed according to their means.' By December enough money had been raised to stave off the sale, and Isadora, relieved, set off back to Nice with Seroff.

Then, after a silence of about six months, she heard news of her school in Moscow. Irma had taken the students on an extended tour of Siberia and China. Isadora, feeling that her pupils were being used merely to make money, was furious. Calling Irma a 'bandit', she dashed off a letter of protest to the Soviet government. It said:

> This is the first word I have heard from the school for six months, and the first knowledge I have had that they are in China. I wish to protest that this school which I formed at the sacrifice of my fortune and person, and for which I [am] naturally boycotted by all former friends and acquaintances in Europe, should be allowed to pass from my hands and into the hands of private speculation... Comrade Lunacharsky wrote of my school, 'Isadora Duncan wanted to give a natural and beautiful education to every child. The Bourgeois society, however, did not understand this and put her pupils on the stage to exploit them for money. We will know how to act differently.'
>
> I ask *when?*

In Nice, Seroff too caused her some distress. She had moved back into an apartment at the Hôtel Negresco, and one evening was dining there with him and an assortment of guests, among whom were Max Eastman, and an American friend of Seroff's whom he hadn't seen for some years. Her name was Alice Spicer and, after drinking a little too much she went off into the bedroom to lie down. Seroff followed her and, as Max Eastman recalled:

> He locked himself into the bedroom ... and refused to answer Isadora's knocking. She pounded on the door and cried out that she would die by her own hand if he did not let her in. And she did go and put on the long purple cloak in which she was accustomed to dance the *Marche Funebre* of Chopin, and walk solemnly out into the night ... straight on into the blue Mediterranean up to her neck.

Isadora gave Sewell Stokes a subtler version of events:

What really happened was this. I was sitting quite alone, feeling very miserable, when suddenly I knew that I didn't want to go on sitting there any more. I said to myself that I just didn't want to go on living any more; that nobody wanted me to. Only it seemed as if somebody else, and not myself, was telling me that. Really a most curious feeling. And when I got up and went out to walk into the sea, I was quite sure that somebody was leading me very gently by the arm. I distinctly remember thinking how wonderful it was going to be, not to have any more worry, and also that none of the responsibility of ending my life would be mine, because somebody else, the somebody who had hold of my arm, was responsible.

Although of course she did not drown herself, and eventually came back out of the sea, reports of the incident, reached Paris and horrified Lotte Yorska and her committee. Reports of their disquiet reached Isadora, and towards the end of December she sent Seroff to Paris to tell them she was all right and allay their fears.

A few days after he left, her agent Will Bradley arrived in Nice with news that he had clinched a deal with Boni & Liveright for her memoirs. For a book totalling 'not less than 70,000 words' she was to receive a total of $1,500, to be paid in monthly instalments, with further payment from any future serialisation. Tommy Smith had also urged Bradley to impress on Isadora the necessity of finishing the book as swiftly as possible.

This put her in something of a panic. She began asking any writer she met for hints on writing. Realising that her only way of getting through the book in a reasonable time would be to dictate it, Bradley suggested to her a method of working. Journalist Pierre Loving recalled:

[He] proposed [she receive] a regular monthly stipend, ... sufficient to cover her own expenses and a secretary's salary... Her secretaries – there was to be quite a procession of them – had to be patient and flexible, willing to drink with her, willing to begin at midnight and work till dawn, if necessary. Isadora rarely got into a talkative frame of mind before evening, and alcohol played its part in untangling the knots in her memory and making the story flow smoothly. She was often irritable and temperamental with her secretaries, but most of them didn't mind. They all felt that they were humble instruments in her service, and the one thing that mattered, after all, was the book.

In February 1927 her work was interrupted when the Hôtel Negresco handed her a bill for nine thousand francs, with a printed note telling her that if she did not pay it that night she would have to vacate her room. She was furious, and sent for the manager. As her old friend Allan Ross Macdougall, who was in Nice at the time, recalled:

In a few minutes he was in the room, bowing deferentially to Isadora reclining on the bed. Looking up sweetly at him she said, 'I do not understand why you bother me with this absurd matter of a bill for a paltry nine thousand francs. After all you know who I am. You know that I have been one of your most famous and regular clients. There have been nights when I spent in your halls double and triple the sum of this bill. I have no money at the moment... My money is all in Paris, tied up in this fight about the house. If I am to get it, I must go there. I am planning to go there tomorrow... If you feel you must have security for this absurd bill, I will leave you my Renault car, which is at present in the garage.

The manager accepted. The Negresco impounded her car and all her trunks, and bought her a first-class train ticket to Paris.

In Paris she decided not to return to the Lutétia, as the management there too had complained about the amount she owed. Will Bradley suggested she try the newly-built Studio-Apartment Hôtel in Montparnasse, and there she went, living on the allowance he was paying her while she completed her book.

She wrote (or rather, dictated) steadily. When people asked her how it was coming along, she had a stock reply, 'Well, I've written twenty thousand words, and I'm still a virgin.' In fact she remained a virgin for too long to suit Boni & Liveright. After they had received the first fifty thousand words they sent her a telegram: ENOUGH OF YOUR HIGHFALUTIN IDEAS SEND LOVE CHAPTERS MAKE IT SPICY.

Although she complained about this to her secretary of the time, she was quite happy that her book should be spicy. She wanted it to be as frank as Whitman's *Leaves of Grass*, or franker. She told Victor Seroff that what it should have were 'pornographic pictures' and lessons in love-making, to shock the sort of gushing women who kept coming up to her and saying, 'Oh, Miss Duncan, your memoirs must be thrilling! We're so anxious to read them!'

As the words flowed out, she received some editorial help from Allan

Ross Macdougall. Seroff also suggested that Mary Desti helped her with her section on Paris Singer. But undoubtedly almost every word in the book is Isadora's.

In many ways she remained at heart American. On 21st May 1927 she joined the crowds at Le Bourget airfield to see the 27-year-old Charles Lindbergh complete the first solo transatlantic flight in his plane *The Spirit of St Louis.* Later in the year, when Sacco and Vanzetti were about to be executed, she joined a protest march to the American embassy, angrily declaring the case 'a blot on American justice.' (Two peaceful radicals, they were accused, probably wrongly, of a hold-up and murder in Boston in 1919. Convicted in 1920 during the great 'Red Scare', they went to the electric chair on 23rd August 1927.)

On 30th April, Mary Desti came back to Paris. She and Isadora had not met since they parted in Berlin, and Isadora and Esenin went back to Moscow. Much had happened to Mary in four years. After her short rest-cure in Paris she had gone back to New York to run Maison Desti. Unfortunately, it had ceased to prosper, and in the spring of 1927 she had had to be bailed out by her former husband, Solomon Sturges. He offered her $1,000 a month, on condition that the money be handed over to his adopted son, Preston. Out of that amount, Preston made her a monthly allowance, and as soon as she got the first cheque she packed her bags and headed for Paris and Isadora.

With her went her English ex-officer husband, Howard Perch. But unfortunately, shortly after they got to Paris, they were walking down the Champs-Élysées and ran into her Turkish husband, Vely Bey, whom she had decided had died in the Great War. She and Howard separated.

As a present for Isadora, Mary had brought from New York a blood-red batik shawl she had designed herself. Two yards long and five feet wide, with eighteen-inch fringes on either end, it was, Mary recalled, 'of heavy crêpe, with a great yellow bird almost covering it, and blue Chinese asters and Chinese characters in black – a marvelous, lovely thing, [it became] the light of Isadora's life. She would go nowhere without it.'

Mary took a small apartment on the boulevard des Capuchines. Isadora hated visiting it, because it happened to be next door to the Olympia music-hall, which was one of the venues where Lisa Duncan had appeared, to some acclaim. Nonetheless, she and Mary began socialising around town together, holding parties at Isadora's apartment and dining out expensively. 'She won't try to economise,' Mary wrote to Preston, 'refuses to eat except at the best restaurants, and wants to drink the most expensive wines – she feels the world owes it to her – well I guess it does.'

Isadora took one short break from drinking heavily. In June she was to dance for one performance at the Théâtre Mogador, an engagement that was to help raise funds for her studio at Neuilly, and which had been organised by Lotte Yorska's committee. To fulfil it she would have to lose weight, and Mary nagged her to do so. For a month she limited herself to one glass of wine at dinner.

She also went to Orcier's Baths to undergo 'bathing and steaming reduction'. But it was an ordeal. As she said to Will Bradley's wife, Jenny, 'I don't dance any more. I only move my weight around.'

In June, Irma's mother died in Hamburg. Irma attended the funeral, and after it came to Paris to see Isadora, having heard of the engagement at the Théâtre Mogador. Isadora was still somewhat suspicious of Irma, but the two met on reasonably good terms. Unfortunately, Isadora's performance had been postponed until 8th July, and Irma had too many planned engagements back in Russia to stay for it. As they parted, Isadora promised to come to Russia when she received the final payment for her memoirs.

At the Mogador, accompanied by the Pasdeloup Orchestra, conducted by Albert Wolff, she danced the *Rédemption*, the second movement of Schubert's Unfinished Symphony, the *Liebestod* from *Tristan*, and the *Ave Maria*, and received a dozen curtain-calls from a celebrity audience that included Yvette Guilbert, Cécile Sorel, Ford Madox Ford, Charles Rappoport, Anita Loos, Mary Miles Minter, Marilyn Miller, her ex-pupil Lisa Duncan, and Mercedes de Acosta, who had come from America specially.

She kept to schedule with her writing, delivering the last pages to Boni & Liveright in August, although the final sections of her book, entitled simply *My Life*, do read as if she was hurrying somewhat. It also ends as she departs for Russia to found her school, but this was not so much a matter of meeting her deadline as of her shrewd suspicion that if she wrote as she would like to about Russia and Esenin, the book might be banned in America.

Mercedes had to go back to America after only a short visit. She was to sail from Le Havre, and Isadora accompanied her on the train to wish her farewell, insisting to a reluctant Victor Seroff that he come too. He came under duress and the resultant quarrel caused a slight coldness between them.

As she was saying goodbye to Mercedes in her cabin, Isadora suddenly begged to come with her. 'I am homesick,' she said. 'I want to go home. Please take me with you. Hide me here in your room until the boat sails and then we will go to see the Captain. He is French, and civilised. He will understand.' As Isadora had no money, no ticket, and no passport, Mercedes reluctantly dissuaded her. After the ship sailed, she found two roses on her pillow – one white and one red. A card beside them said, 'The white reaching toward the sky is YOU, darling; and the red is the earth – ME. I adore you – ISADORA.'

The same month, Will Bradley succeeded in selling the British serial rights to *My Life* for £400, of which £100 was to be paid immediately, and the rest on publication. This money enabled Isadora to settle up at the Studio-Apartment Hôtel, and to set off with Seroff and with Mary Desti for four days in Deauville, after which it was gone.

Her intention, after returning to Paris, was to set off immediately back to Nice. Mary went with her, but Seroff refused, saying he would follow them in a day or so. They were driven to Nice by Ivan Nikolenko, now the companion of Seroff's old friend Alice Spicer, who went along as well. The trouble was, Alice was on a limited schedule, and insisted to Isadora that there could be no loitering, as she had only three days to make the round trip.

Nikolenko was a film-maker, and part of his reason for offering to make the trip was that he hoped to persuade Isadora to at last allow herself to be captured on film. During the trip she did allow him to take a few short shots of her not dancing – shots of her, Alice recalled, 'smoking a cigarette, riding in a car, that sort of thing. Then a very serious Isadora, the wind blowing against her hair – only her profile... She was absolutely lovely – "photogenic" as they say.'

Isadora being Isadora, of course there was bound to be loitering, and at Lyons the party split up, Alice needing to return to Paris. Isadora had also not been happy at the speed with which Nikolenko had been driving, and the parting was somewhat acrimonious. As she and Mary were penniless, Alice offered to buy them second-class train tickets from Lyons to Nice. Isadora indignantly refused (probably offended by the words 'second class', Seroff thought). Mary paid to rent a car and chauffeur by reluctantly using a post-dated cheque. For which, Isadora assured her, Raymond would reimburse her in Nice.

Isadora enjoyed the drive to Nice, singing and laughing like a child, happy in Mary's company. They booked themselves into the Grand Hôtel at nearby Juan-les-Pins. Because of the loitering on the road, Seroff had got there before them, but he stayed only a few days. As he was broke himself, and could find no work in Nice, he explained to Isadora that he absolutely had to return to Paris. He promised to come back when he had earned a bit.

Isadora was crestfallen at his going, and the night after he went, Mary recalled, she and Isadora walked the fifteen miles back to Juan-les-Pins. There they found a small restaurant near the sea – 'a little hut with a kitchen on the end.' It was called 'Tétu' – the surname of its owners. Enjoying the red wine with her meal, Isadora held her glass up to the light to admire its colour, and as she did so, Mary remembered:

> ...her eye caught that of a young man seated behind me who was drinking with three others. I saw her smile and bow as though drinking to someone.
>
> I turned and said, 'Good Heavens, that's a chauffeur you're drinking to.'
>
> 'Oh, Mary, how bourgeois you are! He's nothing of the kind. Have you no eyes! He's a Greek god in disguise, and that's his chariot out there.' She pointed to a lovely little Bugatti racing car with red, white and blue circles around the tail. Sure enough, it was his car. A few minutes [later] they left, and as he drove off she waved to him, and he bowed. She said to me smiling, 'You see I'm still desirable.' Then I knew how badly [Seroff's] desertion had hurt her.

They managed to stay only a week at the Grand Hôtel before the management realised that Isadora was broke. They moved to a cheap hotel near Isadora's studio, which asked for a week's payment in advance. Isadora found that the studio had been padlocked for non-payment of rent, and got the landlords to re-admit her only by promising to vacate the premises permanently on 1st October. Raymond, having reimbursed Mary, was by now flatly refusing to contribute any more to his profligate sister.

Using another post-dated cheque, Isadora and Mary hired another car and chauffeur, and began to spend their days being endlessly driven along the coastal roads. As they went they incessantly sang, and the song they mostly sang was the cheerful but melancholy 'Bye Bye, Blackbird'.

Their fortunes took an upturn when Mary talked the Hôtel Negresco into buying Isadora's impounded Renault, and when her own monthly cheque arrived from Preston. Then, as she recalled, 'there followed such feasting, visiting, restauranting, night-clubbing, as only millionaires might have supported!'

During their socialising, on 10th September, they went to the Carlton at Cannes, and there Isadora bumped into her old lover Francis Picabia,

385

there with his wife Germaine. They greeted each other warmly, and Picabia invited Isadora and Mary to join them at 'the quaintest little restaurant where they make marvellous bouillabaisse.'

The restaurant turned out to be Tétu, and Isadora, deciding this must be fate, gave Madame Tétu her address, asking them to pass it on to the young 'Greek god' if he came in again. Her excuse, Mary remembered, was that 'she was most anxious to buy a car like his.' The old lady smiled wisely and said she was sure he would be there next day.

The next day, 11th September, Isadora's spirits were down again. She had heard from New York that her brother Augustin, whose sight had been failing for some time, was now practically blind. At a lunch in Antibes a few days later, when asked about him, she burst into a long tirade, saying there was no justice on earth and no mercy in heaven, as Augustin was the kindest and most saintly man she had ever known.

On the same day she sent a letter to Seroff saying, 'I miss you dreadfully – We are in a H– of a fix here… Think of me & play Scriabin – perhaps you will be nearer to my spirit when my body with all its material nuisance is not there.' At her studio, she began work on a piece she had not heard until recently, and was enthused by – Liszt's *Symphonie zu Dantes Divina Commedia*.

She was sent the proofs of *My Life* but, reading them, felt appalled, telling writer Glenway Westcott that it was the only thing she had ever done for money in her life, and she was ashamed. Also the style was poor and stilted, and the grammar was poor. She began to weep, and Westcott offered to come in a day or so and look over the proofs with her.

In her financial distress, Isadora begged Mary to contact Paris Singer, who was then at his villa in Cap Ferrat, not far down the coast. Preston had suggested the same thing, so, also on 11th September, she went to Cap Ferrat. But Singer was not inclined to be helpful. For a start, he was by no means as wealthy as he had been. The Florida land boom, in which he had speculated heavily, had collapsed in 1926, losing him a fortune. In addition, he felt that Isadora was by now beyond helping – as far as he could see, her career was now in a downward spiral from which it would be impossible to lift her. He was sorry, but no. Mary returned to Nice with the disappointing news.

Isadora decided the best thing she could do for the moment would be to sell some of the furniture from her studio, and on 13th September she was there with Mary deciding what, when in walked Singer. 'I thought I'd drop in to see if you have had lunch,' he said.

Mary diplomatically left them alone together, and when Singer left, some while later, Isadora chided her, saying, 'I should have loved you to hear all the things he said. He is a lovely, lovely being, and I love him. I believe he is the only one I ever really loved.'

This made Mary laugh. She replied, 'How can you say that, Isadora? Tell me now the absolute truth. Whom above all did you really love the best?'

Isadora thought for a moment, then said, 'Well, to tell you the real, real truth, Mary, I don't know. I seem to love each one of them to the very limits of love, and if Ted, Lohengrin and the Archangel stood before me, I wouldn't know which one to choose. I loved, and still love them all.'

Singer had promised to return the next day with a cheque, and Isadora, relieved, went for a nap in her hotel. While she slept, the 'Greek god' knocked gently on the hotel-room door. Mary answered, and he explained that Madame Tétu had given him the address and said that the lady wanted to buy a car. After some confusion as to whether or not the lady in question was Mary, she told him that Miss Duncan was at present asleep, but if he would leave his card she would pass it on.

When she woke, Isadora was furious at having missed him, telling Mary that she must understand how important this was. The handsome young man was undoubtedly a messenger from the gods.

The next morning, Wednesday, 14th September, Isadora went to the address on the young man's card – the Helvétia Garage. The young man worked there. His name was Bénoit Falchetto, and he was French-Italian. But he was not there at the moment, he was out on a call. He would be back that afternoon. Isadora again lied that she wanted to buy a car, and asked that Falchetto come to her studio at five.

Back at the studio, she was in high spirits. Things were beginning to go right. Will Bradley had informed her that the British serialisation of *My Life* had actually begun, so she would be getting the balance of her fee. With Singer back on the scene, Mary had thought of returning to Paris, but Isadora managed to talk her out of it, saying, 'If you will only stay by me and see the thing through, just stick to me...' Together they would rebuild her school in Paris. 'We'll go to Russia, get the children, and we'll end in a burst of glory yet.'

With Singer expected at four, and the 'Greek god' at five, Isadora went after lunch to have her hair done. Back at her studio, waiting for Singer, she could hardly contain her excitement, dancing around, said Mary, as if she was bursting with some wonderful secret she could not tell to anyone. 'Oh, Mary, Mary,' she would say every so often, then go back to dancing again.

Singer was delayed. Towards five there was a knock at the door, but it wasn't him, it was Falchetto. Mary left for the hotel. When Isadora joined her there an hour later, she was alone but laughing. 'I've lost them both, Mary,' she said. 'I've lost Bugatti and I've lost Lohengrin!... It's no use. I always get caught.'

What had happened was that she had been deep in earnest conversation with Falchetto when Singer arrived at the studio. 'I see you haven't changed,' he said. Both men, taking in the situation, made to leave, but Isadora took charge. She told the embarrassed Falchetto, 'You are coming at nine tonight with the little racing car.' He left, somewhat sheepishly, and Isadora explained that things were not what they seemed, that Mary was interested in buying the young man's car.

Convinced or not, Singer quickly calmed down. He knew Isadora of old, and had loved her for a long time. He apologised for having arrived late. He had been detained, and now must also leave immediately, but he would return tomorrow to take her to lunch and give her the cheque he had promised.

'I don't know if he'll come,' Isadora said to Mary, 'or Bugatti either.' Bugatti, she had discovered, was also a pilot, which she found exciting.

During the early evening Ivan Nikolenko came to Isadora's studio. He showed her the short reel of film he had taken of her on the road to Lyons, and she was impressed. She said yes, she would allow him to film her dancing, because clearly he was an artist. They agreed they would begin next day.

At about eight, Isadora stuck a note for Falchetto on the studio door. It read, '*Suis en face Chez Henri.*' Then she and Mary and Nikolenko went to the café across the road for dinner, Isadora wearing the red batik shawl that Mary had brought her from New York.

Falchetto had not appeared by the time they finished dinner, so all three returned to the studio. Isadora turned on the gramophone and began to dance, singing, 'I'm in love again.' Then the little racing car pulled up outside. Isadora started for the door, and Mary begged her to borrow her black cape, as the evening was becoming chill. But Isadora refused. She would wear her prized red shawl.

Mary ran out first, and begged Falchetto to go carefully, not to go too fast, that he had no notion of what a great person he was driving. 'Madame, you need have no fear,' he answered, 'I have never had an accident in my life.'

As Isadora approached the car, with Ivan following, Falchetto too observed that the evening was chill, and offered to lend her his leather greatcoat, but again she refused.

The car was not in fact a Bugatti. It was a much less famous make, an Amilcar Grand Sport. It had wire-spoked wheels, and was a two-seater, the passenger sitting just slightly further back and to the side of the driver. Falchetto helped Isadora into the passenger seat, then went round to the driving-seat. Isadora, standing, threw the end of her shawl flamboyantly around her neck. '*Adieu, mes amis,*' she cried, '*je vais à la gloire!*'

She sat down, and Mary saw that the long fringes of the shawl had caught in the spokes of the rear wheel, the car having no mudguards. '*Isadora!*' she shouted. '*Ta châle! Ramasse ta châle!*' But as the car roared off, and the wheels turned, the scarf tightened, breaking Isadora's neck and rupturing her jugular vein. She died instantly.

The car stopped after travelling only twenty or thirty metres. Mary at first believed it had stopped because she had shouted, and that everything was all right. Then she heard Falchetto screaming, '*J'ai tué la Madonne! J'ai tué la Madonne!*' The force of the tightening shawl had yanked Isadora out of the car, trapping her head between the body of the vehicle and the rear-wheel tyre, and crushing her nose as her body was dragged along.

On 16th September, after a simple musical service in her studio, with no words and no rites, Isadora's body was taken by train to Paris, to Père Lachaise cemetery, where her children's ashes lay, and there it was cremated. Around ten thousand mourners attended, and again there was only music – Liszt's *Funérailles*, the *Ave Maria*, and Beethoven's *In Questa Tomba Oscura*, sung by baritone Garcia Marsellac. The last piece, as the doors of the furnace opened and her coffin disappeared, was Bach's 'Air on the G String'. Later, her ashes were placed in the columbarium, beneath those of Deirdre and Patrick, and close to her mother.

As Jean Cocteau wrote at the time to Glenway Westcott, 'Isadora's end is *perfect* – a kind of horror that leaves one calm.'

Her memoirs were published posthumously. Dorothy Parker, reviewing them for *The New Yorker* at the beginning of 1928 wrote, 'Here was a great woman; a magnificent, generous, gallant, reckless, fated, fool of a woman. There was never a place for her in the ranks of the terrible, slow army of the cautious. She ran ahead, where there were no paths.'

She was one of those rare artists who created a form so strong and complete in itself that from it there was no going forward. Any variation from the perfection she created could only be a weakening or an imitation. Like James Joyce as a novelist, William Blake as an artist, or Thelonious Monk as a pianist, she could have no direct successors. Indirectly, however, she influenced the whole world of Dance.

She taught the world that Dance was an Art; that it could express deep and subtle Ideas; that it was not only a celebration of Life, but Life itself.

Bibliography

Isadora Duncan

Blair, Fredrika, *Isadora* (London: Equation, 1972)

Dumesnil, Maurice, *An Amazing Journey: Isadora Duncan in South America* (USA: Washburn, 1932)

Duncan, Irma, *Duncan Dancer* (USA: Wesleyan University Press, 1966)

Kurth, Peter, *Isadora: A Sensational Life* (London: Little, Brown & Company, 2002)

Macdougall, Allan Ross, *Isadora: A Revolutionary in Art and Love* (USA: Thomas Nelson & Sons, 1960)

Seroff, Victor, *The Real Isadora* (USA: The Dial Press, 1971)

Stokes, Sewell, *Isadora: An Intimate Portrait* (London: Panther Books, 1968)

Related Topics

Bauer, Harold, *Harold Bauer: His Book* (USA: Norton, 1948)

Bennett, Arnold, *The Journals of Arnold Bennett* (London: Penguin Books, 1954)

Blanchard, Mary Warner, *Oscar Wilde's America* (USA: Yale University Press, 1998)

Cecil, David, *Max* (USA: Houghton Mifflin, 1965)

Cook, R.M., *Greek Art* (London: Weidenfeld & Nicolson, 1972)

Craig, Edward Gordon, *Index to the Story of My Days* (USA: Viking Press, 1957)

De Mille, Agnes, *The Book of the Dance* (London: Paul Hamlyn, 1963)

Dodge, Roger Pryor, *Hot Jazz and Jazz Dance* (Oxford: Oxford University Press, 1995)

Ellmann, Richard, *Oscar Wilde* (London: Penguin Books, 1988)

Gaunt, William, *The Aesthetic Adventure* (London: Jonathan Cape, 1975)

Gaunt, William, *Victorian Olympus* (London: Jonathan Cape, 1975)

Gilbert, Douglas, *Lost Chords* (USA: Cooper Square Publishers (1970)

Graves, Robert, *The Greek Myths* [2 vols.] (London: Penguin Books, 1955)

Holroyd, Michael, *Bernard Shaw* [Vol. 3, *1918–1950: The Lure of Fantasy*] (London: Chatto & Windus, 1991)

Ingersoll, Col. R.G., *Lectures and Essays* (London: Watts & Co., 1945)

Johnston, Alva, *The Incredible Mizners* (London: Rupert Hart-Davis, 1953)

Kendall, Elizabeth, *Where She Danced: The Birth of American Art Dance* (USA: University of California Press, 1979)

Louÿs, Pierre (translated Frances Keene), *Aphrodite* (USA: The Libra Collection, 1960)

Palmer, John, *The Future of the Theatre* (London: G. Bell & Sons, 1913)

Parker, Dorothy, *A Month of Saturdays* (London: Macmillan, 1971)

Pearson, Hesketh, *Beerbohm Tree: His Life and Laughter* (London: Methuen & Co., 1956)

Rose, Sir Francis, *Saying Life: The Memoirs of Sir Francis Rose* (London: Cassell, 1961)

Skinner, Cornelia Otis, *Elegant Wits and Grand Horizontals* (USA: Houghton Mifflin, 1962)

Shaw, Martin, *Up to Now* (Oxford: Oxford University Press, 1929)

Spoto, Donald, *Madcap: The Life of Preston Sturges* (USA: Little, Brown & Company, 1990)

Ursini, James, *The Fabulous Life and Times of Preston Sturges* (USA: Curtis Books, 1973)

Index